Hacker Linux Uncovered

HACKER LINUX UNCOVERED

Michael Flenov

alist

A-LIST, LLC
295 East Swedesford Rd.
PMB #285
Wayne, PA 19087
702-977-5377 (FAX)
mail@alistpublishing.com
http://www.alistpublishing.com

This book is printed on acid-free paper.

Hacker Linux Uncovered

By Michael Flenov

ISBN 1931769508

Printed in the United States of America

05 06 7 6 5 4 3 2 1

A-LIST, LLC, titles are available for site license or bulk purchase by institutions, user groups, corporations, etc.

Book Editor: Julie Laing

Contents

XVI   Contents

Preface

Approved by computer delinquents as an action manual.

Hackers

Approved by system administrators as a defense manual.

Admins

This book is devoted to exploring one of the most popular operating systems installed on servers: Linux. So far, this operating system has not been as popular among home users as among professional administrators. There have been, however, developments of late that make this system likely to capture a good segment of the home-computer operating system market. The operating system is becoming easier to install all the time, and its graphical user interface and the ease of use often give the most popular operating system among home users — Windows — a good run for its money.

This book will be of use to Linux administrators and to those Linux users who want to learn this operating system in more detail. The discussion of the configuration and security issues will come in handy for network security professionals, even those running other operating systems, because the larger part of the information is not tied to any specific operating system.

You will learn how hackers break into servers, and use the knowledge to prevent them from breaking into your server. Because some examples provided in the book can be used not only for defense but also for offense, I would like to give fair warning to young aspiring hackers. Curiosity is a commendable quality, but remember that the law is ever vigilant and always gets its man. If you get away with one break-in, next time you may not be so lucky and may have to spend some time in a company of unfortunate specimens of humankind, where your hacking skills will be of little use to you.

Some material in the book is presented from the hacker's point of view and describes methods of breaking into computer systems. I hope that this information will not actually be put to use. But being somewhat skeptical of the average human integrity, I tried to place more emphasis on defense against breaking in. I also left out some aspects and gave only a general description of others in order not to lead you into the temptation of applying these methods in practice.

You only need to spend a few minutes on programming or on Internet research to finalize my thoughts. Although this book can serve as a starting point for learning break-in techniques, I hope you will not use the acquired knowledge maliciously. If common morality is not enough to keep you from stepping onto the slippery path of computer burglary, remember the legal ramifications of your actions.

Any tool can be used for both useful and destructive purposes. A simple kitchen knife is a good example. It can be used as intended for its kitchen chores or as a defensive or killing weapon. Likewise, the hacker techniques discussed in this book can be used for everyday operating system maintenance as well as for defending against or perpetrating computer system break-ins. I hope that you will not use the acquired knowledge for destructive purposes, which will not add to your good name. As for cracker notoriety, why do you need it? You will be better off directing your efforts toward constructive pursuits.

Despite the obvious strivings by Linux to become an everyday home computer operating system, it is still quite difficult to configure and contains lots of options that most people simply do not need. "Security" is a misnomer when referring to a Linux system operated with its default configuration settings. But no operating system running at the default configuration settings can work reliably and be maximally secure. Software developers cannot possibly know each user's individual needs and strive to make the software work on any hardware configuration. To achieve this, they have to build many extraneous capabilities into their product.

It just happens that being a Linux administrator requires more knowledge and experience than being a Windows administrator. This is because Linux is more complex to configure. In this book, I try to explain this operating system in the most understandable terms; moreover, I try to do this from the hacker's point of view.

"What exactly is the hacker's point of view?" my readers often ask. To answer this question, you should have a clear idea of what a hacker is and what he or she sees in an operating system.

When I am asked how I understand what a hacker is, I answer with the following example: If you can install an operating system and get it working, then you are an administrator. But if you have tuned it up for maximum performance and security, than you are a hacker. Being a hacker means being able to create something better than others can, to make this something faster, more convenient, and more secure. This is what the Linux operating system is, which was created by hackers for the whole world to use.

This book considers the operating system starting from the basics and proceeding to the most complex manipulations with the system. The material is presented in language simple and comprehensible to everyone. This will make it possible for you to acquire essential Linux knowledge without having to use any supplementary literature, because you will learn all the necessary information from one source. For more detailed information, you can take advantage of the **man**, **info**, and **help** files supplied with the operating system.

This book is different from other books on the subject in that the security and performance are considered not in separate chapters at the end of the book — doing this would be a big mistake — but throughout the book as may be necessary. If a person acquires unproductive habits of working with the system, two chapters at the end of the book as an afterthought will not break these wrong habits to teach the right ones. This is why the performance and security of each area considered will be discussed immediately without putting it off until the end of the book.

You can always find instructions on how to simply use or even administer Linux on the Internet or in the software manuals. But information on how to use the operating system effectively is more difficult to come by and is usually gained in pieces from various sources, which makes it difficult to fuse this information into a solid body of knowledge. True security cannot be based on piecemeal information. Overlooking a single, seemingly trivial thing can leave your computer vulnerable to a break-in.

(For supplementary information on computer and network security, I recommend reading another of my books, *Hackish PC*, which provides a good deal of general information concerning computer and network protection.) Although this book deals mostly with the security of the Linux operating system, many of the questions considered can also be of use when building a secure Linux server. Windows security professionals can also derive benefits from the book's information.

The subject of viruses is not treated in the book, because currently the activity of Linux operating system viruses is minimal, which is not to say that there is no such threat. However small it may be, it always exists; but protecting against viruses is similar to protecting against Trojans, of which there are quite a few of the Linux variety. You can obtain more information about virus attacks and protection against them in the already-mentioned *Hackish PC* book of my authorship.

So, start discovering Linux. I am certain that you will see this operating system in an entirely different light and learn many new and interesting things.

Acknowledgments

In each book I write, I try to thank all those who helped me write and publish it. Without these people, the book might not have come into being or might not have its present form.

First, I would like to express my general gratitude to the BHV publishing house, with whom I have been cooperating for several years. Individual "thank-yous" go to the publishing house's management and editors who worked closely with me and helped me make the book as I envisioned it. Especial thanks to the proofreaders who caught and corrected my slips that crept in under the strain of having to produce within tight deadlines, trying to keep the information as current as possible when the book reaches bookstores.

I will never tire of thanking my family — namely, my parents, wife, and children — for being so patient. When I come home after work, it's only to start working the second shift, this time on the next book. Consequently, I am always at the computer at home, which makes communicating difficult because all my thoughts are somewhere in the virtual reality.

Big thanks also go to my friends and acquaintances that helped with advice, ideas, and software.

An individual thank-you goes to the administrators of my Internet service provider, who allowed me to test some of the methods described in the book on their equipment. I tried to be careful when using their systems and not to do any damage to their systems. I would like to believe that I was successful in this respect.

It just so happens that my pets take part in writing all of my books. This book was not an exception, and my cat Chikist lent me his helping paw. Because he is a nocturnal animal, at 11:00 p.m. Chikist starts strolling around the apartment making all kinds of noises. This helped me stay awake and concentrate on the task at hand.

I also want to thank another cat, the Microsoft Office assistant. I used Microsoft Word to write the book, with Linux running on a virtual machine so that I could make screenshots. Whenever my yearling son Cyril was left in my care, I would sit him next to me and he would entertained himself playing with the cat on the monitor while I could go on with my work. Sometimes, however, both the cat and the monitor had to be rescued when my son tried to pat the monitor cat.

The biggest thanks go to you for having bought this book and my steady readers, who also take part in creating my books. My latest books are based on the questions and suggestions from the readers with whom I regularly communicate on the forum of the **www.vr-online.ru** site. So, if you have any questions or suggestions, you are invited to this forum. I will try to answer them to the best of my abilities. Please feel free to express any comments that you may have concerning this book. Your criticism will help me write my next book better.

Chapter 1: Introduction

Once I showed a Windows administrator how to install and work with Linux. He liked the installation process, because it was easy in the latest versions of the operating system. But when we installed and decided to configure the Samba server, there was a flood of questions of the type, "Why does Samba have to be configured? Why can't I just be granted access automatically?" The truth is, Windows administrators are lazy and are used to the operating system doing everything for them. But when their system is broken into, there ensues another flood of questions, this time of a different type: "Why didn't Microsoft provide the tools to disable certain operations?"

As far as users are concerned, once the Linux operating system is installed, it does not require any additional custom configuring. You can start working with any office software and user utilities right away. But network utilities and server programs will not work automatically and require more complex configuring. Practically all operations that can produce undesired results or facilitate intrusions over the network are disabled. The operations are enabled by editing the configuration files or using specialized utilities. The configuration process is rather cumbersome because editing configuration files is awkward and most configuration utilities have the command line interface.

One of the Windows administrators I know gave the following appraisal of Linux based on the complexity of its configuration process: Linux was invented by those administrators who have nothing to do at work so that they could fool around with the configuration files. A week later, the same acquaintance was setting up the Internet Information Server (IIS) service on a server running under Windows Server 2003. His appraisal of this service was the same as for Linux, because by default the IIS version supplied with Windows Server 2003 has all its services disabled and before you can run the server you have to clearly specify what should work and what should not.

Microsoft started designing its operating systems with ease of operation as the foremost goal so that a program installed on the earlier operating systems would work right away without requiring any additional adjustments. With each passing year, Windows security is improving, but at the expense of most functions that make the system easy to use being disabled by default. It is the other way around with Linux. At the inception, it was developed with the security of the system as the foremost concern of its designers. Now, however, this concern has become the secondary priority, with ease of use moving up.

It is rather rough going, because making a system convenient to use detracts from its security and, on the contrary, making a system more secure makes life harder for the users. So manufacturers have to find some reasonable compromise between these two requirements.

1.1. Hacker Attacks

Before starting to explore Linux and its security system, you have to know how hackers can penetrate computer systems. To protect the system effectively, you have to be familiar with the possible ways hackers can use to break into it. To this effect, take a brief look at the break-in process. You must know what hackers think, what food they eat, and what air they breathe. Only in this way can you build an impenetrable firewall for your server or network.

It is impossible to provide a general formula that can be used for all break-ins. Each case is different and requires an individual, creative approach that depends on the system and its security configurations. Computer systems are most compromised by hackers taking advantage of the software errors, and each administrator can have different software on his or her network.

Why do attacks on computers continue to increase with each passing year? The information about the security holes and vulnerabilities in computer systems used to be stored on Bulletin Board Systems (BBSs) and only a few people with special privileges had access to it. So it was these hackers who carried out attacks with impunity, because their level of education and experience was high.

The hacker elite consisted mostly of honest people who conducted their research in the security area with the goal of improving this security, not compromising it.

The way things stand now, any information about vulnerabilities — holes, bugs, and so on — can be found in any corner of the Internet. Now anyone can be a hacker. The freedom-of-information fighters are to blame: How this came to be? Unlimited freedom always leads to destruction in the end. I guess that the urge to destroy is in the blood of all of us. Most of us suppress this, just like we do many other primitive desires, but some give in and use the publicly available information to become crackers.

When breaking into a system, hackers pursue one or a combination of the following goals:

❑ *Obtaining information.* The system is broken into to obtain information that is not available to the common public. Such break-ins are usually directed at stealing business

or financial secrets, software source codes, confidential data, and so on. They are usually carried out by professional hackers fulfilling an order or for personal gain.

❑ *Modifying or destroying data.* All Internet or intranet servers are susceptible to this type
of attack. They can be carried out not only by professional hackers but also by amateurs, including disgruntled employees.

❑ *Denial of Service* (DoS). The purpose of the attack is to render the server's service unavailable without actually destroying any data. These attacks are mainly carried out by
amateurs whose only goal is to do damage.

❑ *Zombification.* This type of attack has become quite common of late. The purpose of
the attack is to put the server under the hacker's control (in the parlance, to turn it into
a zombie) and use it to attack other servers. For example, carrying out a DoS attack
most often requires powerful resources (a powerful processor, broad-bandwidth
Internet access, etc.), which are generally not available on home computers. To carry
out such an attack, a hacker first takes over a poorly-protected Internet server that has
the necessary resources and then uses it to carry out the attack itself.

Attacks can be classified into the following three groups, based on the manner, in
which they are executed:

❑ *Local attacks.* These attacks are executed by an intruder with physical access to the
computer being broken into. This sort of attack is not difficult to protect against because all that is necessary is to restrict physical access to the server by, for example,
placing it in a limited-access room and guarding it.

❑ *Remote attacks.* These are carried out remotely via networks from a physical location
other than where the computer being broken into is located. This type of attack is the
most difficult to protect against. Even the installation of the best firewalls and monitoring and logging software cannot guarantee complete security. Proof of this can be
seen in the many break-ins suffered by some of the world's most protected Internet
servers (Yahoo, Microsoft, NASA, etc.).

❑ *Remote attacks carried out by users of the local network.* Yes, not only bad dudes somewhere on the Internet can be hackers but also the guy next cubicle who may try to
break into your computer for fun, profit, or revenge.

When designing your defenses, you must understand the techniques used by hackers
to break into computers. Only then will you be able to prevent unwanted intrusions and
protect your computers. Consider the main attack techniques used by hackers and how
they are used. To help you understand the process better, I will look at them from the
standpoint of the perpetrator.

I will not consider social engineering. This subject is worth a separate book, and it
makes no sense to only touch on the topic.

1.1.1. Research

Suppose that you want to break into a certain server to test how well it is protected. What should you start with? There is no clear-cut answer to this question. Again, any break-in is a creative process and requires an individual, creative approach. There are no set rules or ready-made templates. However, a few practical recommendations for you to follow can be provided.

Scanning

The first thing to do is test the system's vulnerability by scanning its ports. What for? To find out what services (in Linux, daemons) are installed in the system. Each open port is a service program installed on the server, to which you can connect and make it do certain things for you. For example, port 21 is used by the File Transfer Protocol (FTP) service. If you connect to this port, you will be able to download files from and upload files to the server. You will have to have the corresponding privileges, however, to be able to do this.

First, you need to scan the first 1,024 ports. Many of them are used by standard services such as FTP, HyperText Transfer Protocol (HTTP), and Telnet. An open port is just like a locked entrance door to the server. The more entrances of this type there are, the greater the chances that the lock for one of them will succumb to picking and swing open to let you in.

A good administrator leaves only the most necessary ports open. For example, if your server is used only to serve Web pages but not email, there is no need to keep the mail servers open. The only port that a Web server needs is port 80, so only it should be left open.

A good port scanner reports not only the open-port number but also the names of the service using them. Unfortunately, the service name is not real; it is only the name of the server installed on the port. Thus, the name of port 80 will be given as HTTP. It is desirable that the scanner could save the scanning results to a file and even print them out. If your scanner does not have these features, you will have to write down all the information yourself and save it. You will need this information for your future exploits.

After scanning the first 1,024 ports, you can move on to scanning the rest. Standard services are a rare occurrence in this port range. Why bother scanning them then? Well, there is always a chance that someone has already visited this area and left an open door or installed a Trojan horse on the server. Most Trojan horses keep open ports in the range above port 1,024. So if you are a server administrator, an open port above 1,024 should make you sit up and take notice. If you're a hacker and stumble on an open port above 1,024, you should find out what Trojan horse server is installed on it and find a client for it to control the machine.

This will be all you need to do to break into the server. By using the Trojan horse installed by a stranger, you can obtain access to the server without any great effort on your part. Unfortunately, life is rarely a bowl of cherries and discoveries of this kind are the exception rather than the rule. In most cases, you will have to do all the dirty work yourself.

About ten years ago, ports could be scanned in batches. Nowadays, administrators in ever increasing numbers install utilities on their servers that detect scanning attempts and do everything possible to prevent this process. The subject of protecting from scanning and the utilities used for this will be discussed in *Chapter 12.*

Consequently, because ports cannot be scanned in batches, scanning has become a rather difficult task. This is why professional hackers prefer to do manual scanning. This is done by executing the following command:

```
telnet server port
```

The first parameter is the server address and the second parameter is the port number.

Here, the `telnet` command is executed, which tries to connect to the specified port at the specified server. A successful attempt means that the port is open; otherwise, the port is closed. If no more than five ports per hour are checked in this way, most of scanning-detection utilities will not react; the scanning process, however, will stretch on for weeks.

Sometimes, scanning using various methods of the nmap utility may be helpful. This utility allows scanning be carried out using incomplete cycle packets. But even these methods can be easily detected by modern security utilities.

Because the administrator of the computer you are trying to scan can enter your Internet protocol (IP) address into the suspect list, it is a wise move to conduct scanning from a computer other than your own. To this end, crackers set up Web sites on free servers that allow them to use PHP and Perl scripts. Free servers usually do not require personal data to be provided during the registration, but even if they do, you can simply supply any made-up data because no one is going to check them. As the next step, you establish a safe connection to the server via a proxy server and run your scripts to scan the target's computer.

After the scanning, you will know, which doors are on the server that you can use. But this is not enough; the doors also have to be open. This will take much greater effort.

The most popular scanning tool is the nmap utility. It has conquered the hearts of hackers because it offers a great many features and not all scanning-detection tools can detect it. For example, a scanning-detection program can watch for attempts to connect to several ports sequentially or at once. But nmap may not establish an actual connection.

The process of establishing a connection with a remote server is carried out in several steps. First, the computer sends a request packet to the necessary port of the server. The server answers the request with a special packet. (I will not go into the details of the Transmission Control Protocol, or TCP, because the general idea will suffice for now.) Only then can a virtual connection be established. The nmap scanner can break off contact after the server's first response: It has accomplished its main goal in establishing that the port is open, and there is no need to continue the connection-establishment handshake.

Scanning-detection programs interpret such contacts as errors and do not log them as potential attacks.

Identifying the Server's Operating System

Scanning ports is just the first stage in breaking in. It is similar to casing the place before a robbery. There remains the most important thing to do before attempting the actual break-in: determining the operating system installed on the machine. The specific version of the operating system would also be a welcome piece of intelligence, but you can live without this information in the beginning.

How do you determine, which operating system is in use? This can be done in one of the following ways:

❑ *By examining the implementation of TCP/IP used.* Different operating systems implement the protocol stack in different ways. The program simply analyzes the responses to requests from the server and draws conclusions about the operating system installed based on these analyses. In most cases, the answer is vague, with only the general type of the operating system provided, Windows or Linux, for example. The exact version of the operating system cannot be determined in this way because the protocol stack is implemented in virtually the same manner in Windows 2000, Windows XP, and Windows 2003, so the responses these versions give to the requests are the same. So you can find out that the server runs under Linux, but you cannot find out, under which version. Different versions of the same operating system have different vulnerabilities, so just knowing the basic operating system brand is only half of the information you need to break into the server.

❑ *By examining responses from various services.* Suppose the victim's computer allows autonomous FTP access. All you need to do is connect to the server and check the system prompt. The default welcome prompt looks something like this: "Welcome to the *X.XXX* client FTP Version of FreeBSD Server." The message could reflect the true state of things. On the other hand, it also might not.

If the welcome prompt reflects reality, the administrator is still wet around the ears. An experienced administrator will always change the default welcome message. And a really canny administrator can make the welcome message show something different altogether. For example, a Windows NT 4.0 server can be made to display a Linux welcome message. This will make an unsophisticated hacker waste lots of time using Linux vulnerabilities to break into the Windows NT server. Therefore, don't put too much trust into the welcome message. Try to ascertain the type of the operating system by some other method.

To avoid being fooled, always pay attention to the services used on the server. For example, a Linux server will not serve Active Server Pages (ASPs). Although things like this can be faked, it is not often done. To make an ASP run under Linux, PHP script files are saved with ASP extensions and are redirected to the PHP interpreter. So it looks like the server serves ASP files, but these are actually PHP scripts.

As you can see, the defending side goes to great lengths to make life as difficult as possible for hackers. Most inexperienced hackers believe everything they see and spend lots time trying to break in using methods that have not got the slightest chance of success. Consequently, breaking in becomes too expensive an option, and the hacker gives up.

The hacker's task is to untangle all of the false leads left by the administrator and determine exactly what system he or she is dealing with. Unless this preliminary task has been completed successfully, any further actions would be like looking for a needle in a haystack. The hacker will not even know, which commands to use or what executable files can be infiltrated onto the server.

Hackers like using the nmap utility for determining the operating system. Although the programs main functionality is geared toward port scanning, if run with the −O switch, it will attempt to determine the operating system. There is a chance that this attempt will not succeed, but there also is a chance that it will.

Using Scripts

Now you know, which operating system is running the server, which ports are open, and the services that are sitting on these ports. You should write down all of this information either to a file or on paper. The important thing is that it should be convenient to work with.

This concludes the research part. Now you have enough information to attempt a basic break-in using the vulnerabilities in the server's operating system and services. The information about which vulnerabilities to use can be found by regularly visiting the **www.securityfocus.com** site. Information about new vulnerabilities is updated often on this site, and it is a longstanding and well-known fact that most servers (70% to 90%, depending on the source) simply are not patched. Therefore, you should use all known vulnerabilities on the victim and hope that something works.

If the server is well patched, you will have to wait for new holes to be discovered and for exploits to be written for them. (An exploit is a program written to exploit a specific vulnerability.) As soon as you see a new vulnerability has been discovered and an exploit for it has been written, download the exploit and use it before the administrator patches the hole.

1.1.2. Breaking into a Web Server

Breaking into a Web server involves its own specific considerations. Breaking a server that allows execution of Common Gateway Interface (CGI), PHP, or other scripts requires a different approach than for other server types. The break-in is started by scanning the server for vulnerable CGI scripts. You may find it hard to believe, but research conducted by various companies indicates that many vulnerable scripts are employed on Internet sites.

Scripts are vulnerable because pages are programmed by people, who have an inherent propensity to err. Novice programmers seldom test the incoming parameters, hoping that the users won't change the page code or the Uniform Resource Locator (URL), through which the data necessary for executing certain actions are passed to the server. But I have already considered how to modify page code and fake IP addresses in this chapter. This was possible because the programmers relied on visitors being conscientious. They shouldn't have.

One popular program for site control — PHP-Nuke — contains a parameter vulnerability problem. The program is a collection of scripts used to create a forum, chat, and news service on the site and to control the site's contents. All script parameters are passed through the URL string of the browser, and the error was located in the ID parameter. The developers assumed that only a number would be passed in this parameter, but did not check if this was actually the case. A hacker who knows the structure of the database (which is not that difficult to learn, because the source codes of PHP-Nuke are public) can easily place a structured query language (SQL) request to the database server in the ID parameter and obtain the passwords of all visitors registered at the site. The information is encrypted, but, as you will see later, it would not be difficult to decrypt it.

The problem is aggravated because some programming languages (e.g., Perl) were not intended for use with the Internet. They contain some functions for manipulating the system, and if a programmer inadvertently uses them in his or her work, hackers can take advantage of them to obtain control over the system.

All programming languages have functions that have the potential for misuse, but some languages have more than others. The only more or less secure language is Java. But it places such a drag on system resources that Webmasters are reluctant to use it. In addition, even this language, if used by an unskilful programmer, can leave great gaps that, to hackers, would be like a wide-open hangar door with a welcome sign above it.

Thus, an ignorant programmer is the biggest vulnerability. Because of the shortage of professionals in this area, anyone who completes a crash programming course becomes a programmer. Many such "accelerated programmers" do not have the slightest idea about computer security, which is not about to become a point of complaint for hackers.

So your main task is to add a couple of good CGI scanners into your toolkit. Which CGI scanner should you obtain? It does not matter; anyone of them is better than nothing. Even the worst scanner can find vulnerabilities, about which even the best hackers are unaware. And it just may happen that it will find this vulnerability on the server you are trying to break into. In addition, you should become a frequent visitor to **www.securityfocus.com**, where they regularly put out descriptions of the latest vulnerabilities of various Web site programming languages.

1.1.3. Brute Force

When your attempts to break into a server using your basic brain power have failed, you can always fall back on the brute-force method. No, brute force does not mean that you will have to grab the site administrator by the throat, knock his head on the wall, and demand that he surrender the passwords. Brute force means simply trying different passwords until you hit on the right one.

Look at the statistics. Every security-research project reaches same conclusion regarding the passwords people use: Most beginners use names of their pets, birthdays, phone numbers, and the like as their passwords. A well-compiled password dictionary can let you break into practically any system, because there are inexperienced users everywhere that use these types of passwords. And if these users have high enough privileges, hackers can have a real field day!

Are you still skeptical? Then let me remind you about the famous Morris worm, which used the dictionary method to break into systems. Its own dictionary contained fewer than 100 words. In addition to its own dictionary, the worm used the dictionaries from the compromised computers. But those did not have too many passwords in them either. Using such a primitive algorithm, the worm was able to spread through a huge number of the Internet computers. This was one of the largest-scale infections ever! Yes, it happened a long time ago, but the level of professionalism of the average user has not grown since then. There are many experienced users, but there are many more green beginners.

1.1.4. Local Networks

Hacking a local network is easier than hacking the Internet for the following reasons: The computers are connected using a high-speed connection (10 MB/sec and higher), the traffic of the other network computers can be monitored, fake servers can be created, and firewalls are seldom used because they are mostly used as a shield between the local network and the Internet. Consider the most popular local network hacking techniques.

Traffic Monitoring

Local networks have certain inherent features. For example, if a local network is built using coaxial or twisted-pair cable and hubs to connect the computers, all the network traffic passes through all the computers in the network. Why can't you see this traffic? Because the operating system and the network card are joined in a conspiracy and do not show you the traffic that is not yours. But if you really want to read other people's network traffic, you can obtain a sniffer program and monitor all data that pass through your network card even if they are not intended for you.

The sniffer trick will not work on the Internet; you will see only your own traffic. To be able to monitor the Internet traffic of other participants, you would have to hack into the provider's server and install your sniffer there. This is a rather involved undertaking, fraught with the danger of being found and kicked out. Therefore, sniffers are generally used only on local networks.

Why can you see other people's traffic on a local network but not on the Internet or switched local networks? When the computers are connected into a network using a coaxial cable, they all sit on a common bus serially. The bus can be made into a ring, with the computers at the bus ends connected to each other. When the computers at the bus ends exchange data, all packets pass through the network adapter of the computer (or computers) between them.

Coaxial cable is seldom used as the choice network medium because such a connection is unreliable and its bandwidth is limited to 10 MB/sec.

Since the early 1990s, the preferred network configuration has been the star-connected topology, with computers connected to one central point using a hub or a switch. If the central connecting device is of the hub type (also known as a multiport repeater), all packets that it receives from one of the computers are simply resent to the rest of the network computers. If the central connecting device is of the switch type, the packets are delivered only to the recipient because the switch has built-in routing capabilities.

Switches usually route Medium Access Control (MAC) address-level packets. This type of addressing is used to exchange packets only in local networks (even if data are sent to an IP address). In the Internet, packets are addressed using IP addressing, but far from all switches can handle this type of addressing. In this case, a more intelligent device is needed to send packets to the right place: a router. Like switches, routers send packets only to the computer, to which they are addressed, or to another router that knows where the addressee computer is located.

Consequently, switches in local networks and routers on the Internet make sniffing difficult, because sniffers must be placed directly on the switches or routers.

Intercepting packets is only half of the job: The information contained in them is in a form difficult for humans to interpret. It is mostly just fragments of larger data blocks that have been broken into parts to be transmitted.

Today, you can find any type of sniffer, as well as add-ons for it, on the Internet. Different versions are optimized for different tasks, so you should select the one suited to your particular task. If you are after passwords, you need a sniffer that can isolate the registration information from the overall network traffic. This task is not difficult because, unless the Secure Sockets Layer (SSL) protocol is used, all passwords are sent to the Internet in open text, just like the rest of the information.

The advantage of using sniffers when perpetrating a break-in is that they do not interact with the computer being attacked, which means that they are hard to detect. In most cases, it is simply impossible to know that your traffic is being monitored by someone.

Fake Address

It has already been mentioned that firewalls allow or disallow user access based on a set or rules. But it is not always convenient to disallow all accesses to all ports. For example, access to the management programs can be disallowed for all IP addresses except the one used by the system administrator. Anyone trying to enter the restricted area from a different IP address will be stopped by the firewall.

At first glance, the defense seems perfect. This would be the case were it not for an attack technique called spoofing. This attack is carried out by faking the address of an authorized user to enter the server under attack. Old firewalls and cheaper contemporary examples cannot detect the faked address in the packets. A good firewall should ping the computer trying to connect to ascertain that it is turned on and that this computer is actually requesting the connection to the restricted resources.

Fake Servers

Attacks using fake servers or services are much easier to carry out in local networks than on the Internet. For example, the following well-known fake Address Resolution Protocol (ARP) record attacks can be carried out only on local networks.

As you should already know, when a computer is addressed by the IP address, its MAC address is determined first and then the message is sent to this address. But how can the MAC address be determined when you only know the IP address and do not know the network interface used? This is done with the help of ARP, which broadcasts a request for the computer with the specified IP address to all computers in the network. Only the IP address is provided in the request packet, with the unknown MAC address given as FFFFFFFFFFFFh. If there is a computer with the specified IP address in the network, it replies with a packet, in which its MAC address is specified. ARP operates transparently to the user.

If there is no computer with the specified IP address on the given network segment, a router may reply by sending its own MAC address. In this case, the computer will exchange data with the router, which will resend the packet into another network segment or to another router until it reaches its destination.

But what if the computer that replies is not the specified computer but, instead, an impostor with a different IP address? When sending packets on a local network, computers do not use IP addresses but go by MAC addresses. So the packets will be sent to whichever computer claims that its MAC address corresponds to the specified IP address, regardless of what its real IP address is. The hacker's task, therefore, is to intercept an ARP request and answer it, instead of the intended recipient doing so. In this way, a connection can be taken over.

Suppose that a network computer makes a request to be connected to the server. If you intercept this request and emulate the server's password request, you will discover that computer's password to enter the network. The problem with this method is that it is almost impossible to implement manually. This requires writing a corresponding program, which means you need to have programming knowledge.

1.1.5. Trojan Horses

Using Trojan horses is the stupidest and unreliable method to employ against network administrators, but good enough against regular users, because they are easier to fool. Although there are network administrators not quite up to their position, very few of them will fall for this trick. But who says that there are only administrators on networks? There also are plenty of regular users with high access privileges and trusting souls. They are the ones you can horse around with, so to speak.

A Trojan program consists of two parts: a server and a client. The server needs to be installed on the victim's computer, one way or another, and started. Most often, a Trojan program places itself into the start-up folder, starts automatically with the system, and runs surreptitiously in the background. With the server part planted on the victim's computer, you can use the client part to communicate with the server and make it do all kinds of things, such as rebooting the computer and checking its hard drives for interesting information.

But how do you plant a Trojan horse on someone's computer? The most common way is to send it using email. Simply give the executable file of the server part some intriguing name, attach it to the message, and send it to the victim. The message text should be persuasive enough for the victim to launch the attached file. This is the same method used to insert viruses. If the user falls for your ruse and launches the server part, his computer becomes as good as if it were on your desk.

If the Trojan program is intended to steal passwords, it can send them in a file to an email address specified in advance. The address can be figured out easily by professionals (by examining the Trojan), but this is as far as they will get. Professional hackers are not stupid, and they send their wares from mailboxes they register on free mailbox services under assumed names. When a mailbox is created and checked for mail only through an anonymous proxy server, figuring out the owner is next to impossible (assuming that no secret service agency becomes interested in the case).

Trojan programs are so popular because, by following a few simple rules, the perpetrator will likely remain anonymous. In addition, today's Trojan programs are easy to use.

The danger presented by Trojan horses is indirectly confirmed by the fact that most new antivirus programs check not only for viruses but also for Trojan programs. For example, antivirus programs identify Back Orifice as the Win32.BO virus.

1.1.6. Denial of Service

The stupidest attack thought up by hackers is the DoS attack. The essence of such an attack is that the hacker attempts to make the server stop answering requests for pages. How can this be done? This is often achieved by making the server enter an endless loop. For example, if the server does not check that incoming packets are in the proper format, the hacker may send it a request that will make the server servicing this request endlessly, leaving no processor time for servicing other requests and, thus, denying service to other clients.

A DoS attack can be executed in two ways: by exploiting a bug in the server program or by overloading the server's communications channel and/or resources. The first method requires that the server have a vulnerability and that you know what it is. The most often used vulnerability is the buffer overflow error.

The procedure for the executing a buffer overflow DoS attack is as follows: Suppose that you want to send the string "HELLO" to the server. To accept this string, the server software allocates enough memory to store five characters. The program code may look like this:

```
Program code
A buffer to store five characters
Program code
```

If the program has no provisions for checking the actual size of the data it receives and writes to the data buffer, the buffer is subject to overflow. If a user sends 100 characters instead of just 5, when all these characters are written to the buffer intended to hold only 5 characters, the other characters will be written into the program code area overwriting the code. This means that the program code will be corrupted and will not be able to execute as intended. The program will most likely hang. The server then stops responding to the client requests, and you have carried out a successful buffer overflow DoS attack.

Consequently, the computer was not broken into, no information was touched, but the computer has been put out of the network service. DoS attacks are even easier to execute in a local network. All you have to do is to replace the IP address of your machine with the IP address of the machine under the attack. This will result, in the best case, in the machine under attack becoming inaccessible or, in the worst case, in both machines becoming inoperable.

To execute a resource-overload attack, little or no knowledge is needed about the machine under attack. Here, the stronger machine wins. The resources of any computer are limited. For example, a Web server can organize only so many virtual channels to communicate with clients. If the number of channels exceeds the limit, the server becomes inaccessible.

All you have to do for executing this attack is to write a program whose only function is to keep opening connections. Sooner or later, the connection limit will be exceeded, and the server will not be able to open new connections.

If there are no limitations on the resources, the server will process as many requests as it can. In this case, either the communications channel or the server can be attacked. The choice of the target depends on which is weaker. For example, if a 100-MB/sec channel is serviced by a Pentium 100 server, it is much easier to kill the computer than to overload the communications channel. But if a relatively powerful server is sitting on a narrow bandwidth channel, it is easier to overload the channel.

How can a communications channel be overloaded? Suppose that someone flamed you in a chat room. You find out his or her IP address and learn that the offender uses a simple 56-KB/sec dial-up Internet connection. Even if you use the same connection, you can overload the smart aleck's channel with no problem. You do this by sending an endless stream of large-packet ping requests to his or her IP address. The victim's computer will receive these packets and will have to answer them. If you send enough packets, receiving the ping requests and answering them will be the sole activity of the victim's computer, leaving no channel capacity for anything else and effectively taking your offender out of the chat room. If your channel capacity does not exceed the victim's, you will not be able to do anything but send and receive large ping packets. If you think this price is acceptable to take your revenge, go ahead and have fun.

If you decide to attack a server, your communications channel will be much narrower than the server's total bandwidth, and you will have to determine a weak spot for the attack to be successful. Suppose that the server offers a service for downloading files from other sites and saving them in its storage. To overload the communications channel of such a server, you may ask to download several large files simultaneously. The server will devote most, if not all, of its bandwidth to carrying out your request and, during this time, will leave other clients without service. Your own Internet connection will not be affected by this process.

A wide bandwidth channel is not needed to overload a server's processor. All that is necessary is to send it a time-intensive request. Suppose that you want to attack a server that offers online translation services for Web pages. In this case, you find a page containing lots of text (e.g., a book, a technical manual, or a request for comment) and send the server a bunch of requests to translate it. In addition to the server having to load its channel for downloading the book, it will have to load its processor to translate it. Sending about 100 requests a second to translate, for example, the King James Bible will take the server out of commission. If the server is equipped with protection against multiple requests of the same material, you can send it several large books.

DoS attacks are quite easy to defend against. The server software must control and limit the number of requests that can be submitted from one IP address. But this is only a theory, and a check of this type will only protect you from inexperienced hackers. An experienced hacker will have no problems counterfeiting IP addresses and flooding the server with packets supposedly issued from those addresses. This makes the situation even worse for the server, because, if the attack is conducted over TCP/IP, the server will have to establish a connection for each of those requests.

If a hacker sends a large number of requests to establish connections with different IP addresses, the server will send acknowledgements to those addresses and wait further actions from the computers at those addresses. Because, in the reality, there are no such addresses, waiting is useless. Consequently, filling the server's incoming connection queue buffer puts the server out of service while it waits for a connection with the nonexistent computer. How long this wait will last depends on the time-out value, which can be as large as 5 seconds. During this time, the hacker can flood the buffer with new requests and extend the wait. The process can be repeated for as long as desired.

Distributed Denial of Service

DoS attacks are suitable for attacking servers with narrow bandwidth communications channels. Large servers like **www.microsoft.com** or **www.yahoo.com** are difficult to take out with these attacks because they have wide bandwidth channels and powerful process-ing resources. No hacker can ever match this bandwidth or these processing resources. However, there is more than one way to skin this cat. To match a large server's bandwidth and processing resources, hackers resort to Distributed DoS (DDoS) attacks.

By "distributed" I mean that the communications channels and processing resources of many computer users are allied to execute the attack. However, there aren't too many users who would volunteer their resources for such purposes. Hackers solve the problem of lack of cooperation by taking over users' machines using special-purpose viruses. For ex-ample, the Mydoom.C virus searched in the Internet for computers infected with Mydoom.A and Mydoom.B viruses and used them to attack Microsoft servers. Fortu-nately, this virus did not manage to take over enough machines to execute a full-fledged attack. The Microsoft administration maintained that the servers were working as usual, but some customers did notice some lag in the servicing of their requests.

It is difficult to protect computers from a distributed DoS, because the numerous re-quests are sent by existing computers. It is difficult for the server to determine that these are not bona fide requests but are, instead, directed at taking the server out of commission.

1.1.7. Password Cracking

When a hacker is trying to break into a system, he or she most often uses one of the fol-lowing methods:

- ❑ If he or she already has an account on the server under attack (even if it is just a guest account), the hacker may try to obtain greater privileges.
- ❑ The hacker obtains the account of a specific user.
- ❑ He or she obtains the password file and uses the accounts belonging to other users.

Even when hackers manage to obtain privileged system rights, they still strive to lay their hands on the password file. Succeeding in this endeavor gives them access to the root account (in UNIX systems) and, correspondingly, rights to the entire system. But the passwords are encrypted and the successful hacker will, at most, see the hash sums produced by irreversible password encryption.

When the administrator adds a new user, his or her password is irreversibly encrypted (most often, using the MD5 algorithm), meaning that the plain password cannot be reproduced from the encrypted form. The obtained hash sum is saved in the password file. When the user enters the password, it is encrypted and compared with the hash sum saved in the file. If the results match, the password entered is accepted. The subject of how passwords are stored in Linux will be covered later.

Because the encrypted password cannot be decrypted, it may seem at first that the hash file is of no use. But appearances can be deceiving. Even though the password cannot be decrypted, it can be picked by the brute-force method. There are many programs for this task, John the Ripper (**www.openwall.com/john**) and Password Pro (**www.insidepro.com**), for example.

Why can utilities like these be freely obtained on the Internet by anyone when they can be used for criminal purposes? Any program has negative as well as positive aspects. What should you do when you forget the administrator password or the administrator has forgotten to tell you what it was when you fired him? Reinstall the system? This will take a long time and is fraught with the danger of losing data. It is easier to remove the hard drive, connect it to another computer (or simply load it from a diskette), take the password file, and break the necessary password.

1.1.9. Summary

Each cracker has numerous break-in techniques and instruments in his or her toolkit. The more experienced a hacker is, the more techniques he or she collects and tries against the target server. Having determined the server's operating system and the services running on it, the cracker starts using the attack methods in his or her arsenal one after another.

Any hacker can try password picking. This technique, however, is usually the last one resorted to because it can take too much time and produce no results in the end. In addition, password picking may fail if the server is configured to detect a password-picking attempt and the administrator reacts properly to such attempts. One of the things the administrator could do after detecting that someone is trying to pick the password to the server is configure the firewall to prohibit connections from the IP address, from which the password-picking activity was detected. This will render any other miscreant's actions useless until he or she manages to change the IP address.

The preceding review of hacker attacks is not exhaustive. I tried to provide the most essential basic information. I did not describe any specific break-in methods. Doing this could be considered a call to action, and the purpose of this book is not to add to the already overly large host of crackers. My goal is to show how hackers see the computer and how they use it. This should help you learn more about the computer and make it more secure.

I mainly considered only theory, rather than practice. To implement the break-ins described previously, you would need specialized programs and, for certain tasks, you would have to write custom programs yourself.

You must understand the theory underlying breaking-in well to know what to protect yourself from. Without this knowledge, you will not be able to build defenses capable of deflecting even the simplest hacker attacks. How can you defend yourself without knowing how the attack will be carried out? You can't.

The reliability of your defense is directly proportional to the number of attacks that can be used by hackers against your machine. The Internet is a huge world, and hackers that live in this world use various break-in techniques. To protect your house, you must know what types of criminals are likely to try to break into it. If these are petty juvenile delinquents, a good lock and alarm system will do. But if there is something in your house that may attract really bad guys, you will need window bars, armored doors, and barbed wire on the fence.

It is even more difficult to organize adequate defense on the Internet, because hackers that may try to move into your computer have different degrees of skill and use different attack techniques. It is impossible to foresee, which method will be used against you. You must be ready to defend yourself from any type of attack.

1.2. What Is Linux?

Linux is an operating system whose kernel source codes are freely available for public review and even modification under the GNU general public license. The base of the operating system's kernel was created by a young student, Linus Torvalds, at the University of Helsinki during the period from 1991 (when version 0.2 was released) to 1994 (when version 1.0 was released). The current version is 2.6, released in December 2003, and the development continues. Torvalds wrote a kernel functionally similar to UNIX systems and made it available for public review, asking people to help him improve and expand the capabilities of the new operating system. Quite a few people answered the call, and the project got rolling.

Hackers from different countries joined the project on a voluntary basis and started creating the most controversial operating system. Controversies around Linux arise almost daily, because the operating system has become widespread and customers can have it for free. Some software developers consider this project to have no future, and some (e.g., Microsoft) periodically treat it as their worst enemy.

The first official version of the operating system's kernel, version 1.0, was released in 1994, 3 years after Linux was first announced. Such a rapid development phase was made possible by the large number of professionals who joined in developing Torvalds's interesting idea.

Linux is a multiuser, multitask operating system, which means that several users can execute several tasks at the computer at the same time.

Why has this operating system become so popular, unlike other open-source projects, some of which were implemented even better than Linux? I attribute this popularity to Linux's being created by hackers and for hackers. It is a nice feeling to work with an operating system that you have taken part in creating. Any user can change the source code of the system in any way without fear of being persecuted under the law.

The initial growing popularity of Linux among system administrators was due to the operating system supporting the main UNIX standards, such as Portable Operating System Interface (POSIX), System V, and BSD. With all this, the system was designed for the inexpensive (in comparison with expensive servers like Sun Microsystems or IBM) x86 platform and possessed all the necessary capabilities. Consequently, many individuals and organizations were able to optimize their expenses on information technology infrastructure by migrating some server tasks to the free Linux platform.

One of the first tasks entrusted to Linux was organization of Web servers, and it handled this task superbly. It is difficult to tell the percentage of Web servers being run under Linux currently, but the majority of statistical analyses show that the Linux–Apache combination holds the larger share.

The operating system in its present state allows practically any task to be run under it. There have been numerous free software packages for handling various tasks written for Linux. Computers running Linux are used in diverse areas, including creating special effects for movies.

Another important factor in the operating system's popularity is that it is democratic. You are free to use all of its capabilities and are not forced to use a particular product from a particular developer. Distributives of the operating system usually contain several software packages serving the same purpose; thus, you can have several browsers, several office programs, and so on, in one distribution package. In Windows, this is impossible. I doubt that we will ever see, for example, Microsoft offering Mozilla and Opera in addition to its Internet Explorer in this system. Indeed, why would Bill Gates offer any competitors to his commercial product? In Linux, competition amounts to striving to offer the best product, leaving it up to the user to make the choice.

1.3. Is Open-Source Code Secure?

The contention that open-source code programs are more reliable and secure will hold no water. Windows XP has proven to be highly reliable and secure despite being a commercial product. Most importantly, any bugs in this operating system are timely corrected, with patches that are available for free download and are easy to install.

Those who argue in favor of this assertion believe that an open-source code system is tested by a huge number of people on the code level who discover all possible errors. Yes, testing for errors on the code level concurrently with testing the ready product is easy and effective, but the results of such testing are far from ideal. Even after extensive testing by thousands of users, errors crop up in Linux. Moreover, judging from the army of users that tested the latest Windows versions, you would think that it would finally become the perfect operating system. We know better than that, don't we? Testing is one thing, but running under real-life conditions is another, with unpredictable results popping up.

The advantage of Linux being open source is an excellent value-to-dollar ratio. But although you save a significant deal of money on the cost of the operating system, you incur expenses on its support.

Linux support is rather expensive, so you might encounter problems obtaining timely updates. Moreover, administering Linux is more difficult than administering Windows. It does not have wizards or help windows to make your life easier by telling you what button to press and when to do this. You are supposed to know the Linux commands and be able to use them without outside help. These factors make Linux more difficult for the average home user, and this is why it has not become a common operating system on home computers.

But why is Linux so difficult to master? The answer is simple: Performance and convenience are two incompatible things. Linux is a performance product, and Windows is a convenience product. To do something in Windows, you just need to go through a series of dialog windows, choosing from the available options. But this requires making lots of clicks, which in turn consumes lots of precious time. To do the same thing in Linux, you just launch the console and run the necessary command, which is much faster. But the problem is that you have to remember lots of different commands for all occasions.

Windows uses images and a graphical user interface wherever possible. Graphical utilities in Linux are too unsophisticated and often do not offer many features. This, however, is changing as graphical configuration utilities are becoming available in ever increasing numbers, making the configuration process simpler and easier. It is only a matter of time before Linux becomes easy to use while preserving all of its power and the speed of the command line interface.

Because Linux configuration is a fairly complicated process requiring a high level of proficiency, incorrectly configured systems often become targets of successful hacker attacks. The default configuration of any operating system, be it Windows, Linux, or Mac OS X, is far from ideal. Security is often sacrificed for performance or convenience. For example, some programs may have options that make the administrator's work easier (e.g., the PHP interpreter may have the debug option enabled) but at the same time make it easier for hackers to break into the system. This is why system security is directly dependent only on the person who services it.

You task is not to simply learn to work with Linux but to learn to do so efficiently, meaning that you should be able to configure it for maximum performance and security. This will be your main goal as you use this book.

Nevertheless, Linux security is higher than that of Windows, and this has nothing to do with it being open source. Simply, many security-related aspects in Linux are implemented better than in Windows. Take, for example, memory allocation. When a program is run, it is allocated a certain memory area. In Linux, under normal circumstances a program cannot overstep the bounds of the allocated memory. It can do this only in extreme cases to exchange data with other programs. In Windows, any program can access any memory area. Overstepping the allocated memory area is fraught with the danger of the program mistakenly overwriting a memory area allocated to another program or even to the system itself, causing the system to crash in the latter case.

Starting with Windows 2000, the memory subsystem operation has been improving in this brand of the operating system, but it still has lots of room for improvement. For example, Linux can clear the program's memory area after its termination because it knows exactly how much memory and at what address it allocated memory for the program's needs.

The same maintenance task is more difficult to implement in Windows, so you can only rely on the quality of the application software, which is unlikely to improve. Thus, there is constant memory leakage in this operating system.

1.4. The Kernel

The kernel, the heart of the operating system, implements control over the memory and other computer's resources. The kernel also handles access to various hardware components of the system. For example, until version 2.4 of the kernel was introduced, the only Universal Serial Bus (USB) devices that Linux supported were the keyboard and mouse. But starting with version 2.4, Linux supports USB video cameras, printers, and other devices.

The Linux kernel version is designated using three numbers as follows:

❑ The first number indicates significant kernel changes.
❑ The second number indicates slight changes. This number tells whether the kernel is stable or is intended for testing purposes only and may contain errors. An even number means that the kernel has undergone thorough testing and is stable. An odd number means that the kernel version is in the testing stage and stable operation is not guaranteed.
❑ The build number indicates the release version.

You have to update the kernel yourself, which gives your system new capabilities. Updating to an unstable kernel version, you can take part in its testing. New kernel versions can be downloaded from the **www.kernel.org** site or from the site of the developer of your distribution package.

Updating the kernel not only will give your machine new capabilities for using the hardware components but also will correct errors, which are part of all software, no matter how well tested. It can even increase the efficiency of your system. The most important thing is that you do not have to reconfigure the entire operating system to update the Linux kernel, as is done in some operating systems. I have seen computers whose operating systems were configured just as they had been when they were installed several years ago, with only the kernel and application programs being updated as needed. This is an exception rather than a rule. Usually, the system's hardware has to be upgraded every year or two to increase the performance and thus satisfy the ever-increasing demands of users and new resource-hungry software.

1.5. Distributions

At present, there are dozens of versions of Linux, called distributions. Despite this embarrassment of riches, you can easily see that they are similar to one extent or another, because most of them have the same roots. Many distributions, for example, are built on the base of the Red Hat Linux brand. Although Linux is free, its distributions are not quite so.

Just like Windows or other commercial software, you have to buy Linux from software vendors. Their license agreements, however, are much more generous than those for commercial operating systems. For example, after buying one copy of Linux, you can install it on as many computers as you want to. Usually, vendors modify the installer slightly (this mostly consists of "dabbing some make-up" to the graphical interface), change the list of application software, and then sell it under their brand name. In most cases, however, the system's kernel and the application software are not changed.

But even distributions of different origins almost always use the K Desktop Environment (KDE) or/and GNU Network Object Model Environment (GNOME) graphical shells. If, in an unlikely case, the distribution does not supply these shells, you can easily obtain them from third-party sources and install them yourself. Consequently, all distributions use the same graphical interface, regardless of their origins.

In this book, I will consider the Red Hat distribution of Linux because it is the most widely used (by some accounts, it holds about a 50% share of the Linux market). Don't worry if you are using another distribution: You will not notice any significant differences. The biggest differences among distributions show up mostly during the installation process, but even then only in the way the graphical interface is implemented.

The abundance of distributions is the weakest spot of the Linux operating system. This problem stems from the open-source nature of the software. When you start working with the operating system — or, more exactly, with its application software — you will see that numerous operations are not standardized. For example, you have to press the <Ctrl>+<C> key combination to exit one program, <Ctrl>+<X> to exit another, and <Ctrl>+<Q> to exit yet another one. This is a serious problem that complicates handling the system.

In this respect, Windows is more standardized and is easy to become used to — although in Windows there has been a tendency to march to the beats of different drummers of late. For example, the appearance of programs has become unpredictable. In Windows XP, some programs have kept up with the times and have the XP look, but some have not and have the pre-XP look. Menus and toolbars change from Office 2000 to Office XP to Office 2003. In Linux, despite no standards, all menus and toolbars are the same, and you don't have to become used to new ones from one program to another.

The price for one copy of Linux is much lower than that for Windows. Moreover, the distribution package includes a huge number of application software, such as office applications, Internet utilities, and graphics editors. Consequently, having installed a Linux distribution you can immediately use the system to solve most office and home tasks (not the laundry, though).

Microsoft's Paint, WordPad, and other application programs supplied with the operating system are too unsophisticated for anything but the most basic tasks. To obtain corresponding application software of acceptable performance, you will have to spend thousands of extra dollars. Therefore, the actual price of a ready-to-work Windows-based workstation is much higher than the price of the operating system, because application software is to be purchased in addition to the operating system.

Comparing the combined cost of the operating system and the application software, Linux is significantly less expensive than Windows. Microsoft, however, provides free support for its product; whereas to obtain any decent support for Linux, you must have access to the Red Hat network, which is rather expensive. Thus, support expenses can make the ownership costs of the two operating systems equal. This is why I am not saying that Linux is better than Windows because it is free; that is not quite right. But you will see that Linux is better because it is more flexible, more reliable, and, if it is configured properly, more efficient. These properties are more important than the price, and you will see that all of them are inherent to Linux.

Consider the main Linux distributions available on the market. Remember that Linux is just the kernel, and most of the application software, services, and graphical shells are provided by third-party developers. Exactly which application software is supplied with the operating system depends on the distribution's developer.

In your choice of distribution, you should be guided by what you want the system to do. This is not, however, a mandatory requirement, because any distribution can provide the necessary power and security if you supplement it with third-party software packages.

1.5.1. Red Hat Linux

This distribution is considered the classic and the trendsetter of this operating system, because the creator of Linux, Linus Torvalds, works for Red Hat. You can either purchase this distribution or download it for free from the company's site at **www.redhat.com**. Red Hat produces two versions of its Linux distribution: one for server solutions and one for client computers. The interface of the latter version is becoming increasingly user-friendly and is suitable for any home task.

Installing this distribution has been easy and convenient for a long time. I will consider installing Red Hat in *Chapter 2*, and you will see that there is nothing difficult about it.

All Linux distributions have a bad reputation for not being user-friendly where application software installation is concerned. The latter is usually supplied as the source code that has to be compiled. Red Hat made installing programs, including the Linux kernel, easy with the help of the Red Hat Package Manager (RPM), which may be viewed as a counterpart of the Windows installer.

Many Linux enthusiasts hope that the Red Hat initiatives will make their favorite operating system easy for everyone to use and enable it to move ahead of the competition.

If you are looking for a distribution for a server, I urge you to take a serious look at the Red Hat distribution or one of its clones. Red Hat takes good care of the security of its product and tries to correct any errors in it as soon as possible.

1.5.2. Slackware

It is this distribution that introduced me to Linux. You can download it from **www.slackware.com**. This is one of the oldest and most difficult distributions for home users. There is still no easy and convenient installation utility for it, and most operations have to be carried out in the text mode. You can install the KDE or GNOME graphical interfaces and other utilities that make life easier when using this distribution, but this will not make the installation itself easier.

If you have never worked with Linux, I would recommend that you do not start your acquaintance with this distribution and select a distribution that is easier to work with.

1.5.3. SUSE Linux

I have worked with various software packages produced by German developers and can say that describing their usability as "leaving a lot to be desired" would be a gross understatement. Their programs, at least those that I had the misfortune of working with, are cripples from birth. But the Linux kernel from SUSE (**www.novell.com/linux/suse/**) is a pleasant exception. This distribution has a nice interface, and its huge database of drivers provides excellent hardware support. SUSE programmers have also added a utility collection named YaST to the distribution, which makes administering it much easier. But as you will see, although the ease of use is a desirable quality, maximum efficiency can be achieved only by directly editing configuration files.

I would only recommend SUSE for amateurs or for use on client computers.

1.5.4. Debian

Although many developers of distributions seek commercial gain, many distributions are available for free. The main and largest of such distributions is Debian (**www.debian.org**). This product is created by professionals around the world for their own use, but anyone can use their distribution.

Debian differs from the classical Red Hat, and you may run into problems because some of its configuration files are located in different places than in other distributions. The problems do not end here. Like all noncommercial products, this distribution is more difficult to use than commercial software. Its developers position Debian as a dependable operating system, and they do a good job of it. But they do not care much for regular users, so conquest of the home computer market by this distribution in the foreseeable future is unlikely.

There are many other distributions, spanning the range from large and powerful systems including all necessary software to small distributions fitting on a diskette and running on old computers.

It would be difficult to describe all of them in one book, and there is no need to do so. The main intention of this book is to teach you how to create a secure and efficient system. This is difficult to accomplish because of the large number of distributions; security specifics can differ among distributions and even among kernel versions.

This concludes the introduction to Linux. I will move on to installing this operating system, allowing you to acquire knowledge of it firsthand.

Chapter 2: Linux Installation and Initial Configuration

Installation has always been the most difficult part of all Linux distributions. I remember when installation had to be performed by using several diskettes, following arcane instructions, or typing Linux console commands.

Another difficult task is partitioning disks. Linux requires at least two partitions: the root partition and the swap file partition. Many people are apprehensive of tinkering with disk partitioning, especially if the disk already contains information on it. This apprehension is fully justified, because there is always a chance of losing the information if the instructions are not followed correctly or if the power is lost and the computer is not powered from an uninterruptible power supply (UPS).

During the installation process, any operating system must detect the hardware devices installed, install the necessary drivers, and make other preparations necessary for the devices to function properly. Only about 7 years ago, the list of the supported devices could be read through in a couple of minutes, because many device manufacturers ignored Linux and did not provide their devices with Linux drivers. Moreover, they did not provide the information about their devices that would allow third parties to write drivers for them. Nowadays, reading through the device list will take days, because the penguin (an emblem of Linux) is recognized by all important computer device manufacturers. The system now determines devices rapidly and without errors, requiring no user involvement in most cases.

Today, the entire installation process is performed practically automatically and is no more complicated than that for other operating systems. This is the reason Microsoft has started to feel apprehensive about Linux and its advances into the home computer market. Now any user, even a beginner, can install the operating system on his or her own.

Even though the installation process is easy, I will briefly consider it, giving more attention to its most important moments.

If you already have experience of installing Linux, I still recommend that you read this chapter because you may find some interesting and useful material in it. The main security and efficiency principles are formed starting with the installation stage to be followed and expanded from there.

2.1. Preparing To Install

Which distribution should you install? I cannot give you definite advice in this respect; you have to decide. Select the distribution that meets your requirements and is suitable for the tasks at hand. The descriptions of the main features of the most popular distributions given in *Section 1.5* should be of some help to you in this respect.

I also would like to recommend installing the latest version of both the kernel and the application software of whatever distribution you decide on. The reason for this is, as already mentioned, that the software errors discovered in the earlier versions are fixed in the latest version. To this end, updating your kernel and application software is also highly advisable. If you install an older distribution, you will have to update too many programs. It is better to install all new stuff from the get-go to avoid the trouble of installing updates and put your server in commission right away.

Installation wizards may differ for different distributions, but, as a rule, their windows are often similar, and even the sequence of the performed operations is often the same.

Well then, let's get down to considering the installation process. First, you will have to prepare the hard disk for installing the operating system. If you are installing Linux on a new computer with a hard disk that is not partitioned, and if you are planning on using this operating system only, you don't have to do anything with the disk; simply allocate all available disk space to Linux.

But if you already have Windows installed and want to keep it, you will have to do some work. In this case, you must have some free disk space — free not in the sense of available space on the C: drive but in the sense of disk space not allocated at all. Newer distributions have capabilities to release disk space during the installation. But if your distribution is not one of these, you will have to use a third-party utility, such as PartitionMagic (**www.powerquest.com/partitionmagic**).

Launch PartitionMagic. The main window of the program is shown in Fig. 2.1. The panel on the left contains the tree of all hard disks installed in the system. In this case, there is only one physical hard disk. It is partitioned into only one primary partition, C:, which takes the entire disk space. The graphical depiction of the disk in the right part of the main window shows how much of the disk space is taken by the data (shown in pale orange on the left). The area to the right of it is unoccupied and means the maximum amount of the disk space that can be released from the primary partition.

Your task is to reduce the size of the C: disk, to free the space on the physical disk that can be used to create a new logical disk, on which to install Linux.

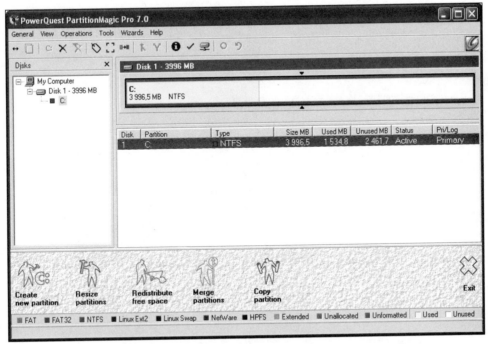

Fig. 2.1. The main window of the PartitionMagic program

Select disk C: in the left panel or at its graphical representation on the right. Click the **Resize partitions** button at the bottom of the window. This will open a dialog window, in which you can specify a new size for the logical disk C:. You should have at least 4 GB or more of disk space to install Linux. So if, for example, the size of the logical disk is 20 GB, specifying the new size as 16 GB will release 4 GB. Click the **Exit** button to apply the changes. The program will ask you to confirm the changes and may inform you of the need to reboot in the Disk Operating System (DOS) mode, to which you should agree. The rest of the procedure will be carried out automatically, and when it is finished, the size of the logical disk will be reduced to the specified, and necessary disk space freed.

2.2. Starting the Installation

Now that you have free disk space, you can start the installer. Insert the installation CD-ROM into the drive and reboot the computer. The first boot device on your computer must be specified as the CD-ROM drive. If this is not the case, enter the basic input/output system (BIOS) setup and set the CD-ROM drive as the first boot device and the hard disk drive as the second boot device. This procedure varies for different motherboards, BIOS manufacturers, and even BIOS versions. Therefore, consult the user's manual for your motherboard for the specific information.

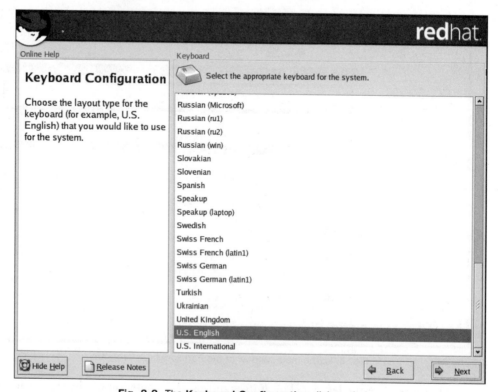

Fig. 2.2. The **Keyboard Configuration** dialog window

First, you will see text lines on the screen reporting the results of testing the computer, installed hard disk drives, CD-ROM drives, mouse, video card, monitor, and other hardware. This may seem unfamiliar and intimidating, but there is nothing unusual about this. Windows also tests the system during the boot process; it simply does not show the results to the user.

After it finishes testing the hardware, the Linux installer switches into the graphical mode and opens the dialog window to select the language to be used during the installation. Select the language you are most comfortable with, and click the **Next** button.

This will open the **Keyboard Configuration** window (Fig. 2.2). Select the necessary keyboard layout and click the **Next** button again.

The next step is selecting the mouse type. The installation program does not trust its own judgment in this respect, and rightly so. Almost always when I install Linux, the installer determines the mouse as the two-button PS/2 type. It does not even attempt to look for the third button. It's no big deal, because almost always only two mouse buttons are used in Linux. I, however, always select a three-button mouse.

The mouse selection dialog window contains a list of mouse manufacturers in the left panel and a list of known devices of the selected manufacturer in the right panel. To keep things simple, select the **Generic** manufacturer (this configuration will work with devices from any manufacturer); in the list in the right window, select the device with the correct number of buttons and connection. The mouse-connection type is shown to the right of the mouse in parentheses and can be one of the following:

- ❑ PS/2 — The modern port for connecting input devices such as the keyboard and mouse.
- ❑ USB — Becoming an increasingly common universal interface used with various devices.
- ❑ Serial — Also known as the COM port and is used in older mice and computers. It is difficult to find a mouse with this interface nowadays.

The next step after selecting the mouse is to select one of the following installation types:

- ❑ **Personal Desktop** — This type of installation is most suitable for personal computers or laptops. Software used mostly on client computers will be installed.
- ❑ **Workstation** — Software packages necessary for network client stations will be installed.
- ❑ **Server** — Server software will be installed (Web server, mail server, etc.).
- ❑ **Custom** — Here you decide, which software packages to install.

Different distributions may offer other choices than the first three just listed, but most of them should include the **Custom** item. I recommend selecting this type of installation so that you have control over which software packages to install.

The next step is selecting the disk, onto which to install the operating system. This may present some difficulties, so I will describe this process in more detail.

2.3. Disk Partitioning

You have the choice of either partitioning the disk manually or having the installer partition the disk automatically. The choices for automatic partitioning are the following:

- ❑ **Remove all Linux partitions on this system** — Selecting this option will remove only Linux partitions (if there are such from previous Linux installations). No other partitions (such as 32-bit File Allocation Table, or FAT32, and the new technology file system, or NTFS) will be removed.
- ❑ **Remove all partitions on this system** — Selecting this option will remove all existing partitions on your hard disk (or disks, if you have more than one hard disk drive). This option is suitable when the operating system being installed will be the only one on the computer. In this case, the installation program will select how much disk space to allocate to specific operating system components.
- ❑ **Keep all partitions and use existing free space** — If there already is an operating system on this computer that you want to keep and you have released disk space using a partition utility (such as PartitionMagic), you should select this option. The installation program will create disks for Linux based on the amount of free space on the physical disk.

2.3.1. Disk Naming

In Linux, the disk-naming method is different from the one used in Windows. There are no disks A:, C:, etc. in Linux. Instead, disks are named as /dev/hdnX, where n is the physical disk letter (assigned as a, b, c, etc.) and **X** is the primary or extended partition number or the logical disk number. There can be up to four primary partitions or three primary and one extended partitions on a physical disk. Consequently, numbers from 1 to 4 are reserved for the primary and/or extended partitions. Logical disks in the extended partition are given numbers starting with 5.

It may seem complicated at first, but the following example should make it simple. Suppose you have two physical hard disk drives on your system. The first drive is partitioned into a primary partition and an extended partition. Furthermore, you divide the extended partition on the first physical drive into two logical drives. The second hard drive has one primary partition and one extended partition. Linux labels this arrangement as follows:

/dev/hda — The first physical hard drive
    /dev/hda1 — The primary partition on the first physical drive
    /dev/hda2 — The extended partition of the first physical drive
        /dev/hda5 — The first logical disk on the extended partition of the first physical drive
        /dev/hda6 — The second logical disk on the extended partition of the first physical drive
/dev/hdb — The second physical hard drive
    /dev/hdb1 — The primary partition on the second physical drive
    /dev/hdb2 — The extended partition on the second physical drive
        /dev/hdb5 — The logical disk on the extended partition of the second physical drive

The first logical disk on the extended partition of the first physical hard drive was assigned the number 5. The number 6 was assigned to the second logical disk on the extended partition of the first physical hard drive. The logical disk on the extended partition of the second physical hard drive was also given the number 5.

2.3.2. Linux File Systems

Now, look at the file systems supported by Linux. This operating system supports various file systems, including the FAT, FAT32, and NTFS Windows file systems. It is advisable, however, to install Linux on its own Ext2, Ext3, or ReiserFS (often shortened to just Reiser) file system. The Reiser file system is the latest development and is based on a concept called journaling. This makes this file system more stable and the after-crash recover process much faster. Thus, it is preferable to install Linux on this file system.

To help choosing the optimal file system, consider the basic operating principles of the main file systems. With the Ext2 file system, the data are cached first and only then written to the disk, which makes file operations highly efficient. However, if there is a power outage or the system crashes, some of the data in the cache may not have been written to the disk and the file system will become corrupted. The next time the operating system boots, it will detect that the integrity of the file system has been corrupted and will run the fsck (a rival of the Windows' scandisk) disk-checking utility to detect and correct any potential damages. This will restore the disk's operability but not the data. Moreover, the scanning process takes a long time, which adversely affects the speed, with which the server is put back into operation. Consequently, be prepared for the system to take a longer time to boot after a crash.

With the Reiser file system, data are also cached before being written to the disk. But unlike with Ext2, after the data were written to the disk, their integrity is checked and only if the write was successful is the cache cleared. In case of a crash or power outage, upon the next boot, the journal record is used to detect corrupted data and to "back out" these data, thereby preventing most data corruption and restoring the disk operability more rapidly than with other file systems.

The Reiser file system has another advantage over other file systems. Data are usually written to the disk in blocks. Assume that the size of a block is 1 KB. Then, for example, a 100-byte file written to the disk in FAT32 will occupy the whole block, with 90% of the block space being wasted. Consequently, the amount of data that can actually be stored on a disk will be slightly less than the disk size; if lots of small files are stored on the disk, the waste will be even greater. The Reiser file system provides more efficient use of the disk space.

Disk waste in Windows can be demonstrated by opening a file's **Properties** window (Fig. 2.3). Take note of the **Size** and **Size on disk** parameters. The former is the file's size and the latter is the disk space the file occupies. The size of a disk cluster is 4 KB, or 4,096 bytes. The file is 973 bytes larger than the cluster size, so another cluster is allocated to store these 973 bytes. No more data can be stored in the second cluster, resulting in more than 75% of its storage space being wasted.

When 1,024 100-byte files are written to the disk, each of the files is allocated a 4-KB cluster. This will result in 4 MB of disk space used to store only 100 KB of data: a waste of almost 95%.

The Reiser file system provides more efficient use of the disk space by allowing several small files to be written to one cluster.

The Ext3 file system is another journaling file system, which is analogous to the Reiser file system. Currently, it is the default file system in most modern Linux distributions. It is difficult to compare the performance of the Reiser and the Ext3 files systems, but from the reliability standpoint I advise you to agree with the developers and use the latter.

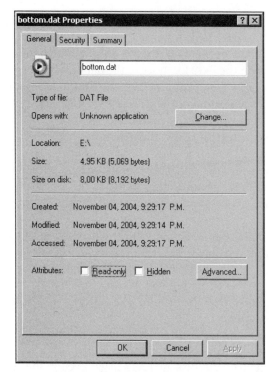

Fig. 2.3. The file **Properties** window

2.3.3. Manual Partitioning

If you intend your machine to be a server, I urge you to partition the disk manually. By default, the installation program creates only two partitions for Linux: the root partition and the swap partition to use as virtual system memory. This arrangement is far from efficient and can prove unsafe. Select the **Manually partition with Disk Druid** item. This will open the **Disk Setup** dialog window (Fig. 2.4).

The large panel in the lower right part of the window contains the list of disks, including the free disk space. In this case, there is only one disk: /dev/sda. Below the disk name, there usually is the table of the disk partition. As can be seen in Fig. 2.4, there are no partitions on this disk.

To create a partition in the free disk space, click the **New** button. This will open the **Add Partition** dialog window (Fig. 2.5).

Select the file-system type in the **File System Type** dropdown list. As was already stated, the most preferable file system for Linux is Ext3, and this is the type of the file system I recommend that you select.

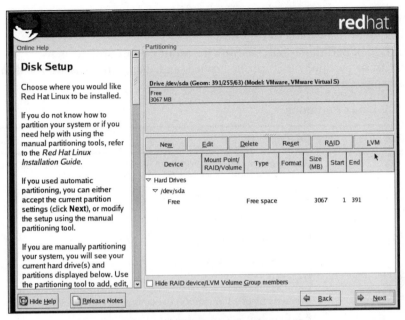

Fig. 2.4. The **Disk Setup** dialog window

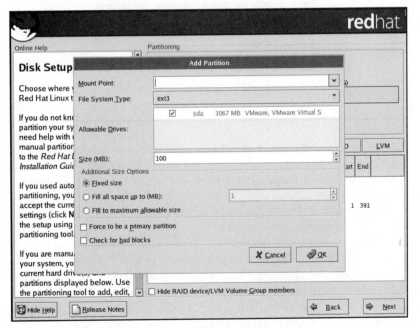

Fig. 2.5. The **Add Partition** dialog window

The size of the new partition is set in the **Size (MB)** list box, either by typing it into the entry field or by using the scroll buttons.

The type of partition is selected from the **Mount Point** dropdown list.

The list of partitions that can be created, and their functions are listed in Table 2.1. The exact list varies for different distributions.

Table 2.1. Linux Partitions

Partition	Description
/	Root partition. While in Windows a path starts with the name of the disk, in Linux the path starts with the root (depicted with a slash).
/bin	System's main executable files.
/boot	Files necessary to boot the system.
/dev	Represents the devices attached.
/etc	Stores system configuration files.
/home	User files.
/lib	Contains binaries to support executables.
/opt	Optional software packages.
/proc	Files used for mounting the virtual file system.
/sbin	Executable files of the main (root) user.
/tmp	Temporary files.
/usr	Stores system files.
/var	Log, spool, or lock files.
swap	Swap file.

Note that, with the exception of the first and the last partitions in the table (root and swap, respectively), the names of all partitions start with a slash. This is because the root and the swap partitions are mandatory, while the rest of the partitions can be represented as folders in the root partition.

The swap partition always has to be a separate partition with its own file system. It cannot be represented as a folder in the root. The size of the swap partition should be at least that of the installed system memory. I recommend making the swap partition at least 3 times the size of the installed system memory: It is possible that the memory will be extended in the future, but changing the size of the swap file is a little complicated, requiring you to edit the /etc/fstab file or use disk partitioning tools, such as fdisk.

Linux requires at least two actual partitions: the root partition (denoted as /) and the swap partition. The root partition can have any file type except the swap file type. The swap partition can only have the swap file-type system. The root partition is used to hold all files, and the swap partition is used as virtual memory to supplement the system memory. The rest of the partitions listed in Table 2.1 do not have to be created as actual disk partitions but can be represented as folders in the root partition.

At first, all of this may seem complicated, especially if you have only worked with Windows before. But the capability to house numerous operating-system files in their own partitions is a powerful one. Two partitions are enough when you have only one physical hard drive on a home computer. If you have two physical hard drives, you will benefit from creating three partitions as follows:

- ❏ / — On the first physical hard drive to hold all system files
- ❏ swap — On the first physical hard drive
- ❏ /home — On the second physical hard drive to hold user files

It is advisable to connect the disks to separate controllers; this will allow the system to work with them practically in parallel. In this way, the performance of the operating system may be raised significantly, because Linux can work with the system and user files simultaneously.

If you are setting up a server, the /home and /var folders are better to set up on separate physical hard drives. Placing these folders on logical disks will not produce the results desired.

How large should you make the partitions? The size of the swap partition should be set depending on the amount of system memory installed, as was mentioned earlier. If the /var and /home partitions are placed on separate physical drives, 4 GB will be enough for the root partition, although it can be made larger.

It is better not to economize on the size of the /var partition; make it 10 GB. This partition stores the log, World Wide Web (WWW), and FTP files. These files grow in size rapidly, and if they fill up the entire available space, the system may crash or even become inaccessible. Hackers sometimes take advantage of this circumstance when organizing DoS attacks. I will consider various aspects of these attacks more than once in this book. Some security specialists recommend placing this partition on the largest physical disk, where most often the /home partition is also located. Following this advice, however, will affect the performance adversely. Placing logs on a separate physical disk makes it possible to write to them concurrently with servicing the rest of the partitions. This means that while on one physical disk the user is working with his or her files in the /home partition, on the other physical disk the system is storing all information about the user's activity. If both partitions are on the same physical disk, they cannot be accessed in parallel.

If necessary, the /var and /home partitions can be placed on the same, the largest, physical disk. But, in this case, allocate to the /home partition all disk space left after other partitions. This partition is used to store user data, which usually become voluminous. Economizing on the space here will soon result in users complaining about not being able to save results of their games on the server. But if the technical characteristics of your system allow this, place the /var and /home partitions each on an individual physical hard disk, as large as you can afford, and you will have no problems.

For a test system, the simplest arrangement, with two partitions (the root and the swap), will suffice.

After partitioning the disk, the new partitions have to be formatted. Some especially smart distributions will carry out this operation without asking any questions.

2.4. Boot Loader

The system must know how you intend to boot it. The boot loader is configured in the **Boot Loader Configuration** window (Fig. 2.6). Whereas the boot loader for Windows must be installed in the Master Boot Record (MBR), a boot loader for Linux can be installed in the MBR, can be installed in the /boot partition on any other disk, or can be unused. (To select where to install the boot loader, check the **Configure advanced boot loader options** checkbox.) In the latter case, Linux can be booted into only from a diskette or using some other complicated method.

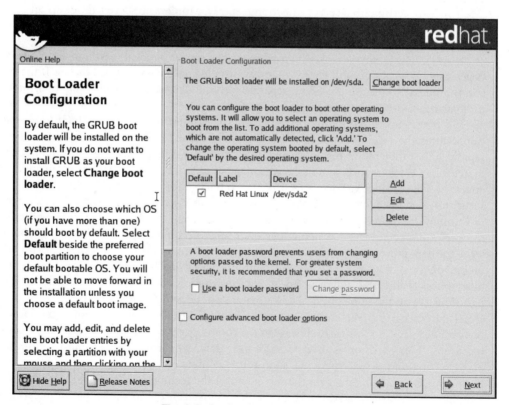

Fig. 2.6. Configuring Linux boot loader

There exist many boot loaders for Linux. Most distributions offer the choice between Linux Loader (LILO) and Grand Unified Bootloader (GRUB). The default boot loader for Red Hat is GRUB. Unless you have some compelling reason to boot into Linux from a diskette, install the boot loader of your choice into the MBR. For this, you have to check the **Configure advanced boot loader options** checkbox, click the **Next** button, and select the appropriate choice in the dialog window that opens.

When the system is powered on, the boot loader will give you the choice of into which operating system to boot: Windows (if you have this operating system installed), Linux (or any of its kernels, if you have more than one installed), or any other system you have installed.

If you have selected not to install the boot loader into the MBR, I strongly recommend creating a bootable diskette. It may come in handy in case the Linux boot loader on the disk becomes corrupted, and it is the only way to boot the computer into Linux if you installed it without a boot loader. Depending on the Linux distribution, you will be given an opportunity to create a bootable diskette during the installation process.

2.5. Network Configuration

If there is a network card installed in your computer, the driver installation dialog window will open. If the necessary driver is not in the list, select none. This does not mean that the network card will not work; simply, a universal driver will be installed for it. After the installation, you will be able to install the card's proper drivers to make it work at its full capacity.

The next step is configuring the network. If there is only a single Dynamic Host Configuration Protocol (DHCP) server in your network, you can leave the default settings. If there are more servers in your network or the addresses have to be assigned manually, clear the check mark in the **Configure using DHCP** checkbox.

If you do not know how TCP/IP works, you can specify 192.168.77.1 as the address. The value of the **Mask** field must be 255.255.255.0. I will cover the network configuration subject in a greater detail in *Section 3.6*, including how to change the connections parameters. In the **Host** name field, specify the computer's name.

2.6. Root Password

The last thing that needs to be done before installing packages is to set the system administrator (root) password (see Fig. 2.7). In Linux, like in Windows XP Professional (not to be confused with Windows XP Home Edition), the system cannot be entered without a password, as can be done in Windows 9x. You have to provide the user name and the password; only then will you be given access to certain areas and functions of the operating system. Exactly with which areas and functions you will be allowed to work in depends on your privileges.

The installation program only checks to ensure that the password is of a certain length, which should be no shorter than six characters for the administrator. Because the root user has complete system rights, the administrator password must be as difficult to pick as possible.

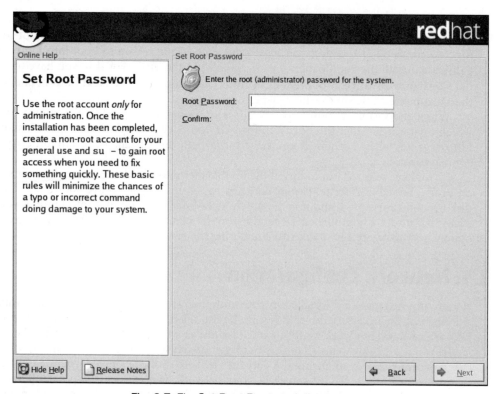

Fig. 2.7. The **Set Root Password** dialog window

All computer security specialists unanimously ask their users to use complex passwords, but few of the latter follow those recommendations. Names, meaningful words, birthday dates, and the like should not be used for passwords. These passwords can be easily compromised by a simple dictionary-search method and, if there is already a dictionary of likely passwords available, this search will not take long.

It is advisable to generate random passwords containing lowercase and uppercase letters, digits, and other allowed characters. A password should be at least 8-character long; 12 characters are more desirable. In the latter case, it will take much more time for the hacker to pick it.

When I need to generate a password, I start a word processor (the standard Notepad will do) and randomly hit the keyboard keys, periodically switching between the uppercase and the lowercase options. You may say that a password generated this way is too difficult to remember. I firmly believe it is better to spend a couple of days memorizing a strong password than to lose some important data.

If you don't feel like doing this, there is a simpler method of generating passwords, but the reliability of the passwords generated using it is accordingly lower. You start with some word as a base, "generation," for example. It is sufficiently long, but, on the other hand, can be easily picked using the dictionary method. To make it stronger, replace the original letters with the letters located in the keyboard row above and to the left of them. Using this method, letter "g" is substituted with letter "t," letter "e" is substituted with digit "3," and so on, the resulting password being t3h34q589h. This password is as easy to remember as the starting word, but, at the same time, is more difficult to pick using the dictionary method.

Other variations of this method can be used, like replacing the original letters with the letters to the right of them. Some replacement letters can also be uppercase, which makes the password twice as difficult to pick.

As you can see, the method is surprisingly simple, but the passwords it produces are sufficiently difficult to pick.

2.7. Installing Packages

The next stage is selecting application software components to install. This is a rather important moment, and it is at this point that many users make their first and the most terrible mistake: They select all available packages. The names and functions of many packages do not tell much to most users, so beginners cannot form a clear idea what they need to install. But this does not mean that all available packages are to be installed.

On my testing system, I have Linux with all available packages installed. I use this system to test new programs and to check the operability of individual modules. But I do not install anything unnecessary on my work systems.

Any Linux distribution contains an incredible amount of application software, especially server programs. You have a Web server, an FTP server, and much other software. If you install all available application-software packages, you will make your computer a public thoroughfare, especially if all these packages start automatically on the system boot. Moreover, it will take much too long for the system to boot, comparable to booting Windows XP on a Pentium 100 machine.

There will be numerous ports opened and various services running in the operating system, about which you do not yet have the slightest idea as to their function and operation. As you know, there is no bug-free software. It is only a matter of time before bugs are detected and, hopefully, corrected. If there is only one buggy daemon (a server program that processes client requests), any hacker can penetrate your system and do whatever he or she likes in it.

For a work system, I start by installing the bare operating system, to which I then add only the necessary components. Additional components can be installed at any time, but removing an installed component is sometimes tricky.

During the installation, the software packages to install are selected in the **Package Group Selection** dialog window (Fig. 2.8), which contains a list of all components that can be installed divided into groups. Packages that are to be installed by default have their checkboxes marked. No server program is installed by default, which is just fine. However, if you know that you need to install some server, you can put a mark into its checkbox to have it installed automatically.

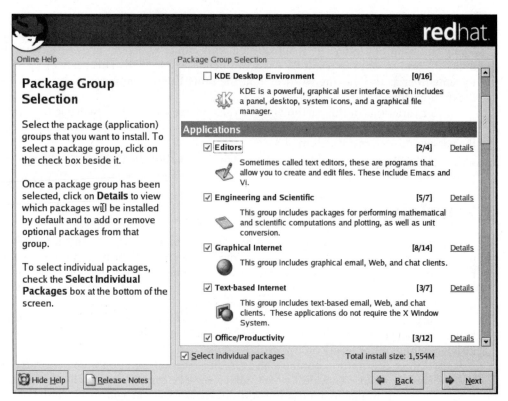

Fig. 2.8. The **Package Group Selection** dialog window

Linux components can usually comprise more than one application. For example, the **Editor** component contains four text editors. To change which particular text editor will be installed, click the **Details** label to open the list of the available components. Here you can view components that are available, and select those you want to install.

Take your time and go through all the packages in the list. Select only the most necessary components; you will be able to add other components after the installation. Remember that during the installation stage, you are laying the foundation for the future efficiency and security of your system.

Do not install anything that is unnecessary. If you do not use a program, you, naturally, will not keep track of and apply updates to fix any potential bugs. Hackers can take advantage of these bugs to penetrate your system. Thus, by installing a program that will be just sitting there unattended, you are leaving an extra door, through which hackers can enter your system.

Having selected all necessary software packages, click the **Next** button. This will take you to the **About to Install** dialog window (Fig. 2.9). This is the last point, at which you can go back to the beginning of the installation process or safely abort the installation.

Clicking the **Next** button will start the process of writing the system to the hard drive, which cannot be undone. The installation process will take a little while, during which you can make yourself a cup of coffee and even watch a short movie.

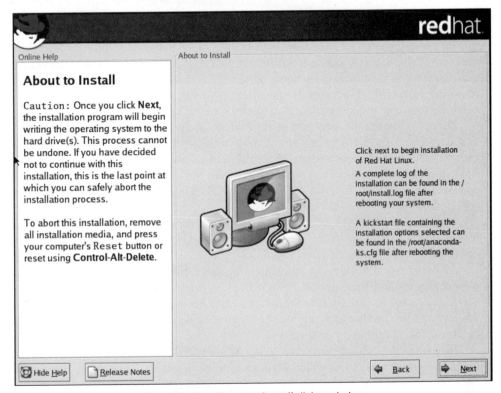

Fig. 2.9. The **About to Install** dialog window

While the installation is under way, let me tell you more about this process so that you will have the necessary knowledge when it is time to configure the system. Suppose that you must have three servers on your network: a Web server, an FTP server, and a news server. The security aspects of running all three servers on one computer will be far from ideal. I always install individual servers on separate computers and advise that you don't economize on hardware but do the same.

Each running daemon is a potential security hole. You already know that all software packages have bugs in them and that administrators are often not the first ones to find this out. Assume that a bug was discovered in the Apache server. This sort of thing happens rarely of late, because the program has been well debugged, but you can imagine such a situation for the sake of an example. Moreover, the bug may be not in Apache but in the Web server that it services, or in the PHP/Perl interpreter. In any case, a hacker can take advantage of this hole to obtain access to your computer. Once in the computer, he or she can easily obtain access to, for example, the FTP server and download all secret data that you may have on the computer. But if you have only a Web server running on the particular computer, the access to confidential data using the FTP server will not be that easy. The most that the hacker will be able to do is deface or destroy the site. And even though this is not pleasant, restoring the home page or even the entire site is much easier than reconstructing all FTP or news-server data.

To prevent the malefactor from penetrating other network computers after breaking into one of them, you should set a different password for each computer. Some administrators are too lazy to memorize many passwords and use one password everywhere. I will cover the password subject in more detail in *Chapter 4*, but for now you should know that you have to use an individual access password for each system.

Daemons are not the only potential problem. Many programs are included into Linux as source codes and have to be compiled before execution. Programs taking advantage of the vulnerabilities of Linux systems also come as source codes. To use them, the malefactor uploads such a module on a server and executes the program. To make it impossible to compile source codes, I advise you not to install development libraries and the GNU C (GCC) compiler.

Program installers are seldom used in Linux; therefore, all configurations are performed when the source codes are compiled. With GCC unavailable, the malefactor will have problems executing malicious code.

An experienced hacker can assemble a program from the source codes on his or her own computer and then upload it onto the compromised server for execution, circumventing the need for the GCC compiler. A novice hacker, however, may be nonplussed by not having the compiler available on the target machine. And any problem faced by hackers is a victory for the security specialist.

If you are just cutting your teeth in the Linux world, I recommend that you install the linuxconf software package, which makes administering tasks much easier. When learning your way around Linux, you will see that many of its settings are configured by manually editing configuration files. This task has been made easier of late by numerous configuration utilities with a graphical interface, linuxconf being one of them.

But if you are not daunted by the task of configuring the system manually, I recommend going about it this way: Configuration utilities with graphical interface often introduce unsafe parameters into the system configuration, or allow service access rights that are too privileged. It is a good idea, therefore, to examine the modifications made by the program, a task that requires excellent knowledge of the structure and content of the configuration files.

After the files are copied to the disk, the system offers to configure the video system. This is done in the **Monitor Configuration** dialog window (Fig. 2.10).

Select the correct video card and monitor and the display characteristics. If you make a mistake here, you will have to start your work with Linux with the command line instead of the graphical interface. Later in this chapter, I will show you how to configure the monitor from the command line.

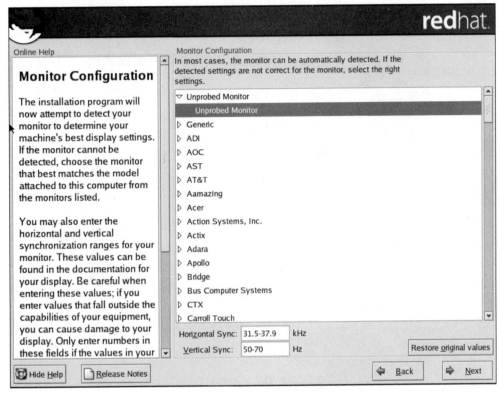

Fig. 2.10. The **Monitor Configuration** window

2.8. First Boot

When the newly-installed system boots for the first time, a few more things need to be set up at this stage: The license agreement must be accepted, the date and time must be set, a system user must be created, and so on (Fig. 2.11).

The most important of these is creating a system user. This is done in the **User Account** dialog window (Fig. 2.12). You can use the root account for working with the system, but this is not recommended. It is advisable that even the administrator enters the system as a regular user (perhaps, with slightly higher privileges to access the necessary functions). The root account should be used only for the most extreme needs.

After finishing the first boot setup, the system boots.

The first stage of the boot process in Linux is the same as in Windows: The memory is tested, disks are determined, and information about the hardware system is displayed. When this process is over, the dialog window of the boot loader selected in *Section 2.4* is displayed (Fig. 2.13).

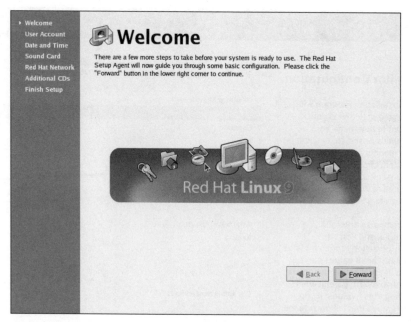

Fig. 2.11. The first-boot **Welcome** dialog window

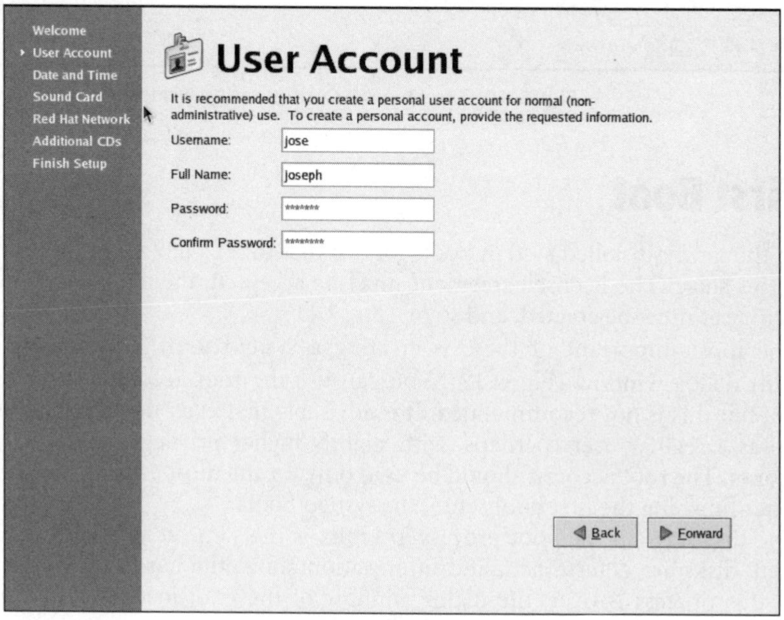

Fig. 2.12. The **User Account** dialog window

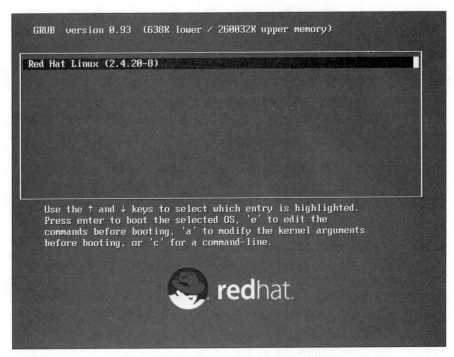

Fig. 2.13. The boot loader dialog window

Because I have only Linux installed, the only option is to boot into this system. If you had other operating systems or Linux kernels installed, they would also be offered for booting in the boot loader menu. Windows and Linux can peacefully coexist on the same computer. I must note, however, that Windows XP and older Linux boot loaders, such as LILO, do not get along with each other. It looks like Windows XP would brook no competition and kill LILO. Modern Linux loaders are more capable and can stand up for themselves.

Boot loaders in some Linux distributions, including Red Hat, may use the command prompt instead of a graphical menu to select the operating system. After the computer starts, a command line prompt to enter the necessary operating system is displayed as follows:

```
LILO boot:
```

The default operating system is loaded by simply pressing the <Enter> key; alternative operating systems are loaded by entering its name from the keyboard and then pressing the <Enter> key. Instead of typing the operating system into which to boot, you can use the keyboard arrow keys or the <Tab> key to navigate through the available choices.

After the selected operating system (Linux in this case) starts booting, information about devices detected, versions of various modules, and so on, is displayed on the black background as white text (Fig. 2.14).

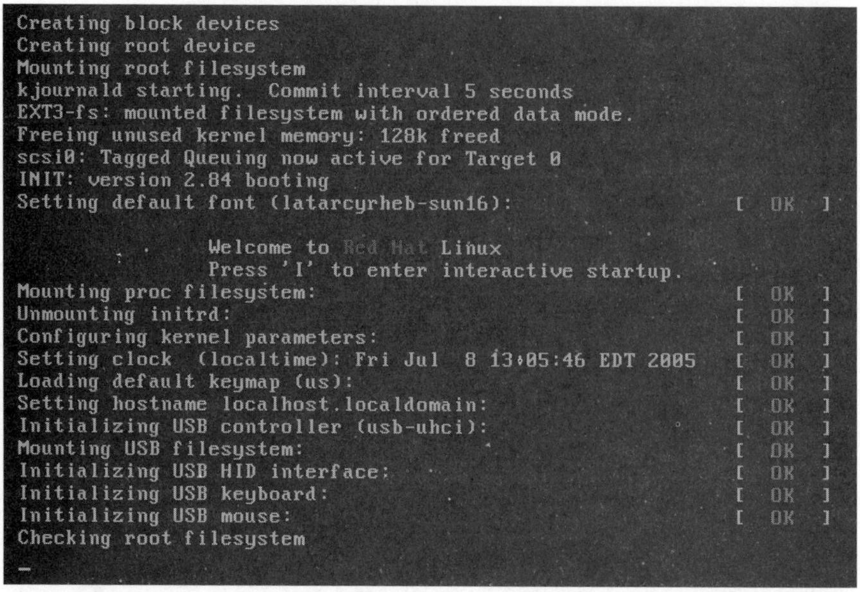

```
Creating block devices
Creating root device
Mounting root filesystem
kjournald starting.  Commit interval 5 seconds
EXT3-fs: mounted filesystem with ordered data mode.
Freeing unused kernel memory: 128k freed
scsi0: Tagged Queuing now active for Target 0
INIT: version 2.84 booting
Setting default font (latarcyrheb-sun16):                    [  OK  ]

                    Welcome to Red Hat Linux
                    Press 'I' to enter interactive startup.
Mounting proc filesystem:                                    [  OK  ]
Unmounting initrd:                                           [  OK  ]
Configuring kernel parameters:                              [  OK  ]
Setting clock  (localtime): Fri Jul  8 13:05:46 EDT 2005    [  OK  ]
Loading default keymap (us):                                [  OK  ]
Setting hostname localhost.localdomain:                     [  OK  ]
Initializing USB controller (usb-uhci):                     [  OK  ]
Mounting USB filesystem:                                    [  OK  ]
Initializing USB HID interface:                             [  OK  ]
Initializing USB keyboard:                                  [  OK  ]
Initializing USB mouse:                                     [  OK  ]
Checking root filesystem
```

Fig. 2.14. The Linux booting process

At one point you will see the message saying "Welcome to Red Hat Linux. Press 'I' to enter interactive startup." (See Fig. 2.14.) Pressing the <I> key will make the system ask your confirmation before loading another service. This is a handy feature in case the system becomes corrupted and some service causes the system to hang. For example, in my experience, installing the sendmail daemon often causes problems. When this happens, the operating system cannot boot. The situation is resolved by simply rebooting the computer, entering the interactive mode, and refusing to load the sendmail service.

Linux is a multiuser operating system. This means that several people can work on the same machine at the same time. The operating system needs to know the current user, so after it boots the system will ask you to enter your login and password. The login identifies you, and the password prevents someone else from entering the system under your name.

The user identification process in the text mode starts with the prompt to enter your login:

```
localhost login:
```

Then you have to enter the password to prove to the operating system that you are who you say you are.

If you prefer to use the graphical interface to enter the system, you can do this in the dialog window like the one shown in Fig. 2.15. I say "like the one" because the login window may differ in different Linux distributions.

Fig. 2.15. The login window

Before entering your login, take a good look around the window. There is menu in it containing the following four items:

☐ **Language** — The default language is English, but you can choose any other available language. Linux supports an extensive choice of languages that is constantly expanding.

☐ **Session** — This allows you to select the graphical interface. In this book, I will mostly use the KDE and GNOME interfaces because they are the most commonly used. Which graphical interface you select is up to you.

☐ **Reboot**

☐ **Shut down**

The **Session** menu item has an interesting subitem: **Failsafe**. Select this item if there are errors in the system configuration and the graphical interface cannot launch. This will open the command line console before the graphical interface launches, and in it you can correct the problem.

After setting the necessary parameters, enter your login and password. Thus you can enter the graphical world of Linux. But which account should you log in under? During the installation you set the system administrator (root) password and added a user during the first-boot configuration. I strongly recommend entering the system under the user account, because the root account allows the highest rank of privileges. This totalitarian control often caused grief when administrators inadvertently deleted some important data when conducting some system testing.

Working under the root account makes it easier to break into the computer through seemingly the simplest applications. Suppose you logged in as root and then decided to do some Web surfing. The browser that you launch for this will have the root privileges. If there is a vulnerability in the browser allowing hard disk access, miscreants can take advantage of this loophole to break into your computer and have access to whatever the root user does.

If, on the contrary, you logged in as a regular user, only the areas and functions available to this user account can be accessed. The system files in this case are more secure. Should it become necessary to raise your privileges to root, for example, to perform some system task requiring root privileges, you can always do this from a user account as long as you know the administrator password. This is done by executing the su (switch user) command with the name of the user whose privileges you want to obtain as the parameter.

To obtain administrator privileges, enter the command as follows:

```
su root
```

or

```
su -
```

When you enter the command, the system will ask you to supply the appropriate password. If you enter the password of the user whose privileges you want to obtain, you will obtain the privileges requested. Having obtained the necessary privileges, you can do with the system what the new privileges allow. With administrator privileges, you are allowed to do everything.

Again, Linux is a multiuser operating system, and it supports several consoles. By default, you enter the first console. To switch to another console, press the <Alt> key and one of the <F1> through <F6> keys. This will open another console with the login screen, in which you can log into the system as the same or another user.

The multiple console feature is a handy one. For example, in one console you can start a program that takes a long time to execute, then you can switch to another console and continue with other tasks in it. You can return to the first console at any moment to check the program's execution.

If, at installation, you selected the option to boot into the graphical mode, at the first boot a window will open, in which the system will offer to let you use the selected default graphical shell. In the successive boots, unless you specify otherwise, the system will boot into this graphical shell.

You can switch into the graphical mode from the text mode at any time by entering the startx command in the command line. In this case, the graphical shell will be loaded without asking you to provide the password because you have already identified yourself (when logging into the system in the text mode).

You may have to log into the system in the text mode if the graphical login window cannot be displayed for some reason, for example, because of configuration errors. In this case, executing the startx command will have no effect, because the graphical shell will not be able to load, and you will have to configure the display settings anew. Most Linux configuration information is stored in text files, which often have to be edited manually. Graphics configuration information is also stored in text files, but it is not necessary to edit them manually. You configure the system with the help of the special setup utility with the graphical interface. Enter the setup command in the command line. This will open the window shown in Fig. 2.16. Select the **X configuration** item in the list. The system will, most likely, determine the video card and the drivers necessary; however, it may have problems properly identifying the monitor and selecting the video modes it supports. In most cases, this task requires human intervention.

All possible monitor modes will be listed, and you can specify any number of them. However, I recommend selecting only the mode that you feel most comfortable working with. Make sure to test the selected graphical mode to ensure that it works properly. If the configuration settings selected are acceptable, the program will offer to let you enter the system using the graphical mode.

The configuration can be performed using the mouse, but, if for some reason the mouse is unavailable, it can be done using the keyboard. Use the <Tab> key to move from one button to another, the space bar to select menu items, and the <↑> and <↓> arrows to move between list items.

The last time I had problems configuring a video card (a cheap Chinese job on the S3 chipset) was about 3 years ago under Red Hat 6.1. Modern distributions have no problems determining hardware components of the system, especially brand-name ones.

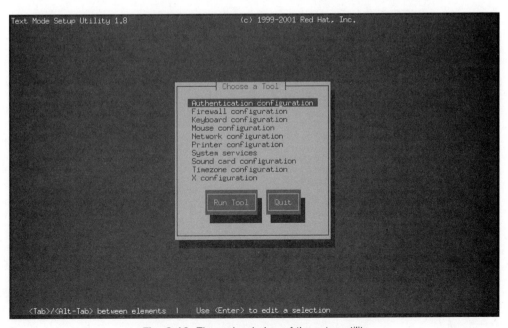

Fig. 2.16. The main window of the setup utility

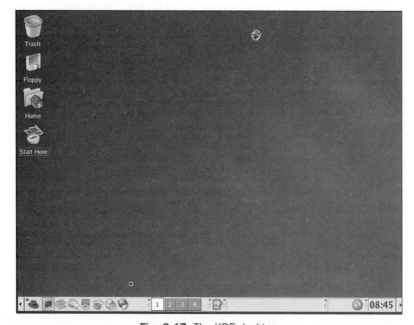

Fig. 2.17. The KDE desktop

Fig. 2.18. The GNOME desktop

I hope that you have managed to enter the graphical mode. If an error happens during logging into the system, the computer hangs, or the display becomes distorted, loading of the graphical shell can be stopped by pressing the <Ctrl>+<Alt>+<Backspace> combination. This will take you into the text mode.

Fig. 2.17 shows the KDE graphical shell, and Fig. 2.18 shows the GNOME graphical shell.

There is the **Taskbar** located at the bottom of both desktops. It contains the following controls:

- ❐ The leftmost button (the one depicted as a red hat) is used to open the main menu. It is an analogue of the **Start** button in Windows. The main menu contains all programs and utilities installed on the computer.
- ❐ Next are the rapid program-launch buttons. The red-framed button on both desktops launches the terminal program.
- ❐ The empty space to the right of the rapid-launch buttons is the actual task bar; the icons for the running programs — tasks — are displayed here. The task buttons can be used to switch among running tasks.

After this brief introduction to the graphical environments, a short description of the terminal window is in order. This is a simple but powerful text tool to control the system. Common home users are mostly interested in games and office programs and have no need for this tool. But it is simply a must for administering and fine-tuning Linux.

Open the terminal window to see what it looks like. In most distributions, it is a window with the black background and white text. After launching, a command prompt is displayed that can look like the following:

```
[root@Flenov root]:
```

What does it mean? First is the name, under which you entered the system, root in this case. The computer name follows the @ character, then space, and then the name of the current folder.

2.9. Moving Around the System

When you enter the operating system, it launches a unique environment for each user. The environment comprises user directories, configurations, and a command shell.

User directories are located in the /home directory and are named by the user's name. For example, the full name of the root user's directory is /home/root/. The files of the root user are stored in this directory.

When a user enters the system, his or her directory becomes the current directory. Thus, when the root user enters the system, the /home/root directory becomes the current directory, and all commands will be executed in this directory until another directory becomes current.

There are several command shells in Linux, and each of them offers specific features. I will consider the Bourne Again Shell (bash), because it is the one used most often.

When I was only cutting my teeth on Linux, after I installed it for the first time, I could not turn it off correctly for a long time because I did not know what command to use to do this. I borrowed a Linux reference book from an acquaintance to find out how to power down the system properly. The description of the power-off procedure, however, was buried in the depths of the book, and it took me about a month to read through to it. During all this time I powered off the system by turning off the computer.

So that you do not go through the same process, here is how to power down the system. This is done using the shutdown command. The command takes several parameters, the two most commonly used of which are -r to reboot and -h to halt the computer after the shutdown. Also, the time, at which to shut down the system, must be specified at the end of the command.

For example, to reboot the system right away, enter the following command:

```
shutdown -r now
```

To shut down the computer immediately, enter this command:

```
shutdown -h now
```

Do not shut down the computer in any other way; always use this command. Powering down the computer using the power button on the system block is fraught with the danger of losing data that were loaded into the memory but not saved to the disk.

If you want to enter the system under another name while working in the text mode, you can do this with the help of the exit command.

To exit the system when working in the graphical mode, click the main menu button and select the **Log Out** item. This will unload the graphical shell, after which the login screen will be displayed, in which you will be able to enter the system under another name or reboot the computer.

2.10. Help

Some operating systems are famous for being easy to use and for offering informative help. But I will never tire of repeating that efficiency, reliability, and being easy to use are not always compatible. There are many commands in Linux, and each of them can be used with numerous parameters. It is impossible to remember all of the commands and their parameters, so the developers have provided an extensive help program for the operating system.

To obtain information about how to use a command or a program, enter its name followed by one of the following switches: -h, -help, or -?. Different programs use their own switches and display short information about how to use the program.

More detailed information can be obtained by using the man command as follows:

```
man name
```

Here, name is the name of the command or the program. For example, to view the description of the shutdown command, enter man shutdown in the command line.

To exit a help program, type -e. This will produce the message "Quit at end-of-file (press RETURN)." Press the <Enter> key and then move to the end of the help file, at which point the man program will terminate.

Pressing the <q> key will terminate the man program immediately.

If you are installing a licensed version of the operating system, it may be accompanied by the installation and user's manual. Most often, the information contained in these manuals is superficial. But some distributions come with detailed documentation or even whole books.

2.11. Configuration Basics

Before considering Linux configuration issues in depth, I want to establish some basic rules applicable to any operating system or service. If you follow these rules, you will be able to build a really secure system, be it a single server or a computer network.

2.11.1. Everything Not Permitted Is Prohibited

When configuring the access parameters, you should adhere to the following rules of minimization:

❐ Run as few programs as possible. This concerns not only whole services but also their components. Suppose that you use the Apache Web server. This program has many features, among which is support of the PHP and Perl interpreted languages. Site programmers, however, normally use only one of these languages; consequently, there is no reason to enable both of them on your Apache server. If the site uses PHP, Perl should be disabled, and vice versa. If your site uses both script languages, you should fire your programmers: Mongrel systems are much more difficult to make secure.

❐ Enable as few options as possible. Most administrators do not like to bother with configuring the system and allow complete access to all features that they think may be used. But such an approach is incompatible with security. The feature that you make available for a user may never be used by the latter but can be used by malefactors to break into your system and cause you lots of grief. For example, a folder may be opened for shared access on client computers on the argument that the users may have to exchange data. Maybe they will, but maybe they won't. Open folders for shared access only when the need for this arises.

The minimization principle will be often be recalled when I describe various aspects of Linux configuration, and prohibition will be the starting point when I analyze examples.

2.11.2. Default Settings

Default settings are intended for training purposes only, and most often enable all features so that you can evaluate the program's capabilities. Enabling all features violates the second rule of minimization.

If configuring the program does not involve many commands and parameters, it can be configured from scratch. But if the procedure is complex (a good example is configuring the sendmail program), the best option is to start with the default settings and then modify them as necessary. Don't try to configure a complex program from scratch. More likely than not, you will forget something and make some error with the configuration. Configuration files are difficult to work with because they are in the text format and the names of all parameters must be written without the slightest error. If at least one character is entered incorrectly, the parameter will not function properly or at all, and the operating system or the service will work with errors.

When writing a parameter name or a file system path, pay close attention not only to spelling but also to the use of the uppercase and lowercase characters. Linux is case-sensitive where names of files and directories are concerned. The same applies to some configuration files.

2.11.3. Default Passwords

During the installation, many services set default passwords. This problem is especially serious in Linux, because installation programs use RPM packages that most often do not even offer to change the default passwords. If I were in the developers' shoes, I would make it impossible to start services with no or default passwords.

For example, after the installation, the administrator account for the MySQL database is named *root* (not to be confused with the Linux root account) and requires no password to log into the database. There is no reason to have a database account with the same name as the operating system's most important account and without a password to boot. After installing MySQL, immediately change the database administrator's account name and set a password for it.

Before putting a system into commission, make sure that all of its passwords have been changed. Here another example using MySQL. Administrators rarely use this database themselves; they only install it. The configuration is usually performed by the programmers, who tune databases to their personal preferences and, for some reason, like to use default passwords. I am a programmer and, when developing databases, use default passwords, hoping that the administrator will take care of changing the passwords, but, as stated earlier, they seldom do.

Not only application programs and operating systems but also network devices, such as routers and intelligent switches, use default passwords. These devices have a built-in protection and authorization system. When initializing this system, the manufacturers don't bother with inventing account names and most often use Admin; the password is usually left blank altogether. This is a big oversight. A good idea in this case would be to use the device's serial number as its password. It is easy for the manufacturer to come up with and for the user to remember but difficult for hackers to pick. But even using the serial number does not guarantee total protection, because if a hacker sees the device, he or she can take a crack at its serial number being used as the password.

Lists of default passwords for various devices have been available on the Internet for a long time; thus, do not forget to change the passwords after installing a device.

2.11.4. Universal Passwords

BIOS manufacturers used to install universal access codes into their chips, which made it possible to enter the system without knowing the main password, installed by the administrator. For example, one of the Award BIOS versions used AWARD_SW as a universal password. Starting with version 4.51, this "service" is no longer available.

If it is possible to disable the universal-password feature, you should do this immediately. Otherwise, replace the equipment or programs. Leaving this feature in place will cancel out whatever other measures you may undertake to secure your system.

2.11.5. Security versus Performance

I already mentioned that security and performance pursue two different goals. Configuring the server for maximum security requires enabling such services as logging, firewalls, and the like, which lay their claim on processor resources. The more services enabled, the more system resources they use.

Each service can be configured in different ways. For example, the logging mode can be configured to log only the most important information. This reduces the workload on the hard drive but increases the chances of an attack going unnoticed. The other extreme is to configure logging to log all messages. Contrary to what you may think, this will not enhance the security, because the increased resource consumption facilitates carrying out a successful DoS attack.

When configuring a server and its services, you must be guided by the principle of necessary sufficiency. This means that you should do everything possible to make the server secure while keeping its performance as high as possible. To ascertain that this balance is achieved, the server should be tested at the maximum workload possible. The latter is defined as twice the number of requests per minute that the server is expected to service. If the server is up to the task and can handle all client requests with processor resources to spare, the system can be put into service. Otherwise, either the configuration should be changed or the computer's capacity should be enhanced.

Chapter 3: Welcome to Linux!

In this chapter, you will start becoming acquainted with Linux. I hope that you have the system installed, because it would be preferable to immediately try everything described. This way you will understand and remember the material better.

We will take a close look at the file system, the main configuration files, and commands for everyday work. Linux can work in two modes: graphical and text. Many authors for some reason consider only the text mode. This intimidates those readers who are used to Windows with its intuitive interface. I will consider both modes in parallel. Nevertheless, the console will be given more attention, because many problems often can be solved much faster using the console than using graphical utilities. I will try to show you the advantages of using the console over using the mouse. Commercial servers often are placed in separate rooms and often are not even equipped with a monitor. They are controlled through a remote console without using Linux graphical features. Why, then, waste memory by loading bulky graphics libraries, files, and other resources? You will be better off to preserve it for other, more useful things.

The graphical mode, however, is useful for working with user utilities. It can also be useful when doing the initial server configuration. Taking into account that not all Linux computers are used as servers and that workstations can run under this operating system, a convenient and easy-to-use graphical interface for Linux is simply a must.

As you can see, being able to work in two modes is one of the advantages of Linux, not a shortcoming. If you were to unload the graphical shell in Windows and leave only the command-line interface, you could conserve memory resources and increase the reliability of this operating system. When graphics libraries are not used, they cause no problems.

Remember those blue screens of death caused by buggy video card drivers? You will not see those in the Linux console.

If you are configuring a home computer or a small network, you can leave the graphical shell in place. But for a commercial server demanding maximum availability, I recommend that you use the text mode so that you make the server secure against failures, and increase its performance.

3.1. Linux File Systems

Before moving on to system configuration, you need to acquire better knowledge of the Linux file system. I touched briefly on the structure in *Section 2.3* when considering disk partitioning. Partitions that can be created in Linux, which are nothing but main folders, are listed in Table 2.1.

I will consider the commands for working with files and directories a little later. For now, I want to show you only the Midnight Commander program. This is the best tool for solving all of the tasks described earlier. Most distributions, including Fedora Core, contain this program. It is launched by entering the mc command in the console command line and pressing the <Enter> key. As you gradually get to know this utility, you will come to love it for its convenience and power; for now, I will only consider its main features.

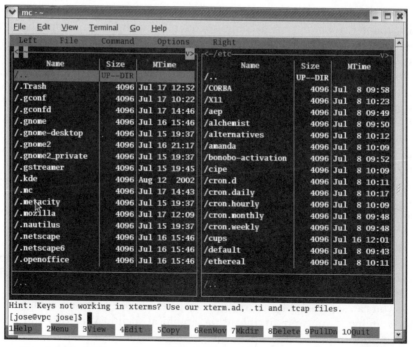

Fig. 3.1. The Midnight Commander program launched in the terminal window

Fig. 3.1 shows Midnight Commander running in the terminal window. The program's window is divided into two panels; in each panel, shown are files and folders of the current directory. Folder names start with slashes. Use the <Tab> key to switch between the panels.

The right panel shows the contents of the root folder. This is the highest level of the file system. Examining the names of the folders in this panel, you will see that most of them are those listed in Table 2.1. Each of these folders can be placed in its own disk partition, if you chose to do so during the installation. But even in this case, the file system will look as one whole.

In *Section 2.3.3*, the root directory was mentioned, designated in Linux as /. This directory is the top of the pyramid in the directory hierarchy. For example, user folders are stored in the /home folder. Then, /home/flenov is the path to the subfolder of user Flenov. To move to a directory, you double-click it with the mouse. Or you can select the needed directory using the <↑> or <↓> key and then press the <Enter> key.

There is always a folder named /.. at the top of the list of folders and files in any folder. There is actually no folder with this name. This is only the pointer to the parent directory of the current folder. For example, moving to folder /.. from the /home/jose folder, you move one level up to the /home directory.

Below the Midnight Commander window (see Fig. 3.1), you can see the command prompt. This is the same prompt as in the terminal and is used in the same way. Farther below, legends for the <F1> through <F10> keys are located. The functions of these keys are as follows:

- ❐ F1 Help — Displays the help file for the program.
- ❐ F2 Menu — Displays the menu for the main Midnight Commander commands.
- ❐ F3 View — Displays the selected file.
- ❐ F4 Edit — Opens the selected file for editing using the built-in text editor.
- ❐ F5 Copy — Copies the selected file of the folder. Selecting a file and pressing the <F5> key opens the copy operation confirmation window. By default, the selected file or folder is copied to the current directory in the opposite Midnight Commander panel.
- ❐ F6 RenMove — Moves the selected files or folders. By default, the selected objects will be moved to the current directory in the opposite Midnight Commander panel.
- ❐ F7 Mkdir — Creates a new folder in the current folder.
- ❐ F8 Delete — Deletes the selected files or folders.
- ❐ F9 PullDn — Calls the Midnight Commander pull-down menu, which is located at the top of its window.
- ❐ F10 Exit — Terminates Midnight Commander.

The names of configuration files and folders start with a period. Be careful when moving or editing them. These files need to be given maximum protection, which I will talk about later in various sections of the book.

3.1.1. Main Commands

Now, consider the main commands of the file system that will be used in the book, and learn more about the Linux file system itself.

pwd

The pwd command displays the full path of the current directory.

ls

The ls command displays the contents (files and folders) of the specified directory. If the directory is not specified, the command displays the contents of the current directory. By default, all configuration files (whose names start with a period) are hidden. To display them, the ls command is used with the -a switch:

```
ls -a
```

To display complete information about catalog contents instead of only folder and file names, the ls command is used with the -1 switch. If more than one switch must be used, they are entered as follows:

```
ls -al
```

This command, however, will display the contents of the current directory. To view the contents of a directory other than the current one, for example, /etc, the necessary folder is specified after (or before) the switches:

```
ls -al /etc
```

NOTE

You can obtain more detailed information about the ls command from the help system by executing the following command: man ls.

The result of the ls -al command may look as follows:

```
drwx------ 3 Flenov FlenovG 4096 Nov 26 16:10 .
drwxr-xr-x 5 root    root    4096 Nov 26 16:21 ..
-rw-r--r-- 1 Flenov FlenovG   24 Nov 26 16:10 .bash_logout
-rw-r--r-- 1 Flenov FlenovG  191 Nov 26 16:10 .bash_profile
-rw-r--r-- 1 Flenov FlenovG  124 Nov 26 16:10 .bashrc
-rw-r--r-- 1 Flenov FlenovG 2247 Nov 26 16:10 .emacs
-rw-r--r-- 1 Flenov FlenovG  118 Nov 26 16:10 .gtkrc
drwxr-xr-x 4 Flenov FlenovG 4096 Nov 26 16:10 .kde
```

By default, the list of a folder's files and subfolders is displayed in several columns. Consider what information is displayed in each column using the first line as an example:

❑   drwx------ indicates access rights. I will consider them in more detail in *Chapter 4*. For now, you should know that the first letter, "d," means the item is a directory.

- ❑ The number 3 indicates the number of hard links.
- ❑ Flenov is the name of the file's owner.
- ❑ FlenovG is the group, to which the file belongs.
- ❑ 4096 is the file size. Because a directory has no file size, the 4096 value is not the actual file size but just a placeholder, and all directories have this value in this column.
- ❑ The sixth column shows the date and time the file was last changed.
- ❑ The final column gives the file name.

cat

The cat command displays the contents of the file specified in the command's argument. For example, to view the need.txt text file, the cat command is entered as follows:

```
cat need.txt
```

To view a file located in a folder other than the current one, the full path to the file has to be specified:

```
cat /home/root/need.txt
```

tac

The tac command is a version of the cat command, only it displays the specified file in the reverse order, that is, starting from the end of the file.

cd

The cd command is used to change the current directory to the one specified as its argument:

```
cd /home/flenov
```

To move from the /home folder to the /flenov subfolder, only the subfolder's name has to be entered as the argument:

```
cd flenov
```

To move a level up from the current subfolder, the destination folder is specified as two periods (..):

```
cd ..
```

As you already know, two periods designate the parent folder of the current folder, or the folder one-level up the current one.

cp

The cp command is used for copying files. The following copying options are available:

- ❑ Copying the contents of a file to another document in the same folder.

  ```
  cp /home/root/need.txt /home/root/need22.txt
  ```

  The preceding command copies the contents of the source file /home/root/need.txt to the destination file /home/root/need22.txt.

❏ Copying a file to another folder.

```
cp /home/root/need.txt /home/flenov/need.txt
```

or

```
cp /home/root/need.txt /home/flenov/need22.txt
```

Note that the destination file can have either a new name or the same name as the source file.

❏ Copying several files to another folder. All source files are listed as parameters; the destination folder is given as the last parameter.

```
cp /home/root/need.txt /home/root/need22.txt /home/new/
```

In the example above, files /home/root/need.txt and /home/root/need22.txt are copied to the /home/new folder. Files from different folders can be copied to one folder as follows:

```
cp /home/root/need.txt /home/flenov/need22.txt /home/new/
```

In the preceding example, files /home/root/need.txt and /home/flenov/need22.txt are copied to the /home/new folder.

❏ Copying a group of files or all files in a folder.

But what if you have to copy all files whose names start with an n from one folder to another? Isn't there an easier way than listing all of them? Relax, there is. You simply use the n* mask, where * is a wildcard that stands for the rest of the file's name after the n character:

```
cp /home/root/n* /home/new/
```

If all files whose names start with ra and end in t need to be copied, the ra*t mask is used.

mkdir

The mkdir command creates a new directory. For example, a directory named newdir is created in the current directory by the following command:

```
mkdir newdir
```

rm

The rm command deletes a file or a directory. The directory being deleted must be empty.

```
rm /home/flenov/need22.txt
```

The names of the files can be given using the same * wildcard character as in the cp command. To delete a directory, the following switches may have to be specified:

❏ -d — Remove a directory.
❏ -r — Remove the contents of the directories recursively.
❏ -f — Do not prompt to confirm the deletion. Be careful when using the last switch, because the files specified will be deleted without the system asking for any confirmation. Make sure that you have written correctly the names of the files you want to delete.

The following is an example of deleting a directory:

```
rm -rf /home/flenov/dir
```

df

The df command is used to determine the amount of free space on a disk or a partition. If no device is specified, the information about all currently-counted file systems is displayed.

The following listing is an example of the command's execution results:

```
Filesystem 1k-blocks  Used     Available Use%  Mounted on
/dev/hda2  16002200   2275552  12913760  15%   /
none       127940     0        127940    0%    /dev/shm
```

The columns contain the following information:

- ☐ Filesystem — The disk whose file system is mounted
- ☐ 1k-blocks — The number of logical blocks
- ☐ Used — The number of used blocks
- ☐ Available — The number of available blocks
- ☐ Use% — The percentage of the used disk space
- ☐ Mounted on — The mount point (the mounted-on directory)

mount

The mount command is used for mounting file systems. The command is rather difficult to understand and use, and it is normally used by system administrators.

In Windows, you are used to diskettes, CD-ROMs, and other removable media becoming available immediately after they have been placed into the corresponding drive. The same media are handled differently in Linux, and many people cannot get used to this circumstance. I am one of those many, because I still cannot adjust to the idea of having to execute additional commands even though I understand how they work and that they must be used.

In Linux, for a CD-ROM to become available, you have to execute the mount command specifying the /dev/cdrom device as a parameter:

```
mount /dev/cdrom
```

Then the contents of the CD-ROM can be viewed in the /mnt/cdrom directory as if they have become part of the file system.

Why is the CD-ROM mounted onto the /mnt/cdrom directory? And how did the system know where to mount it if the mount directory was not specified in the command? Mounting a CD-ROM requires much more data than the command mount /dev/cdrom can provide alone. These data are stored in two system files that describe the main default devices and parameters: fstab and mtab. Let's examine these two files.

The contents of the fstab file look as follows:

```
# /etc/fstab: static file system information.
#
# <file system> <mount point> <type>  <options>              <dump> <pass>
/dev/hda2  /        ext3     defaults,errors=remount-ro       0      1
```

/dev/hda1	none	swap	sw	0	0
proc	/proc	proc	defaults	0	0
none	/dev/shm	tmpfs	defaults	0	0
none	/dev/pts/	devpts	gid=5,mode=620	0	0
/dev/cdrom	/mnt/cdrom	iso9660	noauto,owner,kudzu,ro	0	0
/dev/fd0	/mnt/floppy	auto	noauto,owner,kudzu	0	0

There are two entries for the main disks in the file. The file's contents are presented in six columns. Take a look at the first disk entry. It describes mounting of the hda2 disk. In my file system, this is the main disk, so the second parameter is /. This means that the disk will be mounted as the root. The third column describes the file system, which is ext3 in this case. The ro parameter indicates that the device is mounted for read-only. The rw value for this parameter means that the device is mounted for both read and write.

The penultimate entry in the file describes the CD-ROM device. Take a good look at the second parameter: /mnt/cdrom. This is how the system knows, which directory to mount the CD-ROM device on. The fourth column displays mounting options, which can be used to describe security parameters. In this case, there are several options specified for the CD-ROM: noauto, owner, kudzu, ro. The ro parameter specifies that the CD-ROM is mounted for read-only operations. It would be logical to mount all devices that could be used by hackers to extract information from the server for read-only operations.

The contents of the mtab file are similar to those of the stab file:

# <file system>	<mount point>	<type>	<options>	<dump>	<pass>
/dev/hda2	/	ext3	rw,errors=remount-ro	0	0
proc	/proc	proc	rw	0	0
none	/dev/shm	tmpfs	rw	0	0
none	/dev/pts	devpts	rw,gid=5,mode=620	0	0
none	/proc/sys/fs/binfmt_misc	binfmt_misc	rw	0	0
/dev/cdrom	/mnt/cdrom	iso9660	ro,nosuid,nodev	0	0

If you created some on separate disks, you can configure them also. Earlier, I recommended placing the /home partition containing user directories on a separate disk. If you followed my advice, there may be another entry in the file looking similar to the following:

```
/dev/hda3    /home    ext3    rw,errors=remount-ro   0  0
```

Take a look at the fourth parameter. It specifies mounting options, which can be manipulated to enhance the security of the system. The options are separated by commas. The options in this case are rw, errors=remount-ro. Other available mounting options are the following:

❒ noexec — Disables file execution. If you are certain that the partition should have no executable files, you can use this option. For example, on some systems, the /home directory is only intended for storing documents. Setting the noexec parameter for this partition will prevent hackers from placing into this partition the programs that can be used to break into the system. Actually, it will be possible to place programs into this partition but impossible to execute them.

❑ `nosuid` — Disables the effect of Set User IDentifier (SUID) and Set Group IDentifier (SGID) bits in programs. There should be no programs with these bits set in the /home partition so that privileged programs can be prohibited explicitly. SUID and SGID programs will be explained in *Section 4.5*.

❑ `nodev` — Disables access to character or special device files on the partition.

❑ `nosymfollow` — Disables soft links.

The `nodev` and `nosymfollow` options are not that important security-wise, but they can be useful in certain situations.

Using the `noexec` parameter to protect the system from break-ins is an exercise in futility, because an experienced hacker can run any program if execution of binary files is allowed on at least one partition. And execution is always allowed for the partition containing the /bin folder and other folders, in which files necessary for system operation are stored.

Suppose that your site uses Perl language. If a Perl interpreter is accessible for execution, a hacker can launch Perl scripts in any partition, including those with the `noexec` parameter set. Launching a script from the command line will produce a message about access rights violation. But the following command will launch the program:

```
perl file.pl
```

Even though file.pl is located in the partition, in which execution of binary files is disabled, the command will execute because execution of the Perl program is allowed. The program, in turn, reads a file, which also is an allowed operation, and executes the file in its address space.

Recall that in the mtab file using SUID and SGID programs is disabled for the CD-ROM drive. The same should be done for at least the /home and /tmp partitions. This will prevent users from creating privileged programs in their directories, which in turn will prevent many potential attacks.

Try to mount the CD-ROM drive on a directory other than the default one. For this, you have to create it first:

```
mkdir /mnt/cd
```

Now, execute the following command:

```
mount /dev/cdrom /mnt/cd
```

If you have two operating systems installed on your computer — Windows and Linux — the disk's file system is most likely FAT32 or NTFS. The following two commands allow you to access FAT32 devices on Linux:

```
mkdir /mnt/vfat
mount -t vfat /dev/hda3 /mnt/vfat
```

The first command creates the /mnt/vfat directory, on which the FAT32 disk will be mounted.

The second command mounts the /dev/hda3 disk on the just-created directory. Assume that this is the disk containing a Windows file system. The -t option specifies the type of the mounted file system. It is a mandatory option when mounting a device not described in the /etc/fstab file. Because the necessary information for the CD-ROM is in the /etc/fstab file, you did not have to indicate the file system when mounting the CD-ROM. The vfat parameter specifies the FAT32 file system. This is the name used by Linux to designate this file system.

More information about the mount command can be found by running the man mount command.

umount

When the CD-ROM is mounted, this device is blocked and the disc cannot be removed until the device is unmounted. A mounted device is unmounted using the umount command.

Thus, a mounted CD-ROM is unmounted by the following command:

```
umount /dev/cdrom
```

fdformat

Before a diskette can be used, it has to be formatted. Diskettes are formatted using the fdformat command.

tar

In the course of using this book, you will sometimes install various programs that come in tar.gz archives. Most often, these programs are stored as source code. Files stored in tar.gz archives are extracted using the following command:

```
tar xzvf file_name.tar.gz
```

The command creates a folder with the same name as archive (only without the extension), into which the extracted files are placed. For now you just have to be able to unpack archives and install additional software and third-party utilities.

rpm

Today, most programs are supplied not as source code but in RPM packages. These are easier to install because they are already compiled. To install an RPM program using Midnight Commander, select the necessary package and press the <Enter> key. This will open the package as a directory and allow you to view its contents.

An RPM package always contains an executable install file. The program is installed by executing this file.

To install an RPM program without using Midnight Commander, execute the following command:

```
rpm -i package
```

An already-installed package is updated by executing the rpm command with the -U parameter as follows:

```
rpm -U package
```

If you want to observe the installation progress, execute the command using the –v option. This command will look as follows:

```
rpm -iv package
```

which

Sometimes you want to know, in which folder a certain program is installed. This can be done with the help of the which command with the target program's name as the parameter. The command searches the main folders containing executable files. For example, to determine, in which folder the ls program, used to view folder contents, is installed, execute the following command:

```
which ls
```

It will display **/bin/ls** on the screen. If your operating system supports command aliases, the alias will also be displayed:

```
alias ls='ls -color=tty'
        /bin/ls
```

3.1.2. File Security

I will consider the access privileges in detail in *Chapter 4*. Access privileges are the cornerstone of security, but you cannot rely solely on this tool. Additional tools are necessary for preserving the system's integrity. At the least, you should be able to monitor changes in the files, the main objects of the operating system. Files are where information is stored, and information is what hackers are after. Hackers strive to read, modify, or even destroy information; consequently, you should know how to control it.

Modification Time

The simplest control method is to monitor the file modification time. Suppose that your system was penetrated at 10:30 a.m. To find out what files have been changed, you can search for all files whose modification time is later than this time. This is easy to implement but not very effective, because the modification time can be edited using the touch command. The complete command looks as follows:

```
touch parameters MMDDhhmmYY file_name
```

The date parameters are in uppercase, and the time parameters are in lowercase. The format is somewhat unusual but not impossible to remember. If the year is not specified, the current year is used.

Consider an example. Suppose you want to set the modification time of the /etc/passwd file to January 21 of the current year at 11:40 a.m. This is done by executing the following command:

```
touch 01211140 /etc/passwd
```

Now execute the `ls -l /etc/passwd` command to ascertain that the date and time have been changed as intended.

The `touch` command can also be used to create files stamped with the necessary date.

Although the modification time can be changed easily, the hacker may forget, run out of time, or not have enough privileges to do this.

Thus, all files that were modified after January 21, 2005, 11:40 a.m., can be found by executing the following sequence of commands:

```
touch 0121114005 /tmp/tempfile
find /etc \(-newer /tmp/tempfile \) -ls
find /etc \(-cnewer /tmp/tempfile \) -ls
find /etc \(-anewer /tmp/tempfile \) -ls
```

The first command created a file named tempfile with the reference modification date in the temporary /tmp directory.

The next three commands actually search for files. Each of them has the following structure:

```
find directory \parameter( -search_criterion file_name \) -ls
```

The functions of each part of the command are the following:

- `find` — The search program.
- `directory` — The directory, in which to conduct the search. In the example, I specified the /etc system directory, in which all configuration files are stored.
- `parameter (-search_criterion file_name)` — The search criterion and the reference file name. The search criteria can be one of the following:
  - `-newer` — The file's modification time is later than that of the reference file.
  - `-cnewer` — The file's status was changed later than the time, at which the reference file was modified.
  - `-anewer` — The file was accessed more recently than the reference file.
- `-ls parameter` — Files meeting the criterion are displayed on the screen (as when the `ls` command is executed).

Checksums

The modification time file-control method, while providing some degree of security, is far from perfect. The best file control method is the checksum calculation. Suppose you want to monitor changes to the /etc directory. You can do this by executing the following command:

```
md5sum /etc/*
```

This command calculates the checksum of the files specified in the parameter. The following listing is an example of the command's execution results:

```
783fd8fc5250c439914e88d490090ae1  /etc/DIR_COLORS
e2eb98e82a51806fe310bffdd23ca851  /etc/Muttrc
e1043de2310c8dd266eb0ce007ac9088  /etc/a2ps-site.cfg
```

```
4543eebd0f473107e6e99ca3fc7b8d47   /etc/a2ps.cfg
c09badb77749eecbeafd8cb21c562bd6   /etc/adjtime
70aba16e0d529c3db01a20207fd66b1f   /etc/aliases
c3e3a40097daed5c27144f53f37de38e   /etc/aliases.db
3e5bb9f9e8616bd8a5a4d7247f4d858e   /etc/anacrontab
fe4aad090adcd03bf686103687d69f64   /etc/aspldr.conf
...
```

The command's execution results are displayed in two columns. The first column displays the file's checksum; the second column displays the file's name. Checksum can be calculated for files only. Attempting to calculate a checksum for a directory will result in an error message.

In the example, checksums for all files in the /etc folder are displayed. But, unless you have a photographic memory, it is difficult to remember all the information displayed. It would be more convenient to write the results to a file, which can then be used to analyze any changes. The following command saves the results to the /home/flenov/md file:

```
md5sum /etc/* >> /home/flenov/md
```

The current status of the checksums of the files in the **/etc** directory is compared with their checksums stored in the /home/flenov/md file by executing the following command:

```
md5sum -c /home/flenov/md
```

A list of all files will be displayed. Those whose checksum has not changed will be marked "Success." Modify one of the files, for example, by executing the following command:

```
groupadd test
```

I will not go into the details of this command now; it will suffice if you know that it modifies the /etc/group file. Check the checksums of the files again:

```
md5sum -c /home/flenov/md
```

Now, the /etc/group file with be marked with an error message because its checksum has been changed. Consequently, even if some smart hacker fixes the modification date of the files he or she fiddled with, you can easily detect the intrusion by checking the checksum of the files in question. And it is much more difficult to doctor the checksum.

Files to Keep an Eye on

Some administrators monitor only configuration files. This is big mistake on their part, because hackers may attack not only configuration but also executable files. That Linux is an open-source product has its advantages and disadvantages.

One of the disadvantages is that professional hackers are skilled programmers. It is no problem for them to modify the source code of some utility, adding functions that they need in the process. In this way, hidden doors are often opened in the system.

Therefore, you should monitor changes not only of configuration files but also of all system programs and libraries. In particular, I recommend monitoring the /etc, /bin, /sbin, and /lib folders.

Notes Concerning Working with Files

Linux is quite liberal concerning file names. Any characters can be used, with the exception of /, which is used as a directory delimiter, and 0, which is used as the end-of-the-file-name indicator.

There is a complication, however: Invisible characters can be used in file names. Hackers can take advantage of this by naming their creation using only invisible characters, and users will not see such a file.

Consider an example using the linefeed invisible character. Suppose that a hacker named his file hacker\nhost.allow. In this case, the \n sequence denotes linefeed, meaning that the name will be displayed as two lines as follows:

```
hacker
hosts.allow
```

Not all programs can process this type of name properly. If your file manager does not work correctly, it will display only the second string — hosts.allow — and the administrator will not suspect that there is anything to be feared in this name.

Another way to hide a file is to use a period (or two periods) and a space for its name. The file whose name is a period is a pointer to the current directory. The administrator may not notice that there are two files named . (because the space in the impostor's name is invisible) in the list displayed by the ls command.

Spaces can be inserted anywhere in a file name — in the beginning, in the middle, or in the end — and, unless you are looking carefully, you will not notice anything wrong. Spaces at the end of a file name can be displayed by adding the / character to the file name. This can be done by executing the ls command with -F option.

Yet another way to hide, or rather to disguise, a file is to use characters that look similar to characters in legitimate files' names. Take a look, for example, at this file name: hosts.a11ow. Can you see anything suspicious? It is difficult to notice anything out of the ordinary during a cursory examination of this name. But upon closer inspection you may realize that those two "l"s are not letters at all but two instances of the digit "1" (one).

Hackers often use this trick. Another substitution of this type is using letter "b" instead of letter "d." Although these two letters look quite different when compared by themselves, when they are placed among other characters, the substitution is often overlooked because when we see something often the brain tends to interpret little irregularities as what it expects to be there and not as what really is seen.

Thus, paying close attention is an administrator's main weapon. Any little thing must come under the microscope of your scrutiny, and you should see what is there and not what you expect.

3.1.3. Links

There may be documents in your system that are shared among several users. Consider this situation on an example. Suppose that several users need to be able to access the /home/report file. One way to make this happen is to give each user his or her own copy of the file. But this is easier said than done, because several copies of the same file used by several users present a synchronization problem. Moreover, it is difficult to put modifications from several files into one whole, especially if the same portion of the file was edited. Who is to decide whose modifications apply to the common file?

This problem is solved with the help of hard links and symbolic links. To understand the idea of links, you have to understand what a file is and how the operating system stores it. When a file is created, disk space is allocated to it. The file's name is just a directory link to the area of the disk where the file is physically located. Consequently, several links to the same file can be created, which is allowed in Linux.

The `ls -l` command displays detailed information about files in the current directory in the following format:

```
-rw-r--r--   1 Flenov    FlenovG    118 Nov 26 16:10 1.txt
```

Executing the command with the `-i` option (`ls -il`) adds the file descriptor to the information displayed:

```
913021 -rw-r--r-- 1 Flenov FlenovG 118 Nov 26 16:10 1.txt
```

The descriptor in the preceding string is the number at the beginning of the string, which indicates the physical location of the file.

A hard link points directly to the file and has the same descriptor. Consequently, a file cannot be physically deleted until all hard links have been deleted. In essence, a file name is a hard link to the file's physical location.

Hard links are created by the `ln` command as follows:

```
ln file_name link_name
```

This command will create a hard link named `link_name` pointing to the same physical file as the `file_name` file name.

To be able to practice the material that will be considered, create a text file; name it 1.txt. This can be done by executing the following command:

```
cat > 1.txt
```

Press the <Enter> key and type a few lines of text; finish by pressing the <Ctr>+<D> key combination. Now you have a file to experiment with.

Create a hard link to the 1.txt file. This is done by executing the following command:

```
ln 1.txt link.txt
```

Execute the `cat link.txt` command to display the contents of the link.txt file. As you can see, it is identical to the contents of the 1.txt file. Now execute the `ls -il` command to view the contents of the folder. There should be the following two lines in the list of the folder files:

```
913021 -rw-r--r--   2 root   root    0 Feb 22 12:19 1.txt
913021 -rw-r--r--   2 root   root    0 Feb 22 12:19 link.txt
```

Note that the file descriptors of both files (the numbers in the first column) are the same. The number 2 in the third column means that there are two links to the physical file.

Now, modify the contents of either of the two files. This is done by executing the following commands:

```
ls > link.txt
cat 1.txt
```

The first command saves the execution results of the `ls` command (a list of the contents of the directory); the second command displays the 1.txt document. As you can see, the contents of both files have been changed and are the same.

Now try to delete the 1.txt file and then view the contents of the directory and of the link.txt file. This is done by executing the following sequence of commands:

```
rm 1.txt
ls -il
cat link.txt
```

Although the 1.txt file has been successfully deleted, the contents of the link.txt hard link remain unchanged. In other words, the physical file has not been deleted; only the 1.txt name it was referenced with has been. Note that the number of links for the link.txt file, shown in the third column, has decreased to one.

A symbolic link points not to the physical file but to the file's name. It gives some advantages but creates lots of problems. A symbolic link is created by specifying the -s option with the `ln` command. For example:

```
ln -s link.txt symbol.txt
```

The results of the command's execution displayed by the `ls -il` command are the following:

```
913021 -rw-r--r-- 1 root   root 519 Feb 22 12:19 link.txt
913193 lrwxrwxrwx 1 root   root 8 Feb 22 12:40 symbol.txt -> link.txt
```

Now, the file descriptors for the files are different. Also, the first character of the second column entry for the symbol.txt file is l, which signifies that you are dealing with a symbolic link. The third parameter is 1, and the last parameter contains the name of the file pointed to by the link after the -> character combination.

Remove the main file, then try to view the contents of the symbol.txt link:

```
rm link.txt
ls -il
cat symbol.txt
```

The first command removes the link.txt file. The second command displays the contents of the directory. Make sure that the link.txt file is not there. If you are using the Red Hat distributive, the `ls` command displays different file types in different colors. Otherwise, replace the second command with `ls -color=tty -il`.

This would display the symbolic link name and the file, to which the link points, on the red background. This indicates that the link is broken; that is, it points to a nonexistent file. The `cat symbol.txt` command attempts to display the contents of the file, to which the link points. Because the file does not exist, it produces an error message.

Of interest is that attempting to write to a soft link file (symbol.txt in this case) whose main file (link.txt in this case) does not exist automatically creates the main file. This is a huge shortcoming; consequently, you should ensure that a file has no symbolic links before deleting it.

Another shortcoming of symbolic links lies in their access rights, which will be considered in *Chapter 4*.

Yet another minus of links is that a file, to which a hard or soft link exists, is locked when opened for editing. Suppose that a link exists to the /etc/passwd or the /etc/shadow file. Locking one of these files will make it impossible to enter the system.

To prevent hackers from taking advantage of locking, the rights for writing to the system directories should be limited. Users normally should be given rights to write only to their /home directory and the /tmp directory. When files are shared, it may be necessary to have access to other user directories. But even in this case, the access should be limited to the /home directory, where user directories are located.

With all of the security-related shortcomings of links, the question arises, "Is it wise to use them?" I recommend using links only in extreme cases, when other ways of solving the problem are even worse. But be careful when doing this.

3.2. System Boot

Some administrators pay no attention to the system booting process. The main thing they are interested in is how it works. Even though there is no direct relationship between these two aspects, many programs are started during the system boot, which take up memory, thereby lowering the system's productivity.

Moreover, fast booting allows the system to be put back into operation rapidly after a crash. All computers have to be rebooted at one time or another to restore their full functionality lost because of software errors, power interruptions, and so on. The faster you can do this, the fewer complaints you hear from irate users.

All necessary system settings should be configured during the boot so that you would not have to configure anything manually after the boot. Manual configuration may take a long time, and it is just too dull and boring to go through the same routine every time the system boots.

3.2.1. Start-up

I will start considering optimization of the boot process by returning to the setup utility. Start it in the terminal; you should see a window like the one shown in Fig. 2.16. Open the System services section. You will see a window with a list of all installed services. Services that start automatically are marked with an asterisk. If you need some daemon, but do not use it often, it makes no sense to start it automatically and open a door for hackers. I recommend clearing the automatic start flag for such a service, starting it manually only when you need it running, and terminating it when you no longer need it.

For example, sometimes I debug Web scripts requiring MySQL on my server. Keeping the database running all the time is a waste of memory and an extra door into the system. Therefore, I only run MySQL when I need it and stop the service when I am done with the debugging.

I strongly recommend that you follow the same course of action and clear the automatic start asterisk from all services that need not start with the system boot. The necessary daemon is selected by highlighting it using the <↑> or <↓> keys and clearing the asterisk with the spacebar key. When finished, use the <Tab> key to move to the **OK** button and hit the <Enter> key to save the changes. The services that are already running will remain so, but they will not start the next time the system boots. Reboot the computer and ascertain that the system functions properly and that only the necessary daemons started automatically.

If you are using the KDE or GNOME shell, you can use a graphical utility for configuring automatically launched daemons. The utility is located in the **Services** section. Clicking the **Start Here** icon on the desktop will open a window containing shortcuts to the main system configuration utilities. The shortcut to the **Services** section should be among them.

There also is another way to start this utility. Open the main menu, select the **System Settings** item in it, select the **Server Settings** item in the submenu, and finally select the **Services** item in the next submenu (Fig. 3.2). In the future, I will denote a sequence of menu items by simply listing them delimited with a slash, as follows:

Main Menu/System Settings/Server Settings/Services

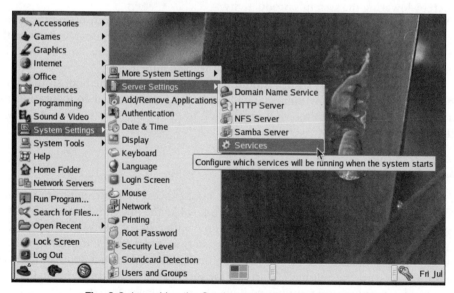

Fig. 3.2. Launching the Services utility from the Main Menu

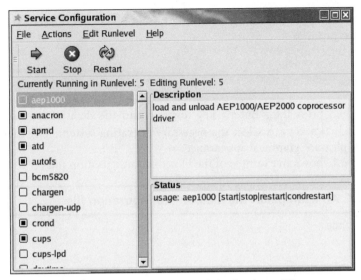

Fig. 3.3. The main window of the Services utility

The main window of the Services utility is shown in Fig. 3.3. There is a two-column list of services in the center of the form. Placing a check mark in a service's checkbox will make the service start automatically. Check marks are placed by double-clicking the necessary service's checkbox.

A selected service can be started, stopped, paused, or restarted using the corresponding toolbar buttons or **Actions** menu items. Any modifications of the services' automatic start have to be saved. This can be done by clicking the **Save** button or executing the **File/Save changes** menu sequence.

IMPORTANT

Never start services that you do no use. Only those programs that you or the server users require regularly should be started automatically. If a daemon is used only occasionally, it should not be started automatically. Instead, start it on an as-needed basis and terminate it immediately when it is no longer needed. Services that are not necessary are best removed altogether to eliminate the temptation to exploit them.

3.2.2. LILO Boot Loader

As you already know, the LILO program makes it possible to boot into Linux or another operating system that may be installed on the computer. All boot configuration settings are stored in the /etc/lilo.conf configuration file. LILO assumes control over the computer after BIOS testing but before the operating system takes over. Older LILO versions issued a simple text prompt:

```
LILO
```

or

```
LILO boot:
```

You could press the <Enter> key to boot into the default operating system or use the <↑> and <↓> keys to select the necessary operating system. The modern boot loader has a more pleasant graphical appearance.

Listing 3.1 shows an example of the lilo.conf configuration file.

Listing 3.1. An example of the lilo.conf configuration file

```
disk=/dev/hda
bios=128

boot=/dev/hda
prompt
timeout=300
lba32
default=linux-2.4.18

image=/boot/vmlinuz-2.4.18-5asp
initrd=/boot/initrd.2.4.18-5asp.img
label=linux-2.4.18
root=/dev/hda2
read-only
```

Each line in the file specifies a certain boot parameter. There are numerous boot options. You can obtain detailed information on all of them in the documentation supplied with the operating system, but for now I will consider only the main options. Most parameters are assigned values. This is done as follows:

```
Parameter=Value
```

To the left of the equals sign is the name of the parameter, and to the right is the value assigned to it. Some of the possible parameters that a lilo.conf configuration file may contain are the following:

❑   `boot=/dev/had` — Specifies the boot device.

❑   `map=/boot/file_name` — Indicates the boot map. If this parameter is omitted, the /boot/map file will be used by default.

❑   `timeout=300` — Shows the time the boot loader waits for the user to select the operating system to load before loading the default operating system.

❑   `lba32` — Enables `lba32` addressing (32-bit addressing of disk blocks). This parameter may cause problems with older hard drives that do not support logical block addressing (LBA).

❑   `default=linux-2.4.18` — Specifies the default operating system, into which to boot. In this case, `linux-2.4.18` is specified.

❑   `image=/boot/vmlinuz-2.4.18-5asp` — Specifies, which Linux kernel to boot. Most often, this line is given as `/boot/vmlinuz`.

❑   `label=linux-2.4.18` — Gives the name of the operating system shown in the LILO screen.

❑   `root=/dev/hda2` — Indicates the disk, on which the root file system is located.

❑   `read-only` — Specifies that the root partition is read-only and cannot be modified during the boot process.

This information will suffice for now. Most of the options not considered are obsolete and are needed only when old computers are used. Based on my experience, I can state that the parameters just listed will be enough. Now, edit the lilo.conf file when compiling the kernel to provide boot options.

The configuration file can be edited in any text editor. I normally use the text editor built into the Midnight Commander program. Launch Midnight Commander. Most likely, the current folder will be your folder, for example, /home/root. You have to move to the root folder. Move to the upper level directory by selecting the /.. entry in the directory content list and pressing the <Enter> key. This will take you to the /home directory. Repeat the process, and you will be taken to the root folder.

In the root folder, select the /etc folder and press the <Enter> key to open it. Select the lilo.conf file and open it for editing by pressing the <F4> key. This will open a basic text editor. Edit the necessary parameters; press the <Esc> key to exit the program. If the file has been changed, the program will ask whether you want to save the changes. Agree if you want to.

If you have never edited configuration files, try doing this now. For practice, you can try to change the time Linux waits for the user to select the boot method (from the hard drive or diskette) before booting using the default method.

In Linux configuration files, there are entries that are called comments. A comment is text that is ignored by the program and is used by the programmer to supply some explanations or to temporarily disable some parameters. A comment entry starts with the # character. All that follows this character on the same line is ignored by the system. For example:

```
# This is a comment.
boot=/dev/hda
timeout=300 # This entry specifies the timeout.
# lba32
default=linux-2.4.18 # This entry specifies the default OS.
```

In the preceding example, the first line starts with the # character and will be ignored by the system. In the third line, the comment follows the parameter. This means that the parameter will be read but the explanation following it will be ignored.

In the fourth line, the # character in front of the `lba32` parameter will make the system treat this parameter as a comment; that is, the system will simply ignore it as if it were not there.

Comments are handy to temporarily disable some options. If you simply delete a parameter, you may forget to put it back; but when a parameter is commented out, you just have to delete the # character to put it back.

LILO can be used to prevent unauthorized booting. This may be necessary, because it is possible to execute commands during the boot process. If a malefactor gains physical access to your computer, he or she can easily boot into the single-user mode and subsequently break the root password or execute some commands.

If the LILO boot loader screen is a simple text prompt (which is characteristic for Red Had distributions), a command during the boot process is executed by entering the name of the operating system to boot into followed by `init=command`:

```
Linux Boot: linux init=command
```

To prevent unauthorized booting, LILO has to be protected with a password. This is done by adding the following line in the configuration file after the `image` keyword:

```
password=your_password
```

The following listing is an example of setting the boot password to `qwerty`:

```
image=/boot/vmlinuz-2.4.18-5asp
password=qwerty
initrd=/boot/initrd.2.4.18-5asp.img
label=linux-2.4.18
root=/dev/hda2
read-only
```

If there are different versions of the operating system installed on a system, a separate password has to be specified for each of them. The following example demonstrates LILO giving an option to boot into one of the two kernel versions, with each requiring its individual password:

```
image=/boot/vmlinuz-2.4.18-5asp
password=qwerty
initrd=/boot/initrd.2.4.18-5asp.img
label=linux-2.4.18
root=/dev/hda2
read-only

image=/boot/vmlinuz-2.6.2
password=123456
initrd=/boot/initrd.2.6.2.img
label=linux-2.6.2
root=/dev/hda2
read-only
```

I will explain how to configure LILO for booting into two kernels in *Section 3.8.4.*

If the `password` parameter is added before the `image` description, the specified password will apply to all operating systems and kernels that are loaded with LILO.

But the password only disables the booting, and not the feature of being able to execute commands when the system is started. To disable this capability, add the keyword `restricted` to the lilo.conf configuration file after the password-setting line, as follows:

```
image=/boot/vmlinuz-2.4.18-5asp
password=qwerty
restricted
initrd=/boot/initrd.2.4.18-5asp.img
label=linux-2.4.18
root=/dev/hda2
read-only
```

The modifications to the configuration file are made effective by executing the `lilo` directive from the command line. This will write the new parameters to the boot area, and the next system booting will take them into account.

3.2.3. init

LILO launches a program that initializes booting into the operating system by configuring the necessary equipment, loading drivers, and mounting hard drives. After this process finishes, the `init` program is launched, which finalizes the booting.

The `init` program, like most other Linux utilities, has its own configuration file (Listing 3.2). This file is named inittab and is located in the /etc folder.

Listing 3.2. The inittab configuration file

```
#
# inittab        This file describes how the init process
#                should set up the system
#                in a certain runlevel.
#
# Author:        Miquel van Smoorenburg,
#                <miquels@drinkel.nl.mugnet.org>.
#                Modified for RHS Linux by Marc Ewing and
#                Donnie Barnes
#

# Default runlevel. The runlevels used by RHS are:
#   0 - Halt (Do NOT set initdefault to this)
#   1 - Single user mode
#   2 - Multiuser, without NFS (The same as 3, if you
#       do not have networking)
#   3 - Full multiuser mode
```

```
#    4 - Unused
#    5 - X11
#    6 - Reboot (Do NOT set initdefault to this)
#   id:5:initdefault:

# System initialization
si::sysinit:/etc/rc.d/rc.sysinit

# What to do in single-user mode.
~~:S:wait:/sbin/sulogin

l0:0:wait:/etc/rc.d/rc 0
l1:1:wait:/etc/rc.d/rc 1
l2:2:wait:/etc/rc.d/rc 2
l3:3:wait:/etc/rc.d/rc 3
l4:4:wait:/etc/rc.d/rc 4
l5:5:wait:/etc/rc.d/rc 5
l6:6:wait:/etc/rc.d/rc 6

# Things to run in every runlevel
ud::once:/sbin/update

# Trap CTRL-ALT-DELETE
ca::ctrlaltdel:/sbin/shutdown -t3 -r now

# When our UPS tells us power has failed,
#  assume we have a few minutes of power left.
# Schedule a shutdown for 2 minutes from now.
# This does, of course, assume you have powerd installed
# and your UPS connected and working correctly.
pf::powerfail:/sbin/shutdown -f -h +2 "Power Failure; System Shutting Down"

# If power was restored before the shutdown kicked in,
# cancel it.
pr:12345:powerokwait:/sbin/shutdown -c "Power Restored; Shutdown Cancelled"

# Run gettys in standard runlevels
1:2345:respawn:/sbin/mingetty tty1
2:2345:respawn:/sbin/mingetty tty2
3:2345:respawn:/sbin/mingetty tty3
4:2345:respawn:/sbin/mingetty tty4
5:2345:respawn:/sbin/mingetty tty5
6:2345:respawn:/sbin/mingetty tty6

# Run xdm in runlevel 5.
# Xdm is now a separate service.
x:5:respawn:/etc/X11/prefdm -nodaemon
```

At the beginning of the file, information is provided in comments about the module and the author followed this with a description of the runlevels supported by the system. Some distributions have as few as two runlevels; Red Hat clones support seven runlevels. These are the following:

- ❐ 0 — Operating system halt.
- ❐ 1 — Single-user text mode. It is rarely used and then only by administrators to perform critically important modifications.
- ❐ 2 — Local multiuser text mode (no network support).
- ❐ 3 — Multiuser text mode with network support.
- ❐ 4 — Currently not used. This may be used in the future.
- ❐ 5 — Graphical mode.
- ❐ 6 — System reboot.

In addition to the seven runlevels just listed, there also is the S runlevel. It corresponds to the single-user mode and is used in script files, but sometimes the inittab file also uses it.

Let's get acquainted with the file's structure now. Each of its lines (with the exception of comments and empty lines) has the following structure:

```
identifier:runlevels:action:process
```

That is, each line consists of four arguments delimited with a colon. The function of each parameter is as follows:

- ❐ identifier — A unique, random value number for a string. There can be no two strings with the same identifier in the file.
- ❐ runlevels — Runlevels, for which the specified action is to be taken. For example, if the action is supposed to work at the second and third runlevels, this parameter should be 23. This is not the number 23 but two digits, "2" and "3," which are not separated by spaces or any other delimiters. If the action is supposed to be executed on all runlevels, this parameter should be left blank.
- ❐ action — The action to be taken. This can take on one of the following values:
  - boot — The process is executed once, during the boot. In this case, the runlevels parameter is ignored.
  - bootwait — This is equivalent to specifying both the boot and the wait parameters; that is, the process has to be executed during the boot and the init program must wait for its termination.
  - ctrlaltdel — This specifies that the system is set to shut down and reboot in response the <Ctrl>+<Alt>+<Del> combination. There should be no accidental or unplanned reboots. The rebooting option is a drawback, because anyone who can physically get to the computer can press this combination out of curiosity, spite, or selfish ends. I recommend disabling this option by commenting it out.
  - initdefault — The line with this parameter is processed only once, during first access to the init file, and specifies the runlevel, into which to enter after system boot. If the runlevel of this line is 5, the operating system will boot into the graphical

mode. If you want to boot the operating system into the multiuser text mode with network support, change the value of the parameter to 3 (see the description of the runlevels). It is possible to specify more than one level (which I do not recommend doing); in this case, the maximum runlevel will be selected.

- off — This will disable process execution, which is equivalent to commenting the line out or even deleting it. But if this process is already under way, the signal to terminate the program is passed to it.
- once — This will execute the process one time only.
- powerfail — The process will be executed when the power fails; init does not wait for process completion. This works only if the computer is powered from a UPS communicating with the computer over a special interface (usually, USB or COM port).
- Powerokwait — The process will be executed when init is informed that power has been restored.
- powerwait — The process will be executed when power is lost. The init program waits for the process to finish before going on. It assumes that the computer is powered from a UPS, which informs init about the power loss.
- respawn — This will restart the process whenever it terminates. This is necessary to keep critical programs always running.
- sysinit — The process will execute during system boot before the login prompt is displayed. The operating system waits for the process to finish.
- wait — This indicates that the program will wait for the process to finish. The init program will not execute any other commands until the process finishes. For example, if the disk has to be checked, the boot process must be suspended until the disk check has been completed.

❑ process — This is the process to be executed.

Now, consider a few lines from Listing 3.2 to see what they mean and to learn to control them for enhancing the system's productivity.

The first line after the comments is the following:

```
id:5:initdefault:
```

You already know that the initdefault parameter specifies how the system will be booted. In this case, the init file will be executed at runlevel 5, that is, in the graphical mode.

Then there are the following interesting lines:

```
l0:0:wait:/etc/rc.d/rc 0
l1:1:wait:/etc/rc.d/rc 1
l2:2:wait:/etc/rc.d/rc 2
l3:3:wait:/etc/rc.d/rc 3
l4:4:wait:/etc/rc.d/rc 4
l5:5:wait:/etc/rc.d/rc 5
l6:6:wait:/etc/rc.d/rc 6
```

As you can see, for each runlevel there is an entry, in which a program is executed. The program is the same for all runlevels — /etc/rc.d/rc — but the parameter passed to it corresponds to the entry's runlevel.

What is the function of the rc program? Its main task is to kill all current processes and to launch new processes corresponding to the new execution mode. For example, you want to move from runlevel 3 (the full multiuser mode) to runlevel 1 (the single-user mode). The switch is carried out as follows: All multiuser mode programs are terminated, after which only single-user mode processes are activated. This entire process is carried out by the /etc/rc.d/rc program.

Open the /etc/rc.d/ folder and inspect its contents. In addition to the rc program, it contains folders for each runlevel named rcX.d, where X is a number in the range from 0 to 6, corresponding to the runlevel. Each of these folders contains scripts whose names start with the letter "K" or "S." When a runlevel is exited, the K-scripts are executed; they kill all processes running at the runlevel. When a runlevel is entered, the S-scripts are executed, which activate all processes necessary for the given runlevel.

Scripts are not edited manually, and the system manages the files without your participation. However, you should know about this boot feature. For example, you do not want a certain daemon to run when the system boots into level 3. You can do this by simply deleting the corresponding script from the /etc/rc.d/rc3.d folder or changing its name to start with a letter other than "S."

The /etc/rc.d/init.d folder contains scripts that launch, stop, or restart system services. It is these scripts that are used when switching from one runlevel to another.

Of interest is also the following line:

```
ca::ctrlaltdel:/sbin/shutdown -t3 -r now
```

It is executed at all levels, because there is no second, runlevel, argument. The third parameter is ctrlaltdel. This means that when the <Ctrl>+<Alt>+<Del> key combination is pressed, the command specified in the fourth parameter will be executed. In most operating systems, this key combination is used to reboot the system. The command that is executed here is /sbin/shutdown -t3 -r now. As you already know, the shutdown command issued with the -r option reboots the system. Its -tX argument sets the delay, where X is the number of seconds to wait until rebooting.

Consequently, pressing the <Ctrl>+<Alt>+<Del> key combination runs the command that reboots the system after a 3-second delay.

Now, take a look at the entry that is executed at power failure:

```
pf::powerfail:/sbin/shutdown -f -h +2 "Power Failure; System Shutting Down"
```

The entry is executed at all runlevels. The shutdown command is also used in this entry, but with different options. These are the following:

- ❏ -f — Cancel disk check
- ❏ -h — Halt after shutdown
- ❏ +2 — Time in minutes until shutdown

Next, in the quotation marks, is the message that will be displayed on each console. In the graphical mode, a window with the same message will be displayed to all users.

Note that the time specified until shutdown is only 2 minutes. This is a short time, because a plain UPS can power a computer up to 20 minutes. Taking into account that in most cases servers are not equipped with a monitor or, if they are, that the monitor is usually turned off, the UPS can last up to 40 minutes. So I recommend checking how long your UPS can last and adjusting the timeout correspondingly to avoid unnecessary shutdowns.

Now, take a look at what happens when the main power is restored:

```
pr:12345:powerokwait:/sbin/shutdown -c "Power Restored; Shutdown Cancelled"
```

This entry executes in levels 1 through 5 and cancels the shutdown if the main power is restored before the timeout specified in the shutdown entry expires. It cannot be used on runlevels 0 and 6 for obvious reasons.

The shutdown is cancelled by executing the shutdown command with the −c option and displaying a message to the effect that the main power has been restored and the scheduled shutdown has been cancelled.

Now consider the following entries:

```
1:2345:respawn:/sbin/mingetty tty1
2:2345:respawn:/sbin/mingetty tty2
3:2345:respawn:/sbin/mingetty tty3
4:2345:respawn:/sbin/mingetty tty4
5:2345:respawn:/sbin/mingetty tty5
6:2345:respawn:/sbin/mingetty tty6
```

Here, session logins for six terminals (ttyX, where X is the number of the terminal, or the virtual console) are defined. This is no good, because hackers can use any of the consoles to penetrate the system as the administrator. To prevent this, logins on all terminals but one should be disabled. This can be done by replacing the respawn action with the off action.

Actually, there is a better way of doing this: by configuring the tty settings in the /etc/securetty file. An example of the contents of this file is shown in Listing 3.3.

Listing 3.3. The contents of the /etc/securetty file

```
vc/1
vc/2
vc/3
vc/4
vc/5
vc/6
vc/7
vc/8
vc/9
vc/10
```

```
vc/11
tty1
tty2
tty3
tty4
tty5
tty6
tty7
tty8
tty9
tty10
tty11
```

This file lists all consoles and terminals, from which a user can log into the system as the root user. The first 11 entries define 11 virtual consoles; the rest of the entries assign terminal windows. To permit login from only one terminal, delete all ttyX entries except for tty1. This will leave all terminals operable, but only the first one can be used to log in with root rights.

Virtual consoles are switched by pressing the <Alt> key at the same time as one of the <F1> through <F6> keys.

The last entry in the inittab file executes only on runlevel 5:

```
x:5:respawn:/etc/X11/prefdm -nodaemon
```

This entry executes the /etc/X11/prefdm shell script, which switches the system into the graphical mode and displays the corresponding login window (considered in *Section 2.8*). You can use the prefdm shell script to switch to the graphical mode from the text mode.

If you want that the init program only to reexamine the inittab configuration file, it is run with the q argument:

```
/etc/init q
```

To switch to another runlevel, execute the following command:

```
telinit X
```

Here X is the runlevel, to which you want the operating system to switch. This command is convenient to use if you are working at runlevel 5 and want to switch to the text mode, which is at runlevel 3. If you try to exit the graphical mode using the regular system means, the operating system will not switch to the text mode and the login prompt will remain graphical.

Executing telinit 6 will reboot the system (according to the function of runlevel 6). And executing telinit 0 (switching to runlevel 0) will shut down the system, the same as running the shutdown -h now command.

I would recommend, however, not switching to runlevels 0 and 6 to reboot and shut down the system, correspondingly, but using the shutdown command with the appropriate arguments.

3.2.4. Interesting Boot Settings

Here I want to briefly consider a couple of files that, although not critical, affect the boot process in a way.

Before the login prompt is presented, some text information is displayed on the screen. Most often, this is the name of the distribution and its version. This information is stored in the /etc/issue file, and you can easily modify it using any text editor, including Midnight Commander.

After successful login, a text message can also be displayed. The text is stored in the /etc/motd file and is by default blank in most distributions. The file can be used to provide different information to the system's users, for example, reminding them to change the password the first day of a month.

3.3. User Registration

In this section, I will consider the process of registering users in the system. This should help you better understand the security system used in Linux during the authorization process.

You already know, from *Section 3.2*: The `init` program loads several `getty` virtual consoles. Any user attempting to exploit any of these virtual consoles has to undergo the authorization procedure, for which he or she must provide the login (user name). The login entered is passed to the `login` program, which in turn requests the password.

The `login` program compares the user name entered with the list of names in the /etc/passwd file and the password with the corresponding entry in the /etc/shadow file. The passwords in the file are encrypted. The password entered by the user is also encrypted, and the result is compared with the encrypted password stored in the /etc/shadow file for the user name specified.

Why is the verification process so complex? The reason for this is that all passwords stored in the /etc/shadow file are encrypted with an irreversible algorithm (most often, the MD5 algorithm is used). This means that the plaintext password cannot be obtained from the encrypted password using mathematical means; it can only be picked using the enumerative or the dictionary methods. There are many simple programs that do this. The simpler and shorter the password is, the faster it is picked. If the password is complex and more than 8 characters long (or, even better, more than 16 characters long), picking it may take too much time and discourage the hacker.

If the user identification is successful, the `login` program executes all automatically-loaded scripts and launches the shell (the command line) that will be used to interact with the system. If the verification fails, the system returns control to the `getty` console, which starts the login process anew.

Consequently, unless the user passes the login authorization, access to the command shell will be denied and only the `getty` console will be available, which can only ask for the user's name and pass this name to the `login` program.

Next I will consider some problems that may arise when logging into the system and how these problems can be solved.

3.3.1. Shadow Passwords

In older Linux versions, the user list and the passwords were stored in the /etc/passwd file. This was a security risk; all users had to have access to this file because many innocent programs require user names. For example, when the `ls` command (view the contents of the current folder) is executed, it needs to have access to the user list to obtain the names of the file owners. Because the file can be read by any user, the encrypted passwords contained in it can also be read by any user. This makes it possible for a user to pick any of the passwords by the enumeration or the dictionary method.

To protect the passwords, all modern Linux versions store them in the /etc/shadow file, to which only the administrator has access. The /etc/passwd file remains accessible to anyone, but now no passwords are stored in it. Take a look at the /etc/passwd file's structure. For an example, I took three first lines from my file:

```
root:x:0:0:root:/root:/bin/bash
bin:x:1:1:bin:/bin:/sbin/nologin
daemon:x:2:2:daemon:/sbin:/sbin/nologin
```

Each entry contains seven items of user information delimited by colons. Their functions, in order of their appearance, are as follows:

- ❐ *User name* — The name typed when logging into the system.
- ❐ *Password* — The encrypted password. If shadow passwords are being used, this field contains an x character
- ❐ *User identifier* (UID) — The unique numerical UID corresponding to the given user name.
- ❐ *Group identifier* (GID) — The unique numerical GID.
- ❐ *User information* — Optional information such as the user's full name, address, and so on.
- ❐ *Home directory* — The absolute path to the directory, in which the user starts working when entering the system.
- ❐ *Shell* — The shell (a command interpreter) that will execute the user's commands. If the user is not supposed to have a command interpreter, the /sbin/nologin file is specified.

Now, examine the entry for the root user. The first parameter is the user's name, which is, of course, root. The password is not shown in the file. It is represented by the x (or !!) character, the password itself being stored in the corresponding entry of the /etc/shadow file.

The next two parameters are the unique UID and the unique GID. There can be no two entries with the same UID in the file. The system uses the GID to determine the group, to which the user belongs, and define the rights granted to this group and, accordingly, to the user.

The user information parameter can contain any data; it has no effect on the system's operation. It is used to provide additional information about the user that the administrator may deem necessary.

The next parameter is the user's home directory. This directory is opened for the user when he or she enters the system.

The last parameter is the command interpreter that will process user requests. The most common command interpreter is /bin/bash. If the user's commands are not supposed to be executed, this parameter is set to /sbin/nologin. The shell parameter for the bin, daemon, and many other accounts is set to /sbin/nologin, because these accounts are not used to enter the system but are only intended for providing internal security for certain programs.

Now, examine the /etc/shadow file structure. Three entries from this file will be enough for an example:

```
root:$1$1emP$XMJ3/GrkltC4c4h/:12726:0:99999:7:::
bin:*:12726:0:99999:7:::
daemon:*:12726:0:99999:7:::
```

Each entry contains several parameters delimited with a colon. Of interest to us are only the first two parameters: login and password. The login (the user name) is used to map the entry in the /etc/shadow file to the corresponding entry in the /etc/passwd file. The actual encrypted password is stored in the second parameter. An asterisk in this field means that this account is locked and the user is not allowed to log in. Thus, accounts for users bin and daemon cannot be used to log into the system.

3.3.2. Password Recovery

What should you do when you forget the password or if a hacker compromised your system and changed the password? This situation cannot be called pleasant, but neither is it unsolvable. If your account has the rights to access /etc/shadow, you can edit this file; otherwise, you can recover the password by booting from a diskette.

Having booted from a diskette, log into the system as root and mount the hard drive (or the partition), on which the /etc directory is located. This is done by executing the following command:

```
/sbin/mount -w hda1 /mnt/restore
```

Now, the /mnt/restore directory (this directory must exist before the command is executed) points to the primary partition of your hard drive, and the file with the password is at the /mnt/restore/etc/shadow path. Open this file in any text editor and remove the root password by simply deleting all text between the first and the second colons. The following is what I obtained in my /etc/shadow file:

```
root::12726:0:99999:7:::
```

Now boot into the system as usual and log in as root. The system will not even ask you to enter the password, because there is none. Do not, however, forget to set a new password, because failing to do this is a security risk.

You can do this by running the passwd root command and following the instructions.

3.3.3. Authentication Modules

The authentication method based on only files — /etc/passwd and /etc/shadow — is somewhat outdated and makes few features available. The developers of the Linux kernel are trying to remedy the situation by adding new encrypting algorithms. These attempts, however, are purely cosmetic; a cardinal solution is needed.

Sun Microsystems has offered a new solution to implement the authentication process: Pluggable Authentication Modules (PAMs).

The advantage of module authentication is that programs do not have to be recompiled to use them. Modules have been developed for the main authentication methods, such as Kerberos, SecureID, and Lightweight Directory Access Protocol (LDAP).

The configuration files for each service that may use PAMs are located in the /etc/pam.d directory. In most cases, you will not have to create these files manually, because they are installed when the program is installed using the RPM package. But you should know their structure in case there is a need to change some parameters.

Each entry in the configuration file contains four fields delimited by spaces. These are the following:

❐ *Module interface* — Can be one of the following types:
   • `auth` — These modules authenticate users and check their privileges.
   • `account` — These modules distribute system resources among users.
   • `session` — These modules support sessions and register users' actions.
   • `password` — These modules set and verify passwords.
❐ *Control flag* — Defines the module's parameters. The following three values can be used:
   • Required
   • Optional
   • Sufficient
❐ *Module path* — Indicates the full path to the module's file.
❐ *Module arguments*

The following is what the /etc/pam.d/ftp FTP service configuration file looks like:

```
#%PAM-1.0
auth        required /lib/security/pam_listfile.so item=user sense=deny
file=/etc/ftpusers onerr=succeed
auth        required /lib/security/pam_stack.so service=system-auth
auth        required /lib/security/pam_shells.so
account     required /lib/security/pam_stack.so service=system-auth
session     required /lib/security/pam_stack.so service=system-auth
```

This information is all you need to know. The service program takes care of the rest without your participation.

3.4. Linux Processes

To control your computer efficiently, you should thoroughly know your server and the processes that run on it. An intruder that breaks into your computer may try to surreptitiously run a program that gives the hacker root rights. A host of such programs can be found on the Internet, including various Trojan horse programs.

A process is a program or its child. A process is created when a program is launched. Each program runs with certain rights. Services that are activated during the system boot have root (complete) or nobody (no) rights. Programs that are launched from the command line have the rights of the user that starts them, unless its SUID or SGID bit is set, in which case the program has the rights of its owner.

There are two main process types: background and foreground. A terminal can have only one foreground process. For example, having launched the man program, you will not be able to execute any other commands until you terminate man.

Those who are familiar with Midnight Commander may ask how it is possible to execute commands while working in Midnight Commander. The answer is simple: processes can spawn child processes. So Midnight Commander is the parent process, and the commands that are executed from it are its child processes. Closing Midnight Commander closes all its child processes.

3.4.1. Mode Switching

All services run as background processes. That is, they do their job in parallel with whatever else you are doing on the computer. However, not only services but also any program can be run in the background mode. It is done by issuing the command to launch the program and following it with a space and the & character. For example, execute the following command:

```
man ls &
```

You will not see the help file but only the following string displayed on the screen:

```
[1] 2802
```

The terminal is now ready to accept other commands, because the terminal's foreground process launched the man ls command in the background mode and itself remains in the foreground.

But what does the message displayed in response to the command mean? The sequential number of the background process launched is shown in the square brackets. This number will successively increase. Because this is the first command issued, the number in the square brackets is 1. A separate count of background processes is kept for each user. If you log into the system on another terminal and launch a background process, you will see something like the following:

```
[1] 2805
```

The number in the square brackets is 1 again, but the next number is, and always will be, different than the one for the first command on the first terminal. This number is the Process IDentifier (PID) of the process created and is unique for all users. This means that if you launch a process number, for example, 2802, no process launched by any other user will ever have this PID.

Remember the identifiers in the preceding two examples; you will need them later.

You can find out what processes are running by executing the `jobs` command. It displays the following result:

```
[1] + Stopped        man ls
```

In this case, you can see that the process number, `[1]`, is loaded into the memory and the status of the `man ls` command is `Stopped`.

But what is the purpose of sending a command into the background execution mode? You can use this feature to run in the background a program that takes a long time to complete, while you can engage into other tasks in the foreground. You can switch the command running in the background to the foreground. This is done by entering the `fg %X` command, where `X` is the process number shown in the square brackets. Try executing this command with `X = 1`; this will bring the `man ls` process to the foreground and display the `man` page for the `ls` command.

It is only logical to expect that if a background process can be made the foreground, the reverse is also possible. It is indeed. The process can be returned to the background by pressing the <Ctrl>+<Z> key combination. This will put you back into the command line mode. Execute the `jobs` command to ascertain that `man ls` is still running in the background mode.

If the program that you want to return to the background accepts system commands, you can do this by executing the `gb %X` command instead of using the <Ctrl>+<Z> key combination. Here, `X` is the process number.

3.4.2. Process Termination

To terminate a process, it has to be returned to the foreground and stopped by one of the methods available. Most often, the program will provide the information on how to terminate it. If this is not the case, you will have to read the program's `man` page (displayed by executing the `man program's_name` command) or other documentation for the program.

Background-only processes, as to be expected, cannot be brought into the foreground mode. They are stopped using special commands, which usually look like the following:

```
service's_name stop
```

Sometimes, processes can hang. Yes, even Linux is not free of this curse. A foreground process can be terminated using the <Ctrl>+<C> or <Ctrl>+<Break> key combination. But this method does not always work for all programs. If a process refuses to terminate when asked nicely, it is terminated using the `kill` command. To terminate a process with the identifier given in the square brackets, issue the following command:

```
kill %n
```

Here, n is the number of process given in the square brackets. For example, the man program in the earlier examples is terminated by entering the following in the command line:

```
kill %1
```

Right afterward, run the jobs command. You should see the following message on the screen:

```
[1] + Terminated        man ls
```

Executing the jobs command again will produce no information about the man program.

A process launched by another user whose PID is known is terminated by the following command:

```
kill n
```

Here, n is the PID of the process. Note that it is entered without the % character. Then the kill command looks for the process with the specified PID and sends a signal for its termination.

3.4.3. Displaying Process Information

Information about running processes can be displayed using the jobs command. To spy on what other users in the system are doing, the ps command is executed. Running this command without any options displays the following information:

```
PID   TTY       TIME    CMD
1652  tty1    00:00:00  bash
1741  tty1    00:00:00  ps
```

The four columns display the following information: the PID; the terminal, on which the program was started; the execution time; and the command being executed.

But this list of processes is far from complete. To display all running processes launched from the current terminal, the ps command is executed with the -a switch. The processes launched from all terminals are displayed by executing the ps command with the -x switch added. If you also want to display the name of the user to whom the process belongs, add the -u switch. The resulting command looks as follows:

```
ps -axu
```

The information it displays is this:

```
USER PID %CPU %MEM VSZ  RSS TTY STAT START TIME COMMAND
root 1   0.0  0.1  1376 452 ?   S     14:25 0:05 init
root 2   0.0  0.0  0    0   ?   SW    14:25 0:00 [keventd]
root 3   0.0  0.0  0    0   ?   SW    14:25 0:00 [kapmd]
root 5   0.0  0.0  0    0   ?   SW    14:25 0:00 [kswapd]
root 6   0.0  0.0  0    0   ?   SW    14:25 0:00 [bdflush]
root 7   0.0  0.0  0    0   ?   SW    14:25 0:00 [kupdated]
root 530 0.0  0.1  1372 436 ?   S     14:25 0:00 klogd -x
rpc  550 0.0  0.2  1516 540 ?   S     14:25 0:00 portmap
```

The status of the processes is shown in the STAT column. It can be one of the following:

☐ S (sleeping) — This is the normal status for services, which only wake up to service client requests.

☐ R (running) — This indicates that the process currently is being executed.

☐ T (traced or stopped) — This process is currently being debugged or stopped.

☐ Z (zombied) — The process has hung and can be killed without any adverse consequences.

☐ W — The process has no resident pages.

☐ < — This is a high-priority process.

☐ N — This is a low-priority process.

These are the main process statuses that you can observe on your system.

A question mark in the STAT column means that the process was started at the system boot stage and does not belong to any of the shells.

The preceding is just a small excerpt from the results returned by the ps -axu command. There are many more processes running in a system, and even with the minimal number of services running, the list may not fit into one screen. I like saving the results of the ps command in a text file so that I could examine it at my leisure in any text editor. This is done by executing the following command:

```
ps -axu >> ps.txt
```

To see what processes are run by other users, you can execute the w command. The output it produces looks similar to the following:

```
10:59am  up 37 min,  2 users,  load average: 0.00, 0.00, 0.00
USER    TTY    FROM  LOGIN@   IDLE   JCPU    PCPU  WHAT
root    tty1   -     10:24am  0.00s  0.82s   0.05s w
flenov  tty2   -     10:39am  8:13   0.85s   0.03s grotty
```

You can see that there are two users in the system at the given moment. The root user is working on the tty1 terminal, and the user Flenov is working on the tty2 terminal. The LOGIN@ column shows when the user logged into the system. What the user is doing at the given moment is shown in the WHAT column.

The JCPU and PCPU columns can be used to evaluate the extent of the system's workload. If your computer is working sluggishly, you can see the processes that take up too much of the processor time in these columns.

The ps command displays static information about the processes. You can check the current resource usage with the help of the top program. It displays current processes sorted in descending order by the processor and memory usage (Fig. 3.4). Thus, you can tell at a glance which service or program takes up too much of the system's resources and puts a drag on the computer.

If my computer starts slowing or hiccups periodically, I launch the top command in a separate terminal and switch to it when necessary to check the workload that the processes place on the system.

```
11:44am  up  1:22,  2 users,  load average: 0,00, 0,00, 0,00
58 processes: 46 sleeping, 1 running, 0 zombie, 11 stopped
CPU states:  0,0% user,  0,5% system,  0,0% nice, 99,4% idle
Mem:   255884K av,  248416K used,    7468K free,       0K shrd,   60188K buff
Swap:  514040K av,       0K used,  514040K free                   61472K cached

 PID USER      PRI  NI  SIZE  RSS SHARE STAT %CPU %MEM   TIME COMMAND
1847 root       16   0  1036 1036   824 R    0,3  0,4   0:00 top
 859 mysql      15   0  4300 4300  1644 S    0,1  1,6   0:00 mysqld
   1 root       15   0   452  452   400 S    0,0  0,1   0:04 init
   2 root       15   0     0    0     0 SW   0,0  0,0   0:00 keventd
   3 root       15   0     0    0     0 SW   0,0  0,0   0:00 kapmd
   4 root       34  19     0    0     0 SWN  0,0  0,0   0:00 ksoftirqd_CPU0
   5 root       15   0     0    0     0 SW   0,0  0,0   0:00 kswapd
   6 root       25   0     0    0     0 SW   0,0  0,0   0:00 bdflush
   7 root       15   0     0    0     0 SW   0,0  0,0   0:00 kupdated
   8 root       25   0     0    0     0 SW   0,0  0,0   0:00 mdrecoveryd
  17 root       15   0     0    0     0 SW   0,0  0,0   0:00 kjournald
 525 root       15   0   540  540   448 S    0,0  0,2   0:00 syslogd
 530 root       15   0   436  436   376 S    0,0  0,1   0:00 klogd
 551 rpc        15   0   540  540   456 S    0,0  0,2   0:00 portmap
 579 rpcuser    15   0   740  740   636 S    0,0  0,2   0:00 rpc.statd
 683 root       15   0   468  468   412 S    0,0  0,1   0:00 apmd
 737 ident      17   0   896  896   716 S    0,0  0,3   0:00 identd
 750 ident      15   0   896  896   716 S    0,0  0,3   0:00 identd
```

Fig. 3.4. A sample of the results produced by the top program

At the top of the window displayed is the information about the number of users, the overall system workload, and the process statistics: the total number of processes and the number of sleeping, executing, zombie, and stopped processes.

A short set of statistics on memory usage is also displayed: the amount of available, used, and free system memory and the same information for the swap file. In this case, the computer has 256 MB of random access memory (RAM) installed, of which only 7 MB is free; the swap partition is not currently being used. Such a small amount of free RAM available tells me that it would not hurt to increase the system memory. The less the computer resorts to the swap file, the more efficiently it works. That the swap file is not being used at the moment does not mean much. Switching into the graphical mode and launching a couple of resource-hungry applications will quickly use up even this memory.

The top program also displays the processor workload information at the specified time intervals. To exit the program, press the <Ctrl>+<C> key combination.

3.5. Task Scheduling

Quite often, a certain operation has to be run at a certain time. In this respect, I used to rely on my memory and would launch the necessary application at the required time myself. But after failing a few times to do this — due to simply being too busy to pay attention to the clock — I placed this task on the computer's silicon shoulders. Come to think about it, why clutter my head space with what the computer can do much better?

If this reason is not good enough, what if some simple but lengthy tasks need to be performed after work hours? What should the administrator do in this case? Stay at work all night? Of course not. The computer can do everything by itself; you just have to tell it what and when has to be done.

3.5.1. Scheduling One-Time Tasks

The simplest, most reliable, and most beloved hacker tool for launching a program at a certain time is the at command. Its simplest format looks like the following:

```
at hh:mm dd.mm.yy
```

The date can be omitted; in this case, the closest date is used. For example, if the time specified is later than the current time, the current date is used; if it is before the current time, then the following date is used, because the command can no longer be executed during the current day.

Consider the usage of the at command on a real-life example. Suppose that you added a new user at the start of a workday who will work only today and only until 12:00. If after this time you forget to delete the user's account, it will present a large hole in your system's security.

So as not to forget to delete the user, you should schedule the deletion at the same time as you create the account for him or her. You start with executing the at command specifying the time as 12:30. Just in case the user does not manage to complete the job assigned by this time, give him or her an extra 20 minutes. Thus, the final command will be the following:

```
at 12:50
```

After you press the <Enter> key, the prompt to enter the command will be displayed:

```
at>
```

Enter the commands to be executed at the time scheduled. The user is deleted by the userdel command; also, his or her directory is deleted by the rm command. The necessary command sequence is the following:

```
userdel tempuser
rm -fr /home/tempuser
```

The user management subject will be considered in detail in *Chapter 4*; for now, just use these commands. Unless there actually is a tempuser user in your system, the command will not execute, but this is not important because at this point you will be more interested in learning how to run it at the specified time than in actual execution.

Type the preceding commands, pressing the <Enter> key after each one. Press the <Ctrl>+<D> key combination to quit the at command. The system will respond with a text message showing the task identifier and the date and time, at which the commands will be executed. It will look similar to the following:

```
Job 1 at 2005-03-03 12:30
```

The queue of scheduled at tasks can be viewed using the atq command. The results of its execution will look similar to the following:

```
1        2005-01-28 12:40 a root
2        2005-01-28 01:00 a root
3        2005-01-30 12:55 a root
```

In the first column, the task's number is displayed. The task can be manipulated using this number. The second column holds the date for the task's execution; the name of the user who created the task is in the last column.

Now suppose that some urgent processor-intensive job has to be done at the time that the system backup is scheduled to be performed. The backup process will put quite a brake on the other work, and it would be logical to postpone the backup until the job has been finished.

This problem is solved by using the `batch` command instead of `at` to schedule the backup. In this case, the execution of the scheduled task will start when the system load drops below the specified value, which is 0.8% by default.

3.5.2. Scheduling Recurrent Tasks

The `at` command is quite simple and easy to use, but it can be used to schedule only a one-time task. Many administrator tasks (backup, for example) must be run on a recurrent basis. Suppose that your system has to be backed up every day at 10:00 p.m. Preparing the `at` command every day is not much fun; most likely, you will tire of doing this after a week at the most and will be looking for a way to optimize the task. A script file is not convenient either, because you will have to remember to run it.

The answer to this problem is using the `cron` program. Using this program requires you to have the `crond` daemon installed and running. It is also advisable to include it in the start-up.

The `crond` daemon is controlled with the help of the `crontab` program. A new entry is added to the schedule by executing the program without any parameters. The program will respond with a blank line, into which the date template and the necessary command can be entered. The format of the filled line is as follows:

```
minutes hours day month day_of_week command
```

The day of the week is specified by a number from 0 to 7, where both 0 and 7 denote Sunday. This is because in different countries the week starts on different days of week: in some it starts on Monday, and in others the week begins on Sunday. In the former, weekdays are denoted by numbers from 1 to 7, and in the latter they are numbered 0 to 6.

Parameters that are not used are filled with an asterisk.

Consider a few examples. Here is the first one:

```
00 5 * * * /home/flenov/backup1_script
```

Here, only the hours and minutes are specified. Because the other parameters are not specified, the command will execute daily at 05:00. The second example:

```
00 20 * * 1 /home/flenov/backup2_script
```

This command executes the same script file every Monday (the weekday parameter is 1) at 20:00. The third example:

```
00 * * * * /home/flenov/backup3_script
```

This command will execute every hour at 00 minutes.

Pressing the <Ctrl>+<D> key combination without entering any commands will delete all previously scheduled tasks. To exit the program without saving the changes, use only the <Ctrl>+<C> key combination.

IMPORTANT

The `cron` service also uses several supplementary directories to simplify the scheduling process. Executable scripts are grouped in the following directories:

- /etc/cron.hourly
- /etc/cron.weekly
- /etc/cron.daily
- /etc/cron.monthly

It seems simple, but on which day of the week and at what time does a weekly script execute? The answer becomes obvious by examining the /etc/crontab/ configuration file of the `cron` service. It contains the following entries:

```
01 * * * * root run-parts /etc/cron.hourly
02 4 * * * root run-parts /etc/cron.daily
22 4 * * 0 root run-parts /etc/cron.weekly
42 4 1 * * root run-parts /etc/cron.monthly
```

The appropriate execution time is specified at the start of each entry in the following format: `minute hour day month dayofweek`.

The execution time can be specified in such a way that scripts from the /etc/cron.monthly directory will execute hourly. So the default names of the execution time directories are purely symbolic and can be easily changed.

Note that there are already scripts in these directories; you should remove all of them that are not necessary to avoid overloading the system, or you should schedule their execution for a different time.

The list of existing tasks (stored in the crontab configuration file) can be viewed by executing the `crontab -1` command. The crontab configuration file can be edited by executing the `crontab -e` command. This will open the file in a text editor, in which you can edit its entries. If you have never worked with this particular text editor, you may have some problems because it is rather specific. If you have any problems, press <F1> to display the help information. Changes become effective immediately upon quitting the editor. To quit the editor without saving changes, type :`q!` and press <Enter>.

All `cron` task information is stored as `test`. For each user, an individual /var/spool/cron/file crontab file is created. The name of the file is the same as the user's name.

The following is an example of the contents of a crontab file:

```
#DO NOT EDIT THIS FILE - edit the master and reinstall.
#(- installed on Thu Jan 27 13:55:49 2005)
#(Cron version--$Id:crontab.c,v2.13 1994/01/17 03:20:37 vixie Exp $)
10 * * * * ls
```

You can edit this file directly, without using the `crontab -e` command.

3.5.3. Task Scheduling Security

In conclusion, I want to give some security advice on working with the at command. Hackers like to use this instruction a lot. For example, a hacker may manage to obtain an account with maximum rights. He or she can then use the at command to delete the account and clean up all the traces of entering the system.

There are two files in the /etc directory that you should configure properly:

❑   at.allow — Only those users listed in this file have the right to execute the at command.
❑   at.deny — Users listed in this file are explicitly denied the right to use the at command.

Similar files exist for the cron service:

❑   cron.allow — Users listed in this file have the right to use the cron service. The file may not be created by default.
❑   cron.deny — Users listed in this file are denied the right to use the cron service.

I have said it many times and will repeat it again: You should maintain a restrictive configuration policy. This means that you start with disabling all services and denying all users all rights; then you enable the services that are necessary and give the necessary rights to those users that require them. But don't try to list all users in the at.deny file. Instead, create the at.allow file and list in it only your account, which preferably is not the root one. If some users complain that they need to use the at command, make sure that they need it before entering their accounts into the at.allow file.

No stray visitors should be allowed to use the at command. Sometimes, it is better to put up with some griping from an unsatisfied customer than to lose control over the system.

If you do not use the at and cron scheduling commands, I recommend deleting the crond service from the start-up, or, even better, deleting it from the system altogether. You cannot control something that you do not use.

The /etc/crontab file is the configuration file for the cron command. I recommend entering the following entry at the beginning of the file:

```
CRONLOG = YES
```

This will enable logging of the commands executed by cron in the /var/cron/log log file.

3.6. Network Configuration

When installed, Linux easily determines the installed network cards. I have never had any problems in this respect. But this is not enough for network operation. You can specify the main connection parameters during the installation. Afterward, however, the settings sometimes have to be modified. You will not reinstall the system to do this, will you?

To transfer data over the network, various protocols have to be installed and configured. In general, a protocol is a set of rules used by two remote devices to exchange data. The rules describe whether a connection has to be established, specify the method for checking the data integrity, decide whether the data transfer is reliable or unreliable, and so on. All this is implemented in the protocol, and your task is to configure it properly.

3.6.1. Linux Addressing

The main protocol used in Linux is the Internet standard TCP/IP. This protocol is installed during Linux installation and only has to be configured. If you have never worked with this protocol, I recommend that you obtain and read some information on this subject. I cannot consider all nuances of TCP/IP in this book and will only consider the fundamental concepts.

For the network to work properly, the following minimal parameters should be configured:

☐ *The address.* Each device in the network must have its address to be able to communicate with other devices in the network. Imagine that there were no addresses for your house. How, then, would mailmen deliver your mail? Computer names cannot be used for this purpose for various reasons beyond the scope of this book.

Devices in a network are addressed using 32-bit-long IP addresses. For convenience, an IP address is divided into four binary octets, each of which is further converted into a decimal number. The four groups of decimal numbers are delimited using periods (dots). The resulting format is called dotted decimal notation.

It is obvious that each group can be no larger than 255. Your Internet interface may have an IP address assigned by the Internet provider.

For local network connections, you have to assign the addresses yourself. I recommend using addresses of the 192.168.1.*x* format, where *x* is a number in the 1 to 254 range (numbers 0 and 255 are reserved). Each computer must be assigned a unique address in this format, with the uniqueness determined by the last number. The third number can be anything but must be the same for all computers in the network. I use the number 77; that is, the computer addresses have the format 192.168.77.*x*.

☐ *The subnet mask.* In conjunction with the IP address, another dotted decimal notation number is used to divide the network into smaller segments. It is called the subnet mask. Whereas your home address can have several components (such as the house or apartment number, street, city, and zip code), a computer address has only two characteristics: the network ID (also called a network address) and the ID of the computer inside the network (also called a host address). The subnet mask determines, which part of the computer address defines the network and which defines the host.

To understand how the mask does this, each of its numbers has to be converted into the binary format. Consider this using mask 255.255.255.0 as an example. In binary format it looks as follows:

```
11111111.11111111.11111111.00000000
```

Now convert the 192.168.001.001 IP address into the binary format:

```
11000000.10101000.00000001.00000001
```

Superimpose the mask on the IP address. The ones in the mask determine, which parts of the IP address are the network address, and the zeros specify the host address.

Ones in the mask must always be located in the left part of the mask, and zeros must be in the right. Ones cannot alternate with zeros. For example, the following mask is correct:

```
11111111.11111111.00000000.00000000
```

This one is wrong:

```
11111111.11111111.00000000.11111111
```

There can be no ones to the right of zeros.

Consequently, with the 255.255.255.0 mask, the first three octets of the IP address define the network ID, and the last octet defines the host ID in this network. Because the maximum value that this octet can assume is 255, this is also the maximum number of computers the particular network can have.

Consider another example.

192.168.001.001 — IP address
255.255.000.000 — Subnet mask

In this case, the first two groups define the network ID, and the last two are the host ID in this network. The number that can be expressed by two octets is much larger than 255; consequently, the network will be much larger.

This allows the following conclusion to be drawn. Hosts (computers) whose IP addresses share the same network ID — that is, are in the same network — can communicate among themselves directly. Computers in different networks cannot see each other. For them to be able to interact, a special device — a router — must be used to connect different networks by passing packets from one network to another.

3.6.2. Viewing Network Connection Information

Information about the current configuration of the network cards and TCP/IP can be obtained by executing the `ifconfig` command. An example of the execution results is shown in Listing 3.4.

Listing 3.4. Information about the network configuration and state

```
eth0 Link encap:Ethernet  HWaddr 00:03:FF:06:A4:6C
     inet addr:192.168.77.1  Bcast:192.168.77.255  Mask:255.255.255.0
     UP BROADCAST RUNNING MULTICAST  MTU:1500  Metric:1
     RX packets:108 errors:0 dropped:0 overruns:0 frame:0
     TX packets:104 errors:0 dropped:0 overruns:0 carrier:0
     collisions:0 txqueuelen:100
     RX bytes:7687 (7.5 Kb)  TX bytes:14932 (14.5 Kb)
     Interrupt:11 Base address:0x2000

lo   Link encap:Local Loopback
     inet addr:127.0.0.1  Mask:255.0.0.0
```

```
UP LOOPBACK RUNNING  MTU:16436  Metric:1
RX packets:122 errors:0 dropped:0 overruns:0 frame:0
TX packets:122 errors:0 dropped:0 overruns:0 carrier:0
collisions:0 txqueuelen:0
RX bytes:9268 (9.0 Kb)  TX bytes:9268 (9.0 Kb)
```

You can see that Listing 3.4 provides information for two interfaces: eth0 and lo. The former is the actual network adapter. Network adapters are named using the ethX format, where X is the number of the device. Device numbering starts with zero. Thus, if there are two network cards installed in your computer, they will be named eth0 and eth1.

The second interface is always named lo (for loopback); its IP address is always 127.0.0.1 and its subnet mask is always 255.0.0.0. This interface is present in any system equipped with a network card. This address does not define any network or a computer. It is used for testing and debugging network applications. It is called loopback because it closes on itself. All packets sent to this address by your computer are also received by your computer.

In addition to the network interface configuration information, the ifconfig command provides lots of other useful information. For example, the RX and TX entries contain information about the number of sent and received packets, respectively.

Another interesting piece of information given for the eth0 network card is the HWaddr (hardware address) parameter. It is also often called the MAC address. This is a 48-bit unique number assigned to the card by the manufacturer. It is unique because each manufacturer has its own MAC address range. Because the lo interface is created by software and does not actually exist, it cannot have a MAC address.

3.6.3. Modifying Network Connection Parameters

The ifconfig command can be used not only to view network connection parameters but also to modify them. For this, it is executed with two arguments:

☐ The network interface whose parameters are to be modified
☐ The parameters

The overall command looks as follows:

`ifconfig ethX parameters`

The main parameters and their functions are the following:

☐ down — Causes the driver for the given interface to be shut down. For example, the eth0 network card can be shut down by executing the ifconfig eth0 down command. If the ifconfig command is executed without arguments immediately afterward, the particular network interface will not be in the information displayed.

☐ up — Activates a disabled interface. For example, the eth0 network card can be put back into operation by executing this command: ifconfig eth0 up.

☐ IP address — If you want to change the IP address, specify its new value as the parameter. For example, if you want to change the current IP address to 192.168.77.3, execute the following command: `ifconfig eth0 192.168.77.3`. With the IP address, the subnet mask can also be modified. This is done by executing the `ifconfig` command as follows: `ifconfig eth0 192.168.77.3 netmask 255.255.0.0`. The new `netmask` value is specified after the `netmask` keyword.

With the IP address and subnet mask modification, the interface can also be started by executing this command: `ifconfig eth0 192.168.77.3 netmask 255.255.0.0 up`.

These are the functions of the `ifconfig` command that you will most likely need in your work. You can obtain more detailed information in the `ifconfig man` page.

3.6.4. Basic Network Tuning

You can find out the computer's (host's) name with the help of the `hostname` command. The same command can be used to change the computer name by executing it with the new name specified as the argument. For example, the following command sets the host name to "server":

```
hostname server
```

The desired network configuration settings are stored in the /etc/sysconfig/network file. Take a look at its contents by executing the following command:

```
cat /etc/sysconfig/network
```

This will display information similar to the following:

```
NETWORKING=yes
FORWARD_IPv4=true
HOSTNAME=FlenovM
```

There is no need to change the preceding parameters manually; this can be done with specialized utilities. The contents of the file were shown only to give you an idea what they are.

3.7. Connecting to the Internet

One of the basic system settings is the Internet connection, which has become an inseparable aspect of any computer. It is difficult to imagine modern life without being able to communicate and exchange information.

The World Wide Web is a prolific source of the most diverse information. You can find various software and documentation there. In *Appendix 2*, I provide some Internet references, from which can be downloaded programs that can make your work with the computer easier and more effective. Of course, you need to have Internet access to be able to do this.

I will not be describing all possible connection configurations, because you find out the pertinent details from your Internet service provider. What I will consider is configuring a modem connection.

Creating an Internet connection is easy if you are using a graphical shell. It is also much easier and convenient to handle Web pages in the graphical mode, using, for example, the Mozilla browser. For this purpose, you should configure one of the Linux graphical shells available; you should use it, however, only in extreme cases and only on workstations, not on active servers.

At present, the simplest and most convenient program for creating Internet connections is KPPP. It is launched by selecting the **Internet/More Internet Applications/KPPP** item sequence in the main menu. A window similar to the one shown in Fig. 3.5 will open.

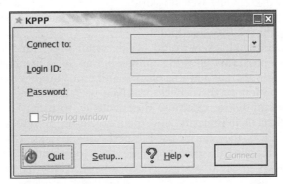

Fig. 3.5. The main window of the KPPP program

Start by clicking the **Setup...** button to specify the parameters for a new connection. In response, the **KPPP Configuration** dialog window will open. Click the **New** button on it. This will open the **Create New Account** dialog window, offering you the options of creating a new account manually (the **Dialog Setup** button) or using a wizard (the **Wizard** button). The wizard contains a list of major Internet providers for different countries, and all you have to do to create a connection is specify the appropriate country and a couple of other parameters. If your Internet service provider is not on the wizard's list, you will have to create the connection manually.

Here, you most often will only have to specify the provider's dial-up phone number. The rest of the parameters can usually be left at their default values.

Once you have created the connection, you only have to select this connection, enter the login and password given to you by your provider in the KPPP main window, and click the **Connect** button. If all settings have been configured properly, in a few seconds you will be in the World Wide Web.

3.8. Updating the Kernel

By updating programs you can obtain new features and correct bugs in their previous versions. The Linux kernel is the core of the operating system and it is updated frequently because of the dynamic development of this operating system. Do not be scared upon learning that such an important piece of software as the kernel has bugs in it: All software does. (I will cover the question of bugs in *Section 14.1.*) To fix bugs in the kernel, you should be able to install a new kernel in your system.

At present, most software is supplied as RPM packages, which are easy to install. The same applies to the Linux kernel. But the newest kernel versions are only available as source codes. This makes the kernel-update process more difficult, but it also gives you an opportunity to tune the system for the maximum productivity. You can install only the necessary kernel components and optimize it for your specific hardware.

Developers of different Linux distributions supply their products with a universal kernel, which can work equally well on various platforms. Also, all distributions that I am familiar with use modules to add new features to the kernel. This is convenient but not always wise from the security standpoint.

Only a few years ago hackers would switch system files with doctored versions that had built-in exploits (programs allowing vulnerabilities in software to be exploited, hence the name) or backdoors. To fight this plague, numerous utilities to prevent changing of the system files and to monitor their checksums have been developed.

This did not stop hackers because they switched to using Linux modules. It is more difficult to monitor their integrity, and their execution produces the same results as the system files; moreover, they can be used to perform any tasks. This hole in system security can be closed by disabling the use of modules, but you should keep in mind that this may also cause problems in the operating system's work. Some hardware manufacturers and utility developers also like to use modules. This can be understood, because modules are easy to install and make it possible to add new or improved kernel features without recompiling the latter. But you already know that the security and the convenience are two incompatible concepts.

3.8.1. Getting Ready to Compile

Before undertaking any steps to compile the kernel, you should prepare for the worst, namely, for the chance that instead of increased performance your update may crash the system. The kernel is the core of the operating system, and any errors while updating it can degrade its operation or even cause the system to become unbootable.

You should also back up any data that you may have on the server. In addition, it is a good idea to make sure that you have a working bootable diskette to help you if after the update you cannot boot the system from the hard drive.

You can create a bootable diskette by executing the following command:

```
/sbin/mkbootdisk ver
```

Here, `ver` is the number of the kernel version installed on your system. If you do not know the kernel version installed, you can find it out by executing the following command:

```
uname -r
```

Suppose that your kernel version is 2.4.20-8. To create a bootable diskette for this kernel, execute this command:

```
/sbin/mkbootdisk 2.4.20-8
```

If the wrong version is specified, the diskette will not be created, because the program looks for the necessary files in the /lib/modules/ver directory, where ver is the version number. In this example, this directory will be /lib/modules/2.4.20-8.

3.8.2. Updating the Kernel Using an RPM Package

The simplest way to install a new kernel is to do this using an RPM package. Installing a kernel is no different than installing any other program. To update the kernel, the following command is executed:

```
rpm -Uvh Package_Name
```

If you want to install a new kernel, the U option has to be replaced with the i option. One of the advantages of Linux is that several kernels can be installed at the same time. Only one of them can be booted into at any given time.

Only the necessary files, modules, and the boot loader are installed from the RPM package, but to be able to boot into the new kernel it has to be registered in the LILO boot loader.

Updating the kernel from an RPM package adds new functions to the kernel and fixes the bugs that it may contain. The main capabilities of the kernel remain the same. The maximum benefits from an updating can only be achieved by recompiling the kernel.

3.8.3. Compiling the Kernel

When updating the kernel from an RPM package, device drivers may be compiled as part of the kernel or loaded separately from it. This kernel is slower but allows drivers to be updated by simply changing the appropriate modules.

When upgrading the kernel by compiling, it can be made monolithic. This means that all drivers will be compiled as part of the kernel, which will increase the kernel's efficiency. This will also make it impossible to update the kernel without totally recompiling it.

I recommend that you learn how to compile, because all new kernel versions are first released as source codes, with the corresponding RPM packages lagging by a week or even longer. All this time, your system will remain vulnerable.

As a rule, the source codes for the kernel are supplied as a tar archive. It is unarchived by executing the following command:

```
tar xzvf linux-2.6.10-rc2.tar.gz
```

The archive name in your particular case most likely will be more sophisticated than in the example. I used the current kernel version at the time this book was being written. You can download the latest kernel versions from the **www.redhat.com** site.

The archive is unpacked into the linux-2.6.10-rc2 directory (which is the same as the archive's name without the tar.gz extension). Open this directory to perform the further steps necessary to compile the kernel.

First, you need to configure the kernel, that is, to specify what functions and features you want to obtain. This can be done using one of the following four utilities:

- ❐ oldconfig — This is a script that installs the default settings values without requiring any user participation. It is invoked by executing the make oldconfig command.
- ❐ config — This is a script that asks you questions concerning the parameters of the future kernel and, depending on your answers, constructs a configuration file to be used during the compilation. It is invoked by executing the make config command.

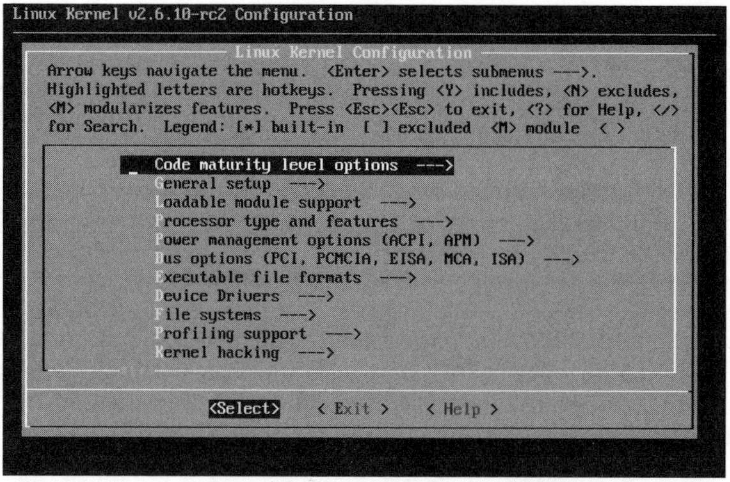

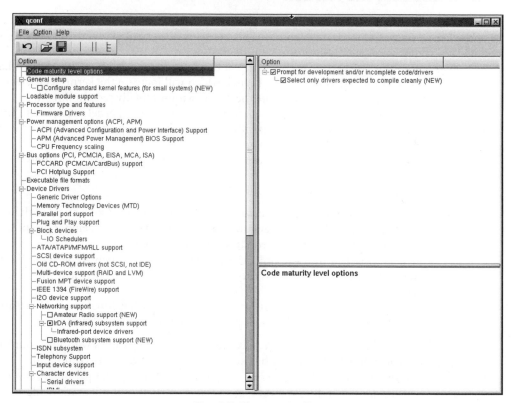

Fig. 3.6. The menuconfig utility

Fig. 3.7. The gconf utility

❑ menuconfig — This text mode utility (Fig. 3.6) is the most convenient way to configure the compilation from the console. It is invoked by executing the make menuconfig command.

❑ qconf (xconfig) — This graphical utility (Fig. 3.7) is the most convenient way to configure the compilation from the Linux graphical shell. It is invoked by executing the make xconfig command.

When configuring the compilation using one of the mentioned utilities, you have to specify whether the resulting kernel is to support modules.

If you want to have two same-version kernels, one supporting modules and the other not, specify different values for the EXTRAVERSION parameter in the makefile file:

❑ EXTRAVERSION=-rc2-module — To compile a modularized kernel
❑ EXTRAVERSION=-rc2-nomodule — To compile a monolithic kernel

In addition to -rc2-module option, you can add a short remark in this parameter, explaining the particularities of the specific kernel version.

Now, execute the following commands to prepare for the compilation:

```
make dep
make clean
```

The following command will take quite a long time to execute, because it will actually be compiling the kernel. While it is occupied with this, you can go and drink a few cups of coffee. The procedure will take an especially long time if you have an underpowered processor and less than 256 MB of RAM.

The compilation is invoked by executing the following command:

```
make bzImage
```

If you opted to compile a modularized kernel version, the following two commands carry out this operation:

```
make modules
make modules_install
```

If you are building a monolithic module use, you can skip these commands, because in this case they are not needed while they take a long time to execute.

All modules are stored in the /lib/modules directory. The make modules command builds the modules of the new kernel, and the make modules_install command installs them into the /lib/modules directory. This directory also contains subdirectories for each of the kernel versions installed in the system.

The compiled kernel is installed by executing the following command:

```
make install
```

This command will copy all files necessary for booting into their proper places. Take a look in the /boot directory. You can see several files in there, including the boot loader for the new kernel version. You can easily tell these files by the number in their names. For example, when I compiled kernel version 2.6.10, files vmliuz-2.6.10 and initrd-2.6.10.img were added to this directory.

3.8.4. Configuring the Boot Loader

Now, look at how to configure the LILO boot loader to load the new kernel, along with the old kernel versions. This is done by adding the following entries at the end of the /etc/lilo.conf file:

```
image=/boot/vmlinuz-2.6.10
label=Linux Kernel 2.6.10
initrd=initrd-2.6.10.img
read-only
root=/dev/hda0
```

The first entry specifies the path to the new kernel. You should specify the correct path, or rather, the file name with its own version number. The `label` entry specifies the text to be displayed for the new kernel option in the boot loader menu. The `initrd` parameter is defined by the boot loader. The last entry specifies the root disk and should be the same as for the old kernel versions, which already are in the lilo.conf file.

After updating the /etc/lilo.conf configuration file, the changes must be recorded in the boot area. This is done by executing the `lilo` command.

Reboot the system; the new boot loader menu will now have the option for the new kernel in addition to the old kernel versions' boot options. But any of the kernels, the new as well as the old, will be loaded using the same configuration files, which is convenient. Should the new kernel compilation turn out to be nonviable, all you have to do is reboot the computer into an old kernel and start troubleshooting the new kernel.

3.8.5. Handling the Modules

The advantage of the modularized kernel compilation is that you can enable only the most necessary functions at boot, thereby decreasing the number of potential vulnerabilities than can be exploited by hackers. But you should be able to control modules (in the same way that you can control services).

The system should boot only with those modules that are used. All other modules are loaded dynamically as the need arises, and unloaded when no longer needed. The following are descriptions of main commands used to control modules.

lsmod

The list of the loaded modules can be viewed using the `lsmod` command. The result of the command's execution looks similar to the following:

```
Module              Size    Used by      Not tainted
binfmt_misc         7428    1
autofs              11812   0    (autoclean) (unused)
tulip               42240   1
ipchains            42216   6
```

```
ide-cd              30240   0   (autoclean)
cdrom               32000   0   (autoclean) [ide-cd]
ext3                62284   1
jbd                 39804   1   [ext3]
```

modinfo

Deciding which modules should be included into the start-up and which should not is not an easy task. And it is important to be able to do this, because every extra module loaded increases the boot time, requires its share of system's resources, and so on. So how are you to decide what is needed and what is not? You should intimately know each module and understand its function.

Information about a module can be obtained using the modinfo command executed with the module in question as the parameter. For example, the following command re-quests information about the ext3 module from the system:

```
modinfo ext3
```

The results of its execution look similar to the following:

```
filename:     /lib/modules/2.4.18-5asp/kernel/fs/ext3/ext3.o
description:  "Second Extended Filesystem with journaling extensions"
author:       "Remy Card, Stephen Tweedie, Andrew Morton, Andreas Dilger,
              Theodore Ts'o and others"
license:      "GPL"
parm:         do_sync_supers int, description "Write superblocks
              synchronously"
```

Some of the information displayed is the file's name and location, the file description, the author, and the license type. The amount of information depends on the module; to tell the truth, in some cases it is so scant that it is impossible to tell the module's function by it.

modprobe

The modprobe command is mainly used by the system to load the installed modules, but it can also be used manually. The command is executed with the name of the module to be loaded as its parameter.

For example, the following command loads the iptable_nat module (it will be con-sidered in *Section 4.12*):

```
modprobe iptable_nat
```

rmmod

The rmmod command unloads the module specified in its argument. When you are finished using a module, do not forget to unload it. Otherwise, it may turn out to be the proverbial straw that broke the camel's back, or, more pertinent, the loophole that hackers use to penetrate your system.

Chapter 4: Access Control

Users must use only their own accounts in the system. Adhering to this policy will increase the degree of security that prevents unauthorized access to your files and, if despite all precautions such access takes place, system logs can be used to determine, which account was used for this.

Regular users should be granted limited privileges, sufficient for carrying out only the necessary operations. You should keep the number of users with extended privileges to a minimum, because accounts of this type require special attention and monitoring. Logging into the system using a privileged account from a computer that could not possibly belong to the owner of the account will indicate a potential or actual break-in.

If you fire an employee, you should immediately delete his or her account to prevent any chance of the account being misused by the disgruntled employee for getting back at you for the firing. In fact, you should delete an account of any terminated employee regardless the circumstances, under which he or she was let go.

You must have administrator rights to manage access rights commands. Administrator rights can be obtained by logging into the system as the administrator or by executing the su command. In either case, you have to know the corresponding password. Another command for obtaining administrator privileges is considered in *Section 4.16*.

Let's move to the specifics.

4.1. Access Rights

Recall the `ls -al` command. It displays the contents of the directory in the following format:

```
drwx------   3 Flenov    FlenovG    4096 Nov 26 16:10 .
drwxr-xr-x   5 root      root       4096 Nov 26 16:21 ..
-rwxr-xr--   1 Flenov    FlenovG      24 Nov 26 16:10 test
```

As you already know, the first column (10 characters wide) displays the access rights. Dissect its contents. The first character indicates the type of entry. It can be one of the following:

- ❑ A dash (-) denotes a regular file.
- ❑ A letter "d" denotes a directory.
- ❑ A letter "l" denotes a symbolic link.
- ❑ A letter "s" denotes a socket.
- ❑ A letter "p" denotes a FIFO file.

It is followed by three groups of `rwx` characters. These groups indicate the access rights for different user categories. The first triplet indicates the access rights for the file's owner, the second for the users belonging to the user's group, and the third for the rest of the users.

The `r` character indicates the read rights, the `w` the write rights, and the `x` the execution rights. No letter means no corresponding rights. Take a look at a few examples.

The access rights in the first entry in the example are assigned as the `drwx------` string. The first character, `d`, means that the entry is a directory. The next three characters, `rwx`, mean that the owner of the directory has the read, write, and execute rights for the directory. For the following two owner categories, the access rights are denoted by dashes, meaning that users of the FlenovG group and all other users have no rights for the directory.

The access rights for the second entry are denoted by the `drwxr-xr-x` string. This is a directory again. The first group, `rwx`, gives all rights to the directory's owner. The next group, `r-x`, allows read and execute rights and disallows write rights to the group's members. The last triplet, also `r-x`, gives the same rights to the group members as to all other users.

The access rights string for the last entry in the example, `-rwxr-xr--`, denotes file access rights, as indicated by the first character, the dash. The file's owner has full rights for the file, as indicated by the first access rights triplet, `rwx`. The members of the file owner's group have read and execute rights but not write rights, as indicated by the second access rights triplet, `r-x`. The rest of the users can only read the file, as indicated by the last access rights triplet, `r--`.

Access rights can also be represented as a sequence of ones and zeros. A one for a certain right means that it is allowed; a zero means that the right is disallowed. Use this notation to write the rights denoted by the `rwxr-xr--` string. Replace the rights-granting characters with ones and the rights-denying dashes with zeros. The resulting combination of ones and zeros should be 111101100. Break this sequence into three groups: 111, 101, and 100. Now convert each triplet into the octal notation using the following formula:

```
Digit1 * 4 + Digit2 * 2 + Digit3
```

Consider the digits obtained — 7, 5, and 4 — as an octal number 754. Remember this number; you will use it when assigning access rights to files and directories. The following is a list of all possible access rights combinations for each position of the octal number (the user type):

- ❑ 0 — All operations are disallowed.
- ❑ 1 — The execution is allowed.
- ❑ 2 — The write is allowed.
- ❑ 3 — The write and execution are allowed.
- ❑ 4 — The read is allowed.
- ❑ 5 — The read and execution are allowed.
- ❑ 6 — The read and write are allowed.
- ❑ 7 — All operations are allowed.

Try to use this list to determine, which rights for each user type represents number 754. Compare the obtained result with the rights denoted by the `rwxr-xr--` string. They should be the same.

NOTE

To have the right to create or delete files, the user must have write rights for the directory. Some beginning administrators are confused by why they cannot delete a file even though they have all rights for it.

4.1.1. Setting User Rights

Access rights to file system objects are modified using the `chmod` command. It can be used to specify new rights to an object in both the symbolic and the digital notation.

First consider the symbolic mode:

```
chmod option rights file
```

The `options` argument can contain any combination of the codes for the user type whose rights are being modified. These are the following:

- ❑ u — Owner
- ❑ g — Group
- ❑ o — All other users
- ❑ a — All user types (the same as `ugo`)

The second argument is prefixed by the action undertaken with respect to the existing rights. This can be one of the following:

- ❑   + — Add rights
- ❑   – — Delete rights
- ❑   = — Replace old rights with new rights

The last argument specifies particular rights or a combination of them. These are the following:

- ❑   r — Read
- ❑   w — Write
- ❑   x — Execute
- ❑   X — Execute only if the file is a directory or already has execute permission for some user
- ❑   s — SUID or SGID bit
- ❑   t — Sticky bit, indicating that the file can only be deleted by the file's owner
- ❑   u — Rights are granted to the file's owner
- ❑   g — Rights are granted to all users who are members of the file owner's group
- ❑   o — Rights are granted to users not included in either of the two preceding types

The chmod command used with numeric arguments looks as follows:

```
chmod rights file
```

The rights argument is a four-digit octal number. The functions of each digit are as follows:

- ❑   The most significant digit sets the sticky bit and can have one of the following values:
  - •   1 — The owner bit
  - •   2 — The SGID bit
  - •   4 — The SUID bit
- ❑   The use of this digit is optional, and it is usually omitted.
- ❑   The next digit, second from the left, sets the user rights. It can have values in the range from 0 to 7.
- ❑   The third-from-the-left digit sets the group rights. It can also have values in the range from 0 to 7.
- ❑   The least significant digit sets the rights of all other users. It can also have values in the range from 0 to 7.

For example, you want the owner and the group to have all rights (expressed by 7 for each user type) and all other users to have only execute rights (expressed by 1). The command to set these rights will look as follows:

```
chmod 771 filename
```

The rights expressed numerically as `771` correspond to the rights expressed symbolically as `rwxrwx--x`. The following command disallows read rights for the group:

```
chmod g-r text
```

After the preceding command is executed, the object's access rights become `rwx-wx--x`. Now, disallow all user categories to execute the file. This can be done by executing the following command:

```
chmod ugo-x text
```

Alternatively, you can execute this one:

```
chmod a-x text
```

After each of the preceding commands is executed, the object's access rights become `rw--wx----`.

4.1.2. Changing User Ownership

File ownership can be changed by the `chown` command as follows:

```
chown owner file
```

The `name` argument sets the new owner of the file. For example, make the root user the new owner of the test file. This is done by executing the following command:

```
chown root test
```

Group ownership of a file can also be changed. This is done by executing the `chgrp` command as follows:

```
chgrp group_name file
```

Here, the `group_name` argument specifies the group that has ownership of the file specified in the `file` argument. For example, the group of the root user is given ownership of the test file using the following command:

```
chgrp root test
```

4.1.3. Safety Rules

In assigning access rights to files and directories, you follow the minimization principle described in *Section 2.11.1*. That is, the default settings must disallow everything. Access is granted only to what is necessary. If a user has no rights for a file, the file should not even be shown in the directory tree.

Giving users unnecessary access to file system objects can end in compromise of the system's security and information leak or even loss. For example, a company's accounting files should be accessible only by those who work with them. Letting everyone see these files may expose the contents to the danger of becoming public property, which is unlikely to contribute to the company's welfare.

The most important safeguard for your system is preventing users from modifying system files. The most important Linux configuration files are stored in the /etc directory.

Only a system administrator should have the right to modify these files. This is how developers of Linux distributions configure the system's default setting, and you should not change them to give users more rights without an actual need for this.

4.1.4. Default Rights

When a user creates a new file or a directory, they are assigned default permissions. Consider this in an example. To create a file, execute an ls command and redirect its output to a file as follows:

```
ls -al >> testfile
```

Examine this file's permissions by executing the ls -al command. The permissions should be -rw-r--r--, meaning that the owner has the right to read from and write to the file and that the group users and all other users have only read rights. Older systems and some distributions may set the default permissions to -rw-rw-r--, granting the group users write rights. Such permissions run counter to the main security principle. But in either case, all users are granted read rights.

This policy is wrong. Suppose you create a file intending to use it to store confidential data. If you forget to change the file's permissions, everyone will be able to view the file's contents.

This situation can be avoided if you understand how a new file is assigned permissions. File permissions are determined based on the mask whose current value is determined by the umask command. The obtained value should be 0022 or 002.

Consider how the mask affects assignment of file permissions. The default permissions for files are set to 666 minus the mask; for directories, permissions are set to 777 minus the mask.

From this, it follows that if the mask's value is 002, permissions for a new file will be set as 666 – 002 = 664, or rw-rw-r-- in the symbolic format. If the mask's value is 0022, the default file's permissions will be set to 666 – 0022 = 644, or -rw-r--r-- in the symbolic format.

The default permissions for new directories are calculated similarly. Thus, with the mask's value at 002, a new directory's permissions will be set to 777 – 002 = 775, or drwxrwxr-x in the symbolic format. If the mask's value is 0022, a new directory's permissions will be set to 777 – 0022 = 755, or drwxr-xr-x in the symbolic format. This means that all users can view the directory's contents.

All this is no good. Although the owner must have access rights sufficient for normal operations with files and directories, all other users are not supposed to have any rights. This can be achieved by modifying the mask. I recommend setting its value to 077. Then the default permissions will be set to 777 – 077 = 700 (or drwx------ in the symbolic format) for directories and to 666 – 077 = 600 (or -rw------- in the symbolic format) for files. Then only the owner will have access rights; all other users having none.

It may seem that I did not get my arithmetic correct in the previous permission calculation, as 666 – 077 should equal 589 and not 600. It cannot be correct when conventional rules are used. Here, the subtraction operation starts with the most significant digit and is performed for each position without borrowing from the higher digit. That is, the first zero in the mask is subtracted from the first six, then each of the sevens in the mask is subtracted from the next two sixes. If the result is negative, it is set to zero.

These permissions are much more acceptable from the security standpoint. A new mask's value can be set by executing the `umask mask_value` command. In this case, it will be `umask 077`.

4.1.5. Link Access Rights

In *Section 3.1.3*, hard and symbolic links were considered. Recall what permissions are given to hard links:

```
913021 -rw-r--r--  2 root  root   0 Feb 22 12:19 1.txt
913021 -rw-r--r--  2 root  root   0 Feb 22 12:19 link.txt
```

As you can see, a hard link to a file has the same permissions as the file itself. There is no reason to expect them to be different, because hard links have the same descriptors as the corresponding files.

The situation is much worse with symbolic links. The following is information for a main file (the first entry) and a soft link to it (the second entry):

```
913021 -rw-r--r-- 1 root  root 519 Feb 22 12:19 link.txt
913193 lrwxrwxrwx 1 root  root 8 Feb 22 12:40 symbol.txt -> link.txt
```

As you can see, the soft link has all permissions set. In practical terms, it means that if you create a symbolic link to the /etc/shadow file and do not modify its default permissions, you can kiss your passwords good-bye: They will be either stolen or deleted. Remember that any operation performed on a symbolic link is actually performed on the file it points to.

If you have to use symbolic links, do not forget the peculiarity of how their default permissions are set. If you cannot rely on your memory, you can carve something like the following reminder on your monitor: "Soft links are created with full permissions!"

4.2. Group Management

What is a group in the context of access rights? Suppose there are 1,000 users in your network, of which 500 require access to the accounting files. How can you grant these users the necessary rights? You can make an effort and grant each of the 500 users the necessary rights to the files individually and relax for a while. Now assume you have to cancel this granting of access rights. Do you fancy executing 500 commands again? Isn't there an easier way to do this? Perhaps writing a program to do this would help. Most likely, it will require as much effort, if not more, as changing each user's rights individually.

On the other hand, you can combine all these users into a group and grant the necessary file access rights to the entire group. Afterward, should you need to deny access rights for the group, you will be able to do this with one command. Don't you think this way is much easier than setting each user's rights individually or writing a program to do this?

In Linux, all users are assigned to one group or another. If the group is not specified when a new user account is created, a new group will be created under the user's name by default.

4.2.1. Adding a Group

A new group is added to the system by the groupadd command. It looks like the following:

```
groupadd [-g gid [-o]] [-r] [-f] group_name
```

The following options can be specified after the command name:

☐ -g gid — This is the group ID. Must be a unique (unless the -o option is used) positive number. In most cases, the group ID does not have to be specified; the system automatically assigns the first smallest available value greater than 500.

☐ -r — This option specifies that a system group is to be created. Such groups are assigned identifiers less than 500. Unless the -g option is also given, the first available value less than 500 will be assigned.

☐ -f — This prevents the creation of groups that have the same name. The command exits with an error, the new group is not created, and the existing group is not altered.

If some options are omitted, their default values are used. The following are some examples of adding a group. The commands' work is explained in the comments following the # character.

```
groupadd testgroup1          # Creating a group named
                             # testgroup1 with a default ID
groupadd -g 506 testgroup2 # Creating a group named
                             # testgroup2 with ID 506
groupadd -r testgroup3       # Creating a group named
                             # testgroup3 with a default
                             # system ID (less than 500)
```

All information about groups is added to the /etc/group file. Open this file either in Midnight Commander or by executing the cat /etc/group command in the console.

There will be the following three entries containing information about the groups added at the end of the file:

```
testgroup1:x:500:
testgroup2:x:506:
testgroup3:x:11:
```

The group name, the password, the identifier, and the user list are presented in four columns, each delimited by a colon.

No identifier was specified for testgroup1; therefore, the system assigned a default ID value. The group ID was explicitly specified for testgroup2. Because the -r option was specified in the last command, the system assigned `testgroup3` the next available default system identifier (11 in this case).

The last column (after the third colon) is empty. It is supposed to contain the user list, but it has not been formed yet.

4.2.2. Editing a Group

Group parameters can be adjusted by editing the /etc/group file directly. I, however, do not recommend this method. Use the `groupmod` command instead. The command takes the same options as the `groupadd` command, only instead of adding a new group it edits the parameters of an existing one.

4.2.3. Deleting a Group

A group can be deleted by the `groupdel` command executed as follows:

```
groupdel group_name
```

Before deleting a group, you have to change the owners of all files pertaining to the group; otherwise, only the administrator will be able to access these files.

A group also cannot be deleted if it has users. Consequently, all group users must be removed from the group before the group itself can be deleted.

4.3. Managing Users

A user can be added using the `useradd` command. The same command is used to change the new user default parameters.

The command looks as follows:

```
useradd options user_name
```

There are quite a few options, most of which you are familiar with from the /etc/passwd file considered in *Chapter 3*. The options and their functions are the following:

☐ `-c` — The comment field of the new user's password file.

☐ `-d` — The new user's home directory.

☐ `-e` — The date when the user account will be disabled. It is specified in the format YYYY-MM-DD.

☐ `-f` — The number of days after the password expires before the account will be disabled. If set to 0, the account is disabled as soon as the password expires. The feature is disabled if set to -1. The default value is -1.

☐ `-g` — The user's initial login group. This can be specified either as a name or as an identifier. In Linux, all users are assigned to one group or another.

☐ `-G, [...]` — Additional groups, to which the new user will belong. The group names are delimited with a comma only, with no space.

❑   -m — Instructs the user's home directory to be created if it does not exist. All files from the /etc/skel directory will be copied to this directory.

❑   -M — Do not create the user home directory. By default, the user home directory is created as /home/user_name. To prevent this from happening, the command must explicitly forbid this.

❑   -r — Specifies that a system account is to be created.

❑   -p — An encrypted password, which can be obtained with the help of the crypt command.

❑   -s — Specifies the user login shell.

❑   -u — A unique identifier. If omitted, the system will assign a random value.

The last argument is the name of the new user account. Consider this process by adding a user account named robert, with all default options:

```
useradd robert
cat /etc/passwd
```

The first command created a new user account named robert. The second command displays the contents of the /etc/passwd file, where all account information is stored. The last entry in this file will look as follows:

```
robert:x:501:501::/home/robert:/bin/bash
```

I have already reviewed the format of the file's entries in *Section 3.3*. The first parameter is the user name. The next field is the password. Because the actual password is stored in the /etc/shadow file, the field contains an x instead of the password. The next two fields are the UIDs and GIDs. In this case, it just happened that the next available values for both of these parameters turned out to be the same, but this is far from an everyday occurrence. The following filled field is the user home directory. By default, all user directories are created in the /home directory and are given the user's name.

Open the /etc/shadow file. Note that there are two exclamation points in the password field of the robert entry. No password was specified when the account was created, so you cannot enter the system using this account. Actually, I do not recommend specifying a password when adding the user. This is simply extra trouble, because it has to be encrypted using the crypt function even though it is not certain that a strong password will be produced. It is easier to create the password after the user has been added using the passwd command:

```
passwd robert
```

The command will display the following prompt to change the password, along with the instructions on how to create a strong password:

```
Changing password for user robert.

You can now choose the new password or passphrase.

A valid password should be a mix of upper and lower case letters,
digits and other characters.  You can use an 8-character long
```

```
password with characters from at least 3 of these 4 classes, or
a 7-character long password containing characters from all the
classes. Characters that form a common pattern are discarded by
the check.

A passphrase should be of at least 3 words, 12 to 40 characters
long and contain enough different characters.

Alternatively, if no one else can see your terminal now, you can
pick this as your password: "trial&bullet_scare".
```

As you can see, the `passwd` command presents some main rules for creating strong passwords and even offers an example of one. I, however, would not use it because it is made of readable words and can be picked by a variation of the dictionary search that joins various words the way `passwd` itself does. This procedure will take much longer than picking a one-word password but much less time than picking a password similar to OLhslu_9&Z435drf. This password cannot be picked using the dictionary method, and it will take years to pick it by the enumeration method.

Now take a look what is in the directory of the new user. Do you think it is empty? Check it out. Open the /home/robert directory and execute the following command:

```
ls -al /home/robert
```

The `-a` option displays all files, including the system files, and the `-l` option displays detailed information. The execution results of this command should look similar to the following:

```
drwx------ 3 robert robert 4096 Nov 26 16:10 .
drwxr-xr-x 5 root   root   4096 Nov 26 16:21 ..
-rw-r--r-- 1 robert robert   24 Nov 26 16:10 .bash_logout
-rw-r--r-- 1 robert robert  191 Nov 26 16:10 .bash_profile
-rw-r--r-- 1 robert robert  124 Nov 26 16:10 .bashrc
-rw-r--r-- 1 robert robert 2247 Nov 26 16:10 .emacs
-rw-r--r-- 1 robert robert  118 Nov 26 16:10 .gtkrc
drwxr-xr-x 4 robert robert 4096 Nov 26 16:10 .kde
```

Note that there are six files and one subdirectory in the directory. The most interesting information is contained in the third and fourth columns, in which the file owner's name and group, respectively, are displayed. All file entries contain the name robert in these columns. But although the user with this name was just created, the group was not. The answer is simple: When a user is created, a corresponding user group is automatically created.

Here is another fine point. The owner of the .. directory, which is the home directory of the robert directory, is root. That is, the user robert is the owner of his directory (/home/robert), but he has no rights to the directory above his (/home).

The user robert has read and write rights to all files and directories in his folder. The users of the robert group and all other users have only read rights, not write rights.

4.3.1. Creating New User Files and Directories

Where do the files in the directory of a newly-created user come from? When a new user account is created, files and directories from the /etc/skel directory are copied into the new user's home directory. Create a file in the /etc/skel directory and check whether it will be copied into the home directory of a user that you will create. To keep things simple, create a new file by executing the following command:

```
ls >> /etc/skel/text
```

The ls command displays the contents of the current directory. The two > characters redirect its output to the text file in the /etc/skel directory. This means that the results of the command's execution will be placed into the specified file. If the specified file does not exist, it will be created. In this way, a new file has been placed in the /etc/skel directory. The contents of the file are of no importance.

Add a new user, and then inspect the contents of his or her home directory:

```
useradd Denver
ls -al /home/Denver
```

You should see that, along with the other files, the text file you created in the /etc/skel directory was copied to the new user's home directory.

I use this handy feature quite often to give a new user the necessary rights, files, documentation, and so on.

One of the files in the /etc/skel directory is bash_profile. It contains the profile of the /bin/bash command interpreter. This file can be used to configure certain user parameters, including the access rights mask. In *Section 4.1*, I described the permissions that are assigned by default to all new user files. I argued that the default permissions are far from ideal from the security standpoint, and I showed how to lower them using the mask command.

Log into the system as robert and inspect the mask using the umask command. Notice that it is 0022, the default value. That is, in *Section 4.1* we changed the then current user's mask, but robert still received the default mask. This exposes his files to the dangers described in *Section 4.1*. To prevent this from happening, I recommend adding the following string at the end of the /etc/skel/bash_profile file:

```
umask 0077
```

Because this file is copied into the home files of all new users, placing this string in it ensures that all new users will receive a proper mask from the security standpoint.

To enhance the security, I do not recommend giving user home directories the same names as their account names. This correspondence may play into the hands of hackers. Once a miscreant knows a user's home directory name, he or she can easily figure out the corresponding user login, and vice versa.

Simply adding some sort of a prefix to a user home directory will make the malefactor's job at least somewhat more difficult.

4.3.2. Modifying the User Default Settings

Now take a look at where the user default settings come from. They are stored in the /etc/default/useradd file. The following are the contents of this file:

```
# useradd defaults file
GROUP=100
HOME=/home
INACTIVE=-1
EXPIRE=
SHELL=/bin/bash
SKEL=/etc/skel
```

This file can be edited manually or with the help of the useradd command. You will see how to do this a little later.

I would like, however, to comment on the GROUP parameter. It equals 100 and, theoretically, all new users are supposed to be placed into this group. But, as you could see in *Section 4.3*, this does not happen. Red Hat ignores this parameter, and by default when a new user is created, a corresponding new user group is also created. This parameter, however, may be used in other distributions; so it is a good idea to check whether it is.

The number 100 is given as the name to a user group with limited rights. It is sort of like a guest password, which gives only the rights to view files.

The useradd command is also used to either display or update default values of the new user's settings. It is done by issuing the command with the -D option and specifying the following options:

- ❑ -g — The new default user group
- ❑ -b — The new default new user home directory
- ❑ -f — The new default number of days after the password has expired before the account will be disabled
- ❑ -e — The new default account expiration date
- ❑ -s — The new default shell (command interpreter)

If no options are specified, the command simply displays the current default values of the new user settings.

I advise you to not ignore the account expiration date option. Assume that your company is being audited and the auditors request access to you databases and certain files. In this case, when creating a new account for the auditors to use, set its expiration date to give them 1 day of work (or whatever they may need). Then you will not have to keep it in your head or write it down in a notebook (which you still have to remember to consult) that on a certain date you have delete this account: It will become inactive by itself.

Some administrators generate temporary users without taking any organized steps for deleting them. This presents a serious security threat, because users of temporary accounts do not normally use strong passwords. Indeed, why bother remembering something like oPih#vg9jG1e that you will have to use for a few days only? By deactivating an account that is no longer needed (automatically or manually), you close one of the passages that can be used by a miscreant to penetrate your system. When you see off a guest and come back into your house or apartment, you lock the entrance door behind you to keep unwelcome visitors out. The same applies to the operating system; once a temporary user leaves, close the door after him or her — that is, remove his or her account.

4.3.3. Modifying a User Account

A user account can be modified directly by editing the /etc/passwd file. However, I recommend using the usermod command for this purpose. It uses the same options as the useradd command, but instead of creating a user account, it modifies the settings of an already-existing one.

You can use this command to add an existing user to an existing group. Do this with the user account robert; assign it to the root group to allow the user perform some administrative functions:

```
usermod -G root robert
```

The command was executed with the -G option, which specifies the groups, to which the user is to belong (the root group in this case). Several groups, delimited by commas, can be specified. More detailed information about the usermod command can be viewed in usermod man.

4.3.4. Deleting a User

A user can be deleted by the userdel command, with the user account to be deleted as the argument. For example, user Denver is deleted by the following command:

```
userdel Denver
```

The user to be deleted cannot be currently logged in.

The command as used here does not delete the user's directory; you have to do this manually. Issuing the command with the -r option will delete the user's home directory, along with the files in it:

```
userdel -r Denver
```

I strongly recommend that you do not use the command in this way. Always delete directories manually, after ascertaining that there are no files that you do not wish to delete in them.

If there are no other members of the group of the user being deleted, the user group can also be deleted by the groupdel command.

4.3.5. A Few Remarks

To completely understand the process of creating user accounts, you have to be familiar with the /etc/login.defs file. The settings used when adding users are stored in this file. Listing 4.1 shows the contents of the file.

Listing 4.1. The contents of the /etc/login.defs file

```
# *REQUIRED*
#   Directory where mailboxes reside, _or_ name of file,
#    relative to the home directory. If you _do_ define
#   both, MAIL_DIR takes precedence.
#   QMAIL_DIR is for Qmail
#
#QMAIL_DIR       Maildir
MAIL_DIR         /var/spool/mail
#MAIL_FILE        .mail


# Password aging controls:
#
#PASS_MAX_DAYS  Max number of days password may be used.
#PASS_MIN_DAYS  Min number of days allowed between
# password changes
#PASS_MIN_LEN   Min acceptable password length
#PASS_WARN_AGE Number of days warning given
# before a password expires
#
PASS_MAX_DAYS         99999
PASS_MIN_DAYS             0
PASS_MIN_LEN             5
PASS_WARN_AGE           7


#
# Min/max values for automatic UID selection in useradd
#
UID_MIN                 500
UID_MAX               60000


#
# Min/max values for automatic GID selection in groupadd
#
GID_MIN                 500
GID_MAX               60000


#
# If defined, this command is run when removing
# a user. It should remove any at/cron/print jobs
# etc. owned by the user to be removed (passed as the
# first argument).
```

```
#
#USERDEL_CMD          /usr/sbin/userdel_local

#
# If useradd should create home directories for users by
# default on RH systems, we do. This option is ORed with
# the -m flag on useradd command line.
#
CREATE_HOME          yes
```

The file contains some interesting settings that can be used to enhance the system security. The function of the parameters is explained in the comments to them. I would only like to expand on one of them:

☐ PASS_MIN_LEN — Minimum acceptable password length. It is used only in the passwd command; the useradd command ignores it. In most distributions, the value of this parameter is 5. I recommend changing it to at least 8. This will make it impossible to set the qwerty password so beloved by so many users.

4.3.6. Cracking Passwords

I want to remind you again about the danger of using simple passwords, not only by the administrators but also by the lowest system user. There are lots of exploits that allow a simple user to raise his or her rights to those of the administrator. But to use such an exploit, the hacker first has to enter the system as that simple user.

To prevent this, all users, no matter what their rights may be, must use strong passwords. If a hacker obtains access to the /etc/shadow file with, for example, 1,000 password entries, the task of picking at least one password becomes significantly easier. As you remember, the passwords stored in the /etc/shadow file are irreversibly encrypted. This means that when picking the password using a straight-search method, each possible combination is also encrypted and then compared with the corresponding entry in the /etc/shadow file. Because the encryption is a rather processor-intensive process, this takes a long time if working with only one entry.

But having 1,000 entries speeds up the process practically a thousandfold, because the encryption has to be done only once, with the result compared with all 1,000 entries. The chances of a hit increase several times.

When hackers lay their hands on the /etc/shadow file, the first thing they do is check for entries, in which the password is the same as the login. You won't believe how often this happens: If the password file is large enough, chances are one out of ten passwords will be the same as the corresponding login.

If this does not work, then the dictionary method is resorted to. Here the chances of a successful hit are close to 100%, because out of ten users there is bound to be one beginner who will use a simple password. You should instruct every new user in the fine art of password creation and periodically run a program to detect weak passwords, such as those made up of common words. If you can pick such passwords, hackers can do this even more easily.

4.4. Typical Rights-Assignment Mistakes

Assigning user access rights on a strictly as-needed basis can make your system significantly more secure. When the access rights are properly regulated, most break-in attempts will be ineffective. For example, once a bug was discovered in one of the Linux services. Thanks to my judicious rights assignment policy, my server was resistant to attacks exploiting this bug. Even if hackers had been able to log onto the server, they could not have changed or deleted anything, because all outside users of this service had only read rights.

So implementing a well-thought-out access rights policy may provide an impenetrable barrier for potential hackers.

Consider a classic example with files and directories. Suppose that directory access permissions are set to `drwxrwxrwx` (or 777), and all files in the directory have `-rw-------` permissions. Theoretically, a file can be modified only by the file owner, but this is not quite so. True, the hacker will not be able to change the file itself; however, he or she can read and write the documents in the directory. This allows the hacker to simply delete the necessary file and create a new one with the same name but with all access rights.

To prevent such a development, you must restrict access not only to files but also to directories.

There are, however, situations, in which directories have to have all permissions. This applies to shared directories used by users to exchange files. At the same time, only the administrator or file owners should be able to delete files in these directories. No user should have the right to delete other users' files. How can the problem of having a directory accessible to all, yet allowing only specific users to control their corresponding contents in it, be solved?

Suppose you have a directory named shared. So that a file could be deleted by its owner, its sticky bit should be set. This is done by executing the `chmod` command with the `+t` option as follows:

```
chmod +t shared
```

Examine the access rights to the directory by executing the `ls -al` command. It should display `drwxrwxrwt`. Note that in the triplet that indicates all other users' access rights, instead of the `x` character there stands a `t` character. It is this character that indicates that the sticky bit is set. Now try to delete from this directory a file belonging to another owner. This will result in the system issuing this message: "rm: cannot unlink 'file_name': Operation not permitted."

Set this bit for all open folders. When they cannot gain access to information, some malicious hackers vent their anger by deleting everything they come across. The sticky bit ensures that hackers can delete only objects that they have created.

In older Linux distributions, permissions for the /tmp directory, in which temporary data for all users are saved, are set to `drwxrwxrwx`. In modern distributions, this directory has the sticky bit set. Check this directory in your system, and if the sticky bit is not already set, set it yourself to prevent users from deleting temporary files that are not theirs.

4.5. Privileged Programs

In *Chapter 3*, I briefly mentioned two permission modes: SUID and SGID. Now I will explain them in more detail. Suppose that a user with limited rights needs to be able to run a high-access-rights program. This can be achieved by setting the SUID bit: The program will execute with the owner access permissions even though the user launching it is not given any additional rights.

The SUID bit can be set by executing the `chmod` commands with the `u+s` option as follows:

```
chmod u+s progname
```

If you examine the file access permissions now, you will see that they have become `-rwsr-xr-x`. As you can see, execute permission (the `x` character) in the owner rights triplet has been replaced with an `s` character, meaning that the program can be run by regular users but with owner rights.

The SGID bit is similar to the SUID bit, but it allows regular users to run programs with group-owner execution rights. This bit is set the same as the SUID bit, only with the `g+s` option:

```
chmod g+s progname
```

In this case, the file access permissions will be `-rwxr-sr-x`. The `s` character in place of the `x` in the group-owner rights triplet means that any user can run this program with group-owner permissions.

The SUID and GUID permissions are quite convenient and useful, but they harbor numerous security problems. For example, when a minimal-rights user launches a root-rights program, the program will execute with the root-access permissions and not with the minimal user's permissions. Should the program contain a bug allowing commands to be executed, these commands will be executed with the access permissions of the program's owner, that is, the root. Consequently, even if hackers cannot execute commands, for which they have no rights, they will be able to do so with the help of a privileged program.

The SUID and GUID bits should be used judiciously; in no case should the owner of an SUID or GUID program be the root or another privileged user. It is better to create a special account for such a program that has only those access permissions that the user needs.

Consider another example. Assume that a guest is not supposed to have access rights to the /home/someone directory, but a program that he needs to use requires this access. So as not to give the guest additional rights, a new user is created that has access rights to the /home/someone directory. This user is then made the owner of the program, and the program's SUID bit is set. Should there be a bug in the program, it can only be exploited to obtain access to the /home/someone directory, with the rest of the disk remaining secure.

This policy is in line with my main rule — Everything that is not permitted is forbidden — and will provide maximum security of the system.

4.6. Additional Protection Features

In addition to the access permissions, any file has attributes that allow it to be secured further. There is, however, a limitation on such attributes' application: They can only be used with the Ext2 and Ext3 file system. But this circumstance can be called a limitation with a reservation, because Ext3 has been the file standard for all distributions for a long time.

The current attributes of a file can be viewed with the help of the lsattr command:

```
lsattr filename.txt
```

Its execution results will usually look like the following:

```
-------------- filename.txt
```

The string of dashes means that none of the attributes are set.
Attributes are set using the chattr command as follows:

```
chattr attributes file_name
```

Using the -R option with a directory will apply the specified attributes recursively to the directory and its contents.

The attributes used by the chattr command and their functions are the following:

- ❑ A — The file's atime record (the time that the file was last accessed) is not modified when the file is accessed. From the security standpoint, this attribute has a negative effect, because the access date can be used to monitor when the file was modified last. I, therefore, recommend not setting this attribute. But if you are running Linux on a home computer and have no need to monitor the access history, you can set this attribute to reduce the number of disk writes (by eliminating an extra write operation when saving the file).

- ❑ a — A file with this attribute set can only be opened in the append mode. This means that any data it already contains cannot be modified or deleted.

- ❑ d — When the backup utility is run, files with this attribute set are not backed up. Setting this attribute allows the size of the backup to be reduced. However, you should only set this attribute to files that are of little importance, such as temporary files.

- ❑ i — This disables any modifications (editing, deleting, renaming, creating links) of a file with this attribute set.

- ❑ s — After a file is deleted, it cannot be restored: Its blocks are set to zeros and then written to the disk. This means that the disk space occupied by the file will be filled with zeros.

- ❑ S — All changes to the file will be written on the disk.

An attribute is set by specifying it prefixed with the + character; it is cleared by specifying it prefixed with the - character. Consider the following examples:

```
chattr +i test
chattr +s test
lsattr test
s--i---------- test
```

In the first entry, the file's i attribute is set, disallowing any modifications to the file. In the second entry, the file's s attribute is set. When the file is deleted, its place on the disk will be overwritten with zeros, ensuring that it cannot be recovered. The command in the third entry displays the file's current attributes, which are displayed in the last entry. You can see that the file's s and i attributes are set.

These attributes are mutually exclusive: The former disallows modification, and the latter requires that the file be completely erased from the disk. What will happen if you try to delete the file? Take a look:

```
rm test
rm: remove write-protected file "test"?
```

In the first entry, you execute the rm command to delete the file. The operating system reacts to the command by asking it to confirm the deletion of the write-protected file (the message in the second entry). As you can see, the operating system detected the file's i (no modifications) attribute. Enter "Y" to agree to the deletion. The system issues an error message and the file remains intact.

Clear the i attribute and list the file's updated attributes:

```
chattr -i test
lsattr test
s------------- test
```

You can see that the i attribute has been cleared. Now the file can be deleted using the rm command without any problems.

4.7. Protecting Services

Many server services will be considered in this book. Their security depends not only on proper configuration of the services themselves but also on the access permissions you assign to them. Hackers often attack certain services looking for bugs that can be used to penetrate the system and, as you already know, there are bugs in any complex software, no matter how secure its developers may claim it is.

While writing this book, I was too busy to make timely updates to my site, which is hosted by a major hosting company. Hackers did not fail to take advantage of this circumstance and carried out a few successful attacks on the site. In a 2-day period, the site's home page was changed twice, and then the miscreants took over the forum. I was forced to remove the forum to a safe place to restore my administrator rights, editing the MySQL database directly.

The hackers carried out the forum break-in by exploiting bugs in the forum's phpBB engine. This is one of the most popular forum engines, and because it is free many site owners use it. Most hackers try to discover bugs in the most popular software, and sometimes they succeed. Only timely updates of the software can help you maintain the upper hand against attackers.

Examine how the attack on my site was carried out, using an abstract site, **www.sitename.com**, as an example. Opening a forum topic causes a reference similar to the following to be displayed in the address bar:

http://www.sitename.com/forum/viewtopic.php?p=5583

Appending a Linux command to this address in the following format will make the server execute the command:

&highlight=%2527.$poster=%60**command Linux**%60.%2527

In particular, the following command can be used to view the contents of the server's **/etc** directory:

&highlight=%2527.$poster=%60**ls%09/etc%09-la**%60.%2527

And the following command will delete the site's home page:

&highlight=%2527.$poster=%60**rm%09index.php**%60.%2527

As you can see, a single buggy forum program line can put the entire server in danger.

But the danger can be minimized by limiting the access permissions of the Web server. This can be done by creating a virtual environment for the Web server to execute in, thereby placing other sections of the server out of the hackers' reach. This will also make the /etc directory inaccessible, and the most that malefactors can do is destroy the site and disrupt the operation of the Web service; everything else will be working uninterrupted. It is much easier to restore one service than the complete server.

After this incident, I spent a whole day surfing the Internet in search for vulnerable forums. It seems like there are many lazy administrators who do not stay current with updates, because I found plenty of vulnerable forums. I believe that these administrators will go through some hard times soon, if they have not already. Sooner or later any vulnerable forum will be discovered by hackers and its owners can only pray that the hacker is just curious and not out to do damage. So I will never tire of reminding people of the need to update all application software, services, and the operating system itself. You will make your administrative life easier by fixing bugs before hackers can find and exploit them.

During my search for vulnerable forums, I also checked for accessible /etc directories to see whether administrators were more security-minded than site owners. You may find it hard to believe, but the /etc directory was accessible on about 90% of the servers I checked. Is this due to administrators being incompetent or lazy? I do not think it makes any difference. Only major servers were protected, with small hosting companies saving by not paying for good administrators.

4.7.1. Protection Principles

Consider the principles to follow in protecting services. You start by creating a root directory for the service. This is done by the `chroot` command, which creates a pseudo-root file system within the existing file system.

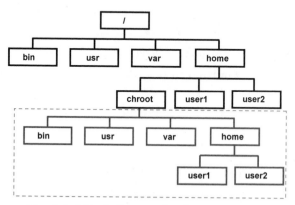

Fig. 4.1. A block diagram of a chroot file system

A program working in a `chroot` environment cannot access any file objects outside of this environment. Take a look at Fig. 4.1, which shows part of a Linux file system. The root directory (/) is at the top of the file system. It contains the /bin, /usr, /var, and /home subdirectories. The /home folder contains user directories. Create a new directory (name it chroot, for example) in this folder to serve as the root for the service you want to isolate. It has its own /bin, /usr, and other necessary directories. The service has to work with these directories, with everything above /home/chroot being inaccessible to it.

The directories that the service can access are enclosed in the dotted line box in Fig. 4.1. The service will work in this environment, considering it the actual file system of the server.

If a hacker penetrates the system through a protected service and decides, for example, to view the /etc directory, he or she will see the contents of the /home/chroot/etc directory but not those of the system's /etc directory. To prevent the hacker from becoming suspicious, all files that the system /etc directory should usually have can also be placed in the /home/chroot/etc directory, but containing incorrect information. Requesting to view, for example, the /etc/passwd file through the vulnerable service, the hacker will be shown the /home/chroot/etc/passwd file, because to the protected service it is the system file.

But there is no need for the /home/chroot/etc/passwd file to contain the true information; any fake data can be placed into it. This will not affect the system's operation, because the operating system will use passwords from the /etc/passwd file and the protected service does not need system passwords.

4.7.2. Setting up a Jail

Linux's built-in `chroot` command for creating virtual environments is too complex and difficult to use. This is why administrators prefer using the Jail program. You can download it from the **www.jmcresearch.com/projects/jail/** site. Place it in your directory and unpack it with the following command:

```
tar xzvf jail.tar.gz
```

This will create a new directory, named jail, containing the program's source code in the current directory. Yes, the source code, because the program is distributed under the GNU general public license.

Now open the jail/src directory (`cs jail/src`) and edit the makefile file in any text editor (Midnight Commander, for example). Skip the parameters at the beginning of the file until you see the following parameters:

```
ARCH=__LINUX__
#ARCH=__FREEBSD__
#ARCH=__IRIX__
#ARCH=__SOLARIS__

DEBUG = 0
INSTALL_DIR = /tmp/jail
PERL = /usr/bin/perl
ROOTUSER = root
ROOTGROUP = root
```

In the first entry, the operating system is specified; it is Linux by default. The next three entries, for the FreeBSD, Irix, and Solaris operating systems, are commented out. Leave them that way. What you have to change is the installation directory, specified in the `INSTAL_DIR` parameter. The latest version (when this book was written) uses the /tmp/jail directory by default. I am puzzled about why this directory is used to install the program: This is a temporary directory accessible to everyone. Earlier versions used the /usr/local/bin directory by default, and this is where I recommend you to install the program. This is the editing that has to be done; do not change anything else in the makefile file.

To execute the ensuing commands, you will need root rights, so either log in as the administrator or grant yourself root rights by executing the `su root` command.

Before compiling and installing the file, make sure that preinstall.sh has execute permission. If it does not, set it using the following command:

```
chmod 755 preinstall.sh
```

Now you are ready to install the program. In the terminal, switch to the jail/src directory and execute the following commands:

```
make
make install
```

If you did everything right, there should now be the files addjailsw, addjailuser, jail, and mkjailenv in the /usr/local/bin directory.

4.7.3. Working with the Jail Program

First create the /home/chroot directory to be used as the root directory for the program to be used to test the system. This is done by executing the following command:

```
mkdir /home/chroot
```

Now the environment for the service has to be prepared. This is done by executing the following command:

```
/usr/local/bin/mkjailenv /home/chroot
```

Inspect the /home/chroot directory. There should be two new directories now: dev and etc. As you know, device descriptions are stored in the dev directory. In this case, the program did not copy the entire contents of the system /dev directory, creating only three main devices: null, urandom, and zero.

The etc directory also contains only three files: group, passwd, and shadow. These are partial copies of the corresponding system files. For example, the passwd file contains only the following entries:

```
root:x:0:0:Flenov,Admin:/root:/bin/bash
bin:x:1:1:bin:/bin:/sbin/nologin
daemon:x:2:2:daemon:/sbin:/sbin/nologin
nobody:x:99:99:Nobody:/:/sbin/nologin
```

The rest of the information in the system's passwd file, including the user robert that you created in *Section 4.3*, has not been copied to the Jail passwd file. The Jail shadow file contains the same information as the corresponding system's file. Make sure that its access permissions are no greater than 600 (`rw-------`).

The /home/chroot/etc/shadow file presents one security problem: It contains the actual encrypted root's password as in the /etc/shadow file. You should either delete or change this password; otherwise, if hackers get a hold of it, they will be able to penetrate the server through another door that not protected by a virtual environment.

Next, execute the following command:

```
/usr/local/bin/addjailsw /home/chroot
```

While this command is executing, it displays information about what files and directories are being copied to the /home/chroot directory. For example, such programs as cat, cp, ls, and rm are copied to the /home/chroot/bin directory, and the service will use these files and not those in the /bin directory.

The program copies those files and directories that it considers necessary, but the service that will work in the virtual environment may not necessarily need all of them. You should delete all unnecessary files, but only after ascertaining that everything works properly.

Now that the necessary programs have been copied and the virtual environment is ready, you can install the service:

```
/usr/local/bin/addjailsw /home/chroot -P httpd
```

The preceding command installs the httpd program (the Apache server) and all libraries it needs into the new environment. The Jail program will determine itself, which components to install.

Now you can add a new user to the virtual environment. This is done by executing the following command:

```
/usr/local/bin/addjailuser chroot home sh name
```

Here, `chroot` is the virtual root directory; in the example, this should be /home/chroot. The `home` parameter is the user's home directory with respect to the virtual directory. The `sh` argument is the shell (command interpreter), and `name` is the name of the user whom you want to add. The user must already exist in the main operating system environment.

The following command adds a specific user (robert) to the virtual directory:

```
/usr/local/bin/addjailuser /home/chroot \
    /home/robert /bin/bash robert
```

The command did not fit into one line, so I carried it to another line with the help of the \ character. (The \ character tells the command interpreter that the command continues in the next line.)

If you did everything right, the program will display the message "Done" to show that the user have been successfully added; otherwise, it will issue an error message.

To run the `httpd` server (the Apache server in Linux), there has to be the apache user in the virtual environment. There is such a user in the real system. Check what its parameters are and create the same user in the virtual environment:

```
/usr/local/bin/addjailuser /home/chroot \
    /var/www /bin/false apache
```

You can enter the virtual environment by executing the following command:

```
chroot /home/chroot
```

You must keep in mind, however, that most commands do not work here. For example, Midnight Commander was not installed into this environment; consequently, you will not be able to run it.

To ascertain that you are in the virtual environment, execute this command:

```
ls -al /etc
```

You will see only a few files, which is just a small part of the contents of the real /etc directory. If you examine the /etc/passwd file, you will see that it contains only the virtual environment users. Should this file be compromised by hackers, they will only obtain these data. The /home/chroot directory will be the only area of the system accessible to the perpetrators; the rest of the file system and system services will be out of their reach.

The Apache server is launched by running the /user/sbin/httpd command from the virtual environment.

4.8. Obtaining Root Privileges

Now that you have enough knowledge about access principles, I can consider typical techniques used by crackers to obtain root rights and to conceal their presence in the system.

Suppose that a hacker obtains a capability to execute commands with root rights. To continue using this account will be too dangerous and provoking. Moreover, the root password cannot be changed.

So how can you log into the system and retain maximum rights at the same time? Recall how Linux manages access rights. The information about user accounts is stored in the /etc/passwd file in the following format:

```
robert:x:501:501::/home/robert:/bin/bash
```

The third and fourth parameters are the UIDs and GIDs, respectively. When a file system object is given access permissions, the system only stores the object's identifiers. In practical terms, it means the following: Suppose there already is a user named robert, who is assigned the identifier 501. When another user account is created and given the same identifier, no matter what its name may be, it will have the same access rights as the original account with this identifier.

Of what use can this possibly be? Check out the identifier of the root user: It is zero. And it is a zero identifier, not the name root, that specifies maximum rights. Now, edit the robert entry in the passwd file, changing the UIDs and GIDs to zero. When done, this entry should look like the following string:

```
robert:x:0:0::/home/robert:/bin/bash
```

Now log into the system as this user and try to open and edit the /etc/passwd file or try to add a new user. You will be successful, even though only the root can edit the /etc/passwd file and add a new user. The system determines the user account's rights using its identifier, which in this case is zero and grants the user maximum rights.

Because the user name is of no importance, I recommend deleting the root user in the /etc/passwd and /etc/shadow files and replacing it with a user with a different name but with the zero UIDs and GIDs. If hackers try to penetrate your system, they will try to pick a password for the root login. They will get nowhere because there will be no such login.

On the other hand, you can leave the root user but change its identifier to greater than zero. I sometimes create a user account named root and set its ID to 501 or greater. When a hacker sees this account, he or she thinks that it possess maximum privileges although it is just a regular user.

Each successful attempt to mislead an attacker increases the chances of him or her panicking. Having entered a system illegally, even a professional hacker experiences a great psychological pressure, fearing to be found out. Quite a few hackers are mentally unstable. It does not mean that they are crazy. They are normal people under normal circumstances, but when perpetrating a break-in they experience great mental pressure and, if something goes wrong, can panic easily.

As you can see, once a hacker has penetrated the system with root rights, he or she may not continue using this account. Instead, the attacker can create another user with any name but with the zero UID and make further exploits using this new maximum-rights account. Server administrators should watch for such shenanigans and prevent any attempts to change UIDs.

UIDs and GIDs can be found with the help of the `id` command. When executed without any options, the command displays the identifiers of the current user. To obtain the identifiers for a specific user, the command is executed with the user name as the argument, as follows:

```
id user_name
```

Examine the identifiers of the user account robert. Execute the following command:

```
id robert
```

It should display the following string:

```
uid=501(robert) gid=501(robert) group=501(robert)
```

If you edited the passwd file as described earlier, the result will be this:

```
uid=0(robert) gid=0(robert) group=0(robert
```

Thus, you can always determine the identifier of any user and his or her real rights.

4.9. Expanding Access Permission

Regulating access is a complicated process. This is the main task of a system administrator, and the system's security depends greatly on it. Any mistake can cause you problems, ranging from being chewed out by the boss to losing your job. In the world, in which information has become the most valuable product, you have to protect it with all available means.

Take your time and check the entire system to ensure the proper assignment of rights. No user, file system object, or program should have any rights it does not need; at the same time, each should have all permissions necessary for proper work.

The method of assigning rights based on the principle "boss," "boss's friends," and "rest of the crowd" is obsolete and does not provide the necessary security. Suppose you have two groups: accountants and economists. Files created by any accountant will have the -rwxrwx--- access permissions and will be accessible to all workers of the accounting department, because members of the owner's group have the same right to the files as the owner.

But what should you do if an economist needs to view files belonging to the accounting group? Moreover, the files not of all accounting group users but of one user only and not all files but a select set. This is a rather difficult problem to solve. Setting access permissions to the accounting files to -rwxrwxrwx will give any user rights to view the accounting information, which is not desirable from the security standpoint.

You could try to solve the problem by using links to copies of the files with other access permissions, but you will become confused in the tangle of different files, copies of files, and file links, all with different access permissions.

The problem can be solved relatively easily using Access Control Lists (ACLs), the way it is done in Windows. The difficult part with this solution is that there is no standard for Linux. In essence, this operating system is a kernel, to which any developer can attach anything he or she desires, so each developer goes his or her own way in solving a particular problem, or simply leaves it alone.

I cannot recommend a universal solution, because there are several different solutions by different developers. This means that whatever solution is used, the system's stability can only be guaranteed for the already-existing Linux kernel versions. There is no guarantee that the ACL system will function error-free when the kernel is updated. This is why I can only recommend that you take a look at the Linux Extended Attributes and ACLs project (**http://acl.bestbits.at/**). If you decide to employ it, you will be doing this at your own risk.

Linux Extended Attributes and ACLs is a product that requires the kernel to be re-compiled after the installation. Its operating principle is based on storing extended attributes for each file. Not all file systems support extended attributes, so make sure your system does so before using ACLs. I consider Reiser and Ext3 the best file systems to use with this software.

After the patch and supplementary programs are installed, you can start working with ACLs. An ACL allows you to assign individual users their own file access rights. The creator of the file remains its owner and has full rights. Other access permissions for the file may not be set.

For example, the access permissions for a file can be set to `-rwx------`. Despite such stringent controls, it is possible to specify other users that will have access to the file in addition to the owner.

Thus, in addition to the main access permissions, there will be a list stored in the system of users that have access to it other than those specified by the main access permission.

If this approach were implemented on the kernel level and were supported by all distributions, I would consider Linux the most secure and stable operating system there is.

4.10. Firewalls

I have considered controlling file access in sufficient detail, but there are other areas, in which access rights have to be controlled. Nowadays, computer operations are impossible without connecting to a local network or to the Internet. Consequently, before putting your server into operation, you have to limit outside access to the computer and to some of its ports.

Computers are protected from attacks originating on the network by firewalls. Some Linux services can also be configured to control network access, but they will be considered separately for each individual service. I would not recommend relying exclusively on a service's network access control capabilities. As you should remember, there are bugs in all software, and if a service's network access control feature is backed up by a firewall, it will not become the worse for it.

A firewall is the foundation of the network security and the first line of defense from external invasion. When a firewall is installed, hackers trying to break into the computer through the network will have to pass through the firewall first, and only after they succeed can they move on and try to enter the file system. At this point, they will have to penetrate the second line of defense: the file and directory access permissions.

Why, then, do I consider the first line of defense after the second? Because a firewall protects only against network attacks, whereas proper regulation of access rights protects against both local hackers and unscrupulous users that have direct access to the computer. Both defense lines are important. Every little thing counts where security is concerned, and you should pay attention to all seemingly-insignificant details.

A firewall can prevent access both to the computer as a whole and to its individual ports used by services. It is not, however, a 100% guarantee against a successful break-in. It just checks that the network packets meet certain requirements; it cannot guarantee that a right packet was sent by the right person.

The simplest way of bypassing a firewall is to use a fake IP address. Once I worked with a company where regular users were forbidden to use the Simple Mail Transfer Protocol (SMTP) and Post Office Protocol (POP3) (connected to ports 25 and 110, respectively). I belonged to this category of users and could not receive or send email. My boss, however, belonged to the privileged class and had this access. Neither could the Web interface be used to access mail services; this capability was blocked at the proxy-server level. But all these security measures did not prevent me from sending an email when I really had to. Here is how I did this:

- ❑ Waited for my boss to leave his office
- ❑ Turned off his computer
- ❑ Changed my IP address to the IP address on his computer
- ❑ Sent the email and changed my IP address back to what it was supposed to be

When my boss came back, he did not make much of his computer being off; he thought that is simply hung and did not suspect a thing. So I used the service I was not supposed to use without any adverse consequences for having done this.

Although there are many ways to bypass a firewall (not counting those made available by bugs), a properly-configured firewall will make the lives of the administrator and the security specialist much easier.

In Linux, the firewall function is performed by a program that filters information based on a set of certain rules clearly prescribing, which packets can be processed or sent onto the network and which cannot. This makes most attacks fail without even having entered the computer, because the firewall does not let the services even see potentially dangerous packets.

A firewall can be installed on each individual computer (to provide protection according to the tasks performed) or at the network entrance (Fig. 4.2). In the latter case, the firewall provides common protection for all of the network's computers.

If there are many computers in a network, installing a firewall on all of them and configuring, updating, and maintaining the numerous firewalls will be quite difficult. Using a single server as a dedicated firewall for the entire network makes this task easier. Better still, if this computer also acts as a gateway or a proxy server for the rest of the network's computers. In this case, any hackers trying to penetrate the network will only see this computer, with the rest of the machines hidden behind the firewall it provides. To break into any of the other network's computer, hackers will have to break into the firewall computer first. This makes the task of protecting the network much easier. Proxy servers are covered in more detail in *Chapter 9.*

But there is one weak link in all firewalls: They are software-implemented and use resources of the server they are installed on. Modern routers can also provide many functions performed by Linux firewalls. On the other hand, Linux systems are often used as routers to keep the cost of the system low by putting to use old computers that cannot be used for any other contemporary task.

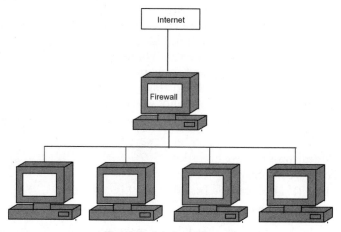

Fig. 4.2. A network firewall

4.10.1. Filtering Packets

The main, but not the only, task of a firewall is filtering packets. There is already a firewall built into Linux, and you do not have to install it separately. In fact, there are two firewalls: `iptables` and `ipchains`. They make it possible to control the Transmission Control Protocol (TCP), User Data Protocol (UDP), and Internet Control Message Protocol (ICMP) traffic going through the computer. Because TCP is the main transport for all other main Internet protocols — FTP, HTTP, and POP3 — filtering TCP traffic allows all these services to be protected.

All requests from or to the Internet must pass through the firewall, which examines them for compliance with the specified rules. Packets in full compliance are let through. But if at least one of the rules is not met, the offending packet may be deleted in one of the following two ways:

- ❑ Denied — Without informing the sending party about this
- ❑ Rejected — Informing the sending party about this

I would not configure my firewall in the latter way; doing so would provide hackers with extra information. It is better to delete offending packets without informing the sending party and have it think that the service is simply unavailable. But this is fraught with the danger of legitimate users experiencing problems in case of incorrect firewall configuration. Suppose that you mistakenly blocked access to port 80, used by the Web service. If a client program tries to access the Web server behind the firewall and does not receive an answer, it will wait until the timeout. The timeout value can be infinite for some programs, and they will hang. You will have to correct the firewall configuration error to let the user work trouble-free.

Moreover, package-rejection messages are sent using ICMP and increase channel traffic. A hacker can take advantage of this to carry out a denial-of-service (DoS) attack to flood your channel with superfluous package-rejection messages. DoS attacks can be directed not only against traffic but also against computer resources. A hacker can run a program repeatedly asking to establish a connection with a disabled port, which will cause your computer to waste resources (processor time, memory, etc.) examining the packets and sending rejection messages. If packets arrive at a fast rate, the server may not be able to handle the load and may stop answering requests from the legitimate users.

Firewall filters can be configured using one of the following two principles:

❐ Everything that is not forbidden is permitted.
❐ Everything that is not permitted is forbidden.

The latter way is more secure, because you start by forbidding everything. Then, as a need arises, you can allow access for specific users to specific services. You should adhere to this policy when configuring your firewall filters for incoming packets.

When starting with everyone being permitted everything, it is easy for the administrator to simply forget to limit some access rights and discover the oversight only when the system is penetrated and damage has been inflicted.

4.10.2. Filter Parameters

Packet filtration is performed by the following main packet parameters: the source or destination port number, the sender or recipient address, and the protocol used. As you already know, firewalls supports three main protocols (TCP, UDP, and ICMP) that form the foundation for all services (FTP, HTTP, POP3, and others).

Note that filtration can be bidirectional. Filtering incoming packets allows any attempts to break into the server to be fended off at the earliest stage.

But why filter outgoing traffic? At first it may seem senseless, but there are important reasons for this. Outgoing traffic can be less innocent than you may think. It may be generated by Trojan horse programs sending confidential information gathered on your hard drive to some email address, or connecting with the author's server to download further instructions from there.

Some specialized programs generate outgoing traffic to bypass the firewall. Suppose you disabled some port for incoming traffic. A hacker can bypass this prohibition by infiltrating a program onto the server that will redirect traffic from the disabled port to an enabled one, similar to OpenSSL tunneling.

It will take a professional all but 5 minutes to write such a program.

There are many loopholes to penetrate your computers, and your task is to close as many of them as possible. Consequently, you must control traffic going in both directions.

Protocols

The base data transfer protocol for HTTP, FTP, and other protocols is TCP. It will make no sense to prohibit it, because this will deprive you of all the niceties of the World Wide Web. TCP transmits data by first establishing a connection with the remote host and only then conducting data exchange. This makes faking the IP address of any of the connection parties more difficult and sometimes even impossible.

UDP is the same level protocol as TCP, but it transmits data without establishing a connection. This means that the protocol simply sends its data onto the network to a specified address without ensuring that this address is reachable first. In this case, there is no protection against faking the IP address, because the attacker may specify any address as the source and the receiving side will see nothing suspicious. Unless there is a justifiable need, I prohibit UDP packets in both directions.

ICMP is used to exchange control messages. It is used by the `ping` command to check the connection with the remote computer and by hardware and software components to inform each other of errors. This protocol is handy, and if it were only used as intended there would not be problems with it. But nothing is perfect in this life, and ICMP has often been used to perpetrate DoS attacks. Forbid this protocol by any means. If exchanging control messages cannot be avoided, try to find another program to do this, but do get rid of ICMP.

Port Filtration

The first thing that you have to pay close attention to is ports. Suppose that your Web server is open to all users. Also suppose that it serves absolutely safe scripts (this is from the realm of fantasy, but suppose this for the example's sake) and/or static HyperText Markup Language (HTML) documents. Moreover, all software is current on updates and has no vulnerabilities. Does all this make the server really secure? Yes, but only for the time being. Sooner or later, you will have to update your absolutely secure scripts (dream on) and static HTML documents. It is doubtful that you will use diskettes as the update vehicle and will need some other way to upload the update. Most often, files are transferred using an FTP service, and this is where you breach a hole in the impenetrable wall of your server fortress.

Only the most secure programs should use the FTP access and the strongest passwords; nevertheless, sooner or later hackers will break into this service. Passwords can be picked, stolen from some user's computer, tricked out of some gullible employee with the help of social engineering, or obtained in other countless ways. If there is a channel leading into the system, it is vulnerable, because hackers will not be trying to break in through nonexistent channels but will concentrate their efforts on something that will eventually yield to their relentless digging. Although the first one to try to break in may walk away with nothing to show for his or her pains, the second, the third, or the hundredth may get lucky, break in on the first try, and destroy everything he can lay his hands on.

So you should establish a policy on the server, according to which port 80 will accept all connections but port 21 (the FTP service) will only accept connections from a certain IP address. Then, unless the would-be computer burglar knows this IP address, all of his traffic will be cut off at the port and he will spend years trying to pick the password.

You should first disable all ports and then start enabling those that are necessary. This advice, however, is difficult to follow for a server that runs a firewall for the entire network, because different computers require different services. Opening all ports on the firewall server would be the same as opening all ports on all of the network's computers. You could use IP addresses to form the rules for the dedicated server firewall, but using a firewall on each of the network's computers would be more practical. In this case, the firewall on each of the computers can be configured to provide the protection required by the particular tasks executed on them. Only port 80 will be seen from the Internet for Web servers, and only port 21 will be visible for FTP servers.

Address Filtration

Based on the preceding information, you can see that IP address can also be used for traffic filtering, although the maximum effect is achieved by combining the port and address filtering.

Suppose that there are two Web servers on your network, which happens quite often. One of the servers is made available for all Internet visitors, and the other services only company users (an intracompany site). In this case, it will be logical to divide the information into two categories: one for internal use and the other for external. Then the closed server can service only the local network traffic regardless of what port it passes through.

The inside server should be isolated from the Internet altogether.

Consider another example. Suppose you have an Internet store and you sell only within your city or town. In this case, you should only allow access to the server from IP addresses within your city and disallow access to all others. But this task is rather difficult to implement.

Filtering out Undesirable IP Addresses

A few years ago, the RegNow (**www.regnow.com**) service (which offers middleman services for developers of shareware programs, providing secure payment services and collecting money from the purchasers) attempted to restrict access from suspicious IP addresses. This was a fully logical step. Some countries, on one hand, teem with hackers and, on the other hand, experience an extreme scarcity of honest software buyers. The executives at RegNow placed African and some eastern European countries — including, because of its penchant for free stuff, Russia — into this category.

This step was justified because carding was flourishing in many of those countries. (Carding is when stolen credit-card information is used to purchase merchandise on the Internet.)

To fight this evil, at least the greater part of it perpetrated by the citizens of those countries, the service disallowed access to their server from whole batches of IP addresses. The effect was nil, because the prohibition turned out to be easy to bypass. All that a lover of free stuff had to do to break through the barrier was use one of the anonymous proxy servers in the United States or Canada. The bona fide customers from the banned countries, on the other hand, experienced serious problems and were not able to use the service to get paid for the services they had provided.

The serious shortcomings of this filter resulted in it being removed shortly after it was put in place, and the RegNow service has not tried to use it since. It is too difficult to filter out all possible proxy servers, and the effect of this filtering is negligible. The problems it causes respectable users, however, may well cost a company its good reputation forever. Thus, sometimes you have to make a choice between security and convenience, and the perfect balance between the two is quite difficult to strike.

Filtering out Incorrect IP Addresses

There was another real-life case, in which a server was stumped by the source IP address. When this server received an invalid data packet, it would issue the sender a message about the data being wrong. The problem was that the attackers were sending packets, in which the source IP address was the same as the destination IP address; that is, both addresses were those of the server the packets were sent to. When the server sent the error message to a packet's sender, it would send the message to itself and would receive the invalid packet again. In this way, the packet would enter an endless loop. Sending thousands of such packets, the malefactors turned the server into a full-time wrong-packet answering machine.

I have not heard of such attacks for a long time, but it cannot be ruled out they will not happen. There are numerous IP addresses that should be filtered out and not let into your network.

Moreover, I recommend filtering out packets from reserved addresses or addresses that cannot be used on the Internet. The following are descriptions of such addresses:

- ❐ 127.0.0.1 — This address is used to specify the local machine (local host); consequently, no packet can originate from this address on the Internet.
- ❐ 10.0.0.0 to 10.255.255.255 — This range of IP addresses is used for private networks.
- ❐ 172.16.0.0 to 172.31.255.255 — This range of IP addresses is used for private networks.
- ❐ 192.168.0.0 to 192.168.255.255 — This range of IP addresses is used for private networks.
- ❐ 224.0.0.0 to 239.255.255.255 — This range of IP addresses is used for broadcasting purposes and is not assigned to computers; consequently, no packets can originate from them.
- ❐ 240.0.0.0 to 247.255.255.255 — This range is reserved for future Internet use.

All of the preceding addresses are invalid for Internet use, and you should not let packets from these addresses breach your firewall.

Linux Filtration Features

The Linux kernel already has built-in functions for filtering packets according to specified rules. But these functions provide bare-bones functionality and require a tool to configure the rules.

Linux offers two application packages for this: `iptables` and `ipchains`. Deciding which of them is better is a close call, because they offer similar functionalities. But many professionals choose `ipchains`. What you choose is up to you.

The Linux kernel contains the following three main rule chains:

❒   Input — For incoming packets
❒   Output — For outgoing packets
❒   Forward — For transiting packets

Users can create their own chains linked to a certain policy; this subject, however, is beyond the scope of this book.

Linux checks all rules in the chain, which is selected depending on the direction of the transfer. A packet is examined for meeting each rule in the chain. If it does not meet at least one rule, the system decides whether to let the packet through and carries out one of the actions specified for this rule: deny, reject, or accept.

This means that if a packet is found not to conform to one of the rules, it is no longer checked for conforming to the following rules in the chain. For example, suppose that you want to open port 21 for yourself only. This can be done by the following chain of two rules:

❒   Prohibit all incoming packets on port 21.
❒   Allow packets originating from address 192.168.1.1 to port 21.

At first glance, everything seems to be right: Access to port 21 is closed to all packets except those originating from address 192.168.1.1. The problem is that a packet arriving to port 21 from address 192.168.1.1 is processed in compliance with rule 1 first, and because "all packets" includes those packets arriving from address 192.168.1.1, the system rejects it and never evaluates it against the second rule.

For the policy to work, the places of the rules have to be swapped. Then an arriving packet is first checked for originating from address 192.168.1.1 and is let through if it is. If it is not, it is evaluated against the second rule, triggering the prohibition for all packets to enter port 21.

Packets routed to other ports do not meet the criteria for the rules and will be processed in the default order.

4.10.3. Firewall: Not a Heal-All

Don't be lulled into a false feeling of security after having installed a firewall: There are many ways to circumvent not just a specific firewall but all of them.

Any firewall is just a security guy at the front door. But the front door is never the first choice as a point of entry for a burglar. Burglars usually opt for the back door or a window.

For example, Fig. 4.2 shows a protected network and the front door: the Internet connection through a dedicated computer running a firewall. But if one of the network's computers happens to be equipped with a modem but without a firewall, this will create a back door to the network, without any doorman standing guard around the clock.

I have seen servers, for which Internet access was permitted from only a certain list of IP addresses. The administrators believed that this measure would protect them from hackers. They are mistaken here, because an IP address is easy to fake.

At one time, I worked with a company where Internet access was controlled by IP addresses. My monthly Internet traffic was limited to 100 MB, while my neighbor had unlimited access. To conserve my traffic, I did not use my quota to download large files but only to view Web pages. When I needed to download something, I did the following:

- ❑ Waited until the neighbor's computer was not in use, for example, when the owner went to lunch.
- ❑ Slightly pulled the network cable on the neighbor's computer out of the network card socket to break the connection.
- ❑ Assigned my computer the IP address of my neighbor and downloaded all that I wanted to download.
- ❑ Having finished, returned the IP addresses and the network cable to their regular places.

In this way I was able to download all I needed over a month.

I then upgraded the process by installing a proxy server on my neighbor's computer and did all of my downloading through it. I was not selfish, so I shared this good thing with my coworkers, and we all connected to the Internet through this IP address with unlimited traffic.

With modern firewalls, simply switching the IP address will not help you enter the system. The identification techniques they use now are much more sophisticated than simple IP-address checking. Switching the IP address may only provide more privileges within the system, and even this is only the case if the network is not configured properly. But administrators worth their salt will not allow such machinations even within the network, using MAC addresses and access passwords to assign access rights.

A firewall is a program that runs on a computer under the control of the operating system (a software firewall) or on a physical device (a hardware firewall). But, in either case, this program is written by humans who, as we all well know, are prone to error. Just like with the operating system, the firewall needs to be updated regularly to repair the programming bugs that are inevitably present in all software.

Consider the port protection. Suppose your Web server is protected by a firewall with only port 80 enabled. Well, that's all the ports that a Web server needs! But this does not mean that other protocols cannot be used. A technique called tunneling can be used to create a tunnel to transfer data of one protocol within another protocol. This was the technique used by the famous Loki attack, which makes it possible to send executable commands to the server within ICMP packets of the echo request type (this is a regular `ping` query) and to return responses within ICMP packets of the echo reply type (`ping` reply).

A firewall is a tool for protecting data, but the main protector is the administrator, who must constantly keep watch over the system security and prevent, detect, and ward off any attack. A new type of attack can penetrate the firewall because the firewall can only recognize those attacks, for which it has algorithm samples in its database. To be able to process a nonstandard attack, the system must be monitored by the administrator, who will be able to notice and react to any unusual changes in the main parameters.

A password or a device like touch memory or smart card is often needed to pass through a firewall. But if the password is not protected, all of the money invested in the firewall will be wasted. Hackers can obtain the password in one of a number of ways and use it to penetrate the firewall. Many systems have been broken into in this manner.

Passwords must be strictly controlled. You must control each user account. For example, if an employee with high system privileges quits, his or her account must be disabled immediately and all passwords, to which the employee had access, must be changed.

I was once called to a company to restore data on its server after they fired the administrator. He considered the termination of his employment unfair and, a few days later, destroyed all information contained on the main server without any problems. Even the well-configured firewall did not stop him. This happened because the firewall was configured by the malefactor himself. This type of thing should never be allowed to happen, and the firewall must be configured so that not even a network administrator can break through.

I always recommend to my clients that only one person knows the highest level firewall password. In a corporation, this should be the chief of the information-processing department. In no case should it be a regular administrator. Administrators come and go, and there is a chance of forgetting to change some password after the next administrator leaves.

4.10.4. Firewall: As Close to Heal-All as You Can Get

From the preceding section, you may get the impression that firewalls are a waste of money. This is not the case. If the firewall is properly configured, is constantly monitored, and uses protected passwords, it can protect your computer or network from most problems.

A quality firewall provides many levels of checking access rights, and a good administrator should never be limited to using just one. If you use only the IP address check to control Internet access, you can start looking for a bank loan to pay your Internet bill, because this address can be easily faked. But a system, to which the access is controlled by the IP address, MAC address, and password, is much more difficult to compromise. Yes, both MAC and IP addresses can be faked. To make sure that they are not, individual computers can be tied to specific port switches. In this case, even if the hacker learns the password, he or she will have to use it at the computer, to which it is assigned. This may require some ingenuity.

The protection can, and must, be multilevel. If you have data that need protecting, use the maximum number of protection levels. There is no such thing as too much security.

Imagine your average bank. Its entrance door will be much stronger than your average house or apartment door and equipped with an alarm system to boot. But if someone comes to do his or her banking in a tank, these protections will be of little use.

A firewall is akin to such an improved door protecting against small-fry hackers, which is what most hackers are. But it will not protect against a professional hacker, or at least not for long.

In addition to protecting the premises with a good door, banks keep their money in safes, which are themselves are placed into vaults. Money kept in a bank can be compared to secret information stored on a server, and it must be provided with maximum protection. This is why banks keep their money in safes equipped with sophisticated locks that take thieves a long time to open. While they are at it, there's more than enough time for the cops to arrive on the scene.

To extend the bank safe analogy to servers, here the role of the safe is played by encryption. So, even if a hacker bypasses the firewall and reach the data on the server, it will take too much time to decrypt them. He or she can be nabbed while still sitting at the desk. But even if the hacker carries the safe away to crack at his or her leisure, meaning downloading the data to decrypt them without being bothered, the chances are great that the information will become obsolete by the time it can be decrypted. The important thing here is that the encryption algorithm and the key are sufficiently sophisticated.

4.10.5. Configuring a Firewall

The easiest way to configure the Linux firewall is to use the built-in graphical utility. Load the KDE graphical shell and select the **Main Menu/System/Firewall Configuration** menu sequence. This will open the **Firewall Configuration** dialog window with two tabs on it: **Rules** and **Options**.

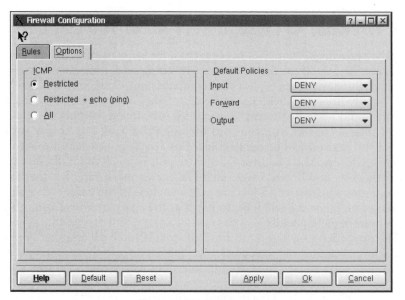

Fig. 4.3. The Options tab

First, open the **Options** tab (Fig. 4.3). Here you can specify default actions for each of the packet types and restrict ICMP packet transit.

On the **Rules** tab (Fig. 4.4), filtration rules can be created, deleted, or edited. A rule is created by clicking the **Add** button. This will open the dialog window shown in Fig. 4.5.

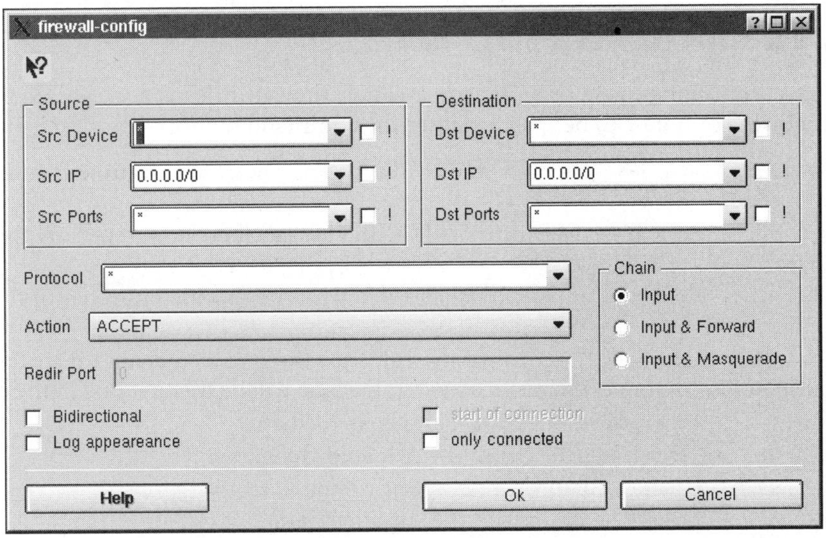

Fig. 4.4. The Rules tab

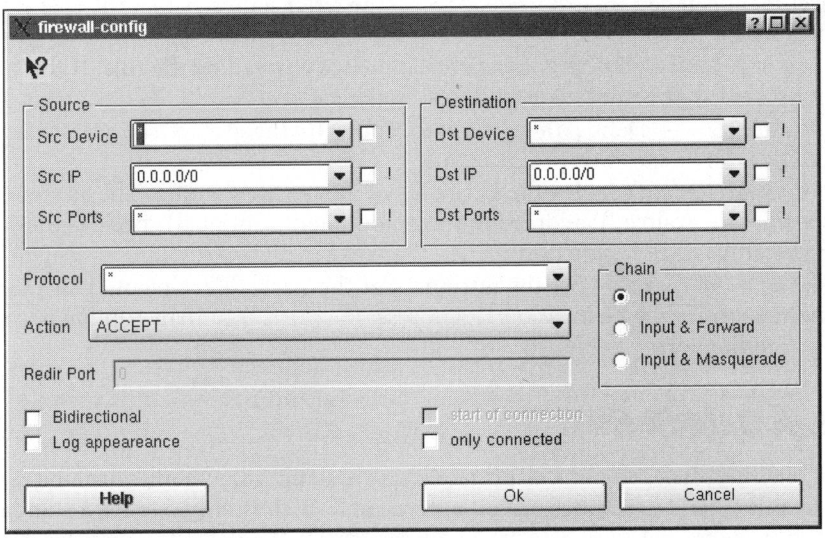

Fig. 4.5. The dialog window for adding new rules

Do not change any settings for now. Just familiarize yourself with the appearance of the Firewall Configuration utility and its capabilities. You can engage in configuration activities later, when you learn how to work with using the ipchains program, which is used to configure the firewall from the command line.

4.11. The ipchains Program

The most commonly used program for creating firewall rules is the ipchains program. The following options can be specified after the command name:

- ❑ -A chain rule — Append a rule to the chain. The chain argument can be input, output, or output.
- ❑ -D chain number — Delete the rule with the specified number from the specified chain.
- ❑ -R chain number rule — Replace the rule with the specified number in the specified chain.
- ❑ -I chain number rule — Insert the rule into the specified chain under the specified number. For example, if number equals 1, the rule will be the first one in the chain.
- ❑ -L chain — View the contents of the specified chain.
- ❑ -F chain — Delete all rules from the specified chain.
- ❑ -N name — Create a chain with the specified name.
- ❑ -X name — Delete the chain with the specified name.
- ❑ -P chain rule — Modify the default policy.
- ❑ -p protocol — Define the protocol covered by the rule. The value of the protocol argument can be tcp, udp, icmp, or all (the latter indicates that the rule extends to all protocols).
- ❑ -i interface — Define the network interface covered by the rule. If this argument is not specified, the rule will extend to all interfaces.
- ❑ --j action — Define the action to apply to the packet. Either ACCEPT, REJECT, or DENY can be specified as arguments.
- ❑ --s address port — Set the attributes of the packet's sender. The address argument specifies the source IP address; the port argument (optional) specifies the source port. Be careful: ICMP has no ports.
- ❑ -d address port — Set the attributes of the packet's recipient. The address argument specifies the destination IP address; the port argument (optional) specifies the destination port.

4.11.1. A Default Filter

Based on the total prohibition principle, the default rule should prohibit any actions. The default ipchains settings permit everything, which is only safe for a standalone computer, not connected to a network. You can check the default setting by executing the ipchains -L command.

It should display something similar to the following:

```
Chain input (policy ACCEPT):
Chain forward (policy ACCEPT):
Chain output (policy ACCEPT):
Chain icmp (0 references):
```

In some distributions, the default ipchains settings may be absent; then the system will issue the following error message:

```
ipchains: Incompatible with this kernel
```

This message can be issued if ipchains is not installed or has been started incorrectly. I have been greeted with this message several times because the distribution's developers did not configure the system default settings properly. This bug is easy to fix and does not require any operations on the kernel.

Open the /etc/rc.d/init.d/ipchains file in a text editor or display it using the cat command. Locate the following entry in the file:

```
IPCHAINS_CONFIG = /etc/sysconfig/ipchains
```

The path to the file in IPCHAINS_CONFIG may be different depending on the particular distribution. In modern distributions, configuration files for services are located in the /etc/sysconfig directory. The configuration file for the ipchains service is appropriately named ipchains. You can check whether it exists by giving the following command:

```
ls /etc/sysconfig/ipchains
```

If the file does not exist, it has to be created. This is done by executing the following command:

```
cat >> /etc/sysconfig/ipchains
```

Now, commands that you enter from the console will be saved to the file. To make the ipchains service work, enter the following command from the console:

```
:input ACCEPT
```

Now press the <Ctrl>+<D> key combination and restart the ipchains service using the following command:

```
/etc/rc.d/init.d/ipchains restart
```

Be careful to specify the full path in the command. Otherwise, the ipchains utility will be started and will not launch the script from the /etc/rc.d/init.d/ directory.

Now the service should start without problems.

For starters, prohibit all traffic. Before moving on to creating rules, I want to make one more remark. You should start configuring any system from scratch, because the default settings often turn out to be not too effective and safe. Execute the ipchains -F command to flush the current rules. It is important to do this operation so that the new rules won't be corrupted by the old ones.

Now specify the default policy. This is done by executing the `ipchains` command with the `-P` parameter and specifying the security policy for each chain:

```
ipchains -P input DENY
ipchains -P output REJECT
ipchains -P forward DENY
```

Note that for the incoming (input) and transiting (forward) packets I specified complete denial, so they will be deleted without any warnings. The default policy rule for the outgoing packets can be specified as REJECT so that the inside clients could be informed of the error when attempting to connect to the server.

Now, your computer is invisible and cannot be accessed from the network. Try to scan the server's ports or ping it. Both actions will produce no results, as if the computer were not connected to the network.

4.11.2. Examples of Adding ipchains Rules

Now you can start specifying rules to allow some access to the server. You should be aware that a rule appended to a chain may not work as intended. There may already be a rule in the chain before the one being added that will prevent packet processing against the new rule. To avoid this pitfall, I place new rules at the head of the chain (by specifying the `-I` and `1` options).

The rule prohibiting everything should be placed at the end of the chain. Rules for a specific action, port, or address should be placed at the head of the chain.

Suppose that all users should be able to work with port 80 (the default Web server port) of the public Web server. This is achieved by executing the following commands:

```
ipchains -I input 1 -p tcp -d 192.168.77.1 80 -j ACCEPT
ipchains -I output 1 -p tcp -s 192.168.77.1 80 -j ACCEPT
```

The port can be specified by either its name or its numerical identifier. Thus, to specify the port by its name, the preceding commands will look like the following:

```
ipchains -I input 1 -p tcp -d 192.168.77.1 web -j ACCEPT
ipchains -I output 1 -p tcp -s 192.168.77.1 web -j ACCEPT
```

Here, the port is specified by its name, web, instead of its numerical identifier, 80. The `ipchains` program will process either argument correctly.

Examine each option of the first command:

- ❑ `-I input 1` — The `-I` option indicates that the rule should be placed in the chain in the specified position. The argument following `-I` specifies the chain, to which the rule is to be added: `input`. The number `1` specifies the position in the chain to place the rule in; that is, it will be the first one in the chain.
- ❑ `-p tcp` — The Web server operates under HTTP, which uses TCP as the transport protocol. Do not forget to specify the protocol explicitly using the `-p` option. Otherwise, you will open access to services on two ports: TCP and UDP. If you are lucky, there will be no program using UDP port 80 at this time.

❑ `-d 192.168.77.1 80` — The rule states that the destination of the incoming packets is port 80 (or `web`) of the server whose address is 192.168.77.1. In the instant case, this is the address of my server. What this means is that I allowed all incoming packets to be received on port 80 of my computer. The address of the sender is not specified in the rule, so packets can come from a computer with any IP address.

❑ `-j ACCEPT` — This option allows packets to be received. If an incoming packet meets the requirements specified by the rule's options (the destination address and port and the protocol in this case), it will be accepted.

So the first rule allows everyone to send requests to the server. But the main function of a Web server is to serve the pages requested by clients. This requires port 80 of my server (192.168.77.1) to be open for outgoing packets. This is achieved by the second command.

Executing the `ipchains -L` command will display the following contents of all your chains:

```
Chain input (policy DENY):
target  prot opt    source      destination  ports
ACCEPT  tcp  ------ anywhere    flenovm.ru   any ->   http

Chain forward (policy DENY):

Chain output (policy DENY):
target  prot opt    source      destination  ports
ACCEPT  tcp  ------ flenovm.ru  anywhere     http ->  any
Chain icmp (0 references):
```

A new entry has been added to the `input` and `output` chains. Note that the IP address of my computer in the `source` and `destination` fields was replaced with its domain name: `flenovm.ru`. The server will do this substitution if it can map the address to the name. Also, the numerical designation of the port is replaced with its symbolic name in the `ports` fields: `http` instead of 80.

I recommend that you study carefully the list of created filters to be able to understand clearly each of its parameters. Consider the structure of rule chains using the `input` chain as an example:

```
target  prot opt    source      destination  ports
ACCEPT  tcp  ------ anywhere    flenovm.ru   any ->   http
```

The first line lists the name of each field in the rule chain filter shown in the second line. There are the following six fields:

❑ `target` — The action that will be performed on the packet meeting the filter requirements. In this case, the `ACCEPT` value means that the packet will be let through; otherwise, the packet is destroyed.

❑ `prot` — The protocol, `tcp` in this case.

❑ `opt` — Extra options. These were not specified in the example, so there are dashes in their place.

❑   source — The packet's source. The word `anywhere` means that the packet can originate on any computer.

❑   destination — The packet's destination. This can be specified by either the computer's name or its IP address.

❑   ports — The ports, specified in the source -> destination format. In this case, the source port can be any, while the destination port can be only 80 (http).

A Web server's contents must be frequently updated, for which purpose an FTP service is normally used. In this case, not just anyone can connect to the server through the FTP port (port 21); only the computer at address 192.168.77.10 can connect. The rules implementing these requirements are added by the following commands:

```
ipchains -I input 1 -p tcp -d 192.168.77.1 21 \
    -s 192.168.77.10  -j ACCEPT
ipchains -I output 1 -p tcp -s 192.168.77.1 21 \
    -d 192.168.77.10  -j ACCEPT
```

The first command allows packets originating from any port of the computer with the IP address 192.168.77.10 to reach port 21 of the server with the IP address 192.168.77.1. The second command allows outgoing packets from port 21 of the server with the IP address 192.168.77.1 to be addressed to the client computer with the address 192.168.77.10.

This, however, will not put the FTP service into operation. An FTP server requires two ports: Port 21 is used to exchange commands and port 20 is used to exchange data. Access to port 20 is opened by executing the following commands:

```
ipchains -I input 1 -p tcp -d 192.168.77.1 20 \
    -s 192.168.77.10  -j ACCEPT
ipchains -I output 1 -p tcp -s 192.168.77.1 20 \
    -d 192.168.77.10  -j ACCEPT
```

Now the computer with the address 192.168.77.10 has full access to the FTP service, which is not available to any other IP addresses. Scanning the server from any computer in your network will show that only port 80 is open; ports 21 and 20 can be seen only from the 192.168.77.10 computer.

Examine the current state of the rule chains by executing the `ipchains -L` command. The displayed information should look similar to the following:

```
Chain input (policy DENY):
target  prot opt    source          Destination  ports
ACCEPT  tcp  ------ 192.168.77.10   flenovm.ru   any -> ftp-data
ACCEPT  tcp  ------ 192.168.77.10   flenovm.ru   any -> ftp
ACCEPT  tcp  ------ anywhere        flenovm.ru   any -> http

Chain forward (policy DENY):

Chain output (policy DENY):
target  prot opt    source          destination    ports
```

```
ACCEPT  tcp  ------ flenovm.ru    192.168.77.10  ftp-data -> any
ACCEPT  tcp  ------ flenovm.ru    192.168.77.10  ftp -> any
ACCEPT  tcp  ------ flenovm.ru    anywhere       http -> any
Chain icmp (0 references):
```

The filters described in this section let through any packets regardless of the interface. This is justified in most cases, but the loopback interface (which always points to the local machine) requires no protection. It can only be used locally; no hacker can connect to your computer through this virtual interface from a remote computer. So it will be only logical to allow all packets through the loopback:

```
ipchains -A input -i lo -j ACCEPT
ipchains -A output -i lo -j ACCEPT
```

Most administrators do not like to allow complete access through the loopback, because the policies for the external and the virtual interfaces will be different. This makes it more difficult to test network programs. A program that works without any problems over the loopback is not guaranteed to function properly over a remote connection, because the firewall filters may interfere with its normal operation.

4.11.3. Deleting ipchains Rules

Try to cancel access to the FTP service by deleting rules from the input chain. I picked the FTP service as an example because here two rules have to be deleted and you have to be careful about how you do this. At first glance, it may seem that the following two commands will produce the desired result:

```
ipchains -D input 1
ipchains -D input 2
```

Do not rush off to execute them. In the preceding commands, the -D option indicates that the specified number rule should be deleted in the specified chain. The order, in which the commands are issued, means that first rule 1 will be deleted and then rule 2. But will this command sequence really achieve the desired result?

Executing the first command will modify the contents of the input chain to the following:

```
Chain input (policy DENY):
target  prot opt   source          Destination ports
ACCEPT  tcp  ------ 192.168.77.10 flenovm.ru  any -> ftp
ACCEPT  tcp  ------ anywhere       flenovm.ru  any -> http
```

The rule for the ftp-data port, the former rule number 1, is gone, which shifted the order of the remaining rules in the chain one position up. Thus, executing the second command intended to delete the rule for the ftp port (port 21) will delete the rule for the http server, which is now the current rule 2, leaving access to the ftp port intact. This mix up is easy to notice and correct with only three rules in the chain. But what if there are a hundred rules? It will be rather difficult to figure out which rule was deleted improperly.

To avoid this problem, start deleting higher numbered rules and proceed downward. In this case, the commands should be executed in the following order:

```
ipchains -D input 2
ipchains -D input 1
```

There is another way of deleting rules from a chain, which is more reliable. To consider it, you will need to create a rule in the `forward` chain. Execute the following command:

```
ipchains -A forward -p icmp -j DENY
```

Here the `-A` option is used, which appends the rule to chain (empty in this case).

NOTE

If forwarding is disabled in your system, the rule will be added but the system may issue a warning. Forwarding will be considered in detail in *Section 4.11.7*.

Investigate what this rule does. It will be triggered by an ICMP packet that has to be forwarded. The `DENY` filter means that the packet will be simply deleted. In this way you will have blocked forwarding of the ICMP traffic. To prohibit ICMP packets altogether, the following rule has to be added:

```
ipchains -A input -p icmp -j DENY
```

Now delete a rule from the forward chain. This is done by executing the same command as used for adding the rule but with the `-D` option instead of `-A` (or instead of `-I`, if you used the insert option to add the rule). The resulting command should look like the following:

```
ipchains -D forward -p icmp -j DENY
```

Execute it and ascertain that the rule has been deleted.

4.11.4. "Everything but" Rules

Rules often have to be specified in the "everything but" format. For example, you have to forbid access to the Telnet port to all except the computer with the 192.168.77.10 IP address. The best way to proceed will be to first allow access to the port for the 192.168.77.10 computer and then forbid access to anyone else. The `input` chain will have the following two rules in this case:

- ❑ Allow connections to Telnet from the 192.168.77.10 address
- ❑ Prohibit connections to Telnet from any address

These rules are based on the assumption that the default policy is to allow connections from any address. In that case, all incoming packets will be checked for compliance with the first rule and either let through (meeting the 192.168.10 requirement) or passed to the second rule (not meeting the 192.168.77.10 requirement). The second rule simply deletes all incoming packets that reach it.

The same result can be achieved with only one command. The rule in this case is formulated as follows:

```
ipchains -I input 1 -p tcp -s ! 192.168.77.10 telnet -j DENY
```

In this command, all TCP packets (as indicated by the -p tcp option) not originating from the 192.168.77.10 address (the -s option) are prohibited (by the -j DENY option) from connecting. The ! character denotes the not-equal logical condition; that is, all packets not originating from the specified source will meet the condition.

This command will work only if the default policy is to allow all packets. Otherwise, packets sourced by the 192.168.77.10 computer will be deleted anyway.

The ! character can also be used with ports. For example, you need allow full access to the server with the exception of the Telnet port from the 192.168.77.12 address. Then the default policy should be denying all traffic and issuing the following command:

```
ipchains -I input 1 -p tcp -s 192.168.77.12 ! telnet -j ACCEPT
```

This command allows full access to the server to all TCP packets from the 192.168.77.12 address with the exception of the Telnet port, the latter prohibition indicated by the ! character in front of the port name.

4.11.5. Network Filters

It is rather difficult to describe each computer individually in large networks. This task is simplified by using group rules. Suppose you have to allow Internet access only to the 192.168.1.x network (the corresponding mask is 255.255.255.0). The first 24 bits in the address (the first three octets) are the network ID, and the last 8 bits (the last octet) are the computer ID in this network. The entire network can be granted access by the following command:

```
ipchains -I input 1 -p tcp -s 192.168.1.0/24 -j ACCEPT
```

Here, the computer address is specified as 192.168.1.0/24. The slash is followed by the number specifying how many bits define the network ID. This means that this filter extends to all computers in this network.

There are three main network categories, which differ by the number of bits in their network IDs. These are the following:

❑ *Category A* — The network ID is the first 8 bits. Networks in this category use addresses in the 01.0.0.0 to 126.0.0.0 range.

❑ *Category B* — The network ID is the first 12 bits. Networks in this category use addresses in the 128.0.0.0 to 191.255.0.0 range.

❑ *Category C* — The network ID is the first 16 bits. Networks in this category use addresses in the 192.0.1.0 to 223.255.255.0 range.

There are some exceptions to this breakdown, which were considered in *Section 4.10.2*. If you are not familiar with TCP, I recommend that you get acquainted with it now. This knowledge will be of great use to you in administering your system.

4.11.6. ICMP Traffic

The protocol that many administrators find most difficult is ICMP, which is required by RFC 792 for the TCP/IP operation. But standards are not always followed in everyday life, and TCP/IP can work on computers, on which ICMP is prohibited.

TCP is the most commonly used protocol, and anyone involved with networks has to deal with it to a varying extent. The UDP in its characteristics is similar to TCP, so most of those who are familiar with TCP have no problems with this protocol either. But few are familiar with ICMP, and many even fear this protocol. Some people even believe that it would cause no harm at the worst and be beneficial at the best to simply eliminate this protocol. This opinion, however, is formed because of lack of understanding of this protocol's importance.

ICMP allows two network nodes to share information about the errors. It is used to send packets not to a certain program but to the computer as a whole; therefore, it does not use any ports. Its packets, however, do have a type and a code. You can view these parameters by executing the `ipchains -h icmp` command.

Most often, ICMP packets are sent in response to a nonstandard situation. Table 4.1 lists the main types and codes of the packets.

Table 4.1. The main types and codes of ICMP packets

Type	Code	Description
0	0	echo-reply — These packets are employed by the `ping` utility to verify that there is a connection with a remote computer.
3	0–7	destination-unreachable — Packets of this type indicate that the addressee is unreachable. Codes provide more specific information: 0 — The network is unavailable. 1 — The computer is unavailable. 2 — The protocol is unavailable. 3 — The port is unavailable. 4 — Fragmentation is required. 6 — An unknown network. 7 — An unknown computer.
8	0	echo-reply — These packets are employed by the `ping` utility verifying that there is a connection with a remote computer to request a reply from the host.
9 and 10	0	These message types are sent by routers.
12	1	This is the wrong IP header.
12	2	There are no required options.

When creating a rule, the type of the ICMP message is specified in the same way as the port for TCP; the code is placed after the -d option. For example, the following command prohibits type 3 code 1 ICMP packets:

```
ipchains -I output 1 -p icmp -s 192.168.8.1 3 -d 1 -j DENY
```

Some administrators do not pay enough attention to ICMP. They make a serious mistake doing this, because ICMP was used to perpetrate many attacks. Moreover, TCP traffic can be transmitted using ICMP messages employing the tunneling technique.

4.11.7. Forwarding

All previously-considered rules only regulate access to the computer. But if a computer is used as a dedicated firewall, it will mostly deal with forward rules.

A firewall protecting the entire network consists, at a minimum, of a computer with two interfaces. One of the interfaces (the modem) faces the Internet; the other (the network adapter) faces the local network. The local network connects to the Internet through this computer, so the firewall forwards the traffic from one interface to the other — that is, from the network adapter to the modem, and vice versa. A computer used in this way is called a gateway. Users do not connect to the gateway but use it only to forward their packets.

It is possible to install services directly on the gateway computer, but I do not recommend doing this. It is preferable not to install them on this computer. Public services should be on the Internet side of the firewall; closed services should be installed on servers within your local network (see Fig. 4.6).

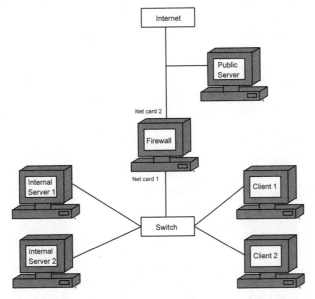

Fig. 4.6. Location of the public and closed service servers

Fig. 4.7. Doubled network protection

This arrangement makes it possible to not create permission rules for the public services for the firewall because it does not protect them. But the local access policy can also be applied on the public server. I do not recommend using public services on your own network. There are numerous hosting companies that specialize in providing this type of service, and you will be better off to let them take care of this for you.

If you place a server providing public services within the network, you will have to create firewall rules allowing all users from the Internet to access it. Such rules were considered in *Section 4.12.2*; but that was only an example, and in real life all public services must be placed outside of the private network.

Each firewall permission is a potential doorway into the local network. If you maintain a public Web server on your network and a bug is discovered in the server's scripts, your entire network will be endangered.

If, for some reason, you have no other way to provide Web service but placing the server on your network, I recommend that you organize the arrangement as shown in Fig. 4.7. This will require an additional server, however, to organize the second firewall.

In the network arrangement shown in Fig. 4.7, Firewall 1 protects the Web server. Its policy should be relatively mild to allow public access to some of the server's ports, such as port 80 for Web site browsing. The important thing is that the filters allow public access to the address of the public server and the designated ports on it only.

The second firewall protects the local network; consequently, its rules must be more stringent and restrict any outside connections. Moreover, there should be no trusting relations between the public server and the local network. Allowing this server to freely connect to any of the ports on the local network negates the whole idea of using this arrangement. Should there be a bug in the Web server's software or the sites it serves, it can be exploited to execute commands on the server and establish connections with the network on behalf of the Web server without even having to break through the second firewall.

Some organizations, in addition to the public servers, place several computers between the two firewalls in the arrangement shown in Fig. 4.7. These are usually obsolete computers creating an appearance of a network to confuse hackers. There is no important information on such sham networks. There are, however, various intrusion-detection tools installed on them to inform the administrators about unauthorized access attempts.

These bogus networks provide a certain level of protection against hackers by taking them off the right track — at least for a while. The machines can have various ports opened and store seemingly important but actually useless information to whet the intruders' appetite and keep them rummaging in the junkyard.

Another way to provide some extra protection for your network is to equip the firewall computer with three network cards. One of the cards provides the Internet connection, another connects the private local network, and the last one connects the public network (see Fig. 4.8). Access to the public interface is quite liberal, and the private interface is protected with all available means.

The arrangement shown in Fig. 4.7 has more effective security than the one in Fig. 4.8. There the local network is protected by two firewalls, which are also easier to configure. The arrangement shown in Fig. 4.8 is simpler and less expensive, because it does not require an additional computer for the second firewall. However, this arrangement provides less security. Once a hacker penetrates this firewall computer, he or she will experience fewer difficulties breaking into the private local network.

But let me return to the subject of forwarding. Fig. 4.6 shows a local network connected using twisted pair to the central switch. Trace the routes that packets in this network can follow. To reach the Internet, a packet from any network computer passes through the switch, enters the firewall computer through one network adapter (call it eth0), and exits the firewall computer through another network adapter (call it eth1) onto the Internet.

The firewall computer must have forwarding permitted to allow packets to pass from one network card to the other. This is done either by writing 1 to the /proc/sys/net/ipv4/ip_forward file (it may contain the default value 0) or by executing the following command:

```
echo 1 > /proc/sys/net/ipv4/ip_forward
```

The kernel must be compiled to support forwarding among network interfaces, because the forwarding process takes place on this level. In addition, the net.ipv4.ip_forward parameter in /etc/sysctl.conf has to be changed to 1.

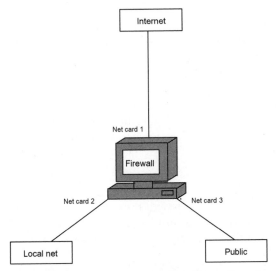

Fig. 4.8. Protecting two networks with one firewall

The subject of allowing Internet access is covered in detail in *Chapter 9*. For now, only the subject of configuring traffic-forwarding security will be considered.

A firewall not only can inspect packets for compliance with the filter rules but also can hide addresses of the network's computers. This is done as follows:

1. A packed placed by a client on the network travels to the firewall with its own IP address.
2. The firewall replaces the IP address of the sender with its own and forwards the packet in its name.

Consequently, all packets sent by any computer of a particular network on the Internet will appear as if they were sent by the firewall computer. This allows the internal organization of the network to be concealed and IP addresses to be saved. Computers within the network can be assigned addresses from one of the reserved address ranges (considered in *Section 4.10.2*), with only the firewall computer assigned a real IP address. This addressing method makes it impossible to connect to the network's computers from the Internet directly, because before any of the network's computers can be broken into, this has to be done to the firewall computer. This makes it much more difficult to break into the network. Inexperienced hackers never become involved with firewalls, because they have neither the extensive knowledge of the security principles nor the great experience required for breaking through a firewall.

Consider a rule allowing the forwarding of packets from the local network to the external interface:

```
ipchains -A forward -i eth1 -s 192.168.1.0/24 -j MASQ
```

Because this is a general rule, I placed it at the end of the `forward` chain using the `-A` option to avoid blocking the filters specific for individual users but interrelated with this rule.

The interface is indicated by `eth1` parameter (the Internet-side network adapter). The address range corresponds to the entire 192.168.1.*x* network. The permission (the `-j` option) is MASQ: address masking. This means that the client's address with be replaced with the address of the firewall computer.

This permission only allows packets from the 192.168.1.*x* network to be sent to the `eth1` interface. This, however, does not mean that the traffic will be able to enter the interface and be forwarded to the Internet. For the firewall to accept user packets, there should be an ACCEPT rule in the `input` chain. It may look as follows:

```
ipchains -A input -i eth0 -s 192.168.1.0/24 -j ACCEPT
```

This filter opens access to the `eth0` network interface to any packets originating at the 192.168.1.*x* addresses.

Now, a rule to permit packets to exit the `eth1` interface has to be added to the `output` chain, and all of your network's computers will have access to the Internet. The IP address of the firewall computer has to be specified as the gateway on all client machines.

If your network is organized as shown in Fig. 4.7, both firewall machines must have forwarding enabled. But address masking is better done on the Firewall 2 machine. This will make the firewall conceal even the local network from the public server.

Frequently, the Internet-side network device is a modem and not a network adapter. In this case, the masking rule for the `forward` chain will look like the following:

```
ipchains -A forward -i ppp0 -s 192.168.1.0/24 -j MASQ
```

The traffic is forwarded to the modem interface, which is denoted by the `ppp0` parameter.

Clients often must have access to Internet resources even though the reverse connection is unwanted. When a TCP-connection request to a remote computer is made, a packet with the `syn` bit set is sent. Regular packets (such as responses to connection requests or data transmissions) are not supposed to have this bit. Consequently, prohibiting TCP packets with this flag set will make it impossible for a remote computer to connect to either the firewall computer or the network. This can be implements as follows:

```
ipchains -I input 1 -i ppp0 -p tcp --syn -j DENY
```

This command places the new rule in the `input` chain. The rule checks for TCP packets with the `syn` flag set (as indicated by the `-- syn` option). Any packets meeting this criterion are deleted.

To mask IP addresses, the corresponding support must be compiled into the kernel, because the address substitution process takes place on the kernel level.

4.11.8. Saving Filter Information

Rules that you create for `ipchains` are stored in the memory. Restarting the system will clear the memory and, naturally, any rules that you set. The operating system does not automatically save rule changes; you have to take care of this yourself. This can be done using the `ipchain-save` utility as follows:

```
ipchain-save > file
```

When I started considering the `ipchains` command, I mentioned the /etc/sysconfig/ipchains file (see *Section 4.11.1*). This configuration file is loaded on the system boot. I recommend saving rule changes in this file by executing the following command:

```
ipchain-save > /etc/sysconfig/ipchains
```

Save the changes every time you change the `ipchains` configuration. Should you have to reload the server for some reason, you will most likely forget to restore the changes.

It is possible to automate the process of saving rule changes, but I do not recommend that you rely on this. It will be more reliable to do this manually.

This file can also be used to restore chain rules. This is done by executing the following command:

```
ipchain-restore < file
```

This is a handy feature. Suppose you want to test a new set of rules but do not want to corrupt the already-configured chains. In this case, you can save the existing state in some file and then experiment all you want. If something goes wrong, you can return to the starting point by restoring the chains from the backup file.

4.12. The iptables Program

The `iptables` program is a new security development for controlling filter chains that has not become popular with most users yet. If you understand how `ipchains` works, you will have few problems mastering `iptables`.

The `iptables` program also employs the `input`, `output`, and `forward` rule chains.

4.12.1. Main Features

The similarities between `ipchains` and `iptables` can be seen in the same commands and parameters they use:

☐ `-A chain rule` — Append a rule to the end of the chain. The chain argument can be INPUT, OUTPUT, or FORWARD.

☐ `-D chain number` — Delete the rule with the specified number from the specified chain.

☐ `-R chain number rule` — Replace the rule with the specified number in the specified chain.

☐ `-I chain number rule` — Insert the rule into the specified chain under the specified number. For example, in the number equals 1, the rule will be the first one in the chain.

☐ `-L chain` — View the contents of the specified chain.

☐ `-F chain` — Delete all rules from the specified chain.

☐ `-p protocol` — Define the protocol covered by the rule.

☐ `-i interface` — Specifies the incoming network interface. Available values are INPUT, FORWARD, and PREROUTING.

☐ `-o interface` — Specifies the outgoing network interface. Available values are OUTPUT, FORWARD, and POSTROUTING.

☐ `-j action` — The action to apply to the packet, called the target in the `iptables` terminology. The main target options are the following:

  • LOG — Record receipt of the packet in the log.
  • REJECT — Delete the packet and notify the sender.
  • DROP — Delete the packet.
  • BLOCK — Block the packet.

☐ `-s address` — The source IP address. As in `ipchains`, the address can be preceded by the `!` argument and followed by the `/mask` network mask.

☐ `-d address` — The destination address.

As you can see, most of the parameters are the same as those for the `ipchains` program. But there are also important differences. For example, the `-o` and `-i` parameters provide an easy way to specify the source and destination interface of a packet. Because the practical aspects of the configuration processes for both services are similar, I will not waste book space on considering the process separately for `iptables` and will only briefly consider the rule-creation process.

In the preceding description of the command options, I considered only the main ones. But if you examine the documentation file, you will see that there are many options that can be used with the `-j` parameter. (If you recall, the `-j` parameter specifies, which actions should be applied to the packet that meets the rule's criterion.)

The configuration process for `iptables` chains is not different from that for `ipchains`. The chain-formation process starts by flushing all contents of the chain. Rules are added to the chain starting with prohibiting everything and then permitting only those actions and packets that will not harm the server. Potentially dangerous services should only be made available to trusted users who require them.

Changes to the `iptables` configuration, as with `ipchains`, must be saved manually to the configuration file (/etc/sysconfi/iptables by default):

```
service iptables save
```

4.12.2. Forwarding

Forwarding in `iptables` is enabled by executing the following command:

```
iptables -A FORWARD -o ppp0 -j MASQUERADE
```

The command allows forwarding to the `ppp0` interface. The `-j` parameter means that you require to hide the source IP address, that is, enable masquerading.

For the Network Address Translation (NAT) table, the command may look as follows:

```
iptables -t nat -A FORWARD -o ppp0 -j MASQUERADE
```

The `-t nat` table option indicates that the `iptable_nat` module has to be loaded. This module can also be loaded manually by executing the following command:

```
modprobe iptable_nat
```

Here, `iptable_nat` is the kernel module that allows the firewall to work with NAT.

4.12.3. Configuring the iptables Program

I will not describe here various prohibitions in detail because I considered those when describing the `ipchains` program. I will just briefly consider the process of creating various rules.

All incoming packets can be prohibited by the following command:

```
iptables -P INPUT DROP
```

All incoming packets will be deleted, or dropped in `iptables` terminology. As with `ipchains`, you should start configuring `iptables` with this command. Note that the `-P` command in used, which sets the default policy for the given chain to the specified target (action). Adding the rule using the `-A` command option (appended at the end of the chain) will prohibit connections of any type.

Some security specialists recommend logging access requests by adding the following filter to the firewall:

```
iptables -A INPUT -j LOG
```

I personally recommend against logging. Public servers have their ports scanned hundreds, if not thousands, of times. To log all of these scannings, you would need a huge hard drive to store the logs. Unless you provide enough space to store the logs, a full hard drive will take down the system. In this way, repeatedly scanning a prohibited port for a certain period will successfully perpetrate a DoS attack.

The following command creates a rule prohibiting the acceptance of echo requests from any computer:

```
iptables -A INPUT -s 0/0 -d localhost \
-p icmp --icmp-type echo-request -j DROP
```

As you can see, creating a filter does not differ significantly from the analogous `ipchains` procedure.

The following command prohibits access to the FTP port:

```
iptables -A INPUT -s 0/0 -d localhost \
-p tcp --dport 21 -j DROP
```

To prohibit access from a certain interface, add the `-i` option and specify the `eth0` interface as follows:

```
iptables -A INPUT -i eth0 -s 0/0 -d localhost \
-p tcp --dport 21 -j DROP
```

Outgoing packets from port 21 are prohibited by the following command:

```
iptables -A OUTPUT -i eth0 -s localhost -d 0/0 \
-p tcp --dport 21 -j DROP
```

A powerful `iptables` feature is the capability to inspect the contents of packets. This is a handy feature when filtering Web requests, for example. You can allow access to port 80, but only to packets that meet the specified parameter requirements. The subject of Web server security will be treated in *Chapter 7*, along with various defense techniques. For now, consider a simple but universal protection technique.

Suppose you want to allow access to the FTP server but prohibit access to the /etc/passwd and /etc/shadow files. The latter is achieved by prohibiting packets containing this particular text. A request packet containing references to these packets will be dropped. The following commands prohibit access to these files using the FTP and the World Wide Web protocol:

```
iptables -A INPUT -m string --string "/etc/passwd" \
-s 0/0 -d localhost -p tcp --dport 21 -j DROP
iptables -A INPUT -m string --string "/etc/shadow" \
-s 0/0 -d localhost -p tcp --dport 21 -j DROP
iptables -A INPUT -m string --string "/etc/passwd" \
```

```
-s 0/0 -d localhost -p tcp --dport 80 -j DROP
iptables -A INPUT -m string --string "/etc/shadow" \
-s 0/0 -d localhost -p tcp --dport 80 -j DROP
```

You also have to take into account the information-protection aspect. Suppose you have a server that receives traffic encoded using the "stunnel" technique, decodes it, and forwards it to another machine. (The stunnel — secure tunnel — technique, which creates an encoded channel between two machines, is considered in *Section 5.2.*) In this case, the firewall will not detect the text to watch for in the incoming packets. But the outgoing packets are decoded and contain commands in plaintext. This configuration requires that both incoming and outgoing traffic be controlled.

Even if stunnel transfers the decoded traffic to another port within the same computer, all types of packets can be controlled on all interfaces to inspect them after decoding.

4.13. Notes on Firewall Operation

A firewall can both protect your computer or network from invasion and make it vulnerable to one. Only carefully configuring your firewall and setting strict access rules can make your system secure.

But even configuring the firewall in the most proper way and creating the most thought-out filters does not guarantee your server will be 100% secure. An unbreakable firewall is a myth. The problem does not lie just with the ipchains or iptables programs. The firewall technology itself does not guarantee total security. Nothing can guarantee you this; if it could, I would not have written this book.

In this section, I will consider some problems that you may encounter when using the firewall. You should have a clear idea of the potential problems so that you could neutralize the danger they present.

4.13.1. Paying Attention

As already stated, only being extremely careful when configuring the firewall can give you higher-than-average confidence in that your system is secure. Examine some of the typical blunders committed when configuring the firewall; this will help you avoid making similar mistakes.

As you should remember, the input and the output chains have three rules apiece. Suppose you no longer require FTP access and disable it. Along with disabling the FTP server, do not forget to delete from the rule chains the rules that allow such access.

Once, an administrator I knew did not delete the rules after disabling the service. Some time later, the FTP service was enabled again, but the IP address, to which the original permission was issued, was now used by another employee. In this case, the person that unexpectedly obtained rights was a loyal company employee and did not intend to misuse them, but you do understand the implications, don't you?

The firewall-configuring task is difficult when IP addresses are assigned dynamically and change constantly. If addresses in your network are assigned using the Dynamic Host

Configuration Protocol (DHCP), you should see to it that computers that require special access and rules were assigned a permanent address (for example, that of the main gateway). This will prevent the wrong person from obtaining a privileged IP address and the real owner from losing it by accident.

Imagine what will happen if, in the example considered in *Section 4.11.2*, IP address 192.168.8.10 is through a fluke assigned to another computer. It will create problems because the user who is supposed to have it does not and the new user may put it to the wrong use.

To strictly control IP addresses, you should use a DHCP server and assign permanent addresses to those computers that require privileged access and for which there are special filters in the firewall rule chains.

Be careful when creating rules. Some services (for example, FTP) may require more than one port to function properly. Unless you open or close all the ports, you will not achieve the desired result.

Be especially careful when configuring the firewall using a graphical shell. When everything is prohibited, XWindows may hang if it loses the network connection with the Linux kernel.

You should also pay close attention to what you are doing when configuring the firewall using a Secure SHell (SSH) protocol remote connection. One wrong move here may break the connection, and the SSH client will disconnect. Then you will have to go to the firewall server and continue configuring it in situ.

Test all connections after each change to the firewall configuration. If you make a mistake, it will be difficult to trace it after several modifications.

To debug problem rule chains, I save the configuration to a temporary file and then print it. It is much easier to see the whole picture on paper than on the monitor. Make sure you specify the correct source and destination parameters (the address and port). Quite often, administrators are not certain about what parameters to specify and act by the seat of their pants.

Go over each chain in your mind, analyzing which packets are let through and which are not. The investigation is best started with the input chain (where packets enter the system). Next, inspect the forward chain and, finally, the output chain. In this way, the complete packet cycle has to be traced. Remember that after the first rule that meets the packet's criteria, no further checks are conducted.

When inspecting rules dealing with TCP, remember that this protocol establishes a connection, meaning that packets have to travel both ways. UDP does not establish a connection and packets can be passed only one way: input or output. But there are exceptions when some programs require bidirectional exchange over UDP.

If some program does not work, make sure that there are the necessary rules for all necessary ports: Some protocols require access to two or more network ports. Next, check that the permission rule precedes the prohibition rule.

Never open access to the specific port on all computers. For example, simply adding a rule permitting incoming packets on port 80 will open this port on all of the network's computers. But far from all computers require access to this port. Thus, when creating a rule, specify not only the port but also the specific IP address, on which it applies.

And don't forget to make backup copies of the configuration (using the `ipchain-save` command). These will come in handy in case of problems with test configurations.

4.13.2. Bypassing the Firewall

A firewall cannot provide absolute security because its operation algorithm, like everything in life, is not perfect. It is based on certain rules, according to which the firewall inspects the traffic passing through the network interface and makes decisions as to whether or not to let it through. But, short of complete prohibition, no filter can provide 100% security because there is no rule that cannot be circumvented.

Most firewalls are vulnerable to DoS attacks. When considering the technology of DoS attacks in *Section 1.1.6*, I said that such an attack is easy to carry out in the following cases:

❑ Your channel's bandwidth is wider than that of the target computer.
❑ A resource-intensive task exists on the target computer, and the attacker can start this task.

A firewall is a complex software system that requires significant technical resources to analyze all transiting traffic. Most of these resources are spent analyzing syn packets, that is, connection request packets. The firewall has to check the parameters of each syn packet against all set rules.

At the same time, no great bandwidth or computer resources are necessary to send syn packets. A hacker can easily flood a permitted server's port with syn packets with random source addresses. The target machine may not be able to handle the great volume of requests that has to be filtered and will queue them, which will prevent it from processing bona fide connection requests.

The problem becomes worse if the firewall is configured to issue error messages. This increases the processor workload because it has to create and send packets to nonexisting addresses or addresses that do not belong to the hacker.

If a client sends data that does not fit into one packet, the packet is broken into several parts. This process is called packet fragmentation. Most firewalls inspect only the first block in a session and consider the rest of them valid. This is logical, because if the first block is valid, why waste the server's resources on inspecting the rest of them?

Packets can be fragmented in such a way that the firewall will let them through. This type of attack can be defended against only if the firewall automatically assembles packets and inspects them assembled. Most firewalls cannot do this.

Firewalls sometimes experience attacks that are successful. If hackers take over the firewall, they will obtain complete access to the network it is supposed to protect. In this case, you can only be saved from complete defeat by an individual firewall on each of the network's computers. Even though the individual workstation firewall security policy may not be as stringent, it may be just enough to prevent the hackers' further invasion into the network.

Any type of firewall can come under attack. Both Linux firewalls and routers with firewall functions can have bugs.

The main task performed by a firewall is to prohibit access to the resources, to which access is restricted. But some resources must be available to everyone. For example, a firewall cannot protect against a break-in taking advantage of bugs in Web scripts on a Web server that is supposed to have free access for Internet users.

Maximum security comes at the price of sacrificing some conveniences. Thus, as I already stated, all outside attempts to connect to the system are best prohibited. Only a network's client can initiate a connection, not a remote computer. This will make it impossible for hackers to connect to the system but may also cause problems for the legitimate network users when, for example, they try to connect to an FTP server in the active mode. As you already know, this service uses two ports: `ftp` and `ftp-data` (`ftpd`). It will be no problem for the user to connect to the server's `ftp` port. To serve a file, however, the FTP server itself has to initiate a connection with the client, which will not be let through by the firewall. This problem has been solved for the FTP service by adding the passive operating mode; the issue remains open for other services — chats, for example.

It is also possible to connect to a protected network through a tunnel on an open port and a permitted address inside the network. This cannot be avoided because there must be at least something allowed.

There can be more than one server in large networks. It was only in one company and movies that I saw network administrators using a separate monitor and keyboard to control each of them. In real life, network administrators are too lazy to work on several monitors and keyboards and use only one computer, controlling the rest of the servers through a remote connection.

But this is not the extent of their laziness. So as not to come to work after hours in case of emergency, they connect to the server's console from home. And this is a serious breach of security that may place the network they are supposed to protect in a serious danger. It's all right if the program used to manage the remote servers encodes the transmitted data in some way, but what if it's just your regular Telnet client? Hackers can intercept the authentication information using a sniffing utility and obtain the same access privileges to the server as the administrator.

4.13.3. Safe Internet

The Internet will not be safe until it is possible to determine the source of each packet that comes from there. The way things are now, any field of the IP packet can be faked to the effect that its authenticity can never be established.

Once that you can never be sure that it is not a wolf in sheep's clothing that is knocking at your server's door, you should take good care to conceal, which permissions and to whom they are given on your server. The less information you make available to hackers, the more secure your server will be. You should also ruthlessly suppress any recognizance moves, for example, port scanning, or tracing, etc.

The tracing principle is as follows: In a network, a packet travels over a certain route to its destination. A packet addressed to another network is delivered there by routers. But for one reason or another, a packet can stray from the destination route and travel endlessly from one network to another. To prevent this, there is the Time-To-Live (TTL) field in the header of an IP packet. This field is set to a certain value by the sender and is decremented by one by each router it passes. When the TTL value reaches zero, the packet is considered lost and is destroyed, with a message sent to the sender that the host is unreachable.

This feature can be used to determine the route a packet travels to its destination. It works as follows: In 99% of cases, packets travel to the destination over the same route. Setting the packet's TTL value to 1 will make the first router it reaches issue an error message, which contains the router's address. The next packet's TTL value is set to 2. The TTL error message for this packet will be issued by the second router it reaches. Thus, sending a series of packets, sequentially incrementing the TTL value of each packet by 1, all routers that the packets pass to reach the specified destination can be established.

A firewall should drop any packets whose TTL value equals 1. This will protect the network but will also reveal that it is protected by a firewall. If a regular packet (with a real TTL value) reaches the addressee but the `traceroute` command to the same destination produces an error message, this means there is a firewall somewhere in the route.

Tracing in Linux is performed by executing the `traceroute` command with the `-I` option and the host's name specified:

```
traceroute -I redhat.com
```

Windows uses the analogous `tracert` command. It is issued with only the host's name to the trace specified.

Executing any of these commands displays the addresses of the intermediate routers in the packet's route. For example, the information displayed may look similar to the following:

```
traceroute to redhat.com (xxx.xxx.xxx.xxx)? 30 hops max, 38 byte packets
1   218 ms 501 ms 219 ms RDN11-f200.101.transtelecom.net [217.150.37.34]
2   312 ms 259 ms 259 ms sl-gw10-sto-5-2.sprintlink.net [80.77.97.93]
...
...
17  638 ms 839 ms 479 ms 216.140.3.38
18  *      *      *          Request timed out.
```

If the firewall lets through ICMP packets, the `traceroute` command can be used to trace the route, even though it may produce an error message. In this case, entry 18 reveals that the timeout value was exceeded. This means that the packet sent was rejected by the server; consequently, the packet with the TTL value of 18 will be dropped.

To continue tracing beyond the firewall, the command has to be issued with the TTL value of 19. The first 17 requests will produce responses, the 18th will be lost, and the 19th will be let into the network. The reason packet 19 is let in is because when it reaches the firewall, its TTL value equals 2. But the first router in the local network will drop this packet.

In real life, however, ICMP packets are prohibited, and this method seldom produces results.

On the other hand, even if you trace the entire route to the destination computer, it does not mean that there is no firewall in the way: It may be there but simply not prohibit ICMP traffic.

A network behind a firewall can also be scanned using the Domain Name System (DNS) server if it is inside the network and is publicly available.

4.13.4. Additional Protection

In addition to the filters based on the firewall rules, supplementary protection mechanisms independent of the firewall configuration or enabled by special settings can be implemented.

One of the popular techniques of bypassing a firewall is faking the source IP address. For example, access to the FTP server is prohibited from all IP addresses except 100.2.2.2. To obtain access to FTP, a hacker can send packets, in which his source IP address is replaced by the permitted address.

But simply replacing a prohibited IP address with the good one will not let the hacker through. The server simply will not respond to packets with the faked IP address. Why? Take a look at Fig. 4.9: The answer to the hacker's query goes to the real owner of the permitted address.

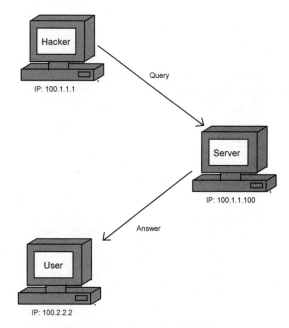

Fig. 4.9. Replacing the IP address

For the server to respond to the hacker's request, special information by which the server can determine the real address of the hacker has to be included in the IP packet.

A modern firewall, including those supplied with Linux, easily detects the swap and blocks fake IP address packets.

4.14. Prohibiting and Permitting Hosts

You may find working with `ipchains` and `iptables` (see *Sections 4.11* and *4.12*) difficult because of the need to know the necessary ports, but this is the most reliable method of providing your server with real security. For simple security goals (for example, temporary protection) there is an easier method: using the /etc/hosts.allow and /etc/hosts.deny files. The former contains a list of hosts allowed access to the system; the latter lists those denied this access.

When a connection attempt to the server is made, the files are checked as follows:

1. If the requesting computer is in neither file, access is permitted by default.
2. If the computer's address is on the list in the hosts.allow file, it is granted access and the hosts.deny file is not checked.
3. If the computer's address is on the list in the hosts.deny file, it is denied access.

The convenience of using these files is that services, to which access has to be limited, can be specified in them for specific hosts. This is done by making an entry in the following format in the file:

```
service: host
```

The `service` parameter specifies the name of the service, to which access has to be restricted. It can also list several services delimited by commas. The host parameter lists addresses delimited by commas (allowed for the /etc/hosts.allow file and prohibited for the /etc/hosts.deny file). Instead of addresses, the `ALL` keyword can be specified, which allows any address or service.

Consider an example configuring these files. For starters, close access to all services by all computers. This is done by adding this entry to the /etc/hosts.deny file: `ALL: ALL`. The resulting file will look as follows:

```
#
# hosts.deny    This file describes the names of the hosts
#               not allowed to use the local INET
#               services, as decided by the
#               /usr/sbin/tcpd server.
#
# The portmap line is redundant, but it is left to remind
# you that the new secure portmap uses hosts.deny and
# hosts.allow. In particular, you should know that NFS
# uses portmap!

ALL: ALL
```

Now specify the following permissions:

☐ The computer with the address 192.168.1.1 can connect to any services.

❏ Only computers with the addresses 192.168.1.2 and 192.168.1.3 can have access to the FTP service. The corresponding file follows:

```
#
# hosts.allow  This file describes the names of the hosts
#              allowed to use the local INET services,
#              as decided by the /usr/sbin/tcpd server.
#

ALL: 192.168.1.1
ftpd: 192.168.1.2, 192.168.1.3
```

If you need to allow the entire network to access a service, this can be done as follows:

```
ftpd: 192.168.1.
```

This entry allows all computers in the 192.168.1.*x* network to access the `ftpd` service. The x character in the last octet means any number.

As you can see, it is much easier to use the /etc/host.allow and /etc/hosts.deny files than to specify rule chains: You do not have to create rules for incoming and outgoing packets here. But the filtration capabilities of these files are too limited and far fewer than those of any firewall.

I recommend using the /etc/hosts.allow and /etc/host.deny files to address temporary security concerns. For example, a vulnerable service can be easily disabled by making a corresponding entry in the /etc/hosts.deny file. If you notice an attack from some IP address, you can prohibit all connections from that address for a few hours with an appropriate entry in the same /etc/hosts.deny file.

You may ask why this can't be done using the firewall rule chains. This is because should you delete or add a wrong rule, the server operation may be disrupted or its security may be lowered. This is why I do not recommend creating temporary firewall rules.

4.15. Advice on Configuring a Firewall

The firewall-configuring task requires an individual approach and depends on the specific tasks the server is to solve. Nevertheless, a few recommendations can be given. These are the following:

❏ Start by prohibiting everything for everyone. People acquire a taste for good things quickly, and once users become accustomed to some service, it will be difficult to wean them from it, even if it is not necessary to them.

❏ If possible, all types of ICMP messages, especially `ping`, should be prohibited. I will return to the subject of the danger posed by network scanning using ICMP packets many times throughout the book.

❏ Prohibit access to port 111. This port is used by *portmapper*, which is necessary for performing Remote Procedure Calls (RPCs) and receiving the results. The `rpcinfo` utility can be used to find out, which RPC services are running on your server. For example, execute the following command:

```
rpcinfo -p localhost
```

The result will look similar to the following:

```
Program vers proto  port
100000   2   tcp    111  portmapper
100000   2   udp    111  portmapper
100024   1   udp  32768  status
100024   1   tcp  32768  status
391002   2   tcp  32769  sgi_fam
```

As you can see, quite a bit of information can be obtained with just one command; thus, port 111 must be closed.

❑ To make controlling access to ports easier, divide the open resources into the following two categories:
- Those for public access, including visitors from the Internet.
- Those for use only within the network. For example, such services as FTP and Telnet are inherently dangerous because they can be used to upload files on the server and to execute commands. If these services are not necessary for Internet visitors, external connections to them should be explicitly prohibited.

4.16. Obtaining Higher Privileges

In conclusion of the security subject, it is necessary for you to become acquainted with the sudo command, which allows programs to be executed on behalf of another user.

I already mentioned in *Section 2.7* that it is highly undesirable to work in the system as the root. The reasons for this are the following:

❑ Programs started by the root run with root rights. Should there be a vulnerability in such a program, it can be used by hackers to obtain root rights.
❑ Entering some command erroneously can impair the entire system. And to make a mistake when entering a command is not that difficult, because Linux provides powerful regular expression capabilities.

If there is no user account without administrator rights in the system, add it now. Then log into the system using this account and try to view the /etc/shadow file by executing the cat /etc/shadow command.

The system will respond with a message that you are denied permission to view the file. Now execute the same command using sudo:

```
sudo cat /etc/shadow
```

The system will respond with the message that your account is not the sudoers (/etc/sudoers) file. This is the file, in which users who are permitted to use the sudo command are listed. An example of this file's contents is shown in Listing 4.2.

Listing 4.2. The contents of the /etc/sudoers configuration file

```
# sudoers file
# This file MUST be edited with the 'visudo' command as root.
# See the sudoers man page for the details on how to
# write a sudoers file.
# Host alias specification

# User alias specification

# Cmnd alias specification

# Defaults specification

# User privilege specification
root       ALL = (ALL) ALL

# Uncomment to let people in group wheel run all commands
# %wheel  ALL = (ALL)         ALL

# Same thing without a password
# %wheel  ALL = (ALL)         NOPASSWD: ALL

# Samples
# %users  ALL = /sbin/mount /cdrom,/sbin/umount /cdrom
# %users  localhost = /sbin/shutdown -h now
```

There is only one entry that is not commented out in this file. This is the following:
```
root    ALL=(ALL) ALL
```
There are the following three fields in this entry:

❑   In the first field, the user (or group) allowed to execute the specified command is designated. I recommend listing specific users here. A hacker can become a member of a group but cannot obtain access to running high-privileged commands as having no rights for this.

❑   In the second field, the name of the machine, on which the permitted user can execute commands as the superuser is specified.

❑   In the third field, the commands that the permitted user can execute as the superuser are listed after the equals sign.

Thus, to enable a regular user to view the /etc/shadow file, the corresponding rights have to be specified for this user in the /etc/sudoers file. You created the regular user robert earlier. Add the following entry for him to the /etc/sudoers file:

```
robert    ALL=ALL
```

Now the user robert can use the `sudo` command to perform any administrator tasks. You can verify this by executing the `cat` command via `sudo` again: `sudo cat /etc/shadow`.

This time the command should execute without any complaints from the system. You will have to enter the administrator's password to use the `sudo` feature.

Giving permission to execute all commands contradicts the secure system principles. Thus, you have to place certain restrictions.

It is difficult for one person to maintain a server that processes numerous user connections daily and runs various services. In most cases, this task is shared by many people. One person is responsible for the system, another maintains the Web server, yet another takes care of the MySQL database, and so on. It is not necessary for all administrators to have the same rights; each of them only has to be permitted to execute those commands that he or she needs to perform the specific task assigned. Thus, rights for each user must to be clearly specified — for example, as follows:

```
robert    ALL=/bin/cat /etc/shadow
```

Note that the absolute paths to the `cat` program and the shadow file are given; otherwise, executing the command will produce an error message.

For example, you want to give some user extended rights and allow him or her not only to view the password file but also to mount the CD-ROM. For this, edit the entry by adding permission to execute the `mount` command:

```
robert    ALL=/bin/cat /etc/shadow, /bin/mount
```

Note that this only gives read permission for the /etc/shadow file by explicitly specifying the `cat` utility to access it with. It makes sense, because it is edited using the `passwd` command. You could simply give permission for executing the `cat` command as follows:

```
robert    ALL=/bin/cat, /bin/mount
```

But in this case a hacker can view any files in the system as root, including those that a regular user cannot see.

No parameters were specified for the `mount` command. In this way, the user can specify the parameters himself or herself. Specifying the CD-ROM as an argument explicitly lets the user mount only this device:

```
robert    ALL=/bin/cat /etc/shadow, /bin/mount /dev/cdrom
```

In the examples considered, the computer parameter was specified as ALL, which means any machine. Never use this value in a real system. Always specify the particular computer, to which the entry applies. Most often, this will be a local server.

The `sudo` utility can be used to execute commands not only as the root but also as any other user. This is done by using the -u option with it. For example, the following command attempts to view the password file as the flenov user:

```
sudo -u flenov cat /etc/shadow
```

If the user is not specified, the sudo program requests the root's password. Giving this password to the user robert is not smart for security, because this kills the whole idea of building such a complex security system. Knowing the root's password, the user can log into the system as the administrator and do whatever his or her heart desires with it.

Never reveal the administrator password to those who are not supposed to know it. Use passwords for other user accounts that have the right to work with the necessary files and programs. In this case, the name of the user that was assigned by the administrator to execute the command will have to be specified.

Another way to avoid having to reveal the administrator password is to allow the user to execute commands without authentication. This is done by adding the keyword NOPASSWD followed by a colon between the equals sign and the list of command as follows:

```
robert    ALL=NOPASSWD:/bin/cat /etc/shadow, /bin/mount /dev/cdrom
```

Now when executing the sudo program the password will not be requested. This is dangerous if you do not list the necessary options but only give the ALL keyword.

```
robert    ALL=NOPASSWD:ALL
```

If hackers obtain access to the user account robert, the sudo utility will give them the ability to execute any commands in the system. If you list only the permitted options, the degree of harm that can be inflicted upon the system if it is compromised decreases to the extent of the dangerousness of the commands the robert user is allowed to execute and the protection of this account (i.e., how long and strong the password is, how diligent the owner is, etc.)

The sudo utility can be used to allow access for editing files. Never use this capability. Launching a text editor to edit even the most innocent file will give hackers too many opportunities. For example:

❐ To execute system commands. Because the editor runs with root rights, the commands will also be executed with root rights, meaning that hackers will have the entire system at their disposal.

❐ To open any other file taking advantage of the root privileges.

I never delegate the ability to edit configuration files using a text editor. If this cannot be helped, I never give root rights for this. The configuration files to be edited are assigned to another owner and the user delegated to edit it will launch the sudo program as this new user, thus avoiding running the editor with root rights.

The following commands are potentially dangerous and should not be executed with root rights by other users:

❐ File editing commands — They would allow a dishonest employee to modify any configuration file, not just the ones specified.

❐ The chmod command — It allows hackers to lower the access rights to configuration files and then edit them even if they only have guest rights.

❐ The useradd command — This command allows hackers to create a zero ID user, thus obtaining rights to the entire system.

❑ The mount command — List only specific devices in the configuration file and allow only trusted employees to execute this command. If hackers are able to mount a device with programs that have SUID bits set or Trojan horse programs, they will be able to take over the entire system.

❑ The chgrp and chown commands — These are used to change the group or file owner. Taking over the ownership of the password file, hackers will be able to read and even edit it.

Another thing to remember when working with the sudo program is that its SUID bit is set, meaning that it executes with the rights of the owner, that is, with root rights. The 1.5.5 through 1.6.5.p2 versions of the sudo program have a memory-allocation bug. This bug can be exploited by hackers to perpetrate a stack overflow attack. You can check your version by executing the sudo command with the -v option. If executed by the administrator, it displays detailed information about the program as shown in Listing 4.3.

Listing 4.3. The sudo program information

```
Sudo version 1.6.5p2

Authentication methods: 'pam'

Syslog facility if syslog is being used for logging: authpriv

Syslog priority to use when user authenticates successfully: notice

Syslog priority to use when user authenticates unsuccessfully: alert

Ignore '.' in $PATH
Send mail if the user is not in sudoers
Use a separate timestamp for each user/tty combo
Lecture user the first time they run sudo
Require users to authenticate by default
Root may run sudo

Allow some information gathering to give useful error messages

Visudo will honor the EDITOR environment variable
Set the LOGNAME and USER environment variables

Length at which to wrap log file lines (0 for no wrap): 80

Authentication timestamp timeout: 5 minutes
Password prompt timeout: 5 minutes
```

```
Number of tries to enter a password: 3
Umask to use or 0777 to use user's: 022
Path to mail program: /usr/sbin/sendmail
Flags for mail program: -t
Address to send mail to: root

Subject line for mail messages: *** SECURITY information for %h ***

Incorrect password message: Sorry, try again.
Path to authentication timestamp dir: /var/run/sudo
Default password prompt: Password:
Default user to run commands as: root
Path to the editor for use by visudo: /bin/vi
Environment variables to check for sanity:
        LANGUAGE
        LANG
        LC_*
Environment variables to remove:
        BASH_ENV
        ENV
        TERMCAP
        ...
        ...

When to require a password for 'list' pseudocommand: any

When to require a password for 'verify' pseudocommand: all

Local IP address and netmask pairs:
        192.168.77.1 / 0xffffff00
Default table of environment variables to clear:
        BASH_ENV
        ENV
        TERMCAP
        ...
        ...
Default table of environment variables to sanity check:
        LANGUAGE
        LANG
        LC_*
```

The displayed is just a fragment of the file, showing the main information. The first entry displays the program version, 1.6.5.p2 in this case. The most interesting items in this listing are the following three lines:

```
Authentication timestamp timeout: 5 minutes
Password prompt timeout: 5 minutes
Number of tries to enter a password: 3
```

The first line sets the time for how long the password is saved in the cache. In this case, it is 5 minutes. If the user executes the sudo command within this time again, the authentication procedure will not have to be gone through.

The following line specifies the time to wait for the user to enter the password. The last line specifies the number of attempts the user can make to enter the password. If the correct password is not entered within this time from the specified number of tries, the program terminates.

Chapter 5: Administration

In this chapter, the questions Linux administrators encounter daily are considered. You will become acquainted with numerous Linux commands, learn how to use them, and discover many useful facts about the system. The information will be illustrated by various examples and interesting facts.

But the chapter is not limited to a simple consideration of commands; this would turn the book into a simple rewrite of Linux manuals. To avoid this, I provide ready-made solutions to administrator tasks that may be of use to you in your everyday work. I hope that the information in this chapter will provide you with answers to many questions and help you solve at least some of the problems you encounter in your work.

Some specialists think that administration is a simple process: All you need is to know commands and execute them at the right time in the right place. But this is only true where pure administrating is concerned. Everything is much more complicated where system security is concerned.

A war is being waged between those trying to break into computers and those protecting against break-ins on the vast expanses of the Internet. The winner in this war will be the one who does his or her homework and reacts faster to the opponent's moves.

5.1. Useful Commands

Consider some programs and commands that can be used to simplify administration tasks and make it more effective. Start with the commands necessary for understanding further material.

5.1.1. netconfig

The netconfig command starts the network-configuration utility (Fig. 5.1). It has a convenient graphical interface, which makes it possible to configure the network parameters without having to deal with the configuration files.

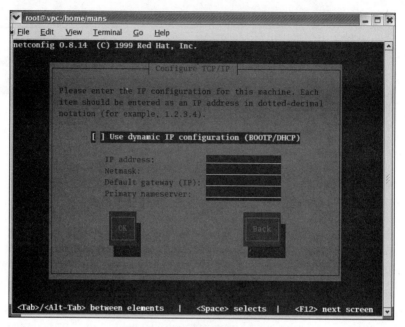

Fig. 5.1. The netconfig window

5.1.2. ping

One of the commands frequently used by administrators is ping. The command sends echo request ICMP packets to the specified system to determine the presence of the other machine.

For example, executing the ping 195.18.1.41 command on my machine displayed the following results:

```
PING 195.18.1.41 (195.18.1.41) from 195.18.1.41 : 56(84) bytes of data.
64 bytes from 195.18.1.41: icmp_seq = 1 ttl = 64 time = 0.102 ms
64 bytes from 195.18.1.41: icmp_seq = 2 ttl = 64 time = 0.094 ms
64 bytes from 195.18.1.41: icmp_seq = 3 ttl = 64 time = 0.094 ms
64 bytes from 195.18.1.41: icmp_seq = 4 ttl = 64 time = 0.095 ms
--- 195.18.1.41 ping statistics ---
4 packets transmitted, 4 received, 0% loss, time 3013ms
rtt min/avg/max/mdev = 0.094/0.096/0.102/0.007 ms
```

The first entry displays the IP address of the computer being probed. If you specify the host name when issuing the `ping` command, you can find its IP address in this way. At the end of the line, the size of the packets to be sent is specified in bytes.

The entries are of the following format:

```
64 bytes from 195.18.1.41: icmp_seq = 1 ttl = 64 time = 0.102 ms
```

This tells you that 64 bytes were received from the address 195.18.1.41. The parameters after the colon and their functions are the following:

❑ `icmp_seq` — The packet number. For each successive packet, this value is incremented by one. If some number is missing, it means that either the ping packet or the reply to it was lost in the Internet. This may be caused by equipment errors, an unreliable cable connection, or one of the routers between the two machines sending the packet the wrong way.

❑ `ttl` — The time-to-live value. This is a number that specifies how many routers the packet can pass on the way to the destination before it is considered lost. The default `ttl` value on most systems is 64, but it can be changed. The value is decremented by one by each router that handles the packet. When it becomes 0, the packet is considered lost and destroyed. Thus, this value can be used to approximately determine the number of routers on the way to the packet's destination.

❑ `time` — The round-trip time. This parameter provides information about the speed of the link. The stability of the link can also be evaluated based on how much this value varies for each packet. Note that the round-trip time for the first packet is almost always longer than that of the successive packets. The rest of the packets should have about the same round-trip time.

If a packet or the reply to it is lost, the program issues a corresponding message. About seven to ten packets are enough to form an idea about the link's quality; the command can then be terminated by pressing the <Ctrl>+<C> key combination. This will display brief statistics about the ping session: the number of packets sent, received, and lost along, with the minimal, average, and maximum round-trip time.

The main switches of the `ping` command are the following:

❑ `-c n` — Send n packets and stop. For example, to send five packets, execute the `ping` command as follows: `ping -c 5 195.10.14.18`.

❑ `-f` — Flood ping. Packets are sent without waiting for the reply. For example, to send 50 packets in this way, execute the `ping` command as follows: `ping -f -c 50 195.10.14.18`. Using this switch with a large number of large packets can put a great load on the network and the computer being pinged, and it may even cause a DoS condition on less powerful systems.

❑ `-s n` — Specify the packet size. For example, a 1000-byte packet is sent by this command: `ping -s 1000 195.10.14.18`. Some older operating system versions contained bugs and would hang when a too-large packet was received. These bugs have been fixed in modern systems.

These are the most often used switches. Additional information on the `ping` command can be obtained in the `ping` man page by executing the `man ping` command.

Not all servers can answer echo requests. Some servers may have their firewall configured not to let ICMP traffic through. In this case, a ping request will produce no response, although the server is functioning normally and can accept other types of packets without any problems.

5.1.3. netstat

The netstat command displays all current connections to the server. The result of its execution looks similar to the following:

```
Active Internet connections (w/o servers)
Proto Recv-Q Send-Q Local Address     Foreign Address    State
tcp        0      0 FlenovM:ftp       192.168.77.10:3962 ESTABLISHED
tcp        0      0 FlenovM:ftp-data  192.168.77.10:3964 TIME_WAIT
```

All information is presented in columns. Consider each of them:

- ❐ Proto — The protocol used by the connection. Most often, this will be unix or tcp.
- ❐ Recv-Q — The number of bytes the user program has not copied.
- ❐ Send-Q — The number of bytes the remote computer did not receive.
- ❐ Local address — The address of the local computer in the computer:port format. The port can be specified by either its name or the numerical identifier. In the preceding example, the port in the first entry is specified as ftp, which corresponds to port 21.
- ❐ Foreign address — The address of the remote computer in the IP:port format.
- ❐ State — The state of the connection.

This command uses numerous parameters; their complete description can be viewed in the help file by executing the man netstat command.

If you suspect that your system has been penetrated, you can use this command to determine, which of the services were used to carry out the penetration and which resources the hackers may be using. For example, if the hackers entered through the FTP service, they are most likely working with files and may be uploading their files to expand their takeover of the system, modifying or deleting system files, or downloading files containing information of interest to them.

5.1.4. lsof

The lsof command is used to display open files. The command is quite powerful and uses various switches. One of its most interesting features is viewing of the open ports by executing the command with the -i switch:

```
lsof -i
```

More detailed information about this command can be found in its man page.

5.1.5. Telnet

The might of Linux and its text console consists of being able to execute commands not only directly at the terminal but also remotely. All you have to do for this is to connect to the Telnet server port with help of a Telnet client.

There are few utilities in Windows that can operate in the command line; therefore, this system requires, and widely uses, graphical mode. The command line in Windows offers rather limited capabilities. To solve this problem, a method of terminal access was created that makes it possible to see the contents of the server's display on the client's screen and work with them as if working directly at the server. But this method is traffic-intensive and is inconvenient over slow communications channels.

Compared with the graphical mode of any operating system, the Linux command line virtually does not use any traffic and can work reasonably well even over the slowest channels, such as cellular phone General Packet Radio Services (GPRS) or home modem connections, which have rather slow speeds.

As you by now understand, the Telnet software consists of the server and the client parts. When a Telnet server is started, port 23 is opened, to which a client computer can connect and execute any commands allowed by the Telnet server.

But that's not all: a Telnet client can be used to connect to other servers. For example, a connection can be made to port 25 and send email messages from the command line by executing Simple Mail Transfer Protocol (SMTP) server commands.

If you have an FTP server installed, you can execute the following command right now:

```
telnet localhost 21
```

In this case, you are connecting to the FTP server on the local computer, as is specified by the `localhost` parameter. To connect to the FTP server on a remote computer, you have to specify its address in place of the `localhost` parameter. The second parameter is the port that the server uses. The FTP server receives control commands on port 21, so this port was specified.

I recommend using a Telnet client only for configuring and debugging services but not for controlling the system. Thus, disable Telnet on all of the network's machines. The utility is not secure because it sends plaintext data, and all attempts to make Telnet secure have failed. One way to secure Telnet is to use it through an Open Secure Sockets Layer (OpenSSL) encrypted channel. But there is another popular method of controlling a server: using the Open Secure SHell (OpenSSH) protocol, which is considered in *Section 5.3*.

Thus, you need a Telnet client, but the Telnet server should be removed from the system.

If you do need to use a Telnet server for some reason, you should do this using a secure communications protocol employing public and private keys (see *Section 5.2*). Then the Telnet traffic will travel encrypted over the network; however, you will still have to undertake additional security measures.

If you have a Telnet server installed, try to connect to it by issuing the `telnet localhost` command. The system will respond with a message similar to the following:

```
Trying 127.0.0.1
Connected to localhost
```

```
Escape character is '^]'.

ASPLinux release 7.3 (Vostok)
Kernel 2.4.18-15asp on an i686
Login:
```

Do you notice anything dangerous in the information displayed? Myself, I see detailed information about the distributive and kernel versions. All this information becomes available to any user even before he or she registers in the system. If hackers see open port 23, they will not have to take pains of learning your operating system and kernel version; all they will have to do is to connect to Telnet to obtain this information.

Telnet being too talkative is the huge security hole that has to be plugged as soon as possible. The prompt messages displayed upon connecting are stored in the /etc/issue and /etc/issue.net files. You can change the prompt messages as follows:

```
echo Text > /etc/issue
echo Text > /etc/issue.net
```

Here `Text` is the text of the new prompt message. You can specify a wrong kernel version to confuse hackers:

```
echo Debian Linux > /etc/issue
echo Kernel 2.4.4 on an i686 > /etc/issue.net
```

So, whatever distribution and kernel version you may have installed, any hacker trying to connect to your computer over Telnet will think that you are using the 2.4.4 old Debian core.

The contents of the files, however, will be restored after the next reboot and Telnet will again show the distribution and core information in the welcome message. You can avoid this by setting the files' `-i` attribute, which prevents file modifications:

```
chattr +i /etc/issue
chattr +i /etc/issue.net
```

5.1.6. r Commands

There are so-called `r` commands in Linux: `rlogin`, `rsh`, `rcp`, `rsync`, and `rdist`. I will not consider them because they are obsolete and present a great security danger. These commands allow remote connection to the system and send their data in plaintext. Although you may need a Telnet client to test services, you have no need for these commands. I only mentioned them so that you will delete them from the system to avoid the temptation of using them yourself and to prevent hackers from exploiting them.

5.2. Encryption

In the early days of the Internet and first network protocols, nobody thought about the security aspects. This issue became important only when actual break-ins started happening. The two biggest oversights in the development of these technologies were allowing data to be sent in plaintext on the network and allowing network equipment to listen to all network traffic.

As was considered in *Chapter 1*, there are two ways to connect computers into a network using coaxial cable. In one, computers are connected to one common bus with the ends of the bus standing free (Fig. 5.2). The other method is just a variation of the first one with the two end computers connected to each other. In the case of the common bus, all computers are connected in series and a packet is placed on the common bus and is available to all computers. Which of the computers receives the packet is decided by its network adapter: It examines all the packets and accepts only those addressed to it for further processing.

All the network cards on the bus can see all packets placed onto it. If you really want to read other people's network traffic, you can find a sniffer program and monitor all data that pass through your network card even if they are not intended for you. Because most protocols process packets in plaintext, any hacker can monitor the network and discover confidential information traveling over it, including access passwords.

Coaxial cable as the choice of network medium is used seldom nowadays, because such connection is not reliable and its bandwidth is limited to 10 MB/sec. Also, the connection concept itself is inherently unreliable. The operation of the entire network may be disrupted if one of the computers fails. The ring topology partially solves the reliability problem, but it does not resolve other issues, such as the slow speed and difficulties constructing, servicing, and using such a network.

The star topology (Fig. 5.3) involves computers connected to one central device, a hub or a switch. The computers are connected using twisted pair wire. This arrangement is more reliable and supports 100-MB/sec bandwidth.

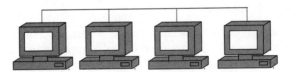

Fig. 5.2. The common-bus network topology

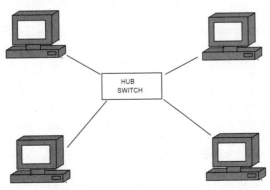

Fig. 5.3. The star network topology

If the central connection device is of the hub type (also known as a multiport repeater), all packets that it receives from one of the computers are simply resent to the rest of the network computers. Thus, any of the network's computers can read packets addressed to any other machine in the network.

If the central connecting device is of a switch type, the packets are delivered only to the recipient, because the switch has built-in routing capabilities. The latter are mostly implemented at the MAC address (also called the physical address) level. A MAC address is a 48-bit unique number assigned to the card by the manufacturer. It is unique because each manufacturer has its own MAC address range. Each computer in the network has a unique MAC address as well and is connected to a separate port on the switch. The switch sends each packet only to the computer, to which it is addressed; the network's other computers will not see this packet.

There also are switches that can handle packets on the IP address (logical address) level, the way it is done by routers. In this case, packets are forwarded based on logical and not physical addresses and a switch can connect entire networks.

But even when a network is connected using a switch, it is possible to eavesdrop on the traffic on the server. Nobody likes this state of affairs, especially when confidential data are involved.

It is unrealistic to redesign the existing protocols, because it is expensive and in some cases simply impossible. But another more convenient, universal solution has been offered: tunneling. Tunneling allows remote access programs from different developers to interact with each other. The technique also supports several authentication methods and data compression and encryption. In general, the tunneling concept can be described (using FTP as an example) as follows:

❑ A program to encrypt traffic is launched on a port, say Port 1, of the client computer. An FTP client connects to Port 1 on the local computer and sends data to this port instead of the remote computer. The encryption program encrypts the data and sends them over the network.

❑ At the remote computer, the same encryption program is started at a certain port. It receives the encrypted data, decodes them, and forwards them in plaintext to the FTP server port.

Fig. 5.4 shows the data encryption process. Thus, all packets are sent via a middleman that encodes them. Currently, the most widely-used encryption protocol is the Secure Sockets Layer (SSL) protocol. It has earned a reputation as a reliable data-exchange tool and has been used to protect Internet transactions. For example, a secure encrypted connection is used when a buying transaction is carried out through an Internet store to protect the credit card information. When the browser connects to the server, the former automatically launches the encryption program on the client computer, via which the server sends and receives encrypted data.

Thus, encryption does not change TCP/IP; data are simply encrypted and decrypted on both the server's and the client's sides. This method is convenient because it can be used to encrypt data sent using any protocol. Should the encryption program have to be modified, for example, to fix a bug or to use a longer key, the protocol will not have to be modified.

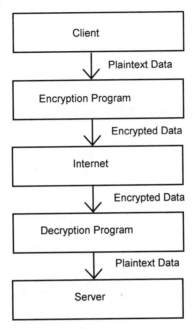

Fig. 5.4. Channel encryption

Fig. 5.5. A secure connection indication in Internet Explorer

Consider an example with the Web service, which works on port 80. The encryption program can be started on the server on port 1080, decrypting all data that passes through the server and passing them to port 80. If you only want to allow access to the Web over the SSL protocol, port 80 can be blocked by a firewall (considered in *Chapter 4*) and allow connections only from the encryption server.

Addresses of sites protected with special keys are prefixed by **https://**. The difference from the regular sites is the "s" letter, which means that the connection is secure. Moreover, when connecting using a browser with SSL enabled, the secure connection is indicated by an icon in the status panel in the lower right part of the browser window. In the popular Internet Explorer browser, this is an icon of a padlock (Fig. 5.5).

But even in Internet Explorer, this icon does not always appear when a secure connection is established. The type of the connection can be determined more precisely by examining the page's properties. Most browsers have a command to view the properties of the loaded page, among which is the encryption used. In Internet Explorer, page properties can be viewed by executing the **File/Properties** menu sequence. This will open a dialog window similar to the one shown in Fig. 5.6. The information about the connection is shown in the **Connection** field. In this case, it shows that the 128-bit encoding SSL 3.0 RC4 protocol is being used.

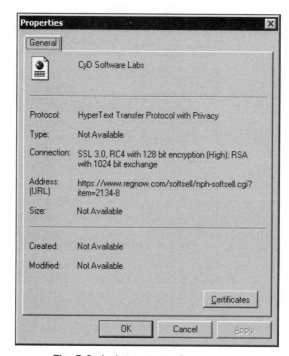

Fig. 5.6. An Internet page's properties

5.2.1. stunnel

The program used most often in Linux for encrypting and decrypting network traffic is stunnel. The program itself only organizes the channel and serves as a middleman. The encryption is performed by the OpenSSL packet, which is included in most Linux distributions. If you don't already have it installed, you can do so by installing the corresponding RPM packet from the installation disc. More detailed information about OpenSSL, as well as the latest updates, can be found on the **www.openssl.org** site.

The OpenSSL operation principle is based on using two keys: public and private. The public key can only be used to encrypt data; the private key is required to decrypt it.

OpenSSL and the stunnel program have lots of parameters, and I will not consider all of them. What I will do is to consider a real-life example and teach you the most often used arguments.

Start the `stunnel` program on the server to decrypt the incoming traffic and forward it to some port, for example, port 25 (used by the sendmail SMTP server). This is done by executing the following command:

```
stunnel -p /usr/share/ssl/cert.pem -d 9002 -r 25
```

In this case, the program was started with the following three parameters:

- ☐ `-p` — After this key, the default SSL authorization certificate is specified. It is created when the operating system or the `stunnel` program was installed and is stored in the /usr/share/ssl/cert/pem file.
- ☐ `-d` — This option specifies that the tunnel is to work as a daemon. The switch is followed by an optional IP address and the port, on which to expect the connection. If the address is not specified, all interfaces of the local computer will be monitored. The port was specified as port 9002. All data coming to it are considered encrypted and will be decrypted for forwarding to another port of the local computer.
- ☐ `-r` — This key is followed by an optional computer name and the port, to which the decrypted data are to be forwarded. If the host is not specified, the data will be forwarded to the local computer's port, on which the SMTP server is supposed to work, which in this case is port 25. If the data are intended for another computer, specify this parameter as `192.169.77.1:25`; here `192.169.77.1` is the IP address of the computer, and `25` is the port number.

Things are much easier with the client. It is launched by the following command:

```
stunnel -c -d 1000 -r 192.168.77.1:9002
```

The `-c` switch means that the tunnel is established for a client. By default, the `stunnel` program launches in the server mode.

The remaining switches are the same as for the server. The `-d` switch indicates the port, on which the connection is expected, 1000 in this case; the `-r` switch is followed by the computer and port, to which the encrypted data are to be sent.

The client program has to be configured to send mail to the port, on which the `stunnel` client is running (port 1000 in this case). The latter will encrypt the data and forward them to port 9002 of the 192.168.77.1 computer. The data on the destination computer are received by the `stunnel` server, which decrypts and then forwards them to the server's port 25.

5.2.2. Supplementary OpenSSL Features

The `stunnel` program was launched on the server with the use of an authorization certificate specified. But how can the authenticity of the certificate be ascertained? The control levels are specified by the `-v` option followed by a number indicating the control level. These are the following:

- ☐ 0 — No check is performed.
- ☐ 1 — If a certificate is present, it is checked for being genuine. A negative result causes the connection to be broken. A certificate is not necessary to establish a connection; it can be established without one.

❏   2 — A certificate must be used at this level. If there is no certificate or if it is invalid, a connection cannot be established.

❏   3 — The use of a certificate is mandatory; moreover, it must be in local storage (on a special list). In this case, the directory, in which certificates are stored, must be specified using the –a option.

An SSL server can decrypt traffic and forward it to the port of the receiving program of not just the local computer but also another remote computer. Thus, the SSL server and the server of the traffic receiver can be located on two different computers. It is desirable that, after decrypting data, the server hide the source client's IP address. This can be done by specifying the –T option.

When the OpenSSL package is installed, certificates and key pairs to be used for encryption are created on the disk in the /usr/share/ssl/ directory.

The protocol to be used can be directly specified using the –n option. The following protocols are currently supported: POP3, SMTP, and network news transfer protocol (NNTP).

For most protocols, there are port numbers that have become standard. There are even names of secure protocols, which are usually obtained by adding an "s" letter to the name of the main protocol. This letter signifies the secure SSL connection. The relevant information is shown in Table 5.1.

Table 5.1. Protocols and the corresponding ports

Protocol	SSL version	TCP port number
HTTP	HTTPS	443
SMTP	SMTPS	465
LDAP	LDAPS	636
TELNET	TELNETS	992
SHELL	SSHELL	614
FTP	FTPS	990
FTP-DATA	FTPS-DATA	989
IMAP	IMAPS	993
POP3	POP3S	995
IRC	IRCS	994

Note that two protected channels are required for FTP. One is used for the control connection, and the other to transmit data. I will return to this in *Chapter 10*, where this protocol is considered.

5.2.3. File Encryption

Some servers are used for storing archive data — access to which, nevertheless, has to be restricted to authorized people only. The best way to protect this information is to encrypt the files. This can be done using the OpenSSL packet.

Not only backup or archive files may have to be encrypted but also confidential information files that are sent over insecure communications channels, for example, through email or a public FTP server.

A file is encoded by executing the /usr/bin/openssl comand as follows:

```
/usr/bin/openssl algorithm -in file1 -out file2
```

There are dozens of encryption algorithms that can be used. The most commonly-used is the Data Encryption Standard (DES) algorithm. You can learn, which algorithms are supported at the OpenSSL site or from the openssl man page.

The -in parameter specifies the input file to be encrypted; the -out parameter specifies the file, into which the encryption results are stored.

A file is decoded by the same command, but with the -d option added. The -in argument specifies the file to be decoded, and the -out argument specifies the file, into which the results of the decoding are to be placed:

```
/usr/bin/openssl algorithm -d -in file2 -out file1
```

Try using the OpenSSL program by encoding the /etc/passwd file. The file is encoded with the DES algorithm, and the results are saved in the /home/passwd file. This is done by executing the following command:

```
/usr/bin/openssl des -in /etc/passwd -out /home/passwd
```

The program will ask you to enter a password and then confirm it to prevent potential entry errors.

Now, verify that the contents of the encoded file are unreadable by executing the cat /home/passwd command.

Decode the encoded file by executing the following command:

```
/usr/bin/openssl des -d -in /home/passwd -out /etc/passwd
```

Encoded in this simple way, a copy of the password file can be safely stored.

5.2.4. Tunneling as Hackers See It

Hackers can use tunneling to achieve their own ends. For example, recently I connected to the Internet using the Asymmetric Digital Subscriber Line (ADSL). The monthly fee covers only 400 MB of the traffic. But for me 400 MB is a pittance. It is barely enough for a week's work in the economy mode because of my numerous contacts. Sometimes I download up to 20 MB a day from my mailbox. The fee for megabytes over the 400 MB monthly limit is rather expensive.

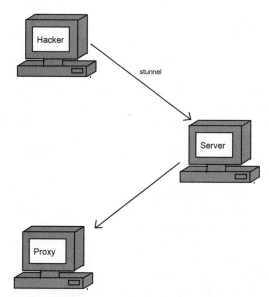

Fig. 5.7. Connecting to the Internet via a Web server

So I had to come up with a solution to circumvent the limitation and to obtain access to unlimited traffic. Like most providers, my provider allows unlimited free traffic from its own servers. Although there is little of use on those servers, this can be fixed easily.

My monthly fee also covers 10 MB of server disk space for a personal Web page. Another home page is not what I am interested in, but the unlimited traffic to and from it is.

By installing a tunneling program on the server, a connection can be organized as shown in Fig. 5.7.

The hacker uses the `stunnel` program to connect to the free Web server located on the provider's machine. From the Web server the traffic is forwarded to some proxy server on the Internet or directly to Web sites. This does not cost any money, because the two-way communication with the Web server is free.

In this way, more than 400 MB can be downloaded, all for free. There should be, however, at least some sort of a Web page placed on the Web server; otherwise, the administrator will notice right away that there is lots of traffic going to the empty Web page and will be able to figure out the tunnel.

Another nonstandard use of tunneling is expanding network access capabilities. For example, some local network may prohibit certain Internet access protocol. In my life, I have worked for companies that allowed access to Web sites only over HTTP. All other protocols were prohibited. The management justified this policy by arguing that users should not be able to send files to the Internet.

Is it possible to circumvent this limitation? Again, place a tunnel on the Web server and you can use any other protocol by hiding all traffic within HTTP. The tunnel then forwards the traffic to the necessary ports under the necessary protocol.

Suppose you need FTP access. Install a tunnel server on port 80 of some Internet server. Access to the Internet server is allowed because a Web service is supposed to be here. Configure the client to connect to the desired FTP server. On your machine, install a client to connect to port 80 of the server. The data that you now transmit will be forwarded to the desired FTP server.

Tunnels of this type do not require encoding and can be implemented with simple programs, for example, Perl scripts. Packets do not necessarily have to be sent using HTTP. Practically any TCP-based protocol will do. You can even hide the necessary protocol in DNS or ICMP packets if these are allowed in your network. Although ICMP can be blocked, it is practically impossible to block DNS, because it is difficult to work in the Internet without it.

As you can see, technology that appears innocent at first glance, which is even intended for providing network security, turns into a break-in tool for the limitations imposed on you by the administrator.

If you are good at PHP or Perl programming, you can write a Web script to access the resources you need on the server. Communicating with the necessary server using the Web browser is like working with mail through the Web interface. Most mail services have this capability and most likely many of you have used it.

5.3. SHH Protocol

It was already mentioned that the Telnet protocol is not very suitable for controlling a remote server because it is far from secure. There is considerable need and an even greater wish to control servers remotely. There are several servers in large networks, and it is inconvenient to scurry about the monitors to configure each of them. Any administrator wants to be able to control the entire network complex without leaving the workplace and to do this over secure channels.

During server management sessions, the administrator sends voluminous confidential information onto the networks (e.g., root passwords) that should under no circumstances be intercepted by eavesdropping utilities. There are numerous programs for providing secure communications. The most popular of them is SSH, which is included in most Linux distributions.

Using this utility, you can administer your network servers remotely from one workplace without having to equip each of them with a monitor and to run to each server every time you have to implement a minor configuration change. This is how I administer my network: from one monitor that I can connect to any system block if the problem cannot be solved over the network.

The advantage of SSH is that this protocol allows commands to be executed remotely but requires authentication and encrypts the communications channel. An important feature is that even user authentication passwords are transmitted encrypted.

Presently, there are two versions of the SSH protocol, numbered 1 and 2. The second version employs a stronger encoding algorithm and fixes some of the bugs found in the first version. At present, Linux supports both versions.

In Linux, the SSH protocol is handled by the OpenSSH program. The native platform of this program is another UNIX-like operating system: OpenBSD, from which it has been cloned to all other UNIX platforms, including Linux. But even now the OpenBSD name can be encountered sometimes in configuration files.

The SSH protocol requires a server and a client for operation. The server waits for connection and executes user commands. The client is used to connect to the server and to send it commands to execute. Thus, both parts of the protocol have to be properly configured for normal operation.

5.3.1. Configuration Files

All configuration files for the SSH protocol are located in the /etc/ssh/ directory. These are the following:

- ❑ The SSH server configuration file: sshd_config
- ❑ The SSH client configuration file: ssh_config
- ❑ The key files for different algorithms:
  - • ssh_host_dsa_key
  - • ssh_host_dsa_key.pub
  - • ssh_host_key
  - • ssh_host_key.pub
  - • ssh_host_rsa_key
  - • ssh_host_rsa_key.pub

What is the reason for so many key files? It is that SSH uses different encoding algorithms, including the two most popular and secure ones: the Digital Signature Algorithm (DSA) and RSA. (The latter abbreviation is composed of the first letters of the last names of its creators: R.L. Rivest, A. Shamir, and L.M. Adleman.) The ssh_host_dsa_key and ssh_host_dsa_key.pub files are used by DSA, and the ssh_host_rsa_key and ssh_host_rsa_key.pub files are used by the RSA algorithm. The remaining two key files — ssh_host_key and ssh_host_key.pub — store the keys to the first SSH version. Each algorithm requires two files: The file with the PUB extension stores the public key, and the file without this extension stores the private key.

Data to be sent to the server are encrypted using the public key. They can only be decrypted with the help of the private key. The private key cannot be picked by any known algorithms within a reasonable length of time. It can, however, be stolen; thus, you should take all necessary measures to prevent this from happening.

5.3.2. SSH Server Main Configuration Parameters

Consider the contents of the SSH server (sshd) configuration file (Listing 5.1). The sshd file is not large, so its entire contents are listed with only some comments deleted.

Listing 5.1. The sshd configuration file

```
#Port 22
#Protocol 2,1
#ListenAddress 0.0.0.0
#ListenAddress ::

# HostKey for protocol version 1
#HostKey /etc/ssh/ssh_host_key
# HostKeys for protocol version 2
#HostKey /etc/ssh/ssh_host_rsa_key
#HostKey /etc/ssh/ssh_host_dsa_key

# Lifetime and size of ephemeral version 1 server key
#KeyRegenerationInterval 3600
#ServerKeyBits 768

# Logging
#obsoletes QuietMode and FascistLogging
#SyslogFacility AUTH
#SyslogFacility AUTHPRIV
#LogLevel INFO

# Authentication:

#LoginGraceTime 600
#PermitRootLogin yes
#StrictModes yes

#RSAAuthentication yes
#PubkeyAuthentication yes
#AuthorizedKeysFile        .ssh/authorized_keys

# Rhosts authentication should not be used.
#RhostsAuthentication no
# Don't read the user's ~/.rhosts and ~/.shosts files.
#IgnoreRhosts yes
# For this to work, you will also need host keys
# in /etc/ssh/ssh_known_hosts.
#RhostsRSAAuthentication no
# Similar for protocol version 2
#HostbasedAuthentication no
# Change to yes if you don't trust ~/.ssh/known_hosts for
```

```
# RhostsRSAAuthentication and HostbasedAuthentication.
#IgnoreUserKnownHosts no

# To disable tunneled clear text passwords, change to
# no here!
#PasswordAuthentication yes
#PermitEmptyPasswords no

# Change to no to disable s/key passwords.
#ChallengeResponseAuthentication yes

# Kerberos options
# KerberosAuthentication automatically enabled if
# the key file exists.
#KerberosAuthentication yes
#KerberosOrLocalPasswd yes
#KerberosTicketCleanup yes

# AFSTokenPassing automatically enabled if k_hasafs()
# is true.
#AFSTokenPassing yes

# Kerberos TGT passing only works with the AFS kaserver.
#KerberosTgtPassing no

#PAMAuthenticationViaKbdInt yes

#X11Forwarding no
#X11Forwarding yes
#X11DisplayOffset 10
#X11UseLocalhost yes
#PrintMotd yes
#PrintLastLog yes
#KeepAlive yes
#UseLogin no

#MaxStartups 10
# No default banner path
#Banner /some/path
#VerifyReverseMapping no

# Override default of no subsystems.
Subsystem       sftp      /usr/libexec/openssh/sftp-server
```

The main parameters that you may have to use are the following:

- ❐   Port — Shows the port, to which to connect on the remote machine. By default, this is port 22. Some administrators like to change this value and to move the server to another port. This action is justified to an extent. For example, if you do not have a Web server, the port normally used by it can be given to SSH. Hackers will think that this is a Web server and will not try to break into it.

- ❐   Protocol — Gives the protocol versions supported. Note that first version 2 is specified, and then version 1. This means that the server will first try to connect over the version 2 protocol and only then over the version 1 protocol. I recommend removing the comments from this line and deleting the 1 number so that only the last protocol version is used. It's high time we updated the client software and started using more secure technologies. Getting stuck on old software only causes losses.

- ❐   ListenAddress — Specifies the addresses to listen for a connection. Your server may be equipped with several network adapters. By default, all of these interfaces are monitored. You should specify only those interfaces that will be used for the SSH connection. For example, often one network adapter is used to connect to a local network, and another one is used to connect to the Internet. If the SSH protocol is used to connect only within the local network, only this adapter should be monitored. It is specified in the address:port format. Several address entries can be made to describe all necessary interfaces.

- ❐   HostKey — Specifies the path to the files containing the encoding key. Only private keys need to be specified, used to decrypt incoming packets.

- ❐   KeyRegenerationInterval — The key can be regenerated during the session in version 1. The purpose of regeneration is to make it impossible to decrypt intercepted packets by later stealing the keys from the machine. Setting this value to 0 disables regeneration. If you followed my recommendation not to use the version 1 protocol (see the Protocol parameter), this parameter does not affect the operation.

- ❐   ServerKeyBits — Gives the length of the server key. The default value is 768; the minimal value is 512.

- ❐   SyslogFacility — Specifies the types of messages to be stored in the system log.

- ❐   LogLevel — Specifies the level of the event to be logged. The possible levels correspond to the system levels, which are considered in *Section 12.5.6.*

- ❐   LoginGraceTime — Gives the time interval, within which the user has to enter the correct password before the connection is broken.

- ❐   PermitRootLogin — Specifies whether the root user can log in using SSH. It was already said that root is the god in the system and its account's privileges must be used with care. If it is not advisable to log in as root regularly, this is all the more so using SSH. Change this parameter to no at once.

- ❐   StrictModes — Specifies whether sshd should check the status of the files and their owners, user files, and home directory before accepting the login. It is desirable to set this parameter to yes because many novice users make their files accessible for writing to everyone.

❑ RSAAuthentication — Specifies whether RSA authentication is permitted. This option is valid for protocol version 1 only.

❑ PubkeyAuthentication — Specifies whether public key authentication is allowed. This option is valid for protocol version 2 only.

❑ AuthorizedKeysFile — Specifies the file storing the public key that can be used for user authentication.

❑ RhostsAuthentication — Allows authentication using the $home/.rhosts and /etc/hosts.equiv files. The default value is no. It should not be changed without a justified need, because this may have a negative effect on the security.

❑ IgnoreRhosts — When set to yes, the ~/.rhosts and ~/.shosts cannot be read. The value should not be changed unless really necessary, because doing so may have a negative effect on the security.

❑ AuthorizedKeysFile — Specifies the file for storing the list of the authorized keys. If a user logs into the system with a key stored in this file, no further authentication is performed.

❑ RhostsRSAAuthentication — When this parameter is set to yes, a host key from the /etc/ssh/ssh_known_hosts directory will be requested. The parameter is used in protocol version 1 only.

❑ IgnoreUserKnownHosts — When the parameter is set to no, computers listed in ~/.ssh/known_hosts should be trusted during RhostsRSAAuthentication. Because you should not trust anyone, it is better to set this parameter to yes.

❑ PasswordAuthentication — When set to yes, a password will be requested. When authentication is performed using keys, the parameter can be set to no.

❑ PermitEmptyPasswords — Specifies whether empty passwords can be used. The default value is no, and it ought not to be changed.

❑ KerberosAuthentication — Specifies whether Kerberos authentication of the user password should be performed. This authentication has been gaining popularity lately because of the security it provides.

❑ KerberosOrLocalPasswd — When set, if the Kerberos password authentication failed, the password is validated using the /etc/shadow file mechanism.

❑ KerberosTicketCleanup — When set, the user's Kerberos ticket cache file is destroyed on logout.

❑ Banner — Specifies whether a warning message is displayed before the login procedure.

5.3.3. The sshd Server Access Parameters

In addition to those listed in Listing 5.1, the following keywords can be used in the sshd configuration file:

❑ AllowGroups — Allows only the users of the specified groups to log into the system. The user group names are listed after the keyword, separated by spaces.

❑ AllowUsers — Allows only the users listed after the key to enter the system. The user names are listed separated by spaces.

❑   DenyGroups — Denies login to users of the specified groups. The user group names are listed after the keyword, separated by spaces.

❑   AllowUsers — Denies login to users listed after the key. The user names are listed separated by spaces. This parameter comes in handy when a user of a permitted group has to be denied login.

I recommend specifying the names of the groups and users that can log into the system over SSH explicitly.

5.3.4. Configuring the SSH Client

The SSH client configuration settings contain even fewer parameters. The global settings for all of the system's users are stored in the /etc/ssh/ssh_config file. But any settings for any user can be redefined in the .ssh_config file in the particular user's directory. The contents of the global configurations file (with some comments omitted) are shown in Listing 5.2.

Listing 5.2. The contents of the /etc/ssh/ssh_config configuration file

---

```
# Site-wide defaults for various options

# Host *
#    ForwardAgent no
#    ForwardX11 no
#    RhostsAuthentication yes
#    RhostsRSAAuthentication yes
#    RSAAuthentication yes
#    PasswordAuthentication yes
#    FallBackToRsh no
#    UseRsh no
#    BatchMode no
#    CheckHostIP yes
#    StrictHostKeyChecking ask
#    IdentityFile ~/.ssh/identity
#    IdentityFile ~/.ssh/id_rsa
#    IdentityFile ~/.ssh/id_dsa
#    Port 22
#    Protocol 2, 1
#    Cipher 3des
#    Ciphers aes128-cbc, 3des-cbc, blowfish-cbc, cast128-cbc,arcfour,
#    aes192-cbc, aes256-cbc
#    EscapeChar ~
Host *
Protocol 1, 2
```

Some of the parameters in this file are the same as in the server configuration file. One of these is the `Protocol` parameter, which specifies the SSH version being used. But in the case of the client, the version 1 protocol should not be disabled. This will not affect the security of the client but will help you avoid problems when connecting to a server that supports only this protocol.

The following are the most common client parameters:

- `Host` — Specifies, to which server the following declarations are to apply.
- `CheckHostIP` — If this parameter is set to `yes`, the IP address will be checked in the known_hosts file.
- `Compression` — Enables (`yes`) or disables (`no`) data compression.
- `KerberosAuthentication` — Enables (`yes`) or disables (`no`) Kerberos authentication.
- `NumberOfPasswordPrompts` — Specifies the number of password entry attempts. If no correct password is entered, the connection is broken.
- `IdentityFile` — Specifies the name of the file containing the private user keys.
- `PasswordAutentication` — Specifies authentication by the password.

5.3.5. Examples of Using the SSH Client

Consider how to connect to a remote server. This is done by executing the following command:

```
ssh user@server
```

For example, to connect to the server flenovm as the user flenov, the following command has to be executed:

```
ssh flenov@flenovm
```

This will be answered by the following message:

```
The authenticity of host 'localhost(127.0.0.1)' can't be established
RSA1 key fingerprint is f2:a1:6b:d6:fc:d0:f2:a1:6b:d6:fc:d0.
Are you sure you want to continue connection (yes/no)?
```

The program informs you that the authenticity of the host `localhost` cannot be established and displays a fingerprint of the RSA key. To continue establishing the connection, enter `yes` from the keyboard. The following message will be displayed:

```
Permanently added 'localhost' (RSA1) to the list of known hosts.
```

This message informs you that the key has been added to the list of the known hosts. This means that the known_hosts file containing the remote system's key was created (or updated) in the .ssh/ subdirectory of your home directory.

The program then prompts you to enter the user's password. If the authentication succeeds, you will be connected to the remote system and will be able to execute commands there as if entering them from its keyboard.

5.3.6. Authentication by Key

Authentication by key is more convenient and more secure than authentication by password. The latter can even be disabled. Accessing the system over SSH is not quite safe. The password can be intercepted when being entered in another program. What is the use, then, of encrypting the SSH connection, if the password can be found when working with other programs?

This can be prevented by using different passwords for each connection. But it is difficult to remember all of the passwords, so it is better to perform authentication by keys, which are protected exceedingly well. All you have to do for this is modify the configuration slightly.

Start by creating a new key. This is done with the help of the ssh-keygen program. It has to be passed the following two parameters:

❐ -t — The key type. This can be rsa or dsa for the second SSH version, or rsa1 for the first version. The rsa key will be used in the example.

❐ -f — The file, in which the private key is to be stored. The open key file will be named the same, but with the PUB extension.

❐ -b — The key length, which should be 512 minimum. The default value is 1024, which you should leave in place.

The key is generated by executing the following command:

```
ssh-keygen -t rsa -f ~/.ssh/myrsakey
```

Note that I specified the place to store the key as the .ssh subdirectory of my home directory, as indicated by the ~ character. SSH will look for all configuration settings in this directory. If you have not connected to the server yet, this path and key do not exist. The situation is corrected by opening the user's home directory and creating the .ssh directory:

```
cd /home/flenov
mkdir .ssh
```

If the file, in which to store the key, is not specified when the key is generated, by default an RSA key file, named id_rsa, will created in the ~/.ssh/ directory. The key file for DSA encoding will be stored in the same directory but will be named id-dsa. I specified the key file name on purpose to show how to do this.

If you did everything right, the program should display the following message:

```
Generating public/private rsa key pair.
Enter passphrase (empty for no passphrase):
```

I recommend specifying a password at least 10 characters long or, even better, a passphrase. The password is submitted by pressing the <Enter> key, after which the program asks you to confirm the password.

If the password confirmation is successful, the following messages are displayed:

```
Your identification has been saved in ~/ssh/myrsakey.
Your public key has been saved in ~/ssh/myrsakey.pub.
```

The first message informs you that the private key has been saved in the ~/ssh/myrsakey file. The public key is saved in the ~/ssh/myrsakey.pub file.

The ~/ssh/myrsakey.pub key file has to be sent to the remote computer for the SSH server to use it for the authentication. The file can be sent over open communication channels, because even if it is intercepted by nefarious individuals, it is useless without the password you entered when the keys were created and without the private key.

The administrator of the remote server has to add the contents of the public key file to the .ssh/authorized_keys file. This can be done by executing the following command:

```
cat myrsakey.pub .ssh/authorized_keys
```

You can now connect to the server using the public key instead of a password to authenticate your identity. But before you do this, make sure that the server configuration file contains the following directives:

```
RSAAuthentication yes
PubkeyAuthentication yes
```

To connect to the server, execute the following command:

```
ssh -i ~/.ssh/myrsakey
```

The -i parameter specifies the public key file. If this parameter is not used, the id_rsa file will be used by default; it is specified in IdentityFile in the SSH client configuration file.

Now the server will ask you not for the password but for the passphrase specified when generating the public key.

```
Enter passphrase for key
```

Setting the PasswordAuthentication parameter in the SSH server configuration file to no dispenses with password checking, and the authentication will be performed based on the keys only. This is sufficient to provide secure communications.

5.3.7. Running X11 in the Terminal

Using the command line to control the remote system allows traffic to be reduced significantly. But sometimes it is necessary to use the graphical mode. I personally do not recommend using the graphical mode for purposes of security and efficiency, but many Windows users simply cannot accept the command line as the only interface. So if you are one of them, the SSH server can redirect X11 (the Linux graphical shell) to your local terminal. For this, the following three directives have to be specified in the sshd_config file:

❐ X11Forwarding yes — Self-explanatory.
❐ X11DisplayOffset 10 — The first display number available to the SSH server. The default value is 10, and there is no reason to change it.
❐ X11UseLocalhost yes — If this parameter is set to yes, the local X server will be used. In this case, the client will work with the local X11 and the service information sent over the network will be encrypted.

If you want to connect to the Linux graphical shell from Windows, you will need a program like X11 for this operating system. I can recommend the X-Win32 client for this, which can be downloaded from this site: **www.starnet.com**.

I do not recommend using X11, because this technology is still in the development stage and there are methods to fake or break into the connection.

5.3.8. Secure Data Transfer

The SSH packet also includes two useful utilities: the sftp server (an FTP server that supports data encryption) and the sftp client (an FTP client to connect to the sftp server). Examine the last line of the SSH server /ect/ssh/sshd_config configuration file:

```
Subsystem       sftp     /usr/libexec/openssh/sftp-server
```

The `Subsystem` directive defines supplementary services. It launches the OpenSSH sftp server.

Working with the sftp client is no different from working with the SSH client. Execute the `sftp localhost` command; the login message, the same as considered in *Section 5.3.5*, will appear. Enter the correct password and you will be taken to the ftp client command line, from which you can send and receive files using FTP commands. This protocol is considered in detail in *Chapter 10*; for now, you only need to know that most of its commands are similar to the Linux file handling commands.

Try to connect to your system through an ftp client. After logging in, you can try executing the `ls` or `cd` commands to verify that the connection is working. To quit sftp, execute the `exit` command. The main FTP commands are listed in *Appendix 1*.

If you have to upload to or download from the server confidential information (for example, accounting files or the password file), you should do this over a secure sftp connection. Regular FTP clients transfer files in plaintext; consequently, anyone can monitor the traffic and obtain information that can be used to compromise your server.

You should keep it in mind, however, that not all FTP servers and clients support SSH encoding. You should ascertain that your software supports this protocol before using it.

5.4. The inetd/xinetd Daemon

To process requests from clients, the server has to be permanently loaded into the memory and connected to a certain port. There is nothing difficult about this, but keeping the program loaded in the memory all the time is not efficient use of the memory resources, especially if the program is large and its services are seldom required. In such a case, it is better to have one service monitoring ports and launching the necessary service when it detects access to a certain port. Linux implements this capability in the older `inetd` and the newer `xinetd` daemons.

How do these daemons decide which service to start? They employ the /etc/services file for this. The file contains a list of services and the associated ports in the following format:

```
name port/protocol  alias
```

- ❑ `Name` — The name of the service to run.
- ❑ `Port` — The port number to monitor.
- ❑ `Protocol` — The `inetd` service can work with TCP and UDP, whose ports do not intersect (and are totally different); thus, the protocol to work with has to be specified explicitly.
- ❑ `Alias` — A name that can be given to the service.

For example, there are following lines in the /etc/services file:

```
tcpmux        1/tcp        # TCP port service multiplexer
tcpmux        1/udp        # TCP port service multiplexer
rje           5/tcp        # Remote Job Entry
rje           5/udp        # Remote Job Entry
echo          7/tcp
...
...
ftp           21/tcp
ftp           21/udp                fsp fspd
...
...
```

I selected these entries on purpose to show your how various services are described.

If you have an old Linux distribution, it most likely still uses `inetd`. As was already mentioned, this old version is a potential security problem. You should update to `xinetd`, which is becoming, if it has not already become, the standard.

I recommend switching to `xinetd` because it contains many additional features that make administration more convenient and the service more secure. For example, it has functions built in to check all successful and unsuccessful connections, to control access, and to only allow access at strictly defined times.

5.4.1. Configuring xinetd

The /etc/xinetd.conf file is the main configuration file for the `xinetd` daemon. The file contains default configuration settings for the services to be launched and the directory, in which the configuration files for specific services are to be stored. The contents of the file are shown in Listing 5.3.

Listing 5.3. The /etc/xinetd.conf configuration file

```
#
# Simple configuration file for xinetd
#
# Some defaults, and include /etc/xinetd.d/
```

```
defaults
{
        instances               = 60
        log_type                = SYSLOG authpriv
        log_on_success          = HOST PID
        log_on_failure          = HOST
        cps                     = 25 30
}

includedir /etc/xinetd.d
```

The `defaults` keyword is followed by the default settings for all services. Any of these values can be changed for each individual service.

The last entry specifies the /etc/xinet.d directory:

```
includedir /etc/xinetd.d
```

This catalog contains configuration files for each service. The files are named after the corresponding services; their contents are similar to the contents of the /etc.xinetd.conf file. Listing 5.4 shows the contents of the /etc/xinet.d/telnet configuration file for the Telnet service.

Listing 5.4. The Telnet service configuration file

```
# default: on
# description: The telnet server services telnet sessions;
# it uses unencrypted username/password
# pairs for authentication.
service telnet
{
        disable            = no
        flags              = REUSE
        socket_type        = stream
        wait               = no
        user               = root
        server             = /usr/sbin/in.telnetd
        log_on_failure     += USERID
}
```

The following are the main parameters that can be edited:

❑   `disable` — If set to `true`, this disables the service.

❑   `flags` — Attributes for the service's execution.

❑   `socket_type` — The type of the socket used. Should be `stream` for TCP, and `dgram` for UDP.

❑   `protocol` — The protocol used to transfer data (TCP or UDP).

❑   `server` — The full path to the daemon's executable program.

❑   `user` — Access rights. In most cases, the value of this parameter will be `root`. This is a normal situation, because the root rights are required for working with ports below 1024. Currently, most services lower their rights according to the settings.

❑   `instances` — The maximum number of program instances that can run simultaneously.

❑   `log_type` — Events to be logged in the specified file or system log.

❑   `log_on_success` and `log_on_failure` — Information to be logged upon a successful or an unsuccessful system login, respectively. The following three values can be used: `PID`, `HOST`, or `USER`.

❑   `per_source` — The maximum number of connections per user. A single user can create several connections, because users like to squeeze everything they can out of the channel by creating several connections working in parallel.

❑   `server_args` — The arguments, with which the server is to be launched.

In connection with the `user` parameter, I stated that the root rights are necessary to be able to work with ports below 1024. What is the reason for this restriction? Unless a user has the root rights, he or she will not be able to launch a service that works with a port in the 1 to 1024 port number range. This protection is necessary because ports in this range are used by important services that regular users are not allowed to run.

Just imagine that hackers who only manage to obtain user rights are able to run the FTP server. This will allow them to upload to and download from the server any files that they desire, which will not make you happy.

5.4.2. Security

You already know that the rights and time to access services using the `xinetd` program can be restricted. This can be done using the `no_access`, `only_from`, and `access_time` commands in the configuration file.

The `no_access` command prohibits access from the specified computers. For example, the following entry in the configuration file prohibits access from the 192.168.1.1 address:

```
no_access 192.168.1.1
```

To prohibit access from an entire network, only its address has to be specified. For example, to prohibit access to all computers in the 192.168.1.x network, the following entry is added:

```
no_access 192.168.1
```

Note that in this case the IP address consists not of four octets, as usual, but only of three.

To prohibit access completely, the following line has to be added to the configuration file:

```
no_access 0.0.0.0
```

Now consider how access can be allowed using the `only_from` command. This command is handy because it can be used to prohibit access from any address and then allow it only from a specified address. Access from any address is prohibited by issuing the command without an argument, as follows:

```
only_from =
```

I recommend including this line in the main configuration file /etc/xinetd.conf and then specifying permitted addresses for each service in its configuration file. For example, to allow access from the addresses 192.168.1.2 and 192.168.1.19, the following entry is added to the configuration file:

```
only_from = 192.168.1.2 192.168.1.19
```

A network is allowed access by the following entry:

```
only_from = 192.168.1.
```

To allow access to all of the network but not to one computer in it, the following two entries can be used:

```
no_access = 192.168.1.1
only_from = 192.168.1.
```

The priority of the prohibition command is higher than that of the permission command, so even though the entire network is allowed access, the 192.168.1.1 computer from this network will not be able to connect.

Next, consider how the access time can be specified. It is logical to allow access to a server working in a company office only during work hours. For example, the following entry allows access only from 8:00 to 18:00:

```
access_time = 8:00 -18:00
```

I, however, would recommend increasing the second value to 19:00, because employees often stay after work and I personally do not like to be pestered about the access rights every day.

The xinetd built-in security functions are quite convenient and powerful, even though they double the access rights that can be configured in the /etc/hosts.allow and /etc/hosts.deny files. I prefer configuring security settings using the xinetd configuration files because the access parameters here are stored in the files of those services that they affect.

5.4.3. Shortcomings of xinetd

Any technology has its shortcoming, and inetd/xinetd is not an exception. When a user connects to one of the ports of your server, the xinetd program parses the port table to locate the service that has to be launched. The process of the looking up the service and its launching may take a little while. But this is not the worst thing. A user can wait a few seconds, but it's a different story with hackers. They can direct a large number of requests to connect to the server, and the xinetd program will consume all of the resources searching for and launching the requested services. In this way, a successful DoS attack can be carried out.

Chapter 6: Samba Style

Initially, FTP was used for exchanging files is Linux. (The protocol is considered in detail in *Chapter 10.*) But the protocol is not convenient to work with because it uses "client–server" technology. For example, to download a file from another computer, an FTP server must be started on that computer. Next, you start an FTP client on your computer, connect to the server on the source computer, and only then download the needed file.

Many local network administrators did not wish to burden themselves with configuring the FTP server for file sharing and started simply allocating a dedicated FTP server with public access for this.

Windows introduced a more convenient way to share files: the **Network Neighborhood** (**My Network Places** in Windows XP) service. This service displays the network's computers, whose shared resources are available to all network users. This is a handy feature, so it's no wonder that users quickly became used to it despite the dangers posed by working with shared resources.

The Samba package was developed to let Windows users see Linux servers in their network environment and perform file operations on them like on Windows machines. The package is often called by its abbreviated name smb and comprises two programs. The server allows local folders to be shared; the client is used to connect to other computers and work with their shared resources.

Samba can be used to make a practical, user-friendly file server. I used to employ a Windows 2000 server for this purpose that was also used as a database server. But a file archive takes too much disk space, consumes network resources, and negatively affects the system security. Therefore, I decided to move the file archive to a separate physical server. The question was what operating system this server should run under. To use Windows 2000 to run a file server would be like using a luxury car for taking trash to a dumpster 20 feet from your house. Linux, which is much less expensive and does not require routine maintenance, is much more suited to this purpose. Once the server has been configured, it can run for years without requiring further attention. Such was the operating system I installed to run my file server, and it has been handling its duties without a hitch ever since.

One of the Samba's powerful features is that is can be remotely controlled using SSH (a remote login utility) or Samba Web-Based Administrative Tool (SWAT).

6.1. Configuring Samba

The main configuration file for Samba is smb.conf, located in the /etc/samba directory (or simply in the /etc directory, for some distributions). This directory also contains the lmhosts file used for mapping host names to their IP addresses (analogously to the /etc/hosts file used by Linux). The Windows disk:\windows\system32\drivers\etc\ lmshosts.sam file is only used for the Samba server's needs.

There also are the following files in /etc/samba directory:

❑   smbusers — This file stores a list of users allowed to connect to the Samba server.
❑   smbpasswd — This file stores passwords for users listed in the smbusers file.

These two files may be not created by default, and you will have to create them manually.

In this case, make sure that the files have correct file permissions. Only the root user can be the owner of these files.

There aren't many parameters in the smb.conf file, so I give a small example of it in Listing 6.1 to help you understand the overall structure of this file. Further, I will consider other Linux servers, which require many more configuration settings.

Listing 6.1. A fragment of the smb.conf configuration file

```
 [global]
# Main parameters
    workgroup = MYGROUP
    server string = Samba Server

;   hosts allow = 192.168.1. 192.168.2. 127.
    load printers = yes
    printing = lprng
;   guest account = pcguest

# Log parameters
```

```
    log file = /var/log/samba/%m.log
    max log size = 0

# Security parameters
    security = user
;   password server = <NT-Server-Name>
;   password level = 8
;   username level = 8
    encrypt passwords = yes
    smb passwd file = /etc/samba/smbpasswd

    unix password sync = yes
    passwd program = /usr/bin/passwd %u
    passwd chat = *New*password* %n\n *Retype*new*password* %n\n
*passwd:*all*authentication*tokens*updated*successfully*
    pam password change = yes
;   username map = /etc/samba/smbusers

;   include = /etc/samba/smb.conf.%m
    obey pam restrictions = yes

# Socket configuration parameters
    socket options = TCP_NODELAY SO_RCVBUF=8192 SO_SNDBUF=8192
;   interfaces = 192.168.12.2/24 192.168.13.2/24

# View configuration parameters
;   remote browse sync = 192.168.3.25 192.168.5.255
;   remote announce = 192.168.1.255 192.168.2.44
;   local master = no
;   os level = 33
;   domain master = yes
;   preferred master = yes

# Server operation parameters
;   domain logons = yes
;   logon script = %m.bat
;   logon script = %U.bat
;   logon path = \\%L\Profiles\%U
;   wins support = yes

# WINS server parameters
;   wins server = w.x.y.z
;   wins proxy = yes
```

```
dns proxy = no

# File presentation parameters
;   preserve case = no
;   short preserve case = no
;   default case = lower
;   case sensitive = no
```

The actual file in your system will be much larger, because it contains numerous comments describing and giving examples of how public directories are configured. I deleted all of those comments to make it easier to orient yourself in the file's contents when considering its directives.

Directives in most Linux and application software configuration files have the following format:

```
Parameter_Name Value
```

The `Parameter_Name` parameter must be one word; no spaces are allowed. It is followed by a space, and then the parameter's value is given.

The Samba server uses a somewhat different format:

```
Parameter_Name=Value
```

The value of the parameter is given after an equal sign. In this way, the parameter name can consist of several words and contain any character with the exception of the equal sign.

6.1.1. Main Settings

The smb.conf file is broken into sections. In the first section, named `[global]`, the server's global parameters are defined. These are the following:

❑ `workgroup = name` — The name of the workgroup the server will appear to be in when queried by clients. When you open the network environment in Windows, you can see all available resources shown by groups. Each group can contain its computers or servers.

❑ `netbios name = name` — This specifies the name, by which the given Samba server is known and will be shown in the network environment. It cannot be the same as the `workgroup` name.

❑ `server string = description` — This is the description of the server shown in the **Comment** field of the server's properties window or of the network environment window in the **Details** view mode). You can enter a comment describing the server into this field, for example, "Main File Server."

❑ `hosts allow = IP addresses/host names` — This is a space-, comma-, or tab-delimited list of IP addresses or names of hosts and networks allowed to access the server. For example, access for all computers from the network 192.168.1.*x* and for one computer from another network with the IP address 192.168.2.1 can be allowed by setting this parameter as follows:

```
hosts allow = 192.168.1. 192.168.2.2
```

❑ printcap name = file — This specifies the file containing descriptions of the printers connected to the system. The default file is /etc/printcap.

❑ load printers = yes|no — When set to yes, this specifies all printers in the printcap file to be loaded for browsing by default. If there is no need for this, set this parameter to no.

❑ printing = style — This specifies the printing style. The following options are available: bsd, sysv, plp, lprng, aix, hpux, and qnx.

6.1.2. Security

The parameters that directly or indirectly affect security are the following:

❑ guest account = name — This is a user name that will be used to access the services specified as guest ok. If your server does not store any confidential information and is used for open file exchange, you can create a guest account; otherwise, allowing a guest login may be a security threat.

❑ log file = file_name — This is the name of the log file, for example, /var/log/samba/%m.log. The %m combination in the file name will be substituted with the name of the user whose activity is logged. Thus, for the user name robert, a log file named /var/log/samba/robert.log will be created.

❑ max log size = n — This sets the maximum log size in kilobytes. There is no size limit if this is set to 0.

❑ security = level — Based on the value, clients decide whether and how to transfer user and password information to the server. The following values are available:

• user — A user must log onto a user security server with a valid user name and password before attempting to access shared resources.

• share — Users don't have to log onto the share security server. A user name and password are required when accessing each particular share.

• server — This specifies the name of the server, on which the passwords are stored. (This is in case the passwords are stored on another server using the password server = Server_Name parameter.)

• security = domain — The user name and password are validated by passing them to a Windows NT primary or backup domain controller, just like a Windows NT Server would do. The password file to use is specified using the smb passwd file = file_path parameter.

❑ encrypt passwords = yes|no — When set to yes, passwords passed through the network are encrypted.. This parameter requires some explanation, because it may cause problems when authenticating from Windows computers.

The problem is that Windows-encrypted passwords are reversible. A password is encrypted on the client and sent over the network to the server, which decrypts it and compares it against the passwords in the password file. In Linux, stored passwords are encrypted irreversibly using the MD5 algorithm. At authentication, the client encrypts the password using the same algorithm and passes it to the server, which compares the encrypted password against encrypted passwords in the password file.

Thus, the encryption and authentication techniques of these two operating systems are incompatible with each other.

For Windows users to be able to authenticate on a Samba server, the password must be sent unencrypted. For this, the value of the `encrypt passwords` parameter should be set to `no`. Moreover, in Windows systems, the value of `EnablePlainTextPassword` must be set to 1. For different versions of Windows, this parameter is located in different keys. For Windows 9*x*, this is the following:

```
HKEY_LOCAL_MACHINE\SYSTEM\CurrentControlSet\Services\VxD\VNETSUP
```

For Windows NT, it is in this key:

```
HKEY_LOCAL_MACHINE\SYSTEM\CurrentControlSet\Services\Rdr\Parameters
```

For Windows 2000 and XP, the parameter is in the following key:

```
HKEY_LOCAL_MACHINE\SYSTEM\CurrentControlSet\Services\
LanmanWorkStation\Parameters
```

If the parameter does not exist, it should be created. It should be of the DWORD type.

If you experience difficulties logging onto the server, switch the system to work with plaintext passwords. In this case, a Samba server will use the /etc/passwd and /etc/shadow files to perform the authentication. It encrypts the plaintext password using the MD5 algorithm and compares it with the encrypted passwords stored in the /etc/shadow file.

If the `encrypt passwords` parameter is set to `yes`, the /etc/samba/smbpasswd file will be used at authentication. (The password file's location and name can be changed with the help of the `smb passwd file` parameter.) This password file is needed because of the differences in the encrypted password-authorization systems used in Linux and Windows.

Do not use plaintext passwords unless necessary. Always remember about network traffic sniffers that can snatch passwords sent on the network in plaintext. If hackers obtain even one password, chances are good they will be able to break into your system.

- ❑ `smb passwd file = file_path` — This specifies the path to the encrypted smbpasswd file. By default, this is the directory, in which Samba's configuration files are located.

- ❑ `ssl CA certFile = file_path` — This parameter specifies the path to the Certification Authority (CA) file, necessary for operation of the SSL protocol used for secure data transfer.

- ❑ `unix password sync = yes|no` — This allows Windows users to synchronize Linux passwords with the Samba password when the encrypted Samba password in the smbpasswd file is changed. If there is no such need, the parameter should be set to `no`.

For this directive to work, the program to change the password has to be specified in the `passwd program` parameter and the program to control the conversation that takes during the password change must be specified in the `passwd chat` parameter. The following is an example of the parameter's use:

```
unix password sync = Yes
passwd program = /usr/bin/passwd %u
passwd chat = *New*password* %n\n *Retype*new*password* %n\
n *passwd:*all*authentication*tokens*updated*successfully*
```

Moreover, the `encrypt passwords` and `smb passwd file` directives have to be used.

❑ `username map = file_path` — This specifies the file containing a mapping of user names from Windows clients to the Samba server. This file is described in more detail in *Section 6.3*.

6.1.3. Network

In this section, the network protocol configuration parameters are considered. These are the following:

❑ `include = file_path` — This parameter allows you to use the smb.conf file from another computer. The name of the file is specified in the `path.%m` format. Here, `path` is the absolute path to the file on the remote machine, and `%m` is the NetBIOS name of the machine, for example, /etc/samba/smb.conf.robert.

❑ `socket options = TCP_NODELAY SO_RCVBUF = 8192 SO_SNDBUF = 8192` — This parameter specifies the protocol options and the sizes of the input and output buffers. In this instance, its values are the following:

- `TCP_NODELAY` — Allows data to be transmitted without delay
- `SO_RCVBUF` — Sets the size of the incoming buffer
- `SO_SNDBUF` — Sets the size of the outgoing buffer

❑ `interfaces = interface_names` — If you have two network cards installed on your computer, each interfacing a different network, this parameter allows users from both networks to work with Samba.

6.1.4. Samba as a Windows Server

Samba can act as a Windows server without workstations running under Windows noticing any difference. This is made possible by the following parameters:

❑ `local master = yes|no` — This option allows a Samba server to become the main local browser on the subnet.

❑ `domain master = yes|no` — This option allows a Samba server to become the main local browser on the domain. Do not set the value of this parameter to `yes` if there is a Windows NT domain controller in your network.

- ❐ `domain logons = yes|no` — If set to `yes`, the Samba server will serve Windows 95/98 domain logons for the workgroup it is in. This will allow Samba passwords to be used when booting on a Windows computer.
- ❐ `logon script = file_path` — If the `domain logons` parameter is set to `yes`, this parameter specifies the batch file to be run when a user successfully logs in. The file can be specified as `%m.bat` (with `%m` replaced with a computer name) or `%U.bat` (with `%U` replaced with a user name).
- ❐ `logon path = path` — Specifies the home directory where user profiles are stored. To use this option, the comments must be removed from the `[Profiles]` section in the default configuration file.

6.1.5. WINS Support

The Windows Internet Naming Service (WINS) is a service for mapping NetBIOS computer names to their respective IP addresses. A WINS database is similar to DNS, only it stores NetBIOS host names as opposed to the domain names used in DNS.

The following parameters are used to configure WINS operation:

- ❐ `wins support = yes|no` — This parameter enables Samba to act as a WINS server.
- ❐ `wins server = w.x.y.z` — This specifies the WINS server address.
- ❐ `DNS Proxy = yes|no` — When set to `yes`, nonregistered NetBIOS names will be looked up with the DNS server.

6.1.6. File Representation

File naming conventions differ between Linux and Windows. For example, in Linux, file names are case-sensitive, and in Windows they are not. This means that DATA.TXT and data.txt are treated as the same file in Windows but not in Linux. This problem can be solved by using several parameters. These are the following:

- ❐ `case sensitive = yes|no` — If set to `yes`, case sensitivity is ignored.
- ❐ `default case = lower` — All file names are depicted in lowercase.
- ❐ `preserve case = yes|no` and `short preserve case = yes|no` — These parameters control whether the case information in file names is preserved.

If there are Windows systems in the network, the preceding values should not be changed. For a homogenous Linux network, case information can be preserved.

6.2. Describing Objects

After all main parameter of the Samba server have been specified, objects to which users can be allowed access can be described. This is done in the sections following the `[global]` section, considered in *Section 6.1.*

6.2.1. Home Directories

Users normally want to work in their own directories. To do so, a user has to have a Linux account, to which his or her directory will be linked. This directory is specified as //server/name, where server is the server name or IP address and name is the name of the user whose home directory is to be viewed.

To allow users' work with their individual directories, the [homes] section has to be described. Consider an example of this section:

```
[homes]
    comment = Home Directories
    browseable = no
    writable = yes
    valid users = %S
    create mode = 0664
    directory mode = 0775
```

The functions of its parameters are as follows:

❑ comment — A text comment, which has no effect on server operation.

❑ browseable = yes|no — Specifies whether the share is seen in the list of available shares in a network view and in the browse list. If set to yes, user folders will be shown in the network environment.

❑ writable = yes — Specifies whether the home directory can be written to. When set to no, users of the service may not create or modify files in the directory.

❑ create mode = 0750 — Specifies permission for created files. In this case, the file owner has full rights, group members have read and execute rights, and all other users don't have any rights. Sometimes, however, the parameter's value should be lowered to 740 so that group users would have only read rights.

❑ directory mode = 0775 — Specifies permissions for created directories. In this case, group users have overly high privileges. I would lower them to 755 to prohibit them from creating files in the new directory. All other users have only read rights, but even this may be too much for them. I would give them no rights by setting the overall rights to 750, or -rwxr-x--- in symbolic notation.

❑ valid users = user_list — Specifies a space-delimited list of users allowed access to the home directories. By default, all users are allowed access, but only few users need it. I, therefore, recommend specifying explicitly those users who need to work with their home directories.

6.2.2. Network Logon

If a Linux server is configured to let a Windows user enter the system through Samba, using it as a domain, comments in the [netlogon] section must be removed.

```
; [netlogon]
;    comment = Network Logon Service
```

```
;    path = /usr/local/samba/lib/netlogon
;    guest ok = yes
;    writable = no
```

The value of the `writable` parameter is set to `no` because users must not have write rights for this directory; scripts that are executed when they log onto the system are stored in this directory. Only the administrator should have the write rights for this directory.

The value of the `path` parameter is the complete path to the netlogon directory. The function of the `guest ok` parameter is the same as that of the identical parameter considered in *Section 6.1*: It governs guest logon. In this case, guest logon is permitted.

Comments in the `[Profiles]` section also have to be removed.

```
;    [Profiles]
;    path = /usr/local/samba/profiles
;    browseable = no
;    guest ok = yes
```

The directory specified in this section stores user profiles, and it should not be seen in the Windows network environment. For this reason, the value of the `browseable` parameter is set to `no`.

6.2.3. Printing

To make printers connected to the Linux server available to users, the `[printers]` sections has to be configured. Its contents are the following:

```
[printers]
    comment = All Printers
    path = /var/spool/samba
    browseable = no
    guest ok = no
    writable = no
    printable = yes
```

By default, the section is already open and registered users already have access to the printers. To make printers available to guest users, add the `public = yes` entry to the section. I do not recommend doing this, because it will give users additional means for playing jokes. For example, I know of a case, in which a worker was sending pictures to all network computers. It may look like an innocent joke, but this interfered with legitimate work and wasted paper and cartridge ink.

6.2.4. Common Access

Quite often there is a need for a directory on a server that can be used to exchange files by all network users. This directory is configured in the `[tmp]` section:

```
;    [tmp]
;    comment = Temporary file space
```

```
;    path = /tmp
;    read only = no
;    public = yes
```

By default, the section is commented out, so the comments have to be removed to enable the directory. Note the path to the shared directory. This is the /tmp directory, in which temporary user files are stored. The `read only = no` and `public = yes` parameters tell Samba that the directory is shared and that files can be written to and read from it by all users.

Even though having this directory is quite convenient, I recommend using it in closed networks only. In networks with access to the Internet, I recommend limiting access to Samba with the help of a firewall. Because the directory is open for writing to anyone, hackers can upload files into it that can be used to obtain root privileges on the server.

6.2.5. Personal Directories

All previously-considered sections of the smb.conf file solve particular tasks and have established names. In some cases, however, the name of a section can be changed without affecting the server operation. I, however, do not recommend doing this, because the new section name may work in one Samba version but not when the server software is updated. In this case, it will be difficult to trace the error causing the faulty operation.

You can, however, create your own sections and describe rights in them. For example, you may want to create a shared directory, in which all users can view files but only users of a certain group can write to. Suppose that this directory is for storing images. This task is accomplished by creating a `[shareimages]` section as follows:

```
;    [shareimages]
;    comment = Share Images
;    path = /home/samba/images
;    public = yes
;    writable = yes
;    write list = @staff
;    printable = no
```

The functions of the section's parameters are the following:

❑ `path = /home/samba/images` — Here is the path to the directory you want to create.
❑ `public = yes` — This makes the directory publicly accessible.
❑ `writable = yes` — Writing to the directory is permitted.
❑ `write list = @staff` — Writing to the directory is permitted only to the members of the `staff` group. All other users can only view the directory's files.

Any previously-considered parameters can be used in custom sections.

6.3. Managing Users

User name information for accessing a Samba server is obtained from the /etc/passwd system file. You can create separate accounts to be used for the Samba server only. These accounts will correspond to the system accounts but can only be used to log onto the Samba server and not onto the system.

Samba user names are described in the /etc/samba/smbusers file. The name and location of the file can be changed using the username map parameter in the smb.conf file. The contents of the /etc/samba/smbusers file are similar to the following:

```
# Unix_name = SMB_name1 SMB_name2
root = administrator admin
nobody = guest pcguest smbguest
```

The list has several uses. For example, it can be used to map DOS or Windows user names to a Linux user name. For example, the maximum rights Window user, administrator or admin, can be mapped to the Linux user with the same function who goes by a different name: root. In this case, the mapping is done in the second entry of the example: root = administrator admin. Even though administrator and admin are different accounts, they will use the same password: the one of the root user.

The file's second function is to accumulate several user names under one user account. For example, you may have to assign the same rights to a group of users. This is done by creating a Linux nobody account, which users will use for their work. Next, Samba users guest, pcguest, and smbguest are created, which will be used to log onto the system.

The information about users allowed access is stored in the /etc/samba/smbpasswd file. Its location and name can be changed by means of the smb passwd file parameter of the smb.conf file. The following is an example of the contents of the smbpasswd file:

```
flenov:0:813D6593C11F1173ED98178CA975D79:[UX      ]:LCT-41FA818F
robert:500:813D6593C11F1173ED98178CA975D79:[UX      ]:LCT-41FA818F
```

It can be seen right away that it is somewhat similar to the contents of the /etc/passwd file. The information in it is divided into several colon-delimited fields. The most interesting of these fields are the first three: the user name, the Linux UID, and the password.

It is inconvenient to add users manually, because it is not easy to encrypt and enter the password into the file. To make this task easier, the Samba package includes the smbpasswd utility. It is used with the following options:

❑ a — Adds a user to the Samba system. The account should already exist in the /etc/passwd file. For example, the following command adds the user robert, which you worked with before:

```
smbpasswd -a robert.
```

In response, the program asks you to enter and confirm the password. This password has no relation to the system password and is only used to log onto Samba. Thus, the system and Samba passwords can differ. I recommend making them different. All Windows versions can store passwords, and this function is not implemented securely in Windows 9x. If the Samba password is the same as the system password and falls into the wrong hands, the system will be compromised.

- x — Removes a user. For example, the following command removes the robert user from the system: smbpasswd -x robert.
- d — Deactivates a user. The following command temporarily deactivates a user without removing him or her from the system: smbpasswd -d robert. After the command is executed, the entry corresponding to the robert user looks as follows:

```
robert:500:813D6593C11F1173ED98178CA975D79:[DUX  ]:LCT-41FA818F
```

Note that the letter "D" was prefixed to the contents of the fourth field. It indicates that this account has been deactivated. In this way, you can easily tell, which accounts are active and which are not.

- e — Activates a user. For example, executing the smbpasswd -d robert command activates the robert user.

Information about additional options for this utility can be found on its man page.

The /etc/samba/smbpasswd file is used if passwords are sent over the network encrypted. In this case, to allow all system users to access Samba, the smbpasswd command has to be executed for each of them. There are scripts to automate this task, but they are ineffective because they do not set a password. Moreover, most often they transfer all users, even including those who should not have access to the system, such as bin, adm, and daemon.

6.4. Using Samba

The Samba service was created mainly for Windows users; however, Linux users have also appreciated all the advantages of this technology, especially because the file sharing implemented in Linux is no worse, and sometimes is even better, than in Windows. The smbclient command is used to work with Samba from Linux.

To connect to the server, at least two options have to be specified: -L (a server's address) and -U (a user name). In response, the program asks you to enter the password. If you are using encryption, enter the system password; otherwise, enter the password specified when transferring the user to the /etc/samba/smbpasswd file (with the smbpasswd command).

To test the server, execute the following command:

```
smbclient -L localhost -U root
```

The system will respond by displaying all shared resources of the server. The result will look similar to this:

```
Domain=[MYGROUP] OS=[Unix] Server=[Samba 2.2.3a]
        Sharename       Type        Comment
        ---------       ----        ----------
```

```
IPC$              IPC      IPC Service (Samba Server)
ADMIN$            Disk     IPC Service (Samba Server)

Server            Comment
---------         ----------
FLENOVM           Samba Server

Workgroup         Master
---------         ----------
MYGROUP           FLENOVM
```

Note that not all directories are shown in this list. For example, the value of the browseable parameter for home directories in the [homes] directory is set to no (see *Section 6.2.1*). This means that these directories will not be shown. This is quite logical, because unauthorized people should not be allowed to view directory names, especially if they correspond to user names or if the directories contain confidential data. Never change this parameter so that hackers will not know what to hack.

To connect to a server's public resource, enter the smbclient command, passing to it the name of the resource in the Universal Naming Convention (UNC) format as follows:

```
\\ServerName\Resource
```

For example, say you want to connect to the home directory of the flenov user. It address is \\192.168.1.1\flenov.

Some explanation is in order. In Linux, the backslash is a service character; thus, each backslash has to be doubled. Accordingly, the command to connect to the resource will look as follows:

```
smbclient \\\\192.168.1.1\\flenov
```

When accessing a resource requiring authorization, the user name possessing the rights to the resource has to be specified:

```
smbclient \\\\192.168.1.1\\flenov -U flenov
```

If the connection to the server is successful, the server will respond with the prompt, at which various file-handling commands can be entered. The prompt looks as follows:

```
Smb: \>
```

Entering the help command or a question mark displays the available commands. These are similar to FTP commands (see *Chapter 10*). To disconnect from the resource, execute the exit command.

Most distributions include a barebones standard Samba packet. But on the Internet, third-party enhancement products can be found, for example, to allow shared resources to be mounted onto the Linux file system as a diskette or a CD-ROM is, or to work with the shared resources in graphical mode the way it is done in Windows.

Chapter 7: Web Server

Although the initial purpose of the Internet was to exchange files, when the first Web browser appeared, the popularity of Web pages started growing by leap and bounds. Nowadays, it is difficult to imagine our lives without the Internet and the Internet without Web pages.

For your server machine to be able to serve Web pages, it must have a Web (HTTP) server program installed. The most widely-used Web server has long been Apache. It is difficult to estimate the share of Apache servers among the total number of Web servers, but it can be said with confidence that they comprise more than half. Even though there are other Web servers for Linux (e.g., TUX), when talking about a Web server for Linux, it is Apache that is meant.

Apache is available as freeware and is distributed under the GNU license. There is also a Windows version of Apache. The developer's official Web site address is **www.apache.org**. Why has this server become so popular? Is it because it is free? The free factor undoubtedly has some influence, but the decisive factor is the server's reliability. The Apache server offers a large choice of features and possesses many important qualities. It is:

- ❑ *Secure* — Many professionals consider this server the safest.
- ❑ *Reliable* — In tandem with Linux, the server can work for years without being reloaded.
- ❑ *Undemanding* — The server does not require any special resources and places a minimal load on the system.
- ❑ *Efficient* — The server rapidly responds to and handles user requests.

There are Apache-based servers that work practically without ever being turned off (available 99.9% of time). Many corporations trust this server with their important data, and I have never heard of anyone who regretted having chosen Apache for this.

The only shortcoming that users complain about is that the server is difficult to configure. This is done by editing a text file, and, because there are a huge number of configuration settings, this may be a demanding task. Also, the abundance of settings makes it easy to set some of them to the wrong values, which may negatively affect system's efficiency and/or security.

Considering the configuration of all existing Apache parameters is beyond the scope of this book; there are just too many of them. But I will consider the most important ones and explain what may affect the server's efficiency and security.

7.1. Main Settings

The main configuration settings of the Apache Web server are stored in the /etc/conf/httpd.conf file (or in the /etc/httpd.conf file for some distributions). The settings for the Web server, virtual servers, and software modules are stored in this file. For Red Hat Linux, all parameters considered are stored in this file unless another location is stated explicitly.

Like most other services, Apache can be configured using a simple and convenient graphical utility. It is launched by selecting the **System Settings/Server Settings/HTTP Server** menu sequence in the main menu. Fig. 7.1 shows the main window of the Apache graphical configuration utility.

The graphical utility is convenient for configuring initial settings, but afterwards you should review the configuration file. For this, you have to know its parameters.

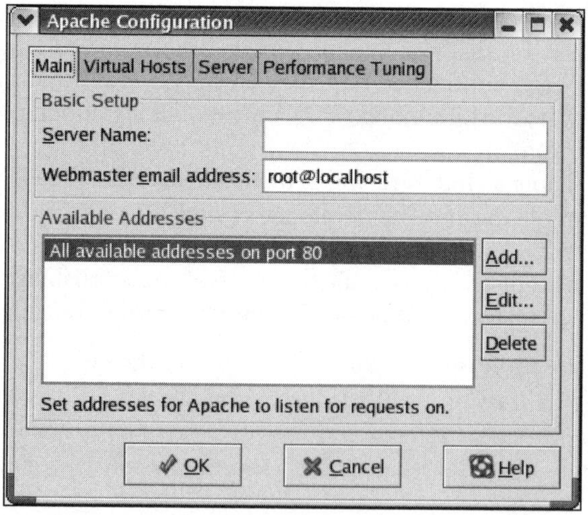

Fig. 7.1. The main window of the Apache graphical configuration utility

The graphical configuration utility should not be used after you edit the configuration file manually because it may interpret the manually-edited values incorrectly and replace them with what it considers to be the right ones. For the changes to take effect, the server has to be restarted. The Apache server reads the configuration file parameters only when it is started.

By editing the configuration file directly, the most secure and most efficient server operation can be achieved. The main parameters of the Apache Web server are the following:

☐ ServerType — Shows the server type. It can have the inetd or the standalone value. If this parameter is set to inetd, such parameters as port specified in the Apache configuration file are ignored, and the parameters specified in the configuration file of the inetd daemon (see *Section 5.4*) are used instead.

☐ ServerRoot — Specifies the root directory, in which logs and configuration files are located.

☐ Timeout — Gives the maximum time to wait when receiving or sending packets.

☐ Port — Specifies the port, on which the service is to work. The default value for public servers is 80. However, this value can be changed for private servers, for example, to 10387. In this case, the page address is specified as ServerName:10387 — for example, www.linux.com:10387/index.htm. This prevents hackers from penetrating the system through the standard Web port unless they scan all ports and find out that port 10387 is used for the Web server. This is a simple but quite effective protection from script kiddies, who possess minimum knowledge about computer security and break into computers only using exploits designed by other hackers.

☐ ServerTokens — When the system is accessed, it returns a header containing detailed information about the system, which includes the versions of Apache, Linux, and all modules. If hackers learn from this header that the server has an older version of the PHP interpreter (or any other program) installed, they will be able to penetrate the server much faster. Talkative parameters have to be disabled to hide information about the server. The ServerTokens parameter can take one of the following values:

- Full — Directs the header to display full information about the server and the installed modules, including their versions. Using this parameter puts the servers in the gravest danger.

- Min — Directs the header to display minimal information: only the server name and the installed modules. Even a simple list of modules without their versions reveals too much information to hackers.

- ProductOnly — Specifies the server, Apache in this case, and will return the server's name without the version. This is what you need.

Experienced administrators can even change the server's name, but this requires them to recompile Apache's source codes. The header is stored in the include/ap_releas.h file as the following two lines:

```
#define SERVER_BASEPRODUCT "Apache"
#define SERVER_BASEVERSION "2.0"
```

Replace the server name and version with other values. Only use a real server name, because a professional hacker will notice the switch.

In earlier Apache versions, the file was located in a different directory.

- ❑ HostnameLookups — If set to "on," the domain names of clients are logged; if set to "off," only the IP addresses are logged.
- ❑ User/Group — Gives the name of the user and group that have rights to run the service. The default value is apache. This user and group should possess the minimal rights in the system, sufficient only for operation of the Web server and its modules. Nothing unnecessary should be allowed.
- ❑ ErrorLog and CustomLog — Specifies the location of the error and custom log files.
- ❑ LogLevel — Specifies the types of messages to log. Possible values are the following: emerg, alert, crit, error, warn, notice, info, and debug.
- ❑ KeepAlive — Indicates whether or not persistent connections (processing more than one request per connection) are allowed. The default value of this parameter is off, so a separate connection must be established to receive each file. This wastes resources. Suppose that a user requested a page with 10 images on it. The client's browser will open 11 connections to service this request: One to receive the HTML document and one for each of the document's images. Setting this parameter to on will allow several requests per connection to be processed.
- ❑ MaxKeepAliveRequests — Specifies the maximum number of requests that can be serviced per connection.
- ❑ KeepAliveTimeout — Specifies the wait in seconds for the next request from the same client. If there are no requests within the time period specified, the connection is broken off.
- ❑ MaxClients — Shows the maximum number of clients that can connect simultaneously. Setting the value of this parameter too high may allow hackers to perpetrate a successful DoS attack against the server by opening too many connections for the server to handle. The default value is 150, but this is enough for only a small server. Apache is capable of processing many more requests, even on not-so-powerful computers. You should set this parameter to a value that will allow the server to process the maximum number of requests without hanging.
- ❑ MaxRequestsPerChild — Specifies the maximum number of requests a child process can serve. To avoid problems during long operation runs, caused by faulty memory (memory is allocated but not released) or resource usage by Apache or the libraries it uses, a child process is terminated when the maximum number of requests is reached. This is not necessary in most systems, but libraries in some systems (e.g., Solaris) suffer from resource leakage.

7.2. Modules

Modules are an important component for configuring an Apache service. They are loaded according to the instructions in the /etc/httpd/conf/httpd.conf file. These look similar to the following:

```
<IfDefine HAVE_PERL>
LoadModule perl_module  modules/libperl.so
</IfDefine>
```

In the first entry, a check is made for whether the HAVE_PERL parameter is set. If it is, the LoadModule command loads the modules/libperl.so module, which is necessary for interpreting Perl scripts.

The next instruction block adds modules:

```
<IfDefine HAVE_PERL>
AddModule mod_perl.c
</IfDefine>
```

By default, all installed modules or the modules included in the distribution are loaded. But this is not an efficient arrangement, because the distribution's developer cannot possibly know what modules a particular user may need. The following main script-support modules can be loaded:

- ❑ perl_module — Perl
- ❑ php_module — PHP
- ❑ php3_module — PHP version 3
- ❑ php4_module — PHP version 4
- ❑ python_module — Python

These modules present the biggest danger for Web servers, because they allow execution of scripts, which can be used to carry out a break-in. For example, a hacker can exploit a bug in a PHP script to execute commands on the server. Well-designed sites use only one Web programming language, and you should load only the module necessary to support the corresponding language.

I recommend using PHP for programming Web pages; this language is flexible in its configuration and can provide great security. My experience has led me to believe that hackers prefer using Perl for creating rootkits. (A rootkit is a collection of utilities that allows execution of commands and covers the hacker's tracks in the compromised machine.) But this is only my opinion. A competent Perl programmer can easily write a program that is both secure and difficult to compromise. A well-protected program can be written in any language, even the most security deficient. On the other hand, a program full of security holes can be written in the most security-efficient language. This depends only on the programmer and his or her level of knowledge and skills.

Modules that are not used should be disabled; this will greatly limit opportunities for break-ins. Remember, a running program is an administrator's enemy and a potential door a hacker can use to enter the system.

Review the modules that are loaded, and delete or comment out those that are not necessary. This will increase the security of the Web server by more than 50%. Why is this so? Although Python is seldom used by hackers, Perl and PHP are popular among them. As mentioned earlier, any program is a potential entry point into the system. Disabling one of the two programs (PHP or Perl) cuts the number of the potential doorways in half.

7.3. Access Rights

In this section, I will introduce to you the main parameters of the /etc/httpd/conf/httpd.conf configuration file. These parameters specify access rights to directories and have the following format:

```
<Directory /var/www/html>
        Order allow, deny
        Allow from all
    </Directory>
```

They can also look similar to the following:

```
<Location /server-status>
   SetHandler server-status
   Order deny, allow
   Deny from all
   Allow from .your-domain.com
</Location>
```

The first block of code sets permissions for a certain directory on the disk (in this case, the /var/www/html directory); the second block of code limits permissions for a virtual directory (in this example, the /servername/server-status directory). If you are familiar with HTML, you should already understand the preceding declarations. For those who do not have this knowledge, I will provide a few explanations for the directory example. The declaration code starts with the following line:

```
<Directory Path>
```

In the angle brackets, the keyword `Directory` is specified, followed by the path to the directory, for which the permissions have to be set. Afterward, commands defining the permissions follow. The block ends with the line:

```
</Directory>
```

The permissions for a directory can be described not only in the /etc/httpd/conf/httpd.conf file but also in the .htaccess file located in the specified directory. The file itself is considered in detail in *Section 7.5.1*; for now, it will suffice for you to know that the permissions specified in the Web server configuration can be redefined.

The permissions are specified using the following directives:

- ❑ `Allow from parameter` — Indicates, from which hosts the specified directories can be accessed. The `parameter` value can be one of the following:
  - `all` — Indicates that access is allowed to all hosts.
  - `domain name` — Specifies the domain name, from which the directory can be accessed. For example, specifying `domain.com` will allow only users of this domain to access the directory from the Web. If you want to protect some files, you can limit access to the folder containing them to your domain or only to the local machine like this: `allow from localhost`.
  - `IP-address` — Restricts access to the directory to the specified IP address. This is handy if your computer has a static address and you want to restrict access to the directory containing administrating scripts only to yourself. The restriction can be to a single computer or to a network, in which case only the network part of the address is specified.
  - `env = VariableName` — If the specified environmental variable is defined, access is allowed. The full format of the directive is the following: `allow from env = VariableName`.

- ❑ `Deny from parameter` — Denies access to the specified directory. The parameters are the same as those for the `allow from` directive, only in this case access is denied from the specified addresses, domains, and so on.

- ❑ `Order parameter` — The order, in which the `allow` and `deny` directives are applied. The following three combinations are possible:
  - `Order deny, allow` — Initially, access is allowed to all; then prohibitions are applied, followed by permissions. It is advisable to use this combination for shared directories, to which users can upload files.
  - `Order allow, deny` — Initially, access is denied to all; then permissions are applied, followed by prohibitions. It is advisable to use this combination for all directories containing scripts.
  - `Order mutual-failure` — Initially, access is denied to all but those listed in the `allow from` and not in the `deny from` directive. I recommend using this combination for all directories storing files used by a certain group of users, for example, administration scripts.

- ❑ `Require parameter` — Specifies users who are allowed access to the directory. The parameter value can be one of the following:
  - `user` — The name of users (or their IDs) allowed access to the directory. For example, `Require user robert FlenovM`.
  - `group` — The names of groups whose users are allowed access to the directory. The directive works the same as the `user` directive.
  - `valid-user` — Access to the directory is allowed to any user that has been authenticated.

❑   `Satisfy parameter` — If set to `any`, access is restricted by using either a login/password procedure or an IP address. To identify users using both procedures, the value should be set to `all`.

❑   `AllowOverwrite parameter` — Specifies, which directives from the .htaccess files in the specified directory can overwrite the server configuration. The `parameter` value can be one of the following: `None`, `All`, `AuthConfig`, `FileInfo`, `Indexes`, `Limit`, or `Options`.

❑   `AuthName` — The authorization domain to be used by the client for verifying the user name and password.

❑   `Options [+ | -] parameter` — Indicates the Web server features available in the specified directory. If you have a directory on your server, into which the users are allowed to upload files, for example, images, it would be logical to disallow execution of any scripts in this directory. Do not rely on being able to prohibit programmatically the uploading of files of types other than images. Hackers will always find a way to upload malicious code to your system and execute it. But you can use the options to disable the Web server from executing scripts.

The keyword `option` is followed by a plus or minus sign, which corresponds to the option being enabled or disabled, respectively. The `parameter` value can be one of the following:

- `All` — Permits all except `MultiView`. The `Option + All` directive allows execution of any other scripts.

- `ExecCGI` — Allows execution of CGI scripts. Most often a separate directory, /cgi-bin, is used for CGI scripts, but even in this directory, execution can be disallowed for individual subdirectories.

- `FollowSymLinks` — Allows symbolic links. Make sure that the directory does not contain dangerous links and that the links in it do not have excessive rights. It was already mentioned in *Section 3.1.3* that links are inherently dangerous; therefore, they should be handled with care wherever they are found.

- `SymLinksIfOwnerMatch` — Follow symbolic links only if the owners of the target file and the link match. When symbolic links are used, it is better to specify this parameter instead of `FollowSymLinks` in the given directory. If a hacker creates a link to the /etc directory and follows it from the Web browser, this will create serious security problems.

- `Includes` — Use Server Side Include (SSI).

- `IncludesNOEXEC` — Use all SSI except `exec` and `include`. If you do not use these commands in CGI scripts, it is better to use this option than the previous one.

- `Indexes` — Display the contents of the directory if there is no default file. Users mostly enter Internet addresses in the reduced format, for example, **www.cydsoft.com**. Here, the file to load is not specified. The full URL is the following: **www.cydsoft.com/index.htm**. When the reduced format is used, the server opens the default file. This may be index.htm, index.html, index.asp, index.php, default.htm, and the like. When the server does not find any such files at the specified path, if the `Indexes` option is enabled, the directory tree will be displayed; otherwise, the error page will be opened. I recommend disabling this option, because too much information is revealed about the structure of the directory and its contents, which can be misused by nefarious individuals.

- `MultiViews` — The view depends on the client's preferences.

All of the directives just described can be used not only in the /etc/httpd/conf/ httpd.conf file but also in the .htaccess files, which can be placed in individual directories and define the permissions for their corresponding directories.

Access rights can be defined not only for directories but also for individual files. The files access rights are defined between the following two entries:

```
<Files FileName>
</Files>
```

This declaration is, in turn, placed inside the directory access rights definition, for example, as follows:

```
<Directory /var/www/html>
        Order allow, deny
        Allow from all
        <Files "/var/www/html/admin.php">
          Deny from all
        </Files>
      </Directory>
```

The directives for files are the same as for directories. In the preceding example, all users are allowed access to the /var/www/html directory; nobody, however, can access the /var/www/html/admin.php file in this directory.

In addition to limiting access rights to directories and files, HTTP methods (GET, POST, PUT, DELETE, CONNECT, OPTIONS, TRACE, PATCH, PROPFIND, PROPPATCH, MKCOL, COPY, MOVE, LOCK, and UNLOCK) can be limited. How can this be useful? Suppose that your Web page contains a script, to which the parameters are sent by users. This can be done using either POST or GET. If you know that the programmer uses only the GET method, you can prohibit the other method so as not to let hackers take advantage of a potential vulnerability in the script by replacing the method.

Also, sometimes only selected users can send data to the server. For example, everyone can execute scripts in a specified directory, but only administrators can load information to the server. This problem is easily solved by separating the rights to use the HTTP methods.

The rights to use the methods are described as follows:

```
<limit MethodName>
 Rights
</limit>
```

As you can see, the process is similar to defining file and directory access rights. Even the same access-rights terms are used, which are placed within the `<Directory>` or `<Location>` definition blocks and affect only the specified directory.

For example, the following definition block can be used to prohibit any data transfers to the server's /home directory:

```
<Directory /home>
  <Limit GET POST>
    Deny from all
  </Limit>
</Directory>
```

Within the rights definition block for the /home directory, the GET and POST methods are limited.

Your task as the administrator is to configure the access parameters for directories and files so that they are minimally sufficient. Users should not be allowed to take any step without your permission. For this, you should base your actions on the "Everything not permitted is prohibited" principle.

Always, first prohibit everything that you can and only then start gradually setting permissions so that all scripts will operate properly. It is better to specify an extra explicit prohibition than to let a permission slip through that can be used by hackers to destroy your server.

7.4. Creating Virtual Web Servers

It is possible to have one physical Web server run more than one virtual Web servers, for example, **www.your_name.com** and **www.your_company.com** These are two different Web sites, but they are located on one server. This arrangement offers the following advantages:

❐ Savings on hardware.
❐ Efficient use of the communication channels for small sites and low server loads.
❐ Savings on IP addresses. Available IP addresses would have long been exhausted if a separate IP address were used for each individual Web site. (Although once the IPv6 protocol is in place, this problem will be less important.) Virtual Web servers can be IP-based or name-based. IP-based virtual hosts are addressed by individual IP addresses. Name-based virtual hosts share the same IP address and are addressed using individual host names.
❐ Simplified administration and security control. It is a rather complex process to configure and secure a Web server; consequently, it is much easier to configure and update software of one physical server than of hundreds of servers.

A virtual server is created by the following directive block:

```
<VirtualHost address:port>
</VirtualHost>
```

The parameters of the virtual server are specified between these tags. For example, the following is a description for a virtual server that uses address 192.168.1.1 and port 80:

```
<VirtualHost 192.168.1.1:80>
    ServerAdmin admin@your_server.com
    DocumentRoot /var/www/your_server
    ServerName your_server.com
    ErrorLog logs/your_server.com -error_log
    CustomLog logs/your_server.com -access_log common

    <Directory /var/www/your_server/>
        AllowOverride none
    </Directory>
</VirtualHost>
```

I will consider only the main parameters used to describe a virtual server. These are the following:

- ❒ ServerAdmin — The email of the administrator to send error messages to.
- ❒ DocumentRoot — The site's root directory, from which files will be served.
- ❒ ServerName — Self-explanatory. If no server name is specified, the server's local IP address is used.

The ErrorLog and CustomLog directives have already been considered. They are followed in the example by specifying access rights to the /var/www/your_server/ directory, which is the root directory of the virtual Web server. Permissions can be set both within the virtual server declaration block and outside of it.

More detailed information can be found in the Apache server documentation.

7.5. Security Notes

There are several directives in the /etc/httpd/conf/httpd.conf configuration file used to control the server's security. These directives can also be used in the .htaccess file. These are the following:

- ❒ AuthType parameter — Indicates the type of user authentication. The parameter value can be one of the following: Basic or Digest.
- ❒ AuthGroupFile file_path — Specifies the name of the file, in which the list of user groups is stored.
- ❒ AuthUserFile file_path — Specifies the file containing user names and passwords. It is advisable to create this list using the htpasswd utility.
- ❒ AuthAuthoritative On|Off — Specifies the access rights check method. The default value is On. If the directive is set to Off and the user does not provide a name, user authentication is carried out by other methods, for example, using the IP address.

❑ `AuthDBMGroupFile` and `AuthDBMUserFile` — These directives are analogous to the `AuthGroupFile` and `AuthUserFile` directives except that the parameter is specified as a Berkley-DB database file.

These directives can help you configure the user-authentication process when accessing certain directories. For example, for a directory that only authorized users can access, you can specify a password file that will be used by the server to control access to the directory.

7.5.1. The .htaccess Files

If a Web server directory must have special permissions, it is advisable to create in this directory an .htaccess file. Permissions described in this file apply to the directory in which it is located. The following listing is an example of the contents of an .htaccess file:

```
AuthType Basic
AuthName "By Invitation Only"
AuthUserFile /pub/home/flenov/passwd
Require valid-user
```

In this file, the authentication type for the current directory is specified as `Basic`. This means that the authentication will be carried out by requesting the user login and password. The text specified in the `AuthName` directive will be shown in the title of the authentication window (Fig. 7.2).

The `AuthUserFile` directive specifies the file containing the list of names and passwords of the site's users. Finally, the `Require` directive is used with the `valid-user` argument. This means that only successfully authenticated users will be able to open files in the current directory.

Fig. 7.2. The user authentication window

In this simple way, unauthorized access to directories containing restricted data (e.g., administrator scripts) can be limited.

As already mentioned, directives such as `allow from` (considered in *Section 7.3*) can be used in the .htaccess file.

For example, access from only a certain IP address, say, 101.12.41.148, can be allowed as follows:

```
allow from 101.12.41.148
```

Combining the `allow from` directive with user authentication will greatly complicate the job for hackers trying to break into the server. Although the password can be stolen, faking the specific IP address necessary to access the directory requires significant effort.

These permissions can also be specified in the .htaccess file:

```
<directory /path>
AuthType Basic
AuthName "By Invitation Only"
AuthUserFile /pub/home/flenov/passwd
Require valid-user
</directory>
```

Which of these two files you choose to use is up to you. I prefer working with .htaccess files because in this case security settings are stored in the directory, to which they apply. But this is not safe, because hackers can obtain access to this file.

The central httpd.conf file is preferable from the security standpoint, because it is located in the /etc directory, which is outside the scope of the Web server root directory, and access to it must be forbidden to regular users.

7.5.2. Password Files

In this section, you will learn how to create and control Apache password files. The file specified in the `AuthUserFile` directive is a simple text file containing user name and password entries in the following format:

```
flenov:{SHA}1ZZEBtPy4/gdHsyztjUEWb0d90E=
```

There are two fields in the preceding entry, separated by a colon. The first field contains a user name, and the second field contains the user password encrypted using the MD5 algorithm. It is difficult to edit this file manually; moreover, there is no need for this because the htpasswd utility is intended for this task.

The utility can encrypt passwords using both the MD5 algorithm and the system's `crypt()` function. Both types of passwords can be stored in the same file.

If you store user names and passwords in a DMB database file (specified by the `AuthDBMUserFile` directive in .htaccess files), use the dbmmanage command to manage the database.

The htpasswd utility is invoked as follows:

```
htpasswd arguments file name password
```

Use of the `password` and `file` switches is optional, depending on the specified options. The utility takes the following main switches:

❐ `-c` — Creates a new file. If the specified file already exists, it is overwritten and its old contents are lost. The following is an example of the command's use:

```
htpasswd -c .htaccess robert
```

When this directive is executed, a prompt to enter and then confirm the password for the user robert will be displayed. After successful completion of this procedure, an .htaccess file will be created that contains an entry for the user robert and the corresponding specified password.

❐ `-m` — Specifies that passwords are to be created using the Apache modified MD5 algorithm. A password file created using this algorithm can be ported to any other platform (Windows, UNIX, BeOS, etc.), on which an Apache server is running. This switch is handy for a heterogeneous operating system network, because the same password file can be used on machines running different operating systems.

❐ `-d` — Indicates that passwords are to be encrypted using the `crypt()` system function.

❐ `-s` — Specifies that passwords are to be encrypted by the Secure Hash Algorithm (SHA) used by the Netscape platform.

❐ `-p` — Indicates no password encryption. I don't recommend using this switch; using it is not prudent for security.

❐ `-n` — Don't update the file; only display the results.

A new user can be added to the file by executing the command without any switches, only passing the file and the user names as the arguments:

```
htpasswd .htaccess Flenov
```

There are two restrictions on using the `htpasswd` command: First, a user name cannot contain a colon, and second, a password can be no longer than 255 characters. These are rather mild restrictions, and both can be lived with. Unless you have masochistic tendencies, it is doubtful you will want to use a password anywhere close to 255 characters long. As for the colon, you'll just have to do without it.

7.5.3. Authentication Problems

Authentication is too simple a method to provide reliable security. When passwords are sent, they are encoded using the basic Base64 algorithm. If the packet containing the user name and password encrypted in this way is intercepted, it can be deciphered in no time. All that is needed to decipher the text encoded using Base64 is to apply a simple function to the text, which produces practically instant results.

A truly secure connection should be encrypted. The `stunnel` utility or HTTPS, which uses SSL, can be used for this purpose. The `stunnel` utility and HTTPS are discussed in more detail in *Section 5.2*.

7.5.4. Server Side Processing

HTML files can be processed directly on the server, the same as PHP files. On one hand, this is convenient, because PHP code can be embedded into HTM files. On the other hand, HTML files present a potential security problem. If hackers modify them, the server can become vulnerable to a break-in.

The `AddHandler` directive is used to allow the server to execute files with a certain extension. The following entries containing this directive can be found in the httpd.conf configuration file:

```
AddHandler cgi-script .cgi
AddHandler server-parsed .shtml
```

If you do not have Perl interpreter installed, you should comment out the first line so that it does not bother you. The second entry presents no danger, but allowing the server to work with HTM or HTML files in this way is not safe. The following line in your configuration file should be either deleted or commented out:

```
AddHandler server-parsed .html
```

If there is a need to allow execution of HTML documents, you can do this in the corresponding .htaccess file. Server processing of HTML files in other directories should be explicitly prohibited. You can do this by adding the following line either to the httpd.conf configuration file or to the .htaccess file in each directory:

```
RemoveHandler .html .htm
```

In this way, you will prohibit execution of HTML files by the server without affecting the SSI instruction. For example, the following code in a SHTML file will be executed:

```
<!--#include virtual="filename.shtml" -->
```

If you do not use SSI (and, accordingly, SHTML files) comment out the following line (by default, it is enabled):

```
AddHandler server-parsed .shtml
```

7.6. The Convenience Factor

The configuration process must be as convenient as possible. Piling up all settings into one /etc/httpd/conf/httpd.conf file will make it difficult to navigate and use them. And the more parameters there are, the greater the chances of letting something undesirable to slip by. Following the ensuing recommendations will make it easier for you to maintain your Web server:

❐   Move all access rights definitions to the /etc/httpd/conf/access.conf configuration file. By default, this file is empty, with everyone using only the /etc/httpd/conf/httpd.conf file. Separating permissions from the rest of the settings will make it easier to orient yourself in the server-configuration settings.

❑ The server's main settings, which seldom change, can also be separated into the /etc/httpd/conf/access.conf file.

❑ Comment all your actions. Many settings remain unchanged for years, but most people have difficulties remembering why they set this or that directive only a couple of months after they did so. For example, you prohibited access to a directory you temporarily used to test scripts to all users. Some time later, you may forget why you did this, and open access to the raw scripts, which may cause a system crash or break-in.

The more convenient it is to control the server security, the fewer mistakes you will make. Parameter grouping and detailed comments help you remember the purpose of the specific settings. This approach to administration also helps you solve problems efficiently as they arise. As you know, in the everlasting war between hackers and administrators, those who know more, are more experienced, and react faster win. The fast-reaction aspect is especially important.

Centralized storage of access rights in configuration files of the Web server is only acceptable for small sites. But these access-rights descriptions become too unwieldy for a hundred or more virtual servers. Even if all permission definitions are stored in the /etc/httpd/conf/access.conf file, its size will be too large to find the necessary information in it efficiently.

For large sites, I recommend describing in the server's configuration files only general rules that cover several directories at once. This can be done because directory paths can be specified using regular expressions. The following is an example that defines rules for everything contained in the /home directory:

```
<Directory /home/* >
    AllowOverride FileInfo AuthConfig Limit
    Options MultiViews Indexes SymLinksIfOwnerMatch IncludesNoExec
    <Limit GET POST OPTIONS PROPFIND>
        Order allow, deny
        Allow from all
    </Limit>
    <LimitExcept GET POST OPTIONS PROPFIND>
        Order deny, allow
        Deny from all
    </LimitExcept>
</Directory>
```

Such regular expressions can be used for creating general rules for different directories. For example, specifying the /home/*/public_html value as the directory assigns the specified rights to all public_html directories in the /home directory unless the permissions are explicitly overridden for individual directories.

7.7. Securing Scripts

As mentioned in *Section 1.1.2,* scripts present a great danger to Web servers. Many a notorious break-in has been perpetrated by exploiting bugs in scripts. You already know that all unused interpreters should be disabled, leaving only those that are really necessary. This will make breaking into the server difficult — but not impossible.

The safest site is one that uses static (HTML) documents without server-side scripts (PHP, ASP, Perl, Python, etc.). If you need an interpreter for your site, limit it to minimal capabilities.

Suppose that your site uses PHP scripts and has functions that access the system. If these functions are used improperly (for example, user-specified parameters are not checked), a malefactor can send such values that may disrupt the server's operation. This book does not teach you how to write correct scripts and how to make them secure, because this is a programmer's job. But you should not rely on programmers' professionalism, because they also are humans, and all humans make errors. What you should do is to take all necessary steps to prevent software bugs from becoming fatal for your server.

The PHP interpreter has a feature called `safe_mode`. This feature can be used to describe the rules for executing certain actions using more secure configuration settings and access rights. But some scripts may not work in this mode, and many administrators disable it. This is not always the right thing to do. You should check first whether the offending script can be rewritten to work; only when this is impossible should `safe_mode` be disabled.

When configuring the interpreter, you should start by prohibiting everything. Afterwards, the necessary options are gradually enabled. It would be the best if you could configure not only the work server but also the server used by the programmers for developing and debugging scripts. In this case, you will be able to control all configuration parameters.

The administrator should act in close cooperation with the Web script programmers. If the programmers require some options for the scripts to be enabled, the person to do this on both servers should be you. The developers should inform you of any changes in the scripts that require changes in the access rights, so that you can make the necessary adjustments.

The administrator and developers should maintain close contact to be able to react rapidly to developments necessitating the use of some extra features. Some administrators like to get rid of the interpreter-configuring responsibilities, shifting this function to their script developers. This is not right, because a programmer is trained to write programs and has no sufficient knowledge to configure with the necessary security level provided.

All PHP interpreter-configuration settings are stored in the /etc/php.ini configuration file. Consideration of this file lies beyond the scope of this book.

7.7.1. Security Fundamentals

At present, most Internet break-ins are perpetrated by taking advantage of bugs in Web page scripts. I'll investigate why this happens.

Most personal site owners are just regular users who want to quickly obtain their own Web page with an extensive feature list. What features does a decent site need? These are a guestbook, forum, chat, polling, and so on. These sections cannot be created using simple HTML and require some sort of programming, for example, Perl or PHP. Regular users do not want to (or cannot) become involved with the intricacies of programming, and they use ready-made engines (payware or freeware) in their projects.

But as you already know, sooner or later bugs are discovered in any software. Widely-used programs, in particular, attract hackers' attention, because breaking these allows them to penetrate the numerous systems, on which these programs are installed.

If you use on your site a forum based on a popular engine, you must understand that sooner or later bugs will be discovered in it and the forum can be used by hackers as an entrance into your server. To prevent this, you should update the Web programs and scripts used on the server regularly.

If you know at least the basic principles of Web application protection, you could write your own forum, which may be more secure than similar products by third parties.

But if you do not know the specifics of the programming language or have no programming skills, you will be better off using software products written by other people. A script written by an amateur can be broken even by a novice hacker without knowledge of the source code, database structure, and other details that facilitate breaking Web scripts.

As they say, damned if you do, damned if you don't. The safest course is to use less popular software developed by professional programmers on your site. It would be even better for it to be closed or even custom-written source code. This entails extra financial expenses, but these are smaller than the costs of restoring the system after a break-in.

If you are responsible for only one Web server, the task of software updating is not a problem. But administrators of hosting companies face a daunting task in this respect, because their servers host hundreds if not thousands of Web sites. It is impossible to monitor all Web sites for regular software updates, but some sort of protection against careless or lazy site owners is still needed. The Jail program (see *Chapter 4*) best suits this task. Using this program, you place a Web service into its own virtual directory. If hackers break a Web program and penetrate the Web service using it, their actions will be limited to the confines of the virtual root directory.

When preparing the material for this book, I found that a vulnerability was discovered in a popular forum engine that made it possible to execute any command on a system hosting a Web site with the forum. This was done by sending a command formatted in a special way through the URL string. I started writing this chapter about a month after the bug was discovered and, remembering this, decided to check a few Internet servers for it. I ran a search of all sites using the vulnerable forum. You may find it hard to believe, but there were hundreds of them.

My attention was attracted by a couple of sites hosted on the server of a major hosting company. I executed the `ls -a / etc` command on both of them. The results were not long in coming: The entire /etc directory was at my disposal with permissions even to delete files. I did not do this even to test the extent of my access rights. I did, however, rename a file on each system and inform the administrators about the vulnerability.

NOTE

I do not recommend doing anything similar yourself. Not all administrators take it well if their sites are broken into, even when this is done with benevolent intentions. Some of them may even notify law-enforcement agencies, which won't bode well for you. Your good intentions may not necessarily be considered in the proper light. When I inform administrators of the vulnerabilities I find in their servers, I do it through an anonymous message.

Placing Apache into a virtual root directory, you only secure the system; all sites located in the virtual directory remain vulnerable. To protect Web sites, you have to look to other ways — for example, by regulating access rights, running several instances of the Apache Web server (each in its own virtual root directory), running dedicated servers for individual sites, or prohibiting insecure PHP functions from executing.

It is difficult and sometimes simply impossible to pick the most effective way to protect multiple virtual servers. For example, one site requires a PHP interpreter, while another requires Perl. You have no choice and must allow both languages.

Based on personal experience, I can suggest using individual physical servers to separate sites according to their requirements, such as the following:

❑   PHP interpreter is used in the safe mode.
❑   Full-rights PHP interpreter is required.
❑   Perl interpreter is used.

You should group sites based on their requirements; this will make administering them easier and simpler.

Important sites should be located on a dedicated server and watched closely. For example, you should not place electronic stores and personal pages on the same server. The latter are often constructed using free modules, which frequently contain bugs; moreover, their owners do not update the site software. Sooner or later, these weaknesses will lead to a break-in into a home page. Once on the server, the miscreant will find a way to penetrate the Web stores located on the server and to obtain confidential financial data. This will put an end to your administrative career.

7.7.2. The mod_security Module

Even though the security of a Web server depends largely on the scripts run on it and the programmers who write these scripts, a server can be protected independently of these factors. An excellent solution to this problem is a free Apache module called mod_security.

The principle of operation of this module is similar to that of a firewall built into the operating system, only it was developed especially for providing interaction with HTTP. Based on the rules set by the administrator, the module analyzes requests from users to the server and decides whether or not let them through to the Web server.

The rules specify what a request may and may not contain. A request usually contains the URL, from which a document or file must be obtained. How can rules for the module be specified to enhance the system's security? Consider a simple example: Unauthorized access to the /etc/passwd file endangers the server's security; consequently, there should be no references to it in the URL string.

Based on this rule, the module checks the URL string. If it does not comply with the rule, the request is rejected.

The `mod_security` module can be downloaded from the **www.modsecurity.org** site. Installing the module allows new request-filtering directives to be specified in the httpd.conf file. The most interesting of them are the following:

- ❑ `SecFilterEngine On` — Enables the request filtering mode.
- ❑ `SecFilterCheckURLEncoding On` — Checks the validity of the URL encoding.
- ❑ `SecFilterForceByteRange 32 126` — Specifies to use characters from the particular range only. There are quite a few control characters (e.g., carriage return and line end) whose codes are less than 32. Most of them are invisible but require the corresponding key presses to be processed. How can such a character be entered into a URL string? This can be done using their codes. For example, the end-of-line character is entered in a URL by typing `%13`. In this case, a URL cannot contain character codes less than 32 and greater than 126.
- ❑ `SecAuditLog logs/audit_log` — Specifies the log file, in which the audit information is to be stored.
- ❑ `SecFilterDefaultAction "deny,log,status:406"` — Specifies the default action. In this case, it is prohibition.
- ❑ `SecFilter xxx redirect:http://www.Webcreator.com` — Provides for redirection. If the rules have been met, the user is redirected to **www.webcreator.com**.
- ❑ `SecFilter yyy log,exec:/home/apache/report-attack.pl` — Launches a script. If the filter is triggered, the /home/apache/report-attack.pl script will be executed.
- ❑ `SecFilter /etc/password` — Prohibits referencing the /etc/passwd file in user requests. Referencing the /etc/shadow file can be prohibited in the same way.
- ❑ `SecFilter /bin/ls` — Prohibits users from accessing commands. In this case, access to the `ls` command is prohibited, which can be used to view contents of directories if a script contains a bug. Access to such commands as `cat`, `rm`, `cp`, and `ftp` should also be prohibited.
- ❑ `SecFilter "\.\./"` — Prohibits dots in URLs. A classic attack is carried out by placing dot characters in a URL.
- ❑ `SecFilter "delete[[:space:]]+from"` — Prohibits the `delete ... from` text, which is most often used in SQL queries to delete data. This string is used frequently in SQL injection-type attacks. In addition, I recommend setting the following three filters:
  - • `SecFilter "insert[[:space:]]+into"` — Prohibits the string used in SQL queries for adding data.
  - • `SecFilter "select.+from"` — Prohibits the string used in SQL queries for reading data from a database.

- `SecFilter "<(.|\n)+>"` and `SecFilter "<[[:space:]]*script"` — Protects against cross-Site Scripting (XSS) attacks.

The preceding are the main methods that can be used to enhance the security of your Web server. Server networks can also be protected in this way. Additional information can be obtained from the developer's Web site.

7.7.3. Secrets Revealed and Advice Dispensed

No matter how carefully scripts may be written and how well they are protected by special modules: Undertaking additional security measures will never hurt. There are several more techniques that can be used toward this goal. In this section, I have collected various recommendations that can help you enhance server security.

Script Restriction

First, restrict script execution to an individual directory. In most cases, this will be the cgi-bin directory: I saw a system once, in which the root directory was specified for this purpose, meaning scripts could be executed from any directory. Don't repeat this mistake, because there are many different Perl programs in the system but they should not be allowed to execute on the Web server.

Backup Copies

Never store backup copies of scripts in directories accessible to Web servers. Consider an example. If a Web page contains PHP scripts, users do not see them in the browser; they only see the results of their execution on the server. To view the source code, some sort of access to the server is necessary, for example, through FTP or Telnet, because Apache does not send this sort of data to clients.

Programmers like to save backup copies of scripts before modifying them, so that if something goes wrong, the old, working version of the script could be restored. Often they save these copies in the same directory as the working script, only with a different extension. For example, old and bak are the two used most frequently.

Because the server does not execute these files, if a file is requested, the source code will be displayed in the browser. We all know that having access to the source code makes finding vulnerabilities in a program much easier.

When a hacker is exploring scripts on the server, there is nothing to keep him or her from checking whether there are backup copies of them. If a hacker sees that there is a file named www.servername.com/index.php on the server, he or she will try to load files www.servername.com/index.bak or www.wervername.com/index.old. Such copies of working script files are often encountered on amateur sites. Learn from other people's mistakes and don't do this on your server.

Any security specialist should prohibit users from accessing backup copies. No matter how often programmers are told not to keep on the server anything unnecessary, such as backup copies, they will continue doing this because they find this convenient. Your task is to store these copies safely — that is, to forbid Web clients to access them.

This can be done with the help of the following directives:

```
<FilesMatch "\.bak$">
 Order deny, allow
 Deny from all
</FilesMatch>

<FilesMatch "\.old$">
 Order deny, allow
 Deny from all
</FilesMatch>
```

7.8. Web Page Indexing

Over the past ten years, the Internet has grown to such dimensions that it has become impossible to find something in it without a good search system. The first search systems simply indexed Internet pages by their contents and then used the obtained database for searches, which produced rough matches. Most languages have words with double or even multiple meanings, which makes search by such words difficult.

The problem lies not only in the words with numerous meanings. There are many commonly-used expressions that are difficult to apply when conducting a search. These factors forced search systems to develop better search algorithms, and now a search can be requested based on a combination of various parameters. One of the today's most powerful search systems is Google (**www.google.com**). It offers many options to make the search more precise. Unfortunately, most users have not mastered these options, but hackers have and use them for nefarious purposes.

One of the simplest ways to use a search system for breaking into a server is to use it to find a closed Web page. Some sites have areas that can be accessed only through a password. Such sites include paid resources, for which the protection is based only on checking the password when entering the system; individual pages are not protected, and SSL is not used. In this case, Google can index the pages on closed sites and they can be viewed through the search system. You just need to have an exact idea what information is stored in the file, and to compose the search criteria as precisely as possible.

Google can be helpful in unearthing quite important information not intended for public viewing, which becomes accessible to the Google indexing engine because of a mistake by the administrator. For the search to be successful, you need to specify correct parameters. For example, the results of entering `Annual report filetype:doc` into the search line will be all Word documents containing the words "annual report."

Most likely, the number of the documents found will be too great and you will have to narrow the search criteria. Persevere and you'll succeed. There are real-life examples, in which confidential data, including valid credit card numbers and financial accounts, were obtained using this simple method.

Consider how indexing of Web pages that are not supposed to be open to public can be disallowed. For this, you have to understand what search systems index. The answer is simple: They index everything they come across — texts, names, picture names, documents in various formats (PDF, XLS, DOC, etc.), and so on.

Your task is to limit the search robots' doggedness so that they do not index the stuff you don't want them to. This is done by sending the robot a certain signal. How is this done? The solution is simple yet elegant: A file named robots.txt containing rules for search robots to follow is placed in the site's root.

Suppose that a robot is about to index the **www.your_name.com** site. Before it starts doing this, the robot will try to load the www.your_name.com/robots.txt file. If it succeeds, it will index the site following the rules described in the file; otherwise, the contents of the entire site will be indexed.

The format of the file is simple: It uses only two directives. These are the following:

- ☐ `User-Agent: parameter` — The value of `parameter` is the name of the search system covered by the prohibition. There can be more that one such entry in the file, each describing an individual search system. If the prohibitions apply to all search systems, the value of `parameter` is set to `*`.

- ☐ `Disallow: address` — This prohibits indexing of the indicated address, specified with respect to the URL. For example, indexing of pages from **www.your_name.com/admin** is prohibited by setting `address` to `/admin/`. The address is specified relative to the URL and not relative to the file system, because the search system cannot know the location of files on the server's disk and operates only with URL addresses.

The following is an example of the robots.txt file that prohibits all search robots from indexing pages located at the URLs **www.your_name.com/admin** and **www.your_name.com/cgi_bin**:

```
User-Agent: *
Disallow: /cgi-bin/
Disallow: /admin/
```

The prohibitions set by the preceding rules also apply to subdirectories in the specified directories. Thus, files located at **www.your_name.com/cgi_bin/forum** will not be indexed.

The following example prohibits the site from being indexed:

```
User-Agent: *
Disallow: /
```

If your site contains a directory with confidential data, you should disallow it to be indexed. But you should not become carried away and prohibit indexing altogether; this will prevent it from being included in searches and you stand to lose potential visitors. According to statistics, the number of visitors directed to sites by search engines is greater than the number of visitors coming from elsewhere.

7.9. Securing the Connection

In *Section 14.5*, various technologies for monitoring network traffic will be considered. These are mostly effective in local networks, with hackers preferring Internet connections because they provide more interesting material and because attacks can be carried out remotely.

How is it possible to intercept traffic between two locations in the United States from Europe? I believe there is no need for the packets' detour to Europe on their way from one U.S. location to another, and they will travel over the U.S. channels. Yet if a hacker makes his or her computer a middleman in the data transfer, sort of a proxy server, this can be done.

What confidential data can the hacker intercept when the client is viewing Web pages? Passwords, credit card numbers, bank accounts, and other sensitive information that people enter on Web forms every day, mostly without even thinking that it may fall into the wrong hands or can be intercepted. The most difficult thing here is to organize for the client to connect not to the real Web server requested but to the hacker's computer. Although people enter the addresses of the sites they want to visit as symbolic names, the actual connection is carried out using IP addresses. The task of mapping symbolic names to the corresponding IP address is performed by DNS servers. It is possible to fool the client with a fake DNS answer or a fake DNS server, thereby redirecting the traffic to the hacker's computer.

Afterwards, the computer in the middle will forward requests from the client to the real Web server and likewise return its answers to the client (Fig. 7.3). In this way, all traffic will pass through the hacker's computer.

But this method is a thing of the past; now it is of little use because of the protection against intercepts provided by HTTPS and an SSL connection.

As you should remember, when establishing an SSL connection, any client program (for example, a browser) and the Web server exchange keys used to encrypt the ensuing data exchange. HTTPS, in addition to the public and private keys, requires signed certificates, which are issued by special companies. The client program checks the certificate and, if it is valid (the digital signature belongs to the authorized company), allows the connection to be made. While the certificates can be faked, it is practically impossible to fake signatures.

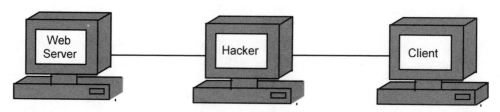

Fig. 7.3. Intercepting traffic

Simply forwarding encrypted data between the client and the server does the hacker no good. The only way to decrypt the traffic is to use the following technique:

1. The hacker generates a key pair and a certificate on his or her computer.
2. The client connects to the hacker's computer and exchanges keys with it.
3. The data sent by the client are encrypted with the key supplied by the hacker, so he or she has no problems decrypting them.
4. The hacker's computer connects to the Web server and obtains its public key.
5. A connection is established between the hacker's computer and the Web server using the key provided by the Web server.

With this arrangement, the client receives a key that was generated by the hacker and has no required signature. This means that a message will be displayed on the client's computer informing the client that the connection is to be established without a signed certificate. This is the moment most users commit a grave security lapse: Having been working on the Internet for a long time, they have tired of paying close attention to various warning messages, so they just automatically click the **OK** button to continue working, thus accepting an unsigned certificate.

The problem with the man-in-the-middle attack can only be solved by protecting the DNS server to prevent hackers from inserting themselves between the client and the server. Never use a proxy server whose origin you are not certain of: It may belong to a hacker, and all your traffic will be at his or her disposal.

Another thing would be training users to pay close attention to all messages displayed by the browser. But this would be difficult to achieve. To make users react to critical information, the browser would have to display it in a format different from the rest of the messages. Seeing a message about a potential danger that stands out from the rest of messages, the user will be more likely to read it. Thus, if the message about connecting to a site without a signed certificate is displayed in a critical-message format, the user is more likely to react to it and break off the connection. Although there are many sites that do not offer signed certificates, it does not mean that they are of the dot-con variety; most of them are quite respectable and protected. It simply costs money to obtain a signed certificate, and not every site owner wants to spend it. Only commercial enterprises offer signed certificates. But even these resources are not free of trouble. A signed certificate is only valid during the specified period, and if the administrator does not update it timely, the certificate lapses.

Users must remember that unless they connect to a site using a secure connection, it is not a good idea to provide credit card numbers to this site. The browser should display this warning in big red flashing letters when connecting to a server without a signed certificate.

Chapter 8: Electronic Mail

Some people use the Internet for viewing Web pages of dubious content, others for finding worthy adversaries for online games, and many for working and learning. But none of us can live without communication. Despite all of the new technologies invented to make communication easier (IRC, ICQ, etc.), electronic mail, or email for short, has remained one of the main communication means and will always remain so. Email was the impetus to local network development, and it was one of the first Internet services to be offered.

For me, an email client has become the main program I use for corresponding with my readers, friends, coworkers, and so on. The people I work with on my books live in different towns and even different countries. My closest partners are more than 600 miles away, and the publishing house office is 1,000 miles away. I don't know how I would be able to handle this arrangement without email, but with it I can live in the south and work for a company located in the north.

How does email operate? The following are the main stages of sending an email:

1. A user creates a message using an email client (an email program), specifies the addressee, and sends the message to an email server. Most often, SMTP servers are used for sending email.

2. After receiving the message, the server determines its destination. The email address consists of two parts divided by the at (@) character: the user name and the server name, for example, **username@servername.com**. The IP address of the **servername.com** server is established using DNS.

3. The source mail server sends the message to the server, on which the recipient is registered.

4. After receiving the message, the **servername.com** server places it into the **username** user's mailbox.

5. The addressee checks his or her mailbox using a mail client and can download message.

The process just described is similar to how the traditional mail operates. The servers play the role of post offices, which sort the mail by its destination addresses, send it to the addressees, and finally deliver it to their mailboxes.

As was mentioned, for transferring messages, mail servers use SMTP, which was developed at the dawn of the Internet. It has long been considered as lacking functionalities, but it is still used extensively.

Several decades ago, the UNIX-to-UNIX Copy Protocol (UUCP) was employed for working with mail. But it was tied to the specific operating system, and its functionalities were limited; therefore, it did not become commonly used and is rarely employed today.

There exist three protocols for receiving mail. These are the following:

❑ Post Office Protocol version 3 (POP3) — This is the most commonly used protocol for receiving mail today.

❑ Internet Message Access Protocol version 4 (IMAP4) — The capabilities of this protocol are greater than those of POP3.

❑ Messaging Application Programming Interface (MAPI) — This protocol is used in Microsoft networks on Microsoft Exchange servers.

The most commonly used Linux mail package is an old sendmail program. The program possesses great capabilities but is rather difficult to use. Because it was developed so long ago, the sendmail server has UUCP capabilities, which are not that common nowadays.

The operating principle of sendmail is quite simple. After receiving a message from a client, the program determines the recipient and enters the service information necessary to deliver the letter into its header. Further actions depend on the server's configuration. Thus, a letter can be sent immediately or placed into storage to be mailed later. Periodically, the accumulated messages are sent to their addressees.

8.1. Configuring sendmail

The /etc/mail/sendmail.cf file is the server's main configuration file. The sendmail server has a bad reputation because it is difficult to configure. Having taken even a brief look at the file's contents, you may feel intimidated by its more than 1,000 lines of information. The mysterious options and parameters only intensify the feeling.

All settings in the sendmail.cf configuration file are grouped into sections. A section is preceded by a header that looks like the following:

```
##################
#   local info   #
##################
```

These comments indicate that the local info section follows them. Some of the sections are the following:

- ❑   Local info — Contains local information and the main information about the server and domain
- ❑   Options — Contains operational settings
- ❑   Message precedence
- ❑   Trusted users
- ❑   Format of headers

It is impossible to consider all of the sendmail configuration settings in this book; it would require a separate book to describe each of its parameters. The goal of this book is to teach you some techniques to enhance the efficiency and security of your system; therefore, I will only consider the settings related to these aspects and how to use sendmail.

To make configuring sendmail easier, the latest versions of this service use a new configuration file: /etc/mail/sendmail.mc. Listing 8.1 shows an example of this file's contents.

Listing 8.1. A fragment of the /etc/mail/sendmail.mc file

```
divert(-1)
dnl # This is the sendmail macro config file. If you make changes
dnl # to this file, you need the sendmail-cf rpm installed and then
dnl # have to generate a new /etc/sendmail.cf by running the
dnl # following command:
dnl #
dnl #       m4 /etc/mail/sendmail.mc > /etc/sendmail.cf
dnl #
include('/usr/share/sendmail-cf/m4/cf.m4')
VERSIONID('linux setup for ASPLinux')dnl
OSTYPE('linux')
dnl # Uncomment and edit the following line if your mail needs to be
dnl # sent out through an external mail server:
dnl define('SMART_HOST','smtp.your.provider')
define('confDEF_USER_ID',"8:12")dnl
undefine('UUCP_RELAY')dnl
undefine('BITNET_RELAY')dnl
. . .
. . .
```

The format of the sendmail.mc file is simpler than that of the old sendmail.cf file, which reduces the chances of making a configuration error. After editing the sendmail.mc file, it has to be converted into the CF format with a special command to turn it into the sendmail.cf file.

I will be mostly considering parameters that have to be set in the sendmail.cf file; if a sendmail.mc file parameter is described, this will be stated explicitly.

In *Chapter 2*, I mentioned that Linux may hang at boot when starting the sendmail service. This happens because the mail server cannot determine the name of your computer. Open the /etc/hosts file. In most cases, there will be only one entry in it:

```
127.0.0.1        localhost.localdomain        localhost
```

This file is described in more detail in *Chapter 11*, where DNS is considered. For now, it will suffice to know that this entry maps IP address 127.0.0.1 to the localhost computer name. In any system, these address and name indicate the local machine. When the localhost name is specified in network applications, this name is converted to IP address 127.0.0.1.

The sendmail program uses the name of the computer specified when Linux was installed as the local machine name. If you have forgotten what this name is, you can use the hostname command to refresh your memory. My machine is named FlenovM. Because sendmail cannot determine the IP address of the machine named FlenovM, it hangs the system. The problem can be fixed by adding the following entry to the /etc/hosts file:

```
192.168.77.1        FlenovM        FlenovM
```

Replace FlenovM with the name of your computer and specify its IP address. Now, sendmail can be placed into the start-up and it will work without a hitch even using default settings.

Each new user is automatically created a mailbox with the same name as the user name. Mailbox files for all users are stored in the /var/spool/mail directory. Thus, the mailbox for the root user is located in the /var/spool/mail/root file.

For working with mail, you need a mail client to send and receive messages to and from the server. There is a host of such programs; some Linux distributions offer up to seven clients. Which one you choose is up to you and your preferences.

You can do without a mail client and connect to the server directly using the Telnet service, especially because Telnet commands are quite simple and easy to use. When using Telnet, mail is sent using port 25 (the SMTP port) and received at port 110 (the POP3 port).

8.2. Mail Operation

I will consider mailbox operations using the KMail client as an example. You should have this graphical mail program if you are using the KDE graphical shell. It is launched by executing the **Internet/More Internet Applications/KMail** main menu sequence. This will open the program's main window, shown in Fig. 8.1.

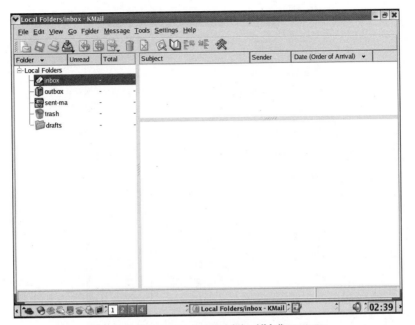

Fig. 8.1. The main window of the KMail program

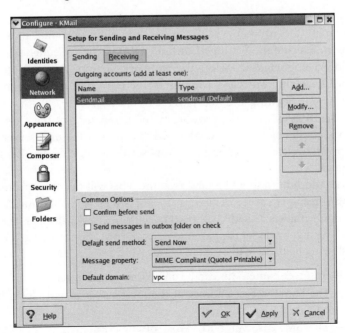

Fig. 8.2. The network configuration window

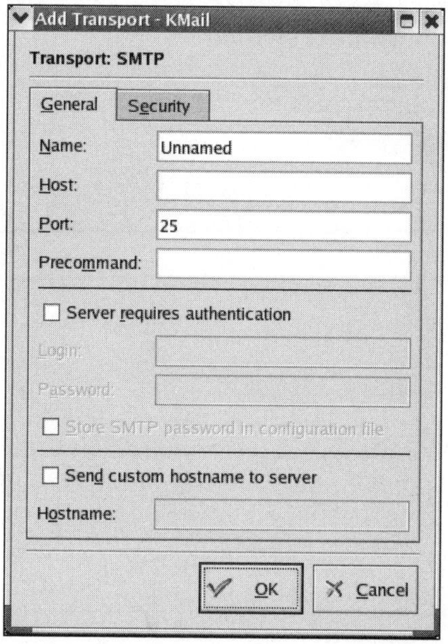

Fig. 8.3. The SMTP server configuration window

The program does not know yet, with which mailbox you want to work; you will have to configure it. Execute the **Settings/Configure KMail** menu sequence. This will open the configuration dialog window. Select the **Network** section; this will open the **Setup for Sending and Receiving Messages** window in the right part of the configuration window with two tabs on it: **Sending** and **Receiving** (Fig. 8.2).

On the **Sending** tab, you have to specify the parameters of the sending server. By default, the local sendmail is already configured, but what if the mail server is located on another computer? Delete the existing account (select it and click the **Remove** button) and then create new one.

Click the **Add** button to add a new account. This will open the protocol selection dialog window, offering a choice of two protocols: **SMTP** and **sendmail**. Select SMTP, because it is more universal, and click the **OK** button. This will open the **Add Transport** window. in which you will set the parameters of the SMTP server (Fig. 8.3).

The following fields have to be filled in this window:

☐ **Name** — A server name. This can be any name you choose.

☐ **Host** — The SMTP server address. If the local server is used, **local host** or **127.0.0.1** can be specified.

☐ **Port** — The SMTP server port. Most often, port 25 is used, but a different port can be used.

If the server requires authentication, check the **Server requires authentication** box and fill in the **Login** and **Password** fields that open.

If you have worked with email before, creating SMTP server parameters should give you no problems.

Next, the receiving part of the server has to be configured. Open the **Receiving** tab; you will see a list of servers on it. Select all existing accounts and delete them. Click the **Add** button to add a receiving server. This will open a window, in which you have to specify one of the following the server types: **Local mailbox**, **POP3**, **IMAP**, or **Maildir Mailbox**. Most often, the POP3 server is used; the process for creating it is similar to that of the SMTP server. You also have to specify the server address, the port (port 110 by default), and a login and password.

Using a local mailbox may be the most interesting thing. Even if an SMTP server is not installed, a directory containing a local mailbox is created, into which security messages, in addition to regular email messages, are sent for the administrator. When working from the console, you will see a message saying "You have new mail;" this means that there is a new message in your mailbox in the local directory. The best way to check this mailbox is to use a mail client.

For this, create a new account so that you can read security messages in a convenient format. Click the **Add** button to open the server type selection window. Select the **Local mailbox** option and click the **OK** button. This will open the **Add account** dialog window shown in Fig. 8.4.

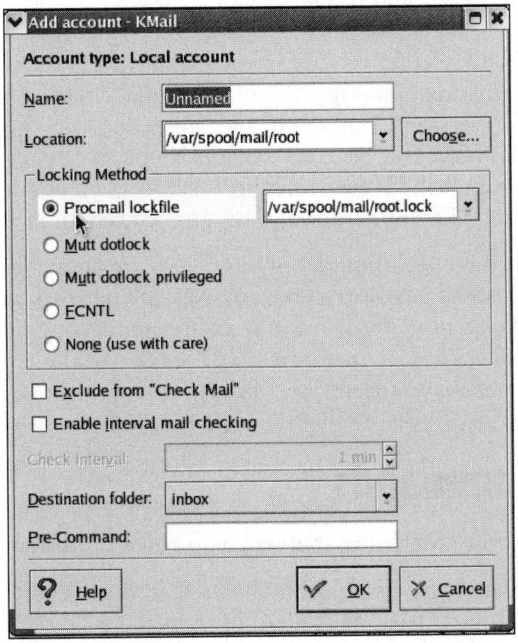

Fig. 8.4. The Local mailbox configuration window

The following fields have to be filled in this window.

- **Name** — An account name. This can be any name you choose.
- **Location** — The mailbox location. By default, all mailboxes are stored in the /var/spool/mail/name directory, where **name** is a user name. The administrator's mailbox will be /var/spool/mail/root.

The rest of the parameters are most often set by default, unless the administrator messed up the configuration.

Try to read mail using different protocols. Make sure that messages come into your mailbox and reach the recipient. Everything should be working all right even with the default settings. Later, some specific settings will be considered to make your mail server more secure; before making any improvements, however, you have to ensure that the basic version is working as intended.

8.2.1. Message Security

Email messages are sent over a network medium in plaintext and can be easily read if intercepted. Thus, you should encrypt confidential messages before sending them.

The most common encryption techniques are the following:

- Secure/Multipurpose Internet Mail Extension (S/MIME) — This standard is mainly supported by Netscape and its clone mail clients. This imposes certain restrictions because not all users are accustomed to using these programs.
- Pretty Good Privacy (PGP) — This encryption program is used in many areas, including encrypting mail messages. Numerous mail clients support this standard. There are several PGP versions, but many specialists recommend using the GNU Privacy Guard (GnuPG) program. No, this version is not any better than the rest, because all of them are based on the same principle. What is good about this version is that it was developed beyond U.S. borders and, thus, out of reach of its key length-limiting laws.

But with any of these techniques, only messages are encrypted. The protocol itself does not use encryption, so all passwords are sent over the network in plaintext and have to be protected. This can be done by using one of the modern standards, such as RFC 1734 (MD5 APOP Challenge/Response) or RFC 2095 (MD5 CRAM-HMAC Challenge/Response), or by resorting to the `stunnel` utility.

8.3. Useful Commands

The following are some commands that will help you administer a sendmail server:

- `hoststat` — Shows the status of the hosts that worked with the local mail server recently. The command is an equivalent of the `sendmail -bh` command, which is inactive by default.

❑ `mailq` — Displays short information about messages waiting in the queue to be proc-essed. The following is an example of the command's execution results:

```
/var/spool/mqueue (1 request)
----Q-ID---- --Size-- -----Q-Time----- -----Sender/Recipient-----
j0IAnST11838    6    Tue Jan 18 13:49    <flenov@flenovm.ru>
                       (host map: lookup (flenovm.ru): deferred)
                       <root@flenovm.ru>
```

The first line tells you that there is one message in the queue. The second line (that is, the first line below the header) displays the date the message was sent (`Tue Jan 18 13:49`) and the sender's address (`flenov@flenovm.ru`). The last line shows the message's recipi-ent: `root@flenovm.ru`.

❑ `mailstats` — Displays message statistics, including the total number of bytes sent.

❑ `sendmail` — This is the sendmail server command. When run with different options, it can provide various types of useful information. Consult its `man` page for more information.

8.4. Sendmail Security

The security of the sendmail service leaves a lot to be desired, with bugs being regularly found in it. Because of this, administrators and programmers have made the service into the butt of jokes. I have heard some of them even making bets on whether a new bug would be found in it within a month.

In this section, I will describe some parameters that can be configured to enhance the service's security.

8.4.1. Telltale Banner

Security problems start at the connection stage. Like most other services, the sendmail service displays a greeting message containing the program name and version.

This information should be made unavailable to hackers. This is achieved by changing the `SmtpGreetingMessage` parameter in the /etc/sendmail.cf file. In older sendmail ver-sions, the value of this parameter was the following:

```
SmtpGreetingMessage=$j Sendmail $v/$Z; $b
```

The most dangerous element here is the `$v/$Z` option, which displays the program name and version. Therefore, it was removed in more recent versions. Now the parameter is set to the following value:

```
SmtpGreetingMessage=$j $b
```

If the value of this parameter in your system contains something in addition to this, you should remove it. You can even set this parameter to display an entirely different service, as follows:

```
SmtpGreetingMessage = $j IIS 5.0.1 $b
```

Any successful attempt to confuse hackers stalls them and gives you a small victory.

8.4.2. Outgoing Mail Only

Mail servers often are used only to send mail. For example, Web servers can have sendmail installed only so that mail could be send from Perl or PHP scripts. If receiving mail is not a part of your server's mission, this mode should be disabled. This can be done by modifying the contents of the /etc/sysconfig/sendmail file as follows:

```
DAEMON = yes
QUEUE = "q1h"
```

The second directive sets the parameters that will be passed to sendmail when it is started. To allow your server to receive mail, change the value of the QUEUE parameter to -bd.

If there is no sendmail file in the /etc/sysconfig directory in your system (as is the case in some distributions), you will have to edit the /etc/rc.d/init.d/sendmail script file. Find in this file the parameters passed to the program, and change them to q1h directly in the script text.

8.4.3. Access Rights

No operating-system service should be allowed to work with root privileges. Should a vulnerability be found in the program's code that allows command execution, the system can be considered already compromised, because commands will be executed as root.

The service should work with the privileges of a user that has access only to the directories and files necessary for the service's operation. In the most recent sendmail versions, this can be implemented with the help of the RunAsUser parameter as follows:

```
O RunAsUser = sendmail
```

By default, this entry may be commented out. If it is, remove the comments. You can also implicitly specify the group with whose rights the program is to run:

```
O RunAsUser = sendmail:mail
```

Here, sendmail is a user name and mail is a group name.

8.4.4. Superfluous Commands

The mail server can process a great number of commands, but not all of them are useful. Make sure that the following entries are in your configuration file and that they are not commented out:

```
O PrivacyOptions = authwarnings
O PrivacyOptions = noexpn
O PrivacyOptions = novrfy
```

All of these options can also be listed, delimited by commas, in one line as follows:

```
O PrivacyOptions = authwarnings, noexpn, novrfy
```

The most dangerous element for the server may turn out to be the vrfy option, which is used to check whether a mailbox exists. The third directive in the example disables this option.

The second directive sets the noexpn parameter. This disables the expn command, which allows the email address and even the user name to be determined by the mail alias name. Hackers can use this directive to build spam mailing lists. They should not be given a chance to collect this information.

8.4.5. Executing External Commands

The mail service has one serious problem: It has to execute system commands, which is always fraught with danger. If a hacker can run such a program with extended privileges, great harm can be done to the system. This is why I recommend lowering the service's rights, but this alone is not sufficient.

To prohibit system commands from execution, sendmail has to be made to work through a secure command interpreter. For this purpose, the smrsh program was developed. The program curtails sharply the number of commands that can be run by sendmail, improving the overall security of the system. The easiest way to make the mail service use this command interpreter is to add the following line to the sendmail.mc file:

```
FEATURE('smrsh', '\user\bin\smrsh')
```

Here, in parentheses, the following two parameters are specified: the name of the command interpreter and the directory, in which it is located. Make sure that this is where the command interpreter is located in your system; otherwise, change the path.

By default, the smrsh interpreter executes commands from the /usr/adm/sm.bin directory. It will not run programs from different directories. If there are only secure programs in the /usr/adm/sm.bin directory, your system will be less vulnerable.

8.4.6. Trusted Users

The sendmail service allows a list of users to be created that are trusted to send messages without warnings. This list is saved in the /etc/mail/trusted-users file. I do not recommend entering real users into this list.

But the file can be useful under certain circumstances. You can add the Apache user to it to allow letters to be sent from Web scripts.

8.4.7. DoS Attacks

Mail servers are often subjected to DoS attacks because they have to accept connections from any users to service the mailboxes. Consequently, ports 25 and 110 are, most often, publicly available.

The sendmail service can be made more secure against DoS attacks by properly setting the following parameters:

- ❑ `MaxDaemonChildren` — This parameter sets the maximum number of simultaneous processes. It can be used to protect the processor from excessive workloads. Its default value is 12. This value can be set higher for a more powerful processor to use its resources more effectively. For a less powerful processor, the value can be lowered.
- ❑ `ConnectionRateThrottle` — This parameter specifies the maximum number of connections per second per daemon. By default, the value of this parameter is 3. It should not be raised unless you are certain that your server can handle the increased number of connections.

8.5. Mail Bombing

The first time I was mail bombed was almost ten years ago. Once I left my email address in a chat room (I had never done this before). As my bad luck would have it, there was a beginning hacker sitting there who flooded my mailbox with mail bombs.

So what is a mail bomb? Mail bombing sends a massive amount of email to a specific person or system. A huge amount of mail may overfill the victim's mailbox, making it impossible to receive legitimate messages.

At first, it may seem that this attack is easy to protect against: All you have to do is increase the mailbox size or remove the size limit. But this is the worst thing that could be done: With a limited mailbox size, a successful mail bomb attack will take out only one mailbox. With an unlimited mailbox size, a successful DoS attack can be carried out against the entire server.

Mail messages are the only way for an unauthorized person to upload information onto a server. When an email message is received at a server, it is stored on the server's hard drive until it is downloaded by the user when the mail is checked. Sending a constant flow of messages to a mailbox of unlimited size will fill the entire hard drive, and the server will no longer be able to receive messages into any of its mailboxes.

The worst situation that can be caused by mail bombing is when mailboxes are located in the default directory, which is /var. If this directory is filled, the server will no longer be able to write service information to it. The /var directory is also used to store security logs. If these logs cannot be updated, the server will become inaccessible.

Thus, the mailbox disk space must be limited. It is preferable to lose one or even a few mailboxes than to lose the entire server.

There is no foolproof defense against mail bombing. You can, however, make it more difficult for the perpetrator to carry it out. This can be done with the help of the parameters considered in *Section 8.4.7*. Moreover, the maximum size of a single message that can be received to a mailbox can be limited to a reasonable size using the `MaxMessageSize` parameter. This will make the miscreants' job more difficult because they will have to send many small messages instead of one large message.

8.6. Spam

The scourge of the Information Age is unsolicited mail, or spam. Spam makes up a large part of email traffic, and the existing techniques of fighting it do not always produce the results desired.

Thus, one of ways to fight unwanted mail is to prohibit incoming mail from servers found guilty of sourcing spam messages. But spammers keep finding new ways to get around the prohibitions, including using public or zombied servers.

If your server has been zombied and is used to send spam, this exposes you to the following dangers:

❑ Extra traffic expenses if you pay by volume
❑ Extra processor workload because spam mailings are usually carried out on a mass scale and consume a lot of the processor time, thereby loading the communication link

Moreover, your server may be entered on a spam blacklist, resulting in all your outgoing correspondence being filtered out and not reaching the recipients. The latter can be viewed as a successful DoS attack against your mail service.

8.6.1. Blocking Incoming Spam

Unsolicited incoming mail has the following undesired consequences:

❑ It incurs extra traffic expenses, as already mentioned.
❑ The attention of your workers or network users is distracted by the irrelevant mail.
❑ Spam messages are often bulky, requiring additional disk space for storing them.

There are many more ways to fight spam than those described here. But those described are sufficient for you to start taking steps against electronic junk mail.

Filtering Servers

The sendmail program has an option to filter out servers, from which the spam is received. The best way of doing this is to add a prohibiting directive to the sendmail.mc file. The problem is, however, that this directive has a different format for different sendmail versions.

Thus, for version 8.10 it looks like the following:

```
FEATURE(dnssbl, 'spam.domain.com',
'550 Mail not accepted from this domain')dnl
```

For version 8.11, it looks like this:

```
HACK('check_dnsbl', 'spam.domain.com', '', 'general', 'reason')dnl
```

In both directives, the `spam.domain.com` item has to be replaced with the name of the domain whose mailings you want to block. This method is ineffective, because often quite innocent servers would be on the receiving end of such prohibitions.

Once, my software sales server was placed on a spam list. Those were the times when a server could become blacklisted deservedly or for no reason. When I would mail the registration keys to the people who bought my software, about 10% of the messages would be returned marked as spam. This kept some of my customers from using the software they bought. This went on for a month until spam blacklists were judged to be ineffective.

Filtering Messages

More precise filtering involves blocking messages by their contents. A special program analyzes all information passing through the server and looks for typical signs of spam mailings. If a message is judged to be spam, it is deleted.

This method is the most effective; however, it is difficult to tell by the text of a letter whether it is spam. Hackers are constantly looking for new ways to circumvent such filters, so the percentage of filtered out spam is not high. The program can be configured to delete all messages, in which "buy," "sell," and other words typical for spam occur. However, there is a chance that this filter will delete some of your good mail.

I will not be recommending any specific spam-filtering programs, because I don't know any that would offer an ideal solution. But if you decide to use such a program, you may as well take a look at SpamAssassin (**spamassassin.apache.org**). It implements many checks to effectively detect undesirable messages.

In addition, you can modify the value of the `MaxRcptsPerMessage` parameter of the sendmail server, which sets the maximum number of message recipients. More than 100 recipients is a good indication of a spam message. It is not, however, always so, because mailing lists in some organizations can have 1,000 employees. In this case, important messages can be lost. To prevent this, the mail program should be configured to send messages in batches of no more than 20 recipients at a time.

8.6.2. Blocking Spam Remailing

When configuring your mail server, you should make it unavailable to be used by hackers for mailing spam. The following configuration settings will make using your server for mass mailings ineffective:

❏ By default, SMTP does not require authorization, so any user can connect to the server and send mail. This can be prevented by doing one of the following:

- Configure the firewall to prohibit from connecting to the SMTP port those users who do not belong to your network. This defense is used most often by providers and administrators of private and corporate networks. You should have no problems implementing this method, because I have considered it several times in this book.

- Allow mail to be sent only within a certain period (e.g., 10 minutes) after receiving mail by POP3. This allows the server to authorize the client when the mail is checked and to use the obtained authorization data for creating a firewall or some other permission to access SMTP. When this permission is active, mail can be sent from the authorized IP address.

- Use SMTP authorization. The original mail-sending protocol did not contain the user-authentication requirement, so not all servers support this feature. But sendmail and other powerful mail programs offer an SMTP user-authentication feature.

❏ In addition, you should disallow a large number of messages to be sent from the same IP address. In this respect, 20 messages is an acceptable number. A user should not be able to send more than 20 letters within 10 minutes.

❏ Disallow the mailing of letters to a large number of recipients listed in the **CC** field.

There also are other methods, but those just described ought to be enough.

The more recent sendmail versions by default permit remailing of messages only from the computers specified in the /etc/mail/access file. The contents of the file are shown in Listing 8.2.

Listing 8.2. The /etc/mail/access file

```
# Check the /usr/share/doc/sendmail/README.cf file for a description
# of the format of this file. (search for access_db in that file).
# The /usr/share/doc/sendmail/README.cf is part of the sendmail-doc
# package.
#
# By default, we allow relaying from localhost...
localhost.localdomain          RELAY
localhost                      RELAY
127.0.0.1                      RELAY
```

You can place the following directives into this file to allow mailings only from the local network computer or from the server:

```
localhost                RELAY
your_domain.com          RELAY
```

This method is effective only when the integrity of the local network's computers and servers has not been compromised. But if hackers obtain access to the network, they can mail any sort of spam from user accounts. This is something that cannot be avoided. If there is at least some sort of permission, hackers can take advantage of it, so your task is to make it difficult for them.

It is not always possible to prohibit mailings; therefore, you have to resort to other methods — for example, making users check their POP3 mailbox before mailing messages. This can be implemented with the help of the Pop-before-SMTP service (**popbsmtp.sourceforge.net**). The service checks the /var/log/maillog message log file and allows mail to be sent only if it finds that there was a successful POP3 authorization within a certain period.

The POP3 authorization method, however, has one significant shortcoming: If there is an anonymous proxy server or a masking firewall in the route, via which the letters arrive, packets will arrive with a different IP address. This means that all users connected using the same proxy or firewall are automatically considered authorized. Consequently, a search in the log by the IP address will not provide 100% protection.

The most preferable is the SMTP authorization method (SMTP AUTH), described in RFC 2554. The sendmail service supports this extension starting with version 8.10.

If you decide to use SMTP AUTH, make sure that the user's mail clients are configured to authenticate at the server.

8.7. Conclusion

I considered only the skin-deep workings of email, because configuring sendmail requires a book of its own. More detailed sendmail configuration information can be found in the documentation supplied with the operating system located in the /usr/share/sendmail-cf directory. Also, running a search for "configuring sendmail" in any Internet search system will produce a huge list of hits on this subject.

If this is still not enough, you can buy a book on the subject, for example, *Sendmail* by Bryan Costales and Eric Allman, published by O'Reilly Media.

If you are just beginning to work with the sendmail service, I recommend that you start with the default configuration settings and proceed from there.

Chapter 9: Gateway to Internet

You already know how to install and configure a Linux server, secure its connection, and enable the main services. But such services as a Web server and email are used on more than the local network. The maximum advantages materialize when integrated with the World Wide Web.

But it's a dangerous world out there on the Internet. You can run into all kinds of people and learn that life is not a bowl of cherries. Along with law-abiding Internet denizens, evil hackers lurk online.

You have to learn to protect your computer from them. When you build an office or some other building, you make its walls strong enough to resist attempts to break through. The doors must keep dishonest people out. Finally, you equip the finished building with an alarm system.

You have already built your computer walls and taken care to make them strong by securing your local network. Now you have to install doors to enter the network from the outside: the Internet. The door to the World Wide Web in a computer building will play the roles of gateway and proxy server. These are what will be considered in this chapter. In addition to configuring the server, the client has to be configured.

After making sure that the doors are up to snuff, you will install the alarm system: utilities to monitor network traffic activities and to detect unauthorized activities at the doors and in the building. These will be considered in *Chapter 12*.

9.1. Gateway Configuration

One way to access the Internet is to connect through a modem or a dedicated phone line. *Section 3.7* touched briefly on using the KPPP graphical utility to configure both types of Internet connections. I will not develop this subject, because there is nothing to add here in terms of the security. You can easily find numerous documents on the Internet describing how to configure Internet connections using KPPP. I will only make a few remarks in this respect.

If you use the graphical connection-configuration utility, you should know that all scripts are stored in the /etc/ppp and /etc/sysconfig/network-scripts directories. Make sure that you familiarize yourself with the files contained in these directories.

After connecting to the Internet, ascertain that a DNS server (which maps symbolic Internet site names to their corresponding IP addresses) is available. This can be done by pinging some Web site, like this:

```
ping www.redhat.com
```

If there is a response, a DNS server is available; otherwise, you will only be able to address Web pages by using their IP addresses. If the DNS server is not available, you can specify its address manually. You will have to obtain the DNS server address from your Internet provider and add it to the /etc/resolv.conf file as follows:

```
nameserver 191.168.1.1
```

Instead of the 191.168.1.1 value, specify the address given to you by the provider. If the provider gives you more than one address, all of them can be added to the file as follows:

```
nameserver 191.168.1.1
nameserver 191.168.1.2
```

9.2. Proxy Server Operation

Initially, proxy servers were intended for solving a specific task, namely, caching data received from the Internet. For example, you may have a network of a hundred computers that all connect to the Internet using one physical communications link. It is well known that most users load the same pages several times a day. Loading the same page wastes the local server's bandwidth.

Do a simple calculation. Every day you use a search system, for example, Yahoo (**www.yahoo.com**) or Google (**www.google.com**). Assuming that on average, 10 requests are made from each of the 100 computers, about 1,000 loads of the same page will be made every day. I will not calculate how many megabytes this is, for it is already obvious that bandwidth is wasted.

A proxy server solves this problem by storing (caching) a Web page on the local disk the first time it was accessed. The next time a local user asks to access this page, instead of requesting it from the remote server, the local server serves it from the local disk cache.

The economy is obvious. With time, these features have been enhanced and currently offer the following functions:

- ☐ Caching documents received from the network
- ☐ Caching the results of DNS requests
- ☐ Organizing a network access gateway
- ☐ Controlling Internet access
- ☐ Providing anonymous Internet access by hiding addresses
- ☐ Reducing IP address use

In this chapter, the most popular Linux proxy server — squid — will be considered.

To reduce the bandwidth traffic and to increase the loading speed, a special program is installed on the server that provides access to the Internet (Fig. 9.1). When a page, for example, **www.yahoo.com**, is loaded on one of the local network's computers for the first time, all of its contents are saved in the proxy's cache. The next time the same page is requested from the local network, the images it contains are loaded not from the Internet but from the provider's proxy server, and the text (depending on the contents of the page and the changes to it) may be loaded from the source server.

As a rule, the graphical contents of a page take up most of its volume. The text part of a page does not usually exceed 15 KB, but the graphical part can be 100 KB and more. Loading the latter information from the local proxy server makes it possible to reduce the bandwidth load and increase the page-loading speed.

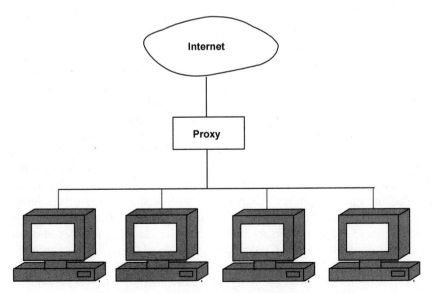

Fig. 9.1. Accessing the Internet via a proxy server

The loading speed is increased because the proxy server is sending most of the Web page data (all graphics and the unmodified text) at the local network rate, which currently is 100 Mb/sec on even the cheapest network equipment. The dial-up Internet connection speed is much lower, ranging from 2 to 8 Mb/sec. At this rate, only text data that do not change are loaded (most often, HTML file contents).

In addition to caching Web pages, a proxy server can cache results of DNS requests. This can also have a positive effect on the productivity. Although humans prefer to use symbolic Web page names, computers convert them to the corresponding numerical IP addresses. Thus, before a page can be loaded, some time is taken for converting the symbolic address to its IP form. However, if the site being accessed has already been accessed, its IP address will be saved in the proxy's cache. So instead of going to a DNS server for the IP address, the proxy will take it from its cache. The DNS subject is discussed in more detail in *Chapter 11*.

As the World Wide Web has been developing and the requirements of its users have been increasing, capabilities of proxy servers have also been growing. Now, a proxy server can perform gateway functions and provide Internet access without additional software or equipment. Moreover, it serves as a shield guarding the network against invasions from the outside. When any of the proxy clients sends a Web page request to the Internet, the proxy server hides the client's IP address and sends the packets on its own behalf. This means that hackers can see only the address of the proxy server and will attempt to break into it and not into the computers it services. This makes it much easier to organize defense against outside attacks, because you can give more attention to one computer, that is, the proxy server, instead of spreading it among all client computers. However, the protection capabilities of proxy servers are too basic and are easily circumvented, so they should be supplemented by a good firewall and an eagle-eyed administrator.

The IP address concealment feature also makes it possible to save IP addresses. Because only the proxy server has the actual Internet connection, only it must have an IP address. The rest of the computers in the local network can have unroutable addresses reserved for private networks (in the 192.168.*x.x.* or 10.*x.x.x* ranges).

There are two types of proxy servers: transparent and anonymous. Transparent proxies simply forward a client's packets to the requested Web server without changing the sender's address. A proxy that conceals the sender's IP address is called anonymous. This server communicates with the external world on behalf of clients under its own name. This feature is often taken advantage of by miscreants. For example, hackers do their break-ins through anonymous proxy servers so that the owners of the burglarized machines will not be able to determine, from which address the break-in was perpetrated.

Today, there are many servers on the Internet claiming to offer anonymous proxy services, but not all them actually do. Some of them make the request source IP available to the system, to which the request is directed; others log all traffic activities, including IP addresses, with the logs available to law-enforcement agencies. Consequently, you can never be sure that the server is as anonymous as it claims to be.

Because not all of a network's computers are allowed Internet access, user authentication can carried out on the proxy server level.

Some proxy versions have a handy feature: They can exchange their cache data. For example, several offices may share one local network, but each of them has separate Internet access through its own proxy server to keep the Internet bills separate. The individual proxies can be combined into a sort of a proxy network so that if one of them does not have the information requested in its cache, it will check the caches of the other proxies for it.

Most often, this cache-sharing feature is implemented using the Internet Cache Protocol (ICP). If one server does not find the requested document in its cache, it sends an ICP request to the other proxies. If one of the proxies gives a positive reply, the information will be taken from its cache.

Using cache sharing does not lead to a significant loading-speed increase when requesting small documents, because it takes extra time to search for the documents in the shared caches. With a large request load on the servers and a sizable cache base, the search time may even be so long that it eliminates any speed load advantages. It still leaves the bandwidth economy factor, which may be important for those who have to watch each megabyte of traffic.

Not all proxy servers will have the main features just considered. It all depends on what purposes a particular proxy was developed for, and some of them are intended to address only one task.

To work through a proxy server, you have to properly configure the program you want to use the proxy with. Consider the Mozilla browser as an example. Launch the browser and select the **Edit/Preferences** menu sequence. A tree of categories that can be configured is located in a pane on the left in the **Preferences** dialog window. Select the **Advanced/Proxies** category sequence to configure proxy server connections. The default is no proxy: **Direct connection to the Internet**. You should select the **Manual proxy configuration** and specify the IP address and port of the proxy server for each protocol (Fig. 9.2).

When configured to use a proxy server, the browser will send all requests to the proxy server, which will then forward them to the destination server. The proxy server always has to be loaded and must listen to the specific port (or several ports for different protocols).

A separate port is allocated for each protocol. For HTTP, intended to load Web pages, most often port 8080 is used; however, this value depends on the server and can be changed. Before using proxy server software, make sure that it has the necessary features and supports the necessary protocols. If the proxy does not support a certain protocol, its traffic will connect to the Internet directly.

To enhance the security of your network, you should configure the firewall to prohibit incoming connections to the ports used by the squid proxy service. For example, for the HTTP proxy port 3128 is used. Prohibiting incoming connections to this port will prevent using the proxy server for purposes other than those it is intended for, for example, breaking into the network.

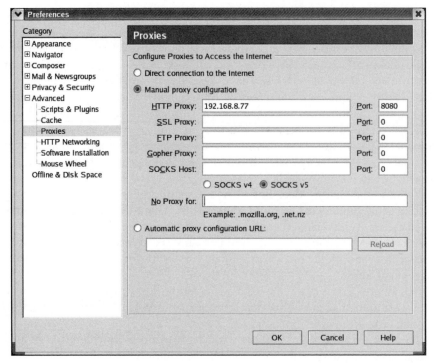

Fig. 9.2. Configuring a proxy server in Mozilla

9.3. Squid

As already mentioned, the most commonly used Linux proxy server is squid. This server has been around for quite a while, and during this time it has gathered numerous features. There is no task that I could not do using squid.

The main configuration file for squid is /etc/squid/squid.conf (in some systems, it is /etc/squid.conf). The file is very large and it would make no sense to list it all here, because a large part of it is detailed comments on how to use its directives.

I will consider the main commands for controlling the proxy server. As usual, all parameters affecting productivity and security will be considered in detail. Other settings will be given a cursory look only; you can obtain detailed information on them from the comments in the configuration file.

9.3.1. HTTP Tags

One of the main reasons for connecting to the Internet is to browse Web pages. When a Web connection is through a proxy server, HTTP has to be properly configured. The following tags are used for configuring HTTP in squid.

In the `http_port` n tag, the n parameter specifies the port number to be used for the connection. The first things that need configuring are the ports, on which the server will track for connections from clients. These directives have the `XXXX_port` format. For an HTTP port, the directive looks as follows:

```
http_port 8080
```

Then you have to configure the browser on the client computer by specifying the IP address of the server running squid and the port allocated by this directive.

The `hierarchy_stoplist` tag provides a list of words that, if found in a URL, cause the data to be retrieved from the source server. I recommend that you add to this list the `cgi-bin` string and a question mark: `hierarchy_stoplist cgi-bin ?`. URLs containing this text point to scripts that may be executed on the server, and it is better not to cache their results.

Consider an example. Suppose that you retrieved a Web page with the URL **www.servername.con/cgi-bin/ping.cgi** that allows the ping command to be executed through the Web interface. Assume that the first time you pinged address 18.1.1.1. The result will be saved in the proxy server's cache. The next time you run the script to ping address 18.1.1.18; the browser, however, will return the result of the first ping, because it will retrieve it from the cache.

Pages containing scripts return varying results, depending on the situation and the parameters specified by the user. Caching these pages will cause the browser to always return the same result: the one stored in cache. So instead of convenience offered by using proxy, you get a headache.

The question mark is often used to pass parameters to PHP scripts; thus, these pages should not be cached either.

The `hierarchy_stoplist` tag prohibits you from retrieving pages from cache. The following two entries prohibit caching pages whose URLs contain the `cgi-bin` string or a question mark altogether.

```
acl QUERY urlpath_regex cgi-bin \?
no_cache deny QUERY
```

I believe you can see that there is no need to cache material that must be provided by the server; this would only waste disk space.

9.3.2. FTP Tags

There are several tags to control FTP proxy operations. The following are some of the main ones:

❑   `ftp_passive on|off` — Specifies the operation mode. If set to `on`, it enables the passive mode. This is the default setting.
    The squid server allows you to work with FTP but may require some additional configuring. For example, if squid is located behind a firewall that does not allow the passive mode, the value of this parameter should be changed to `off`:

```
ftp_passive off
```

- ❐ `ftp_user address` — Specifies the email address to be used as the password during the authentication procedure on anonymous FTP servers.

  No server can determine whether the email address entered is correct, so this check can be disabled. Some FTP servers, however, verify whether the email address is correct. The default string is `ftp_user squid@`.

  However, by default, this entry is commented out in the /etc/squid/squid.conf file. The default email address should also be changed to something like `ftp_user squid@hotmail.com`.

  Any FTP server will accept this address as correct, because it complies with all rules for email addresses.

- ❐ `ftp_list_width n` — The n number sets the width of the FTP listing. This value should be set to fit the width of a standard browser. Setting it too small may cut off long file names.

9.3.3. Cache Configuration Tags

The efficiency and convenience of proxy server operation depend on how its cache is configured. I will try to explain in detail all pertinent tags.

- ❐ `cache_dir type directory size L1 L2 options` — Specifies parameters of the directory, in which the cache will be stored. The main parameters are `type`, `directory`, and `size`. In most cases, the value of `type` is set to `ufs`. It can be set to `aufs` for asynchronous input/output. I do not recommend doing this, because it may cause flawed operation.

  The directory should be located in the largest partition, so that information will not be spread over several disks. But if all you have is one disk with one partition on it, the location makes no difference.

  The default size of the directory is 100 MB. This is sufficient to speed up work for three users. If there are many users in your network and they all have different tastes or jobs (meaning, they visit different sites), the size should be increased. I allocate at least 1 GB of disk space to cache. If the server is allowed to cache large files, the allocated space will be filled in no time.

- ❐ `cache_mem n MB` — Specifies the maximum amount of operating memory to use as a memory cache for objects. The default value is 8 MB. If your machine is only used to run the proxy server, this value can be specified as the difference between the total size of the operating memory and the memory necessary for the operating system's needs. For example, 64 MB is more than enough for an operating system working in the text mode. Thus, if, for example, you have 512 MB of operating memory installed, you can give 448 MB of it $(512 - 64 = 448)$ to the proxy server; the more memory the proxy server has, the more rapidly it will be able to serve frequently requested pages.

- ❐ `cache_swap_low n` — Sets the low-water mark of cache filling. When the percentage of cache filling exceeds the n value, the server starts cleaning it up, removing old objects until the cache filling percentage falls back to the acceptable level.

- ❐ `cache_swap_high n` — Sets the high-water mark of cache filling. This tag is similar to the previous one, only object evection is more intensive to prevent cache overflow.

- ❐ `minimum_object_size n KB` — Specifies the minimum size of objects that can be cached. The default value is 0, meaning there is no minimum threshold.

- ❐ `maximum_object_size n KB` — Specifies the maximum size of objects that should be cached. The default value is 4,096 KB (4 MB). Set this value low to increase the server's speed; however, you will pay an increased traffic penalty for this. If you want to save bandwidth, keep this value high.

- ❐ `maximum_object_size_in_memory n KB` — Specifies the maximum size of objects to be kept in the memory cache. The default value is 8 KB.

- ❐ `ipcache_size n` — Specifies the IP address cache size. The default value is 1,024 KB.

- ❐ `ipcache_low n` and `ipcache_high n` — Specify the minimum and maximum IP address cache filling percentage, respectively.

- ❐ `reference_age parameter` — Specifies objects' lifetime in the cache. Objects whose lifetime exceeds this value can be deleted. The following are a few examples:

```
reference_age 1 week
reference_age 3.5 days
reference_age 4 months
reference_age 2.2 hours
```

The default value is 1 week:

```
reference_age 1 week
```

- ❐ `quick_abort_min n KB` — A situation may arise, in which the connection is broken while an object is being retrieved. If less than the n value remains to be retrieved, retrieval of the object is completed anyway: When the connection is restored, there will be no need to repeat the retrieval. The default value is 16. Setting it to −1 disables the feature.

- ❐ `quick_abort_max n KB` — The same situation as with `quick_abort_min`, only if more than the specified value remains to be retrieved, the retrieval of the object is aborted. The default value is 16.

- ❐ `quick_abort_pct n` — The same situation as with the previous two tags, but only if more than the specified value has been retrieved, the retrieval will be completed.

- ❐ `negative_ttl n minutes` — TTL for failed requests. Negative requests (such as "Connection refused" or "404 Page Not Found") may be temporary, and they should not be cached for long periods. The default value is 5 minutes. If a request to the same address is made after this time, the server will attempt to retrieve the page from the source server instead of serving it from the cache.

- ❐ `positive_dns_ttl n hours` — TTL in hours for successful DNS lookups. During this period, succeeding attempts to access the same lookups to the DNS server will be served from the cache. The default value is 6 hours, which can be increased to 24 hours. A few years ago, IP addresses had a tendency to change often, so TTL values had to be set low. Nowadays, most sites have static addresses, which change only with a change of the host, and major portals have their own permanent IP addresses. Setting this parameter to 0 disables the squid's IP address caching feature.

❑ `negative_dns_ttl n minutes` — TTL for failed DNS lookups. A failure to resolve a DNS address may be caused by some temporary problems with the DNS server and not with the address. These problems are usually fixed in 2 to 3 minutes, and failed lookups should not be cached for longer than this. I set this parameter to 1 or 0, so that users could load the site they need as soon as the DNS server is back in order.

❑ `range_offset_limit n KB` — Caching parameters. If set to −1, the server will download the entire object so that it may cache it. If set to 0, squid does not fetch more than the client requested. The value greater than 0 specifies how far into the file a range request may be to make squid prefetch the whole file. If beyond this limit, the proxy does not cache the result of the range request.

9.3.4. Log Tags

There are several parameters in the squid's configuration file dealing with logs (the latter can be viewed in any text editor). These are the following:

❑ `cache_access_log file` — Specifies the path to the file, in which all user activity (namely, HTTP and ICP requests) is logged. The default value is /var/log/squid/access.log.

❑ `cache_log file` — Specifies the path to the file in which general information about the cache activity is logged. The default value is /var/log/squid/cache.log.

❑ `cache_store_log file` — Specifies the path to the file, in which the activities of the store manager are logged. The log shows, which objects are saved to the cache and for how long, and which are evicted. The default value is /var/log/squid/store.log. However, no utility exists for analyzing the data stored in this log. Besides, there is no practical use for this data; you only waste disk space and system resources to save them. So you will be better off to disable this log by setting the `file` parameter value to `none`.

❑ `log_mime_hdrs on|off` — Indicates whether Multipurpose Internet Mail Extension (MIME) headers will be tracked. If set to `on`, MIME headers will be recorded in the `access` log.

❑ `useragent_log path/filename` — Specifies the file, in which the `User Agent` field from each HTTP request is logged. There is no practical use for this field, and it can be faked easily; thus, it is disabled by default.

Linux logs and various services are discussed in *Section 12.5*. In *Section 12.5.4*, the contents of the squid's main log — /var/log/squid/access.log — are considered.

9.3.5. Cache-Sharing Tags

For several squid servers to be able to communicate with each other to share their cache contents, the corresponding protocol has to be properly configured. This is done using the following tags:

- ❑ `icp_port n` — Specifies the port number to be used for ICP. The default value is 3130. Setting the `n` value to 0 disables the protocol.
- ❑ `htcp_port n` — Specifies the port number to be used for ICP working above TCP/IP. The default value is 4827. Setting the `n` value to 0 disables the protocol.
- ❑ `cache_peer hostname type http_port icp_port option` — Specifies other caches in the hierarchy. The `hostname` parameter is set to the name or address of the cache to be queried. The `http_port` parameter specifies the port where the cache listens for proxy requests. It corresponds to the `http_port` parameter in the squid configuration file. The `icp_port` parameter specifies the port number used by squid to send and receive ICP queries to and from neighbor caches. It corresponds to the `icp_port` parameter in the squid configuration file of the remote system. The `type` parameter can have one of the following values:
  - `parent` — The topmost cache in the hierarchy. Forwards cache misses on behalf of a child cache.
  - `sibling` — May only request objects already held in the cache. Cannot forward cache misses on behalf of a peer.
  - `multicast` — Can query one or more neighboring caches.

The option parameter can take on many different values, and considering them is beyond the scope of this book. Detailed information for each option value can be found in the configuration file comments.

- ❑ `icp_query_timeout n` — Specifies the timeout value in milliseconds. Most often, proxy servers are located in local networks, which have high access speed; thus, there is no need to set this value to more than 2000 milliseconds (2 seconds).
- ❑ `cache_peer_domain cache_host domain` — Limits the domains, for which the neighbor caches can be queried. For example, the following entry allows retrieval from the cache only of data requested from the **com** domain:

```
cache_peer_domain parent.net .com
```

Requests to other domains will be ignored to avoid overloading the proxy server. This tag can be used to configure sever proxy servers, each responsible for its own domain.

9.3.6. Miscellaneous Tags

The following tags I could not place into any specific category, but they are of certain importance and need to be considered:

- ❑ `redirect_rewrites_host_header on|off` — Enables (`on`) or disables (`off`) rewriting of host headers in redirect requests. If rewriting is enabled, the server work in the autonomous mode; otherwise, it is in the transparent mode. The autonomous mode requires extra expenses to implement but allows only one IP address to be used for the external connection for any size of network. The transparent mode is faster but requires each computer to have an IP address to work with the Internet.

❑ `redirector_access allow|deny` — Specifies the list of processes sent to the redirector process. By default, all requests are sent.

❑ `cache_mgr email` — Indicates the email address, to which a notification will be sent should there be problems in the squid operation.

❑ `append_domain domain` — Indicates the default domain. Because users generally request pages from the **com** domain, it would be logical to specify this domain in the directive: `append_domain.com`. Then, if a user enters the address, for example, redhat, squid will automatically append the domain code, taking the user to the **redhat.com** site.

❑ `smtp_port n` — Sets the port number, on which to listen for SMTP requests on sending messages. SMTP is the type of protocol that does not require caching, and using a proxy server will not save on traffic. The feature may come in handy when a gateway cannot be installed and only a proxy is allowed.

❑ `offline_mode on|off` — Indicates the operating mode. If set to `on`, squid will work with the cache without accessing the Internet. If the cache does not contain the page requested, an error message will be issued. To allow squid to address the Internet, the parameter must be set to `off`, which is the default setting.

9.4. Squid Access Rights

This is the sorest subject for any administrator. Yes, access rights to various squid functions are controlled in squid, and they are defined in the /etc/squid/squid.conf configuration file. But because the main emphasis of this book is on the security aspects of Linux, I devoted this subject to a separate section.

9.4.1. Access Control List

The first thing to consider is the ACL, which is a powerful tool for configuring site access rights. Using a list of names, actions or users can be grouped. The tag is issued in the following format:

```
acl name type string
```

The functions of the tag's three parameters are the following:

❑ `name` — This can be any name, preferably descriptive of the actions performed.

❑ `decision_string` — This is a template whose function depends on the type of operation specified in the second argument.

❑ `type` — This parameter can take on the following values: `src`, `dst`, `srcdomain`, `dstdomain`, `url_pattern`, `urlpath_pattern`, `time`, `port`, `proto`, `proxy_auth`, `method`, browser, or user. The functions of the main types, specifying how to interpret the preceding parameter (decision_string), are as follows:

- src — Access is controlled by source IP addresses.
- dst — Access is controlled by destination IP addresses.
- port — Access is controlled by the destination port number.
- proto — A list of protocols is given delimited by a space.
- method — This specifies the type of the method of the request; for example, POST or GET.
- proxy_auth — This requires an external authentication program to check user name and password combinations. With REQUIRED put as a user name (i.e., acl password proxy_auth REQUIRED) allows any valid user name to be accepted.
- url_regex — This instructs the function to search the entire URL for the regular expression you specify.
- time — This indicates the time in the format day h1:m1 – h2:m2. This string can be used to restrict access to only specified days of the week and times of day. The abbreviations for the days of week are the following: s for Sunday, M for Monday, T for Tuesday, W for Wednesday, H for Thursday, F for Friday, A for Saturday.

The configuration file already contains several lists that are ready to use and usually do not have to be edited. These are shown in Listing 9.1.

Listing 9.1. Default ACL rules in the /etc/squid/squid.conf configuration file

```
acl all src 0.0.0.0/0.0.0.0
acl manager proto cache_object
acl localhost src 127.0.0.1/255.255.255.255
acl SSL_ports port 443 563
acl Safe_ports port 80                  # http
acl Safe_ports port 21                  # ftp
acl Safe_ports port 443 563             # https, snews
acl Safe_ports port 70                  # gopher
acl Safe_ports port 210                 # wais
acl Safe_ports port 1025-65535          # unregistered ports
acl Safe_ports port 280                 # http-mgmt
acl Safe_ports port 488                 # gss-http
acl Safe_ports port 591                 # filemaker
acl Safe_ports port 777                 # multiling http
acl CONNECT method CONNECT
```

The preceding list is the minimum recommended ACL configuration.

The first entry specifies an `acl` named `all`. The `src` type of decision string means this list covers all users whose IP address matches 0.0.0.0/0.0.0.0, that is, all users.

The next entry creates an ACL class named `manager`. It defines access to the `cache_object` protocol, as specified by the `proto` type and the `cache_object` decision string. And so on.

Now, try to create your own ACL class. Suppose you have to allow access to the Internet for ten computers in your network with addresses from 192.168.8.1 to 192.168.8.10 (the subnet mask is 255.255.255.0). Access should be denied to all other computers in the network.

When creating the list, you should start by denying access to all and then allowing it only to those who require it. A class for all users already exists in the default list: `acl all src 0.0.0.0/0.0.0.0`. A list for ten computers is named, for example, `AllowUsers`; its decision string is of the `src` type, the decision string itself being the range of addresses in question. Here is how it looks:

```
acl AllowUsers src 192.168.8.1-192.168.8.10/255.255.255.0
```

This ACL class, named `AllowUsers`, includes all computers in the specified address range.

9.4.2. Assigning Rights

After access lists have been created, access rights for each of them can be assigned using the following commands:

☐ `http_access allow|deny ACL_name` — Specifies access rights to HTTP. In the following example, all users, except those specified in the `AllowUsers` ACL, are prohibited access to HTTP:

```
http_access deny all
http_access allow AllowUsers
```

By specifying access rights for the `AllowUsers` ACL, all it takes is one line to allow access for all computers included in this ACL. This eliminates the need to specify rights for each computer and makes the lives of administrators of big networks much easier.

In the previous example, only computers in the 192.168.8.1 to 192.168.8.10 address range were allowed access to the Internet. Access will be denied to any computer trying to access the Internet from any other address.

☐ `icp_access allow|deny ACL_name` — Specifies access rights to the proxy server over ICP. By default, access is denied to all:

```
icp_access deny all
```

☐ `miss_access allow|deny ACL_name` — Specifies rights to receive the MISSES reply. In the following example, only local users have the rights to receive the MISSES reply; all other users can only receive the HITS reply:

```
acl localclients src 172.16.0.0/16
miss_access allow localclients
miss_access deny !localclients
```

9.4.3. Authentication

Using an IP address to limit access rights does not guarantee that the IP address cannot be faked. Moreover, there always exists a possibility that the wrong people can obtain the physical access to the computer allowed access to the Internet. Once they do, what they do with it is up their good, or ill, will.

I used to work for a company, in which each employee was allotted a certain monthly download limit, with the excess paid for by the employee. The authentication procedure was based on the IP address.

NOTE

Authentication does not work if squid is configured to work in the transparent mode.

Once, several employees were noticed to have gone over their traffic limit significantly. This would have been no big deal, except these guys were away on vacation. Someone was faking their IP addresses and using their share of the Internet traffic.

To prevent something similar from happening to you, you should employ supplementary protection by checking the user name and password. This is done using the following directive:

```
authenticate_program path_to_program path_to_pswdfile
```

The directive specifies the path to the external authentication program and the path to the password file. By default, the authenticator program is not used. The traditional proxy-authentication program can be specified by the following directive:

```
authenticate_program /usr/lib/squid/ncsa_auth /usr/etc/passwd
```

The path to the ncsa_auth program may be different for your system.

You must have at least one ACL of the proxy_auth type to be able to use the authentication feature of the proxy server.

Consider the following directives:

- authenticate_children n — Specifies the number of concurrent authentication processes to spawn. One process cannot perform authentication of several clients at once; consequently, while one user is being authenticated, no other users will be able to access the Internet using the proxy server.
- authenticate_ttl n hour — Indicates the time in hours that the authenticated user name–password pair remains cached. During this time, the user can work without having to undergo the authentication process again. The default value is 1 hour; however, if a wrong password is entered, the pair is removed from the cache.
- authenticate_ip_ttl 0 second — Specifies how long a proxy authentication will be bound to a specific IP address. The purpose of this directive is to prevent password sharing. Setting it to 0 will prevent users logging in with the same password from

different IP addresses. For dial-up users, this value can be increased to 60 seconds, so that the user can redial in case of a connection break. However, dynamic IP addresses are normally used for dial-up connections, with a new address given for each connection; consequently, it is not guaranteed that the original address will be given for the repeated call.

❑ `authenticate_ip_ttl_is_strict on|off` — If set to `on`, access from other IP addresses is disallowed until the time specified in `authenticate_ip_ttl` expires.

9.5. Working with Squid

Here I will consider some security aspects of the squid service and the supplementary features that can accelerate Internet operations.

9.5.1. Squid Security

When I first read squid documentation, I found the following two directives interesting: `cache_effective_user` and `cache_effective_group`. If squid is run as root, the user and group identifiers will be replaced with those specified by these tags. The user and group identifiers are set to `squid` by default:

```
cache_effective_user squid
cache_effective_group squid
```

In this way, squid will not work with the root rights, and when an attempt is made to make it do so, the service will itself lower its rights to squid. I do not recommend modifying these directives. There is no need to give the squid service greater rights, because those for the cache directory are sufficient for it.

9.5.2. Site Acceleration

Squid can be used to access a certain site more rapidly by acting as an `httpd` accelerator. At least three parameters have to be specified for this:

❑ `httpd_accel_host address` — This indicates the host name of the accelerated server.
❑ `httpd_accel_port port` — This sets the port, to which the accelerated requests are to be forwarded. Most often, this is the default port (port 80).
❑ `httpd_accel_uses_host_header on|off` — The HTTP header contains a HOST filed in it, which is not checked by squid. This may be a source of security problems. The developers recommend setting the value of this option to `off`. It should be set to on if squid is operating in the transparent mode.
❑ `httpd_accel_with_proxy on|off` — This needs to be set to `on` for the cache to function as both a Web cache and an accelerator.

9.5.3. User Agent Field

Many statistical systems do not take into account or do not allow entry to users in whose requests the User Agent field is blank. This field being blank indicates that the request was channeled through a proxy.

Another company I used to work for limited Internet access by IP addresses. I was the only programmer and the network administrator in my department. Only the department head, his assistant, and I were allowed Internet access. A few hours after I was hired, all other department workers had Internet access. How? Simple: I installed a proxy server on my computer, to which all of my coworkers could connect without having to go through an authentication process. The proxy redirected all requests from my coworkers to the main corporate proxy. Because all these requests were coming from me, the main proxy did not suspect anything.

It could have been suspicious, because there is a small flaw in this charitable solution. This is the User Agent field, which was blanked out when requests passed through my proxy. But there is a solution to this problem: the field can be filled out manually in the configuration file by the fake_user_agent directive. For example, the following line emulates requests coming from a Netscape browser:

```
fake_user_agent Netscrape/1.0 (CP/M; 8-bit)
```

9.5.4. Network Protection

The squid service is a two-edged sword: it can be used both to protect the network and to penetrate it. To prevent outside users from using the proxy server to connect to computers in the local network, the following directives have to be added to the configuration file:

```
tcp_incoming_address downstream_address
tcp_outgoing_address upstream_address
udp_incoming_address downstream_address
udp_outgoing_address upstream_address
```

In the preceding list, downstream_address is the address of the computer with squid installed whose network connection is directed to the local network; upstream_address is the address of the network connection directed to the Internet. If addresses are specified incorrectly, it will be possible to connect to the local network's computer from the outside. The following is an example of squid configured incorrectly:

```
tcp_incoming_address upstream_address
tcp_outgoing_address downstream_address
udp_incoming_address upstream_address
udp_outgoing_address downstream_address
```

9.5.5. Fighting Banners and Popup Windows

It was already mentioned that most traffic from any site is graphics. Most browsers allow the image-viewing feature to be disabled; this, however, will make Web surfing less convenient. Without graphics, some sites become less informative and more difficult to navigate; thus, it is not possible to dispense with graphics display altogether.

But there is a type of graphics that irritates and does not carry any useful information — the graphics we would love to, and can, get rid of. I am talking about banners. Consider how to disable banner display way up on the proxy server level. For this, first define the following rules in the squid.conf file:

```
acl banners_regex url_regex "/usr/etc/banners_regex"
acl banners_path_regex urlpath_regex "/usr/etc/banners_path_regex"
acl banners_exclusion url_regex "/usr/etc/banners_exclusion"
```

The first entry creates an ACL named banners_regex of the url_regex type that allows a complete URL to be searched. The last parameter specifies the /usr/etc/banners_regex file, in which the URLs of banner systems will be stored.

The second entry creates an ACL named banner_path_regex of the urlpath_regex type. The last parameter here specifies the /usr/etc/banners_path_regex file, in which URLs to be disallowed will be defined.

The third entry creates an ACL of the same type as the first one, named banners_exclusion and linked to the /usr/etc/banners_exclusion file. In the first two files, descriptions of URLs or templates to be used for killing banners will be stored. Sometimes, however, you may want to view a particular banner. In this case, its URL can be recorded in this file and the banner will be loaded.

Next, specify the following operators for the created ACLs:

```
http_access deny banners_path_regex !banners_exclusion
http_access deny banners_regex !banners_exclusion
```

Both directives do basically the same: They prohibit loading from the addresses specified in the banners_path_regex and banners_regex lists unless they are included in the banners_exclusion list.

Consider the following fragment of the contents of the /usr/etc/banners_regex file:

```
^http://members\.tripod\.com/adm/popup/.+html
^http://www\.geocities\.com/ad_container/pop\.html
```

As you should remember, this file contains template URL paths, and all addresses that match them will be filtered out.

The first entry describes a template that prohibits loading of addresses of the following type:

```
http://members.tripod.com/adm/popup/popup.html
```

As you can see, it is easy to do away with the popup windows from the **www.tripod.com** site. If you know how to build regular expressions, you will be able to create a similar list for any banner system and cut off the most sophisticated paths of graphical pests. The subject of regular expressions is not considered in this book because it is too extensive and requires a book all for itself

In your fight with banners, be prepared for the resurrection of the banners you thought you had killed off. This is because banners are simply commercials allowing sites to earn money to stay in business. Some especially clever administrators are constantly looking for ways to prevent users from getting rid of banners. One of the ways they achieve this is by changing the addresses, from which the banners are served, to neutralize regular expressions.

9.5.6. Replacing Banners

Even though in most cases banners and popup windows are irritating pests, they provide some artistic dressing for pages. Having eliminated them, you may find pages dull and unattractive. This problem can be alleviated by replacing removed banners and popup windows with your own images, which are stored on the local server and, thus, do not have to be loaded from the Internet.

The tool to implement this task is a redirector. In squid, this is an external program that replaces addresses. For example, if the page code contains an address for a banner and your banner-filter program detects it, the redirector replaces the address of the other guy's banner with the address of whatever you may want to load in its place.

There is only one little problem with this: Linux has no ready program for this task and you will have to write it yourself. Any programming language will do, but I will show an example implemented in Perl. If you know how to program in this language, I am certain you will like replacing banners better than simply killing them using ACLs.

Listing 9.2 shows an example of a classic redirector program. I tried to simplify it as much as possible to make it easier to adapt for your needs.

Listing 9.2. Perl redirector program

```perl
#!/usr/bin/perl

$| = 1;

# Specify the URL on your Web server, to which the images
# are stored.
$YOURSITE = 'http://yourserver.com/squid';
$LOG = '/usr/etc/redirectlog';
$LAZY_WRITE = 1;

if ($LOG) {
  open LOG, ">> $LOG";
  unless ($LAZY_WRITE)
```

```perl
      {
        select LOG ;
        $| = 1 ;
        select STDOUT;
      }
}

@b468_60 = qw (
        www\.sitename\.com/cgi/
        # Add descriptions of the 468 x 60 banners'
        # URLs here.
        );

@b100_100= qw (
        www\.sitename\.com/cgi/
        # Add descriptions of the 100 x 100 banners'
        # URLs here.
        );

@various  = qw (
        www\.sitename\.com/cgi/
        # Add descriptions of non-standard size banners'
        # URLs here.
        );

@popup_window = qw (
        ^http://members\.tripod\.com/adm/popup/.+html
        ^http://www\.geocities\.com/ad_container/pop\.html
        ^http://www\.geocities\.com/toto\?
        # Add descriptions of popup windows' URLs here
        );

# Descriptions of where images are located
$b468_60     = "$YOURSITE/468_60.gif";
$b100_100    = "$YOURSITE/100_100.gif";
$various     = "$YOURSITE/empty.gif";
$closewindow = "$YOURSITE/close.htm";

while (<>)
 {
   ($url, $who, $ident, $method) = /^(\S+) (\S+) (\S+) (\S+)$/;
   $prev = $url;

   # A check for 468 x 60 banners
```

```
$url = $b468_60 if grep $url =~ m%$_%, @b468_60;

# A check for 100 x 100 banners
$url = $b100_100 if grep $url =~ m%$_%, @b100_100;

# A check for non-standard size banners
$url = $various if grep $url =~ m%$_%, @various;

# A check for popup windows
$url = $closewindow if grep $url =~ m%$_%, @popup_window;

# An individual site not included in the list at the
# beginning of the file
$url = "$YOURSITE/empty.gif" if $url =~ m%hitbox\.com/Hitbox\?%;

if ($LOG and $url ne $prev)
   {
     my ($sec, $min, $hour, $mday, $mon, $year) = localtime;
     printf LOG "%2d.%02d.%2d %2d:%02d:%04d: %s\r\n",
             $mday, $mon + 1, $year + 1900, $hour, $min, $sec,
             "$who $prev > $url";
   }

  print "$url $who $ident $method\n";
}

close LOG if $LOG;
```

Save this program in the /usr/etc/redirector file and give squid the rights to execute it. Afterward, add the following entry to the squid.conf file:

```
redirect_program /usr/local/etc/squid/redirector
```

For the program to work, you will have to create the following files on your Web server:

- 468_60.gif — A 468 × 60 image.
- 100_100.gif — A 100 × 100 image.
- empty.gif — An image that will replace all nonstandard banners. It is best to make it 1 × 1 pixels so that it does not spoil the aesthetics of the site's design.
- close.htm — An HTML file to close popup windows. It contains the window.close() JavaScript function to close the windows. Listing 9.3 shows an example of the contents of this file.

All these files should be stored on the Web server in one directory. Don't forget to specify the correct path to this directory in the script's $YOURSITE variable.

I tried to explain the most important code areas in Listing 9.2 with comments. If you have Perl programming experience, you will have no problems making it all work.

Listing 9.3. JavaScript for killing popup windows

```
<html>
<head>
<script language = "JavaScript">
<!--
  window.close();
//-->
</script>
</head>
<body>
</body>
</html>
```

9.5.7. Barring Sites

I had a conversation with an acquaintance not long ago, and he offered a definition of the Internet that I found amusing: The World Wide Web was created for and lives by pornography. Although I do not completely agree with him, I feel he might be partially right in that the sites with sexy content are most frequently visited (if you don't take into account the Microsoft update site, from which users download patches for software from this company).

No employers will be happy if their workers visit sites with illicit content during work hours. This produces not only traffic waste but also other expenses unrelated to work. Parents do not want their children to be exposed to sites like these either, and they strive to shelter their sensibilities from too many facts of life. I am saying this as a father of two children.

Pornography sites can be easily banned using the same methods as those used to kill banners. For example, you could disallow any site whose URL contains the word "sex." But this method can produce false calls. For example, an address may contain the "GasExpo" text in it. Because it contains a letter combination that spells "sex," this site will be barred. This is a real-life example, in which a user was not allowed to load a gas-equipment exhibition site.

Although creating lists of prohibited sites is a difficult task, it is not an impossible one. Currently, most sites of erotic persuasion have folded their activities in the **com** domain and are settling down in other domains, which usually belong to small island nations. In some of such domains, almost 90% of sites are of the adult entertainment nature. These you could bar without any fear that someone won't be able to catch up on the latest in the gas equipment developments.

9.5.8. Limiting Bandwidth

Frequently, when organizing Internet access some users have to be provided a high-speed connection. How can this be accomplished if, by default, all users are peers and can access the Internet at the maximum speed available? You have to establish some priorities to achieve this.

If a user requires a wide bandwidth channel to work with applications requiring a high data-exchange rate (e.g., for presentations), you have to reserve for this user a channel of wider bandwidth than that set aside for the rest of the users. This can be achieved only by borrowing bandwidth from other users.

Limiting the external channel is easy to accomplish using squid. The following example lists the directives used to achieve this:

```
delay_pools 3
delay_class 1 1
delay_class 2 2
delay_class 3 1
delay_parameters 1 256000/256000
delay_access 1 deny all
delay_access 1 allow admins
delay_parameters 2 256000/256000 4000/8000
delay_access 2 allow all
delay_access 2 deny admins
delay_parameters 3 64000/64000
delay_access 3 deny all
delay_access 3 allow bigboss
```

Add this code to the /etc/squid/squid.conf configuration file after the following comment:

```
# DELAY POOL PARAMETERS (all require DELAY_POOLS compilation option).
# ------------------------------------------------------------------
```

Most of the parameters are already set by default and have to be modified.

The first line — delay_pools n — specifies that there will be n number of delay pools (rules describing access speeds) to use. By default, n equals 0; there is no limit on the number of pools. Because you are going to create three pools, n is set to 3.

Next, the pools are actually created using the delay_class n c directive, where n is the pool number and c is the class number.

There are three different pool classes. These are the following:

❑   1 — The download rates of all connections in the class are added together, and the aggregate is kept below a given maximum value. For example, you can limit the download speed from all adult entertainment sites (defined in advance using acl tag) to 32 Kb/sec. If your Internet connection bandwidth is, for example, 256 Kb/sec, no matter how many people try to download hot stuff, they will have only 32 Kb/sec to share, with the rest of the users guaranteed the remaining 224 Kb/sec of bandwidth.

- ❐   2 — The aggregate bandwidth for all connections in the class *and* the bandwidth of each connection in the class is limited. For example, with a 256 Kb/sec Internet connection, you can limit a certain class of users to 128 Kb/sec *and* ensure that no single user gets more than his or her fair share of this bandwidth.

- ❐   3 — The aggregate bandwidth for all connections *and* the bandwidth for each IP range *and* the bandwidth for each connection is limited. Suppose you have four IP ranges (subnetworks) in your local network and an Internet connection speed of 512 Kb/sec. You want to leave 64 Kb/sec available for mail and other service traffic. This leaves 512 − 64 = 448 Kb/sec for all four subnetworks. Each of the four subnetworks is further limited to about 112 Kb/sec. Each user of each subnetwork is then limited to his or her share of the subnetwork's bandwidth, the actual bandwidth depending on the number of users and their download habits.

In the example, I used delay pools class 1, class 2, and class 1 again. I did it on purpose to make the example more illustrative.

Next, speed limits are set on each pool as follows:

```
delay_parameters delay_pool aggregate_bandwidth
network_bandwidth user_bandwidth
```

The `dealy_pool` parameter is the pool number whose bandwidth is being limited. In the example, the following line limits the bandwidth of the first pool:

```
delay_parameters 1 256000/256000
```

Because pool 1 is of the type 1 class (`delay_class 1 1`) — that is, only its aggregate bandwidth can be limited — the directive takes only one parameter: `aggregate_bandwidth` (the value `256000/256000`). The parameter's value consists of two numbers separated by a slash. The first number is the actual speed limit (in bytes per second). The second number is the threshold, in bytes downloaded, when this speed limit kicks in. For example, when downloading a large file, its first 16,000 bytes will be downloaded at the normal speed, whatever it is. But then the limit will kick in and the remainder of the file will download at 4,000 bytes per second (32 Kb/sec).

The number of parameters depends on the pool class. Only two parameters have to be specified for the class 1 pool, which limits the aggregate connection bandwidth:

```
delay_parameters delay_pool aggregate_bandwidth
```

The directive for the second pool class looks as follows:

```
delay_parameters delay_pool aggregate_bandwidth user_bandwidth
```

Thus, the first directive sets the aggregate bandwidth of all connections to 256,000 bytes per second (or 2 Mb/sec). No bandwidth limit is imposed if it is specified as −1.

After the bandwidth limitations for the first pool are specified, access rights to the pool are set by the `delay_access` directive as follows:

```
delay_access delay_pool allow|deny acl
```

The first parameter is the pool number. This is followed by the access or the deny option for the members of the list, given as the last parameter (acl).

In the example, access rights to pool 1 are set for two groups: all and admins:

```
delay_access 1 deny all
delay_access 1 allow admins
```

The first directive bars all users from working at the given bandwidth, and the second gives access to it to only the members of the admins ACL. It is assumed that only administrators are such members.

Next, a description of the bandwidth limitations and access rights for the second pool are given:

```
delay_parameters 2 256000/256000 4000/8000
delay_access 2 allow all
delay_access 2 deny admins
```

The second pool is of the type 2 class. Here, the aggregate bandwidth limitation is specified (256,000 bytes per second), as well as the bandwidth limitation for individual connections (4,000 bytes per second). All users but the administrators will work at this speed.

Finally, there could be some problems if you limit the boss to the bandwidth of 4,000 bytes per second like a regular user. To avoid potential problems, separate permission is given to the boss as follows:

```
delay_parameters 3 64000/64000
delay_access 3 deny all
delay_access 3 allow bigboss
```

The bandwidth limitation feature can be used to bar loading of multimedia files during work hours. Listing 9.4 shows how to configure squid to read Web pages at regular speeds but to limit speeds for loading media files during work hours.

Listing 9.4. Limiting speed for loading media during work hours

```
# ACL describing the network
acl fullspeed url_regex -i 192.168.1
# ACL describing media files that must put the brakes on
# during work hours
acl mediaspeed url_regex -i ftp .exe .mp3 .avi .mpeg .iso .wav
# The period, during which the restriction on the
# download speed of media files applies
acl day time 08:00-18:59

# Two second-class pools are needed.
delay_pools 2
delay_class 1 2
```

```
delay_class 2 2

# The first pool has no restrictions for anyone.
delay_parameters 1 -1/-1 -1/-1
delay_access 1 allow fullspeed

# The second pool restricts daytime speed.
delay_parameters 2 4000/100000 4000/100000
delay_access 2 allow day
delay_access 2 deny !day
delay_access 2 allow mediaspeed
```

I believe the comments to the code are sufficient to understand how it functions. The media file download speed, however, is limited for all users. If you want to make exceptions for certain users from this restriction, you can create an ACL for them (named, for example, `allowfull`) and add the following line at the end of the listing:

```
delay_access 2 deny !allowfull
```

9.6. Browser Caching

In addition to page caching by a central proxy server, page caching can be done by local programs. For example, the Mozilla browser can cache Web pages visited on the local hard drive. When a previously-visited page is requested again, the browser does not retrieve it from the proxy server cache but loads it from its local cache.

Fig. 9.3 shows the dialog window for configuring Mozilla cache. The **Memory Cache** parameter is the maximum operating memory allocated to caching pages. Its default value is 4,096 KB. Using memory cache speeds up operations when browsing the same site, because most of its graphical objects are saved in memory and retrieved from there instead of from the hard drive.

The **Disk Cache** parameter sets the size of the disk cache. Usually, its default value is set to 50,000 KB (about 50 MB). This amount is too small for regular Web surfing and will be used up quickly. If your hard drive allows, I recommend increasing this value. The **Disk Cache Folder** parameter specifies the folder, in which the disk cache is stored.

You can also specify when a page in the cache should be compared with the page on the network. The following four options are available:

❑ **Every time I view the page** — Self-explanatory.
❑ **When the page is out of date** — Ditto.
❑ **Once per session** — Every time the browser is started.
❑ **Never** — The page will always be loaded from the local cache; you can reload it by clicking the **Reload** button on the browser's toolbar.

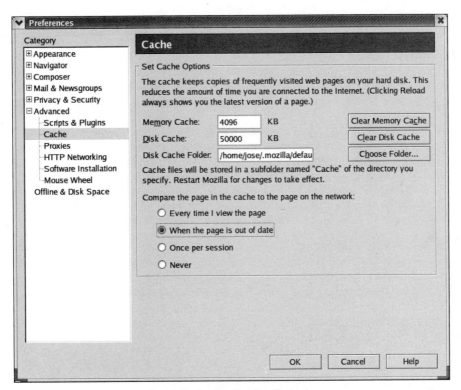

Fig. 9.3. Configuring Mozilla cache

When working with the Internet using a proxy server or local browser caching, you should remember that pages that load can be outdated. To load the fresh version of the page, click the **Reload** button.

Chapter 10: File Transfer

I remember when building a local network was an expensive enterprise, obtaining Internet access was even more expensive, and files had to be exchanged using diskettes. If anyone remembers those times, I am sure those are not fond memories. Diskettes would constantly become corrupted and data they contained would be lost. It was all right if the distance between the source and the destination of the data being transferred was short: You could make another trip. But having to do this over a great distance had a negative effect on the emotional state of the carrier.

Even now, some computers are equipped with 3.5-inch floppy drives, because no cheaper alternative for transferring small volumes of data has been offered yet. But it is difficult to imagine an office not equipped with a full-fledged local network. In some companies, all computers must be connected to the local network. With computers connected into a local network, the need to equip them with floppy disk drives is no longer there, and the latter are simply removed from the machines. If you are itching to ask why, because one never knows when a floppy might come in handy, you have forgotten the main principle of security: There should be nothing unnecessary. This applies not only to software but also to computer hardware.

A floppy disk drive is a hole, through which information can be taken off the computer without any hacking skills but by simply obtaining the physical access to the machine. I know one company whose local network was isolated, and they used to think that this made it impervious. Despite all this seeming security, they lost secret trade information and subsequently their market. And all because of little pieces of plastic that cannot be detected by metal detectors. That's right, floppy disks. Only then were floppy disk drives removed from all of their computers.

Local networks make it possible to get rid of extra hardware and transfer the data more rapidly and reliably. All you have to do is configure the necessary protocols properly and use the network medium to its full capacity.

Currently, the most popular file exchange protocol is FTP. Even though it was developed some time ago, it is remains widely used. Granted, some of its capabilities are not quite up to par for modern requirements.

10.1. FTP Operation

FTP operation requires two software components: a client and a server. Any Telnet client can be used to connect to the server's port 21 and enter commands from the command line. But in these times of graphical interfaces, users desire more convenience than the command line can provide. My favorite FTP client for Windows is CyD FTP Client XP (available from **www.cydsoft.com**). Its main window is shown in Fig. 10.1.

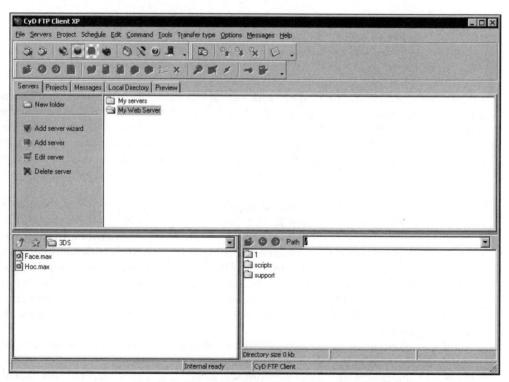

Fig. 10.1. The main window of CyD FTP Client XP

If you urgently need to test the protocol but have no FTP client installed, you can use a simple browser for this, like Internet Explorer or Netscape. This is done by entering the address in the URL field in this format: `ftp://name:password@address`. For example, you could enter `ftp://flenov:mypassword@ftp.my_server.com` or `ftp://flenov:mypassword@192.168.77.1`.

FTP uses two ports for its operation: One port is used to transfer control commands, and the other is used to transfer actual data (files). The client program connects to port 21 and starts sending commands. This port is used by all users and the service that listens to the channel works simultaneously with several connections.

When a client requests data, another connection is opened for the specific user, over which the file is transferred. This is makes the programmer's work convenient, but it is inconvenient for the administrator, who has to configure the firewall.

Most FTP commands are similar to those used in Linux to work with files. This is because when the protocol was developed, the main network operating system was UNIX. Now we have Windows everywhere, but 20 years ago things were different.

10.1.1. FTP Commands

Listing 10.1 shows an example of a client program exchanging commands with an FTP server. Lines originating from the client start with the > character; those originating from the server start with the < character.

Listing 10.1. An example of an FTP command exchange

```
< 220 Flenov Michael FTP Server
> USER Anonymous
< 331 Anonymous access allowed, send identity (e-mail name) as password.
> PASS your@mail.com
< 230 Anonymous user logged in.
> PWD
< 257 "/" is current directory.
> TYPE A
< 200 Type set to A.
> PASV
< 227 Entering Passive Mode (127,0,0,1,13,20).
> LIST
< 125 Data connection already open; Transfer starting.
< 226 Transfer complete.
```

The first line is the server greeting. It is issued right away to port 21. Most often, this line describes the server and its version. In this case, instead of a specific server name, I placed my name. A real server with the default configuration setting will display a line similar to the following:

```
220 flenovm.ru FTP server (Version wu-2.6.2-5) ready.
```

Why did I change the greeting text? I did so because by default it showed the domain name, the name and version of the FTP server, and the prompt message. Do you see anything dangerous in this information? I do: All hackers have to do for finding out what FTP server they are dealing with is to connect to port 21.

Their further actions are easy to predict. If I were those hackers, I would search all Bugtraq databases for information about bugs in the given version of the Washington University FTP daemon (wu-ftpd) service. It is more likely than not that I would find some. Then the administrator of the server can only pray that I do not find exploits to take advantage of the discovered bugs or that the bugs discovered are minor and do not let anything serious be done with the system.

After the server displays the prompt, the client can start sending commands to it. But before this, the client has to introduce itself to the server. This is done by executing first the USER and then PASS FTP commands, specifying the user login and password as the parameter for each, respectively.

FTP servers allow operations with three types of authorization: real, guest, and anonymous. In the first case, you have to pass to the server the real login and password of a user allowed access to the server. After the USER command is executed, the server prompts you to enter the password for the specified user:

```
331 Password required for flenov.
```

When logging in as an anonymous user, the login is given as anonymous (USER anonymous). The server will answer with the following message:

```
331 Anonymous access allowed, send identity (e-mail name) as password.
```

The password to log in as an anonymous user is an email address. The address does not have to be a real one; the server cannot check this. Some servers do not even check the validity of the format of the entered email address, and any text can be entered as the password.

Anonymous user access gives minimal file and directory handling capabilities and is used only to access open file archives. The anonymous access is most often used to publish documents for public access using FTP. For example, software developers set up FTP servers with anonymous access to let users download the software updates or new software versions.

A real user can traverse the entire file system of the server, being limited only by the access rights of the user account chosen to connect to the server.

Guest login access rights are something between anonymous and real login access rights. A guest login has more rights than an anonymous login and it has rights to upload files, but unlike a real login, a guest can only work in its own directory. For example, if a guest is given access to the /home/robert directory, he or she can have full access to its files and subdirectories but will not be able to go above this directory. You can designate any name as guest.

Note that the password in the PASS command is sent in plaintext, which presents a serious problem. Every time some service is considered in this book, you run into the plaintext data transmission issue. It can't be helped now that nobody thought about hackers at the dawn of the Internet. Now you have to develop various methods to hide passwords.

If your server services only anonymous logins, it does not matter that passwords are sent in plaintext. With this type of authentication, any user can connect to the server by specifying any email address as the password. But these servers are only used to store public resources. When a server contains confidential information, access to it is through real password authentication. In this case, the password must be encrypted. You can do this using the stunnel program or SFTP, which was considered in *Section 5.3.8.*

I saw an excellent solution on a public Web server about 10 years ago. To upload data onto the server, a user had to register by filling out a Web form with personal data. Afterward, the user would be issued a password valid for that session only. Files could only be uploaded into a special directory, which could only be written to. The permissions for the uploaded files were given only for read and write, not for execute. With this arrangement, the password can be transmitted in plaintext. Even if a password is intercepted, it cannot be used to log into the server again.

It is easy to implement a one-time password arrangement if your server uses PAMs (see *Section 3.3.3*).

After a successful login to the server, you can execute any FTP commands. However, there is a problem with this — the command set depends on the server. All developers provide the main commands described in the Requests For Comments (RFC). But because the capabilities provided by the standard no longer meet today's requirements, Web server developers add their own functions, which may differ from one developer to another. Thus, if a client program does not behave as you would expect it to in some situations, it does not necessarily mean that there is something wrong with it; it simply may be incompatible with the server it is trying to communicate with.

The main FTP commands are listed in Table 10.1. They may be of use to you when working with Telnet or testing the server.

Table 10.1. FTP commands

Command	Description
USER login	Used to enter the login during the authorization procedure
PASS password	Used to enter the password during the authorization procedure
SYST	Returns the system type
HELP	Returns a list of available commands
LIST	Displays files and directories of the current directory
PWD	Displays the current directory
CWD directory	Changes the current directory to the specified one
TYPE type	Specifies the data transfer type: A for ASCII files, I for binary files
RETR file	Retrieves the specified file from the server
STOR file	Uploads the specified file to the server
ABOR	Aborts the last FTP command or data transfer
QUIT	Terminates the FTP session and exits

10.1.2. Server Messages

The FTP server responds to the commands it receives with messages that provide information about the results of the command execution. Responses consist of a three-digit code followed by optional text. When a response requires more than one line, the code and the text parts are separated with a hyphen in the nonterminal lines and with a space in the terminal line.

You should know the meaning of the response codes to be able to determine the type of errors they indicate.

The meanings of the first and second digits of FTP server response codes are listed in Tables 10.2 and 10.3, respectively.

Table 10.2. The meaning of the first digit in FTP server codes

Code	Description
1	The command has been launched successfully but has not terminated yet; the user has to wait for the command to terminate before issuing new commands. This type of response is given when executing lengthy operations (e.g., file transfer). Another response will be issued when the command terminates.
2	The command execution has been successful; the user can issue new commands.
3	The command execution has been successful, but another command is needed to complete the operation. These responses are given when executing operations involving several actions — for example, during the authentication procedure, which takes two commands. A response code starting with 3 is issued after the USER command during a login authentication procedure.
4	Execution failed, but it may be successful if another attempt is made later. This response may be issued when the server cannot execute the command right away because it is busy executing another operation.
5	Execution failed. This response may be produced by incorrect command syntax or parameter specification.

Table 10.3. The meaning of the second digit in FTP server codes

Code	Description
0	A syntax error
1	A human-oriented help message
2	A connection establishing or terminating message
3	An authentication message
4	Not defined
5	A file system message

Consider an example. Suppose that you see the following message from the server and are thinking about what to do next:

```
331 Anonymous access allowed.
```

Knowing what the code digits mean will help you handle this situation. The first digit, 3, tells you that the previous command was executed successfully but that another command is needed to complete the transaction. The second digit is also 3; that is, the response is an authentication message. When can this response be issued? Of course, after the login was entered. The FTP server is waiting for the password and has informed about this with the 331 message.

As you can see, minimal knowledge is sufficient to figure out what problem has arisen, and to solve it rapidly.

10.1.3. Transferring Files

Because FTP is intended to be used with different systems, two file transfer modes are supported: text (ASCII) and binary.

Suppose that you want to send a text file from a UNIX computer to a Windows computer. In UNIX, the carriage return (<CR>, code 13) character is used as the end-of-line indicator. In Windows, two characters are used for this: <CR> and line feed (<LF>, code 10). The transmitted file will not be quite readable, because all text lines merge into one because of the lack of <LF> characters.

Fig. 10.2 shows the contents of a sendmail.cf file transferred from a Linux server to a Windows server in the binary mode and opened in the Windows Notepad text editor. As you can see, it is difficult to make anything out of its contents, with the <CR> character printed as a rectangle instead of starting each line as a new line.

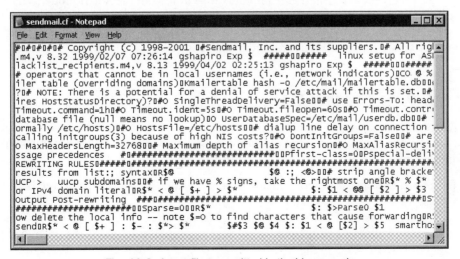

Fig. 10.2. A text file transmitted in the binary mode

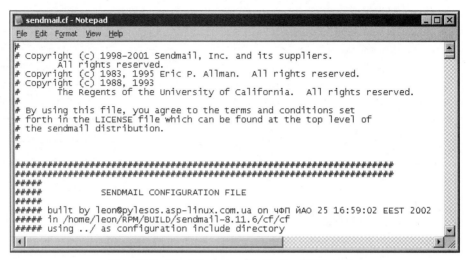

Fig. 10.3. A text file transmitted in the ASCII mode

The end-of-line problem is solved by transferring the file in the ASCII mode. In this case, the text is transmitted line by line and the receiving operating system adds the necessary line-feed control characters itself. Fig. 10.3 shows the same sendmai.cf file transmitted in the ASCII mode. Its contents are easily readable now.

Binary files (such as images or music) must be transferred in the binary mode. In this case, it makes no difference under what operating system the file was created, because it will be properly recognized by any other operating system supporting this format.

If a binary file is transferred from Linux to Windows in the ASCII mode, Windows will replace all <CR> characters (which are a regular occurrence in binary files, although they do not indicate the carriage return operation) with the <CR>+<LF> character combination, and the binary file transmitted will become corrupted.

10.1.4. Data Channel Mode

As already mentioned, FTP operations require two ports: a control port and a data port. Port 21 is the control port, used to transfer FTP commands only. Files are transferred over another port. The process can be described as follows:

1. The client opens the port on the local computer, to which the server is to transfer the file.
2. The client sends a request to the server to download the file, and informs the server of the IP address and the port of the client computer, to which the download is to be performed.
3. The server makes a connection with the client computer and starts data transfer.

This mode, in which the connection is established by the server, is called active. The way the connection is established presents a problem. If there is a firewall installed on the client computer, it is most likely configured to prohibit any connections initialized from outside to prevent unauthorized access to the local network. Only a computer inside the firewall is authorized to establish the connection.

Thus, FTP will not work properly in the active mode if the client firewall is properly configured. If the firewall is configured to allow outside connections, it might as well be nonexistent because it no longer prevents unauthorized outside access.

This problem is solved by the passive FTP mode transfers. This is the default mode on most server and client FTP programs, because almost all modern operating systems have built-in firewalls.

In the passive mode, the connection is established somewhat differently:

1. The client asks to download a file.
2. The server allocates a port to be used for the ensuing data transfer and informs the client of the port number.
3. The client establishes a data connection with the specified port.

In this way, the server only opens its port and prepares to transfer the file; all connections are established by the client. This is more in line with the firewall rules.

10.2. Configuring the wu-ftp Server

According to my observations, the most widely used Linux FTP server is the Washington University FTP (wu-ftp) server. It is included in the main Linux distributions, including Red Hat and its clones. If you have one of these distributions, the server can be installed with packages during the operating system installation, and all you will have to do is configure the service properly. If you don't have an FTP server installed, you can easily install it from an RPM (for a Red Hat system) or another archive.

Modern distributions contain a graphical utility for configuring the FTP server, named kwuftpd. It is launched by selecting the **System/kwuftpd** menu sequence from the KDE main menu. The utility's main window is shown in Fig. 10.4. However, as usual, I will consider fine-tuning using configuration files. Once you know how to configure the FTP service using the configuration files, you will have no problems doing this using the kwuftpd utility.

The configuration information for the FTP server is contained in the following six files:

❑ ftpaccess — Information specifying access rights to the server, the FTP users, and the main security settings.
❑ ftpservers — Information specifying virtual FTP servers.
❑ ftpusers — Information specifying users explicitly forbidden access to the FTP server.
❑ ftphosts — Information specifying access rights to the server for certain hosts. Access can be both allowed and denied.
❑ ftpgroups — Information describing FTP groups.
❑ ftpconversion — Information for configuring on-the-fly file conversions.

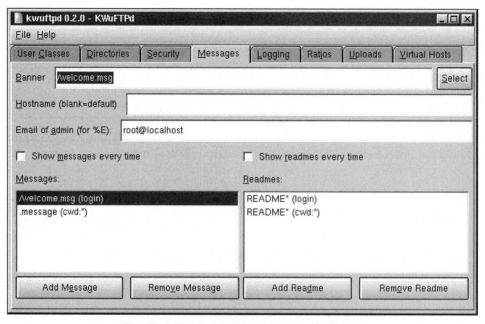

Fig. 10.4. The main window of the kwuftpd utility

10.3. Main Settings of the wu-ftp Server

The main configuration file for the wu-ftp server is ftpaccess. Its contents are shown in Listing 10.2.

Listing 10.2. The contents of the ftpaccess configuration file

---

```
# This file was generated by the KDE
# wu-ftpd configurator.
# (c) 2000 by Bernhard Rosenkrunzer (bero@redhat.com)
class all anonymous,guest,real  *
noretrieve
loginfails 5
private no
banner /welcome.msg
email root@localhost
message /welcome.msg          LOGIN
message .message              CWD=*
readme          README*       LOGIN
readme          README*       CWD=*
```

```
chmod              no          anonymous,guest
delete             no          anonymous
overwrite          no          anonymous
rename             no          anonymous
passwd-check       rfc822      warn
log transfers anonymous,guest,real inbound
log transfers anonymous,guest,real outbound
anonymous-root /home/flenov
```

When configuring the FTP server, the default values of many directives are not changed because they do not affect the server's productivity or security. Although some of the directives play a role in preventing incorrect or inefficient use of the server (e.g., the timeout XXXX directive contributes to timely release of resources), their default values are sufficient for this; moreover, changing values of some directives may have negative effects.

Consider the main directives of this file, which I grouped by categories to make working with them easier.

Information about other features, which will not be considered, can be obtained from the ftpaccess man page.

10.3.1. Access

Access directives define the main rights for accessing the FTP server. Consider the main directives of this category:

❑   class name type address — Organizes user classes by type and address. In the example configuration file (Listing 10.2), there is the following entry:

```
class all anonymous,guest,real  *
```

The class is specified as all. It is followed by an enumeration of the user types that will pertain to this class. In this case, all available categories are included in the class: anonymous, guest, and real. The last parameter is an address template, which in this case is a wild card, that is, any address. Thus, any user, with any address, belongs to the all class.

Classes are a handy concept. You can group certain users into a class and assign them certain rights. For example, you can create a class of users whose IP addresses lie within the address range for your office, company, or country. You then open full FTP access to this class only, prohibiting or limiting access to all others. It is more convenient to assign rights to an entire class at once than to write access rights for each user.

❑   noretrieve type class_name file — Prohibits the specified file from being read. The type parameter specifies the absolute or relative path to the file. The next parameter, class_name, specifies the class, to which the prohibition applies. The all class described previously can either be specified explicitly or not specified, in which case the prohibition will apply to all users. If the file parameter is specified with a full path, the prohibition will apply to this file only. If only the file name is given, access to all files with this name in all directories will be prohibited.

The following directive prohibits accesses to any file named passwd:

```
noretrieve relative passwd
```

Add this line to your configuration file and then connect to the server using an FTP client. For testing the FTP server, I used the gFTP client program. After connecting to the server, I created a file named passwd in the /home directory and then tried to download it to the /home/flenov directory. In response, the FTP client only created an empty file in the directory. But it could not issue any messages because the prohibition on retrieval made it crash. This sort of termination is specific to the gFTP server; other FTP clients should process the error properly and remain operational.

If the FTP server is located on the same physical machine as the Web server, it would be logical to also prohibit reading the .htaccess file, in which the access rights to the Web server directories are defined. FTP users should have no right to even view these rights. It is better to assign rights to specific users only, so that each of them could work only with his or her own .htaccess files, or to provide some other way to edit rights.

Operations with the system directories should be prohibited. For example, the following entry prohibits retrieving any file from the /etc directory and its subdirectories:

```
noretrieve /etc
```

- ☐ `loginfials number` — Indicates the number of unsuccessful attempts to log onto the server, after which a corresponding record is created in the log. The number of login tries in the example file is 5. If a user cannot log in after five tries, chances are this is not a bona fide user but a hacker trying to crack the password by either trying random combinations or using the dictionary method.

- ☐ `private parameter` — Specifies, if set to `yes`, that the SITE GROUP and SITE GPASS wu-ftp server commands can be used to change the group. (Command sets of other FTP servers may not contain these commands.) By specifying the correct group and password, the user obtains the rights of the corresponding group, specified in the ftpgroups file.

- ☐ `deny address file` — Prohibits client access from the specified addresses. When a connection attempt is made from a prohibited address, a message stored in the file specified by the `file` parameter is displayed. The address can be specified as a regular expression.

- ☐ `defumask mask` — Indicates the access rights mask used to create new files. The Linux `umask` command, which specifies the current value of the mask, was described in *Section 4.1.*

- ☐ `limit-time type minutes` — Limits the session's duration. For example, you do not want certain users to hang out for too long on your FTP server. The `type` parameter can be specified as `*` (all users), `real`, `anonymous`, or `guest`. The `minutes` parameter specifies the allowed session duration, after which the connection will be broken off.

- `file-limit direction number class` — Sets the limit on the number of transferred files. The direction parameter can be specified as `in`, `out`, or `total`. For example, the `file-limit total 10` command prohibits transfer of more than ten files in both directions.

- `byte-limit direction number class` — Limits the number of transferred bytes. The directive operates like the `file-limits` command, only it works with bytes instead of files.

- `anonymous-root directory` — Specifies explicitly the directory for anonymous users. These users cannot have their own directory, unlike real users whose root directory when connected to the server is their home directory.

- `guest-root directory` — Makes all guests use the same directory (analogous to the previous command). If each guest must have a personal directory, it is better to create an account for each guest explicitly (see *Section 10.6*).

- `passwd-check type message` — Verifies the password validity for anonymous users, that is, for the email address entered as the password complying with the certain standards. The `type` parameter can have one of the following values: `none` (no check is performed), `trivial` (check for the @ character in the address), or `rfc822` (full check for compliance with the RFC 882 standard). The message parameter can be set to `warn` or `enforce`. In the former case, a warning message is issued, but the user is allowed to proceed; in the latter, the user is denied access.

- `deny-email address` — Denies access if the specified email address is given as the password. Most FTP clients are configured with some arbitrary valid email address for anonymous access — for example, **my@mail.com** — that is rarely changed. Because this address complies with all rules for the email address format, the server cannot determine that it is not a real address. But when this address is specified explicitly in this parameter, users will not be able to use this address as the password unless it is changed to something else. But even this does not guarantee that anonymous users will give their own email addresses as the password.

- `deny-uid identifiers` — Prohibits users with specified identifiers from accessing the FTP server. The `ftpusers` file, considered in *Section 10.5*, performs the same function. This command is convenient because it can be applied to ranges of users. For example, the `deny-uid %-500` command denies access to all users whose user ID is less than 500.

- `deny-gid identifiers` — Prohibits access the FTP server for the users of the group with the specified identifiers. The `ftpusers` command performs the same function.

- `restricted_uid identifiers` — Prohibits guest users with the specified IDs from accessing directories outside their home directory.

- `restricted_gid identifiers` — Prohibits users with the specified group ID from accessing directories outside their home directory.

- `unrestricted_uid identifiers` — Allows guest users with the specified ID to access directories outside their home directory.

- `unrestricted_gid identifiers` — Allows users with the specified group ID to access directories outside their home directory.

❑   `dns refuse_no_reverse file override` — Issues a warning message if the client does not provide a return address, and breaks off the connection unless the `override` parameter is specified.

❑   `dns refuse_mismatch file override` — Issues a warning message if the forward and reverse lookups for the site do not match, and breaks off the connection unless the `override` parameter is specified. I always enable this option and disable it only when real users experience problems working with the server. This is necessary to prevent hackers from faking the IP address to enter the system by circumventing the corresponding check.

10.3.2. Controlling File Upload

File upload is the most dangerous operation for the server. Each user should only be able to access his or her own directory. But what if anonymous users also need to upload files? In this case, you should prohibit uploads by anonymous users to vulnerable directories, into which scripts could be uploaded and executed afterwards.

The `upload parameters` command defines a directory that permits or denies uploads. For example, the following command denies uploads to the /etc directory:

```
upload /etc          no
```

The following command permits uploads to the /home directory:

```
upload /home         yes root root 0600 nodir
```

The third and fourth parameters specify the owner and group that will be set for the file. I specified both of them as root, so that a regular user could not do anything with the document. The fifth parameter specifies the file permission, `0600` in this case. This means that only the administrator can read from and write to it. The last parameter — `nodir` — prohibits directory creation.

The following example allows the user to create directories:

```
upload /home/robert   yes root root 0600 dir 0700
```

The penultimate parameter is `dir`, which permits the user to create directories. The last parameter is `0700`, which assigns exclusive rights to the directory to the administrator. This way, even if hackers upload a malicious program into this directory, they will not be able to execute it because they will not have the proper rights for this.

You should prohibit uploading of files into any system directories open to users for viewing. But if you are using only guest access, where a user can work only in his or her own environment, there is no need for this.

10.3.3. Controlling Operation Rights

The ftpaccess file can also be used to describe the main operations and their permissions. The general format of such commands is as follows:

```
Action yes|no user
```

The value of the `action` parameter can be one of the following: `chmod`, `delete`, `overwrite`, `rename`, or `umask`. The value of the `user` parameter can be one of, or a combination of the `anonymous`, `guest`, and `real` user types, or a user class.

By default, all actions and all users are allowed. But it would be logical to prohibit deleting, renaming, and modifying files or changing their attributes by unauthorized (anonymous) users.

For example, Listing 10.2 contains the following lines to prohibit access to these operations:

```
chmod           no        anonymous,guest
delete          no        anonymous
overwrite       no        anonymous
rename          no        anonymous
```

10.3.4. Informational Directives

These directives are responsible for providing information about the system that the remote user sees when logging into the FTP server. These are the following:

☐ `banner name` — Specifies a text file (in the `name` parameter) whose contents will be displayed to the user when starting the login process. The contents are arbitrary; these may be a greeting, some information, or the FTP server usage rules. You should remember that the banner is displayed before the authentication process; therefore, it should not contain any information that may help hackers break into the system.

☐ `greeting full|brief|terse|text` — Specifies how much information about the system is given to the user before the login. The greeting is a string that may look like this: "220 flenovm.ru FTP server (Version wu-2.6.2-5) ready." As explained in *Section 10.1*, this string is displayed before the authorization process and contains information about the system and the FTP server version. It is not a good idea to display either full or correct information; you are better off showing the least possible amount of correct information or, even better, displaying something that is not true. The meanings of the parameter values as follows:

- `full` — The host name and daemon name and version are displayed.
- `brief` — Only the host name is displayed.
- `terse` — The "FTP server ready" message is displayed.
- `text` — A custom message is displayed.

I like the last option the best. The custom text to be displayed is entered after a space following the text parameter, as follows:

```
greeting text text_string
```

On my servers, I use a custom message saying either `greeting text flenovm.ru FTP Server (MS IIS 4.1.0) ready` or `greeting text flenovm.ru FTP Server (cd-ftpd 2.1.9) ready`.

Neither of these two messages provides any information about what FTP server is installed. The first one may make hackers think they are dealing with the Internet information server from Microsoft, which is used only in Windows systems. This can confuse even an experienced hacker. Unfortunately, this message does not prevent the same hacker from using special utilities to determine that the operating system is actually Linux. Even though these utilities will not be able to determine the exact version of Linux, they establish that the FTP server greeting message is a fake.

In the second case, I specify a nonexistent server. Not being able to find an exploit to break into the server because of the lack of information about the server used, the potential computer burglar may prefer looking for easier prey.

Or you could display that you have the ProFTP server installed, which exists and is often used by Linux administrators.

- ❑ `hostname host_name` — Defines the default host name of the FTP server.
- ❑ `email email_address` — Specifies the administrator's email.
- ❑ `message file type` — Displays the contents of the specified text file in the following cases:
  - When logging into the system if the `type` parameter is specified as `LOGIN`
  - When changing the directory if the type parameter is specified as `CWD=directory` and the user has switched to the specified directory

10.3.5. Logging

Some administrators log activities of anonymous and guest users only. Their rationale for this is that real system users will not do anything damaging to the server that they need for their work. This is fundamentally flawed thinking, because quite a few break-ins are perpetrated by real users; moreover, most often hackers use real user accounts to break in.

It is difficult, impossible with the proper assignment of access rights, to do anything damaging to the server when logged in as an anonymous user or a guest. Only when there is a bug in the server software can this be done. Thus, in most cases malefactors try to obtain access to a real user account for their activities.

Should a nonstandard situation develop, logs will provide you with detailed information about the reasons for this. You can then take steps to eliminate those particular causes. (The logging subject is covered in detail in *Chapter 12*.)

The default file for storing the wu-ftp log is /var/log/xferlog. The history of activity for the last six days can be viewed in the /var/log/xferlog.X file, where X is a number from 0 to 5.

The following are some examples of configuring the wu-ftp server's logging functions:

- ❑ `log commands type_list` — Enables logging of all client commands. The `type_list` parameter's value can be one of the following: `anonymous`, `guest`, or `real`.
- ❑ `log transfers type_list directions` — Enables logging of files uploaded or downloaded by users. The value of the `directions` parameter is a comma-separated list of any of the two keywords: `inbound` and `outbound`.

❏ `log security type_list` — Enables logging of all security violations, such as attempts to execute prohibited commands.

❏ `log syslog` — Redirects the logging messages to the syslog file.

❏ `log syslog+xferlog` — Sends the transfer logs to both the syslog and the xferlog files.

10.4. Creating Virtual Servers

Being able to create a virtual FTP server is a powerful function. When there are 20 virtual Web sites running on a physical computer, it is logical for them to be able to provide FTP services. In this case, each site will be assigned its own access rights.

I will not go into detail on the virtual server subject, because this is beyond the scope of this book. If you desire more information on this subject, you can find it in the documentation (e.g., `ftpaccess man` page). Also, you can create one using the graphical FTP server-configuration utility.

To tell the truth, I am not fond of the virtual server functions of the wu-ftp server. If you need several virtual FTP servers, I advise you to take a look at the ProFTP server, which is, in my opinion, more suitable for this task. The wu-ftp server is too cumbersome to configure for work with virtual servers because its configuration files are spread all over the system.

All virtual FTP servers are defined in the ftpservers configuration file. A virtual FTP server is defined by specifying its IP address and the directory containing its configuration files (which are duplicates of the wu-ftp server configuration files listed previously). If a configuration file for a virtual server is missing, the corresponding file in the /etc directory will be used instead.

10.5. Additional Settings

So far, I have been considering only the ftpaccess configuration file. But you already know that more than one file is used to configure the wu-ftp server. Take a look at them.

10.5.1. Prohibiting Access to Real Users

Because wu-ftp server uses operating system accounts, which are stored in the /etc/passwd file, any real user can automatically work with the FTP server using his or her account and access rights. However, far from all users need this capability.

To prohibit real users from accessing the FTP server, their names should be added to the /etc/ftpusers file. Listing 10.3 shows the contents of the file. Depending on the distribution, the contents may vary.

Listing 10.3. The contents of the /etc/ftpusers file

```
# The ftpusers file is deprecated.
# Use deny-uid/deny-gid in ftpaccess.
root
bin
daemon
adm
lp
sync
shutdown
halt
mail
news
uucp
operator
games
nobody
```

Note that the root user is prohibited access. This is because the administrator has too many rights and if hackers highjack this account, they will obtain complete control over the system. Never allow high-privileged users (administrators and administrator group users) access the FTP server.

If you have to work with files and directories that belong to the administrator, do not do this using the FTP server. The best way to edit such files is directly at the computer. Or you can download the files into your directory and then edit them locally or remotely using a secure terminal.

The best policy would be to prohibit FTP access to all system accounts whose ID is less than 500. This can be done by adding the following entry to the ftpaccess file:

```
deny-uid %-500
```

This way, you can be sure that you don't forget to restrict access to someone — especially if there is more than one user that has the same ID number (for example, 0).

10.5.2. Computers Are Not Allowed

Great administrator wisdom states that a firewall helps those who help themselves. A firewall prohibits access to the server to certain ports from specific computers. The /etc/ftphosts configuration file performs a similar function: It prohibits or allows access from the specified IP addresses or an entire network.

By default, the file is empty, because the software developers cannot know how you intend to go about organizing access. You can enter the following directives into the file:

```
allow name template
deny name template
```

For example, if you want to deny anonymous users access from address 192.168.1.1, add the following line to the file:

```
deny anonymous 192.168.1.1
```

According to the "everything not permitted is prohibited" principle, it may seem that the deny directive is not necessary. This is a wrong way of thinking, because a certain type of users has to be allowed access from the specified address and then all other users must be prohibited access to the FTP server.

10.5.3. Grouping

The ftpgroups file contains descriptions of the groups allowed to use the SITE GROUP and SITE GPASS commands when created. These are nonstandard FTP directives, which few developers support; consequently, users may find working with these commands too inconvenient.

The ftpgroups files contain entries similar to the following:

```
test:ENCRYPTED PASSWORD HERE:archive
```

The description line contains three colon-separated parameters: group name, password, and real (system) group name.

10.6. Guest Accounts

Logging into the FTP server under any real user name allows you to travel over the entire file system. In most cases, however, real users only need to work with their own documents; therefore, guest accounts will suffice for this purpose for all users. Consider an example of how this is done.

First, a new account is created for the user; name it robert_ftp. This is done using the following command:

```
useradd robert_ftp
```

The corresponding entry for this account in the /etc/passwd file should look similar to the following:

```
robert_ftp:x:507:507::/home/robert_ftp:/bin/bash
```

This is a standard new user entry. But this account can be used to enter the system locally, and you only want to give it FTP access. Change the shell for the user to /bin/ftponly. There is no such shell right now, but it will be created a little later. In addition, the /home/robert_ftp directory has to be made a root directory. This is done by adding a directory named . (dot) at the end of the user's home directory path.

The edited entry for the robert_ftp user in the /etc/passwd file should look as follows:

```
robert_ftp:x:507:507::/home/robert_ftp/.:/bin/ftponly
```

Note that the /bin/ftponly shell file does not exist. Create it now. Only one such file has to be created for being used by all guest accounts. The file is created by the `cat` command as follows:

```
cat >> /bin/ftponly
```

The command creates a file named ftponly in the /bin/ directory and redirects all subsequent console input to it. Enter the following text from the console:

```
#! /bin/sh
echo 'You are not allowed to log in interactively'
exit 0
```

Press the <Ctrl>+<X> key combination. This will save the file, terminate the entry mode, and take you back to the regular console mode.

The first command in the /bin/ftponly file displays the message saying an interactive login is not allowed, and the second terminates the session.

Now the /bin/ftponly file has to be made executable. This is done by the following command:

```
chmod 755 /bin/ftponly
```

Thus, you have a new user and a shell file for this user. Attempting to log into the system as the robert_ftp user will display the "You are not allowed to log in interactively" message for a moment, followed by termination of the current login session. Thus, you will not be able to log into the system as robert_ftp.

Instead of the /bin/ftponly file, the /dev/nul device can be used as the shell. This is a null device, which cannot process commands and will not allow the user to enter the system. This device is specified in the /etc/passwd file as the console for all system accounts not intended for local work.

There is one little thing left: Tell the FTP server that the robert_ftp user is a guest. This is done by adding the following entry to the ftpaccess file:

```
guestuser robert_ftp
```

Now, when connecting to the FTP server as robert_ftp, you will only be able to see your directory, which will appear to be the root directory. The rest of the directories above it will not be visible.

On my system, all FTP users work only as guests in their own directories, or anonymously with shared directories. Real FTP user accounts are created only for selected administrators and then only when necessary, because such accounts are more difficult to control.

You only have to restrict access for guest users to a certain directory, with the server protecting the rest. However, there can be problems here. Consider a classic programmer error. Suppose that a user is allowed access to the /home/robert directory and that the server enforces this access by simply checking that any path from this user starts with this string. For hackers, this directory will seem to be the root (/) directory, and they should not be able to reach any higher directories. But take a look at the following command:

```
cat /home/robert/../../../../../etc/passwd
```

It is supposed to display the contents of the /home/robert/../../../../etc/passwd file, but what it displays is the content of the /etc/passwd file. The starting part of the path meets the requirement, so the path is considered to be valid. But then it is followed by multiple /.. character combinations, each of which specifies a higher-level directory. This combination may be repeated in the path string several times, judged sufficient to take the user to the root directory. The final /etc/passwd part will take you to the password file.

Despite being so obvious and easy to avoid, this bug is quite common. All the programmer has to do is ensure that the address does not contain the /.. combination and take proper steps if it does. Although the wu-ftp server does not have this bug now, it may acquire it with an update, when the check may be disabled or deleted. This type of thing sometimes happens, especially if the software is developed by a team and the quality control of the overall product is deficient.

10.7. FTP Server Security

Up to now, I have been explaining how to configure a Linux FTP server. Now I will take a look at some examples of using the server in ways other than as intended, and ways of protecting against this.

Examples that will be considered in this section shocked the Internet community and security specialists, because the FTP server can be used to carry out practically any type of attack: spread viruses, Trojans, and spam; break into servers; and even anonymously scan remote computer ports. In short, FTP server can be used as a hacker tool.

10.7.1. Intercepting Connections

As you should remember, the process of connecting to the FTP server and the subsequent file transfer comprise the following steps:

1. The client connects to the server.
2. The server supplies authorization.
3. The client requests a file transfer.
4. The server opens a port and sends the pertinent information to the client.
5. The client connects to the specified port number and downloads or uploads the file.

Although it is difficult, it is possible to redirect the data connection from the authorized client to another machine. You have to intercept the packet, in which the server sends the port number information, connect to this port before the authorized client can do this, and then upload your information to the server or download information from the server to your machine.

The more dangerous development is the file-uploading part. Because you cut in after the authorization, you can upload any data without problems, because the server does not check that the IP address, from which the connection is made, matches the IP address, from which the request for connection was made.

Most FTP servers today have a built-in function to compare the IP addresses connected to port 21 and to the data port. This makes the attack more difficult to carry out because now the hacker must fake the IP address, which is not an easy task with TCP.

Using IP-address binding does not always solve the problem. If there is an anonymous proxy server or a firewall that masks IP addresses between the FTP client and the server, the FTP server will see not the address of the FTP client but the address of the proxy or the firewall.

You could disable the passive mode, which would dispense with this issue entirely. But this would not be a universal remedy for all security issues. As you will see in the next section, the active FTP mode is also far from secure.

But what did you expect? An active-mode connection can also be intercepted, although this is somewhat difficult to accomplish. When hackers obtain access to a computer connected to an FTP server, all they have to do is to wait until the user of the compromised machine requests a data transfer, and intercept the port.

10.7.2. Scanning Ports

As mentioned in *Section 1.1*, obtaining as much information as possible about the target machine is the initial break-in stage. Port scanning is one of the ways of collecting primary information. It is, however, dangerous to do this from your own computer, so hackers resort to all types of tricks to mask the scan source.

One of the tricks is placing a PHP or Perl port-scanning script on a server and scanning port from there. This method has the following shortcomings:

❑ You need a server that can execute scripts, which is not always easy to come by.
❑ Free servers that can execute scripts require you to register, and keep detailed activity logs. If the registration requirement is no more than a formality that is easily to get around by supplying arbitrary information, the logging part presents a big problem. Most servers nowadays are configured to watch for scanning activities conducted using their resources, and will record and call the administration's attentions to any such attempts. After that, finding the person behind the scan is only a matter of technicalities.

Hackers have come up with an excellent way to make a server scan ports. All you do is connect to an FTP server operating in the active mode.

Refresh your knowledge of how active-mode file transfer is conducted. The FTP client sends the FTP server a request specifying the port on the client computer, to which the server should connect to conduct the file transfer. In addition to the port number, to which the server will send data, the client sends the IP address. But this address does not have to be the client's address! This means that a client whose address is 192.168.1.1 can request the FTP server to connect to any port on a computer with any IP address and the server will be none the wiser. Hackers figured out how to use this peculiarity and make the FTP server scan ports on other computers.

Once I carried out a successful DoS attack on my own server. I made the FTP server scan the computer with the proxy used to connect to the Internet. The proxy server had an attack-detection system installed, which automatically blocked any connection attempts upon detecting any port-scanning attempts. (Such systems are discussed in *Chapter 12*). The scanning was successful, and I went to lunch with the feeling of a job well done. But when I returned, I was swamped with complaints that the FTP server was not working. I checked it out and everything was all right. So I started scratching my head. As it turned out, the FTP server became inaccessible to outside users connecting via the proxy server, because the proxy server detected the scanning and put the FTP server on its black list.

You can use the nmap program to scan ports using the FTP server as follows:

```
nmap -b user_name:password@ftp_server:port
```

As you can see, this entry looks much like the string to connect to the server using a Web browser. If an anonymous server will be used to do the scanning, the user name and the password can be omitted:

```
nmap -b ftpserver:port
```

If the server uses port 21, the port parameter can also be omitted.

One way of protecting against FTP port scanning is to configure the firewall to disable the active mode, that is, to block port 20, which is most often used as the FTP data port. In this case, all connections are initialized by the client only.

10.7.3. Mailings

The FTP server can be used to send email messages. This is done by placing the following text file on the server:

```
HALO mailserver.com
MAIL FROM: name@server.com
RCPT TO: recipient@server.com
DATA
The letter body
.
```

The entries are SMTP server commands and mean the following:

- ❏ HALO mailserver.com — The SMTP server greeting; the mailserver.com parameter has to be replaced with the real server name
- ❏ MAIL FROM: name@server.com — The sender's address
- ❏ RCPT TO: recipient@server.com — The recipient's address
- ❏ DATA — The command indicating that the letter body is to follow

The last line in the file consists of only a period, because the SMTP server interprets the <CR> and <LF> characters as the end of letter. Windows generates this character combination when the <Enter> key is pressed, but Linux only generated a <CR> character. It is only important that the file has some sort of new line delimiter and does not matter what it is, because the file will be sent in the ASCII mode.

Load this file on the FTP server and execute the following two commands:

```
PORT 192,168,1,1,25
RETR filename
```

The first entry is the FTP `PORT` command, telling the server to connect to port 25 of the computer with IP address 192.168.1.1. The first four numbers are the computer's IP address, and the last is the port to connect to. This command can be used to scan server ports manually, but in this case we are after another thing.

The second entry is the command that sends to the server the `filename` file with SMTP commands. The SMTP server sees this as if the FTP server is giving it directives to send the letter, which it will execute. The recipient of the letter will never be able to determine its source. The letter's service information will only point to the FTP server. In this way, malefactors can send anonymous letters without worrying that they will be found out.

The most diverse types of letters can be sent: viruses, Trojans, spam, and so on. Yet another way of using the FTP server to send email messages is to place a large file there and make the server send this file to the SMTP server endlessly. Launching several such processes can be used to pull off a successful DoS attack against a weak SMTP channel.

The only way to protect against such an attack on the SMTP server side is to use mandatory authorization to gain access. In this case, the hacker will have to possess information on a real account that is allowed access to the SMTP server. The FTP server is also protected by authenticating users who want to connect to it. No anonymous connections should be allowed, especially for file uploads.

10.8. Supplementary Information

I have not described all of the wu-ftp server's configuration file directives. There are too many of them; I have described only the most important ones.

You can obtain additional information about a particular configuration file by checking the `man` page for that file.

You can also read the wu-ftp server documentation in the /usr/share/doc/wu-ftpd-X.X.X directory (X.X.X is the version number of the server installed on your machine).

All changes specified in the configuration file become effective immediately. However, clients have to reconnect to the server to start working with the new settings.

The following are some useful FTP server administering commands:

- ❐ `ftpd` — Starts the server with special parameters. There are many possible attributes; information concerning them can be obtained from the `ftpd man` page. I have never had to resort to using the command options because once the server has been properly configured it works steadily.
- ❐ `ftprestart` — Restarts the FTP server.

❑ `ftpshut` — Shuts down the server. For example, to update software, don't just pull the plug on the server; shut it down in an orderly fashion. Use this command with the following options:

- `-l n` — Do not accept any new connections less than n minutes before the shutdown. Specify a time sufficient for the clients to properly finish their server operations.
- `-d n` — Disconnect the connections n minutes before shutting down the FTP server. I recommend setting the disconnection immediately or 1 minute before the shut down.
- `time` — Specifies the shutdown time for the FTP server and is similar to the same parameter in the Linux `shutdown` command. You can shut down the server immediately by specifying the value of the `time` parameter as now; however, I recommend using the +n option (where n is time in minutes until the shutdown) or specifying the exact time in the HHMM format.

❑ `ftpcount` — Displays the number of connected FTP users. When there is something funny going on in my system, I always check whether there are FTP clients connect. If there are, the next thing I want to know who is connected.

❑ `ftpwho` — Displays a list of the connected FTP clients and their corresponding accounts used to establish the connection. Sometimes, it takes only one look to determine the connection is being used by a bad guy — for example, a user who is not to be supposed to be using FTP at this time is shown in the accounts connected list.

❑ `ckconfig` — Checks the FTP server's configuration and displays a report for each wu-ftp server configuration file.

10.9. Summary

FTP itself and FTP servers from various developers have had serious security problems throughout their history. The losses caused by FTP and sendmail bugs combined may even overshadow the losses caused by viruses.

FTP's main problem is that it was created to be user-friendly. Another problem is that it uses two ports. Authorization is performed only when connected to port 21, and data channel operations are conducted without any confirmation of the client's authenticity.

Back when it was created, FTP was needed for data transfer, but today it should be avoided. If you only want to let users download information, consider using HTTP for this. It is more secure, and it can be used to upload files to the server.

Data exchange on a local network can be organized using the Samba server or HTTP. Many administrators do feel like configuring the Web server only for data exchange and install potentially dangerous scripts on it. But keep in mind that FTP can also be dangerous to security. You should choose the lesser of the two evils. If you already have a Web server running, use its capabilities as much as possible; then you will be able to close port 21, thereby protecting yourself against potential problems that can arise from its use.

If you need to use the FTP service yourself for remote file operations, I recommend using the SSH package and the built-in SSH FTP to encrypt data. This type of connection is much more difficult to compromise.

Chapter 11: Network Addressing

Each computer in a network must have its own unique address so that other network members can find it to exchange data. Thus, a network is something akin to a telephone system. To call someone, you have to dial that person's number, not his or her name.

When you are requesting a Web page from a server, you need to know the page's IP address. Once you know the address and send your request to the server, you have to supply it with your own IP address so that the server knows where to return the requested page. Here, an analogy with the regular mail can be observed. If you want to receive an answer to your letter, you have to put your return address on the envelope.

At the dawn of the Internet, the number of computers in it was not that large, and the simplest and most logical method of implementing addressing was selected: using numbers. Still, 20 numerical addresses is about the limit an average human can remember, so for the convenience of humans, hosts are given names that can be easily remembered, for example, **www.webpage.com**.

These two addressing systems are incompatible, and something had to be done about this. This was solved by creating a centralized database of numerical IP addresses and their corresponding symbolic host names. This allows users to enter a symbolic address into a program, which then looks up the corresponding numerical IP address in the centralized database and uses this address to connect to the necessary computer.

This made the situation with remembering addresses much easier for people. Now to visit a site, for example, of the Microsoft Corporation, you have to know not its exact numerical IP address but just an easy-to-remember domain name: **www.microsoft.com**.

11.1. Introduction to DNS

At first, a simple text file was used to store the database resolving symbolic domain names to their corresponding IP addresses. In Linux, this is the /etc/hosts file. When there were relatively few computers on the Internet, this method worked, even if it was somewhat cumbersome to maintain the central database and update local hosts files.

But as the number of computers on the Internet grew, so did the size of the database, until it became impossible for each location to maintain a copy of it. This is when the DNS came into being.

DNS is a distributed database of host names and their corresponding IP addresses; there are thousands of DNS servers on the Internet. The domain namespace has a hierarchical structure, with the root domain indicated by a . (dot, or period). The root domain is followed by subdomains, also separated with a period. The domains after the root are called top-level domains. Some of the top-level domain names are **com**, **org**, **net**, **gov**, **edu**, **ru**, and **de**. In **cydsoft.com**, **cydsoft** is a second-level domain name. Fig. 11.1 shows an example of the domain namespace hierarchy.

The advantages of DNS become apparent not only on the Internet but also in sufficiently large local networks. After DNS was implemented, another of its advantages came to light: The same IP address can be used for several sites. This allows several sites to be maintained on a single server.

IP address resolution parsing of a domain name is carried out from right to left. Suppose you have to resolve the IP address of the **www.cydsoft.com** host. A DNS client program on the user's computer sends a request to a root server to specify, which DNS server services the **com** domain. Then, a query is sent to the **com** domain DNS server to find the **cydsoft** domain. If this domain is found, the address of the DNS server servicing the **cydsoft** domain is obtained. A query to resolve the **www.cydsoft.com** domain name to its IP address is then sent to this DNS server.

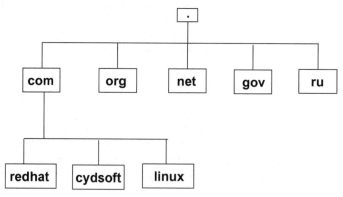

Fig. 11.1. The domain namespace hierarchy

All these operations are performed transparently to the end user, so you will never see all these intricacies when entering an address into a browser. Depending on the browser, a message that the IP address is being looked up (Opera) or that the Web page is being connected to (Internet Explorer) is displayed in the browser's status line.

There also are numerous automatic DNS information-caching servers. Caching DNS information makes it possible not to query the main database all the time but to obtain the necessary address at the nearest server. Caching servers exchange information among themselves and allow any host name to be resolved to its address. Thus, your Internet provider may maintain its own DNS server. In this case, the request to resolve a host name to its IP address is sent to this DNS server. If this server does not have the requested host name information, the request is passed to another DNS server. The request is relayed among various DNS servers until the necessary host name information is encountered; in this way, the IP address for the requested host name can be obtained from the nearest DNS server containing the necessary information in its cache.

DNS servers can not only look up IP addresses by host names but also perform reverse lookups, that is, resolve IP addresses to the corresponding host names. In this case, the IP address is also parsed from right to left. For example, to resolve IP address 190.1.15.77 to the host name, the address in the DNS request is entered as 77.15.1.190 with the .in-addr.arpa suffix added, resulting in this: 77.15.1.190.in-addr.arpa.

11.2. Local hosts File

As already mentioned, initially, the /etc/hosts file was used to resolve host names to IP addresses. This text file contains entries of the following format:

```
127.0.0.1  localhost.localdomain localhost
192.168.77.1 FlenovM
```

Each entry in the file maps a host name to its corresponding IP address. By default, there are only two entries in the file. The first entry is the loopback mapping. For all computers, the localhost name and the 127.0.0.1 IP address specify the local machine. Thus, the local computer can be pinged as follows:

```
ping 127.0.0.1
```

The second entry maps the computer name to the explicitly specified IP address of the machine's network adapter. In this case, the network card's IP address is set to 192.168.77.1; it is mapped to the FlenovM computer name. This means that either the computer name or its IP address can be specified as the parameter for the ping command. The following two commands are identical:

```
ping 192.168.77.1
ping FlenovM
```

When the second command is executed, a request will be made to the /etc/hosts file to obtain the corresponding IP address. Then the echo request will be directed to that address.

But which, the /etc/hosts file or DNS, is referenced first to resolve an address? This depends on the configuration of the operating system. There is the following line in the /etc/host.conf file:

```
order hosts, bind
```

The order directive specifies the order, in which the address resolution systems are referenced. At this setting, first the /etc/hosts file will be consulted, and only if the necessary information is not found in it will the bind command be executed to send a request to the DNS server. This speeds up access to main servers. Suppose that you visit the **www.redhat.com** site every day. When a request is sent to the DNS server, it takes a couple of seconds to resolve the host name to its IP address and to start loading the page.

To speed up the loading, the following entry can be made in the /etc/hosts file:

```
209.132.177.50 www.redhat.com
```

The 209.132.177.50 address corresponded to the **www.redhat.com** site when this book was being written. However, the address can change.

NOTE

If, for some reason, the site will no longer load, delete the corresponding entry from the /etc/hosts file. Then execute the ping redhat.com command to check the communication with the server and to find out its IP address. This will display the IP address, with which the ping messages are exchanged. IP addresses of most sites change rarely, so once a mapping entry is added to the /etc/hosts file, you can save lots of time and nerves, especially when there are problems with the DNS server.

11.3. External DNS Servers

If the necessary mapping information is not found in the local /etc/hosts file, it has to be requested from the DNS server. This requires the IP address of the DNS server to be known. The information about this address is contained in the /etc/resolv.conf file. The contents of the file look similar to the following:

```
search FlenovM
domain domain.name
nameserver 10.1.1.1
nameserver 10.1.1.2
```

The search parameter in the first entry specifies the host name search server. The file on your system most likely also contains this entry, with the name of your computer specified as the server. This parameter can contain a space- or tab-delimited list of several servers. For example:

```
search FlenovM MyServer
```

The local server is searched quickly enough, but searching remote servers may take a while.

In the second file, the `domain` parameter is specified. Users sometimes like to specify computer names without giving the top-level domain name; for example, "redhat" instead of "redhat.com." In the `domain` parameter, the top-level domain name is specified to be used in such cases. Most often, a specific top-level domain name for local networks is specified in this parameter.

The rest of the entries specify the `nameserver` parameter. This is an external DNS server, to which the requests are directed. There can be several such entries; most current distributions have no more than three entries. The `nameserver` entries are queried in the order they are listed in the file until the necessary address has been resolved.

In most cases, a single server is enough, because all of them operate recursively. For example, when a computer requests to resolve the **redhat.com** address, the request is directed to the first DNS server on the list. If this server does not find the necessary address, it forwards the request to another DNS server that is has on its own `nameserver` list.

I, however, recommend specifying two DNS servers. Sometimes, when the first DNS server fails, the second one saves the situation.

11.4. Configuring DNS

Currently, the most common Linux DNS service is `bind`. This service is implemented by the `bindconf` utility, which has a graphical interface and is easy to use. To run the utility, open a console from the graphical mode and execute the following command:

```
bindconf &
```

The ampersand (`&`) specifies that the program is to be run in the background. When a graphical utility is launched in the background, it does not interfere with the console operations. Note, however, that when the console window is closed, all programs launched with the `&` option are also closed.

Fig. 11.2 shows the DNS configuration utility's main window. In the center of the main window, the dialog window for adding a domain is shown. All you have to do for adding a domain is select the zone type and specify the domain name.

Even though DNS can be configured through the user-friendly graphical utility, I will consider doing this using the configuration files for the service. Editing them directly allows the service to be configured more precisely and will also enable you to understand the DNS operation process better.

The main DNS configuration file is /etc/named.conf. Listing 11.1 shows an example of the contents of this file.

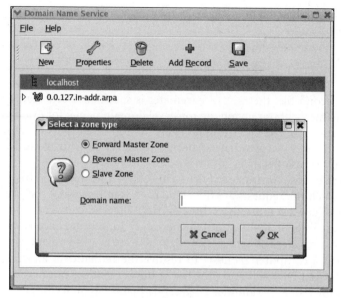

Fig. 11.2. DNS control windows

Listing 11.1. An example of the contents of the /etc/named.conf file

```
options {
        directory "/var/named/";
};

zone   "." {
       type hint;
       file   "named.ca";
};

zone   "sitename.com" {
       type master;
       file   "sitename.zone";
};

zone   "10.12.190.in-addr.arpa" {
       type master;
       file   "10.12.190.in-addr.arpa.zone";
};
```

In this example, the file is broken into four sections of the following format:

```
type name {
 Parameter1;
 Parameter2;

 ...
};
```

The functions of each section are as follows. The first section is options:

```
options {
        directory "/var/named/";
};
```

It contains only one parameter in braces: directory. It specifies the home directory of the DNS server, where all of its files will be stored.

The rest of the sections are of the zone type, with the zone name given in quotation marks. Each of the sections contains two parameters. The type parameter defines the zone type, and the file parameter defines the file containing the description of the zone.

The first zone in the example is described as follows:

```
zone  "." {
        type hint;
        file  "named.ca";
};
```

What is this . zone? Recall the DNS theory presented at the beginning of the chapter. According to this theory, the DNS root domain is represented as a period. Thus, the section describes the root zone. The section type, hint, means that the server will only store links to the DNS server. Because this is the root zone, all links will be to the root servers.

The file parameter specifies the name of the file containing all links to the root servers. Your system may not have this file because the information in it is dynamic. It is the best to obtain the latest version of this file from the **internic.net** server. This is done by executing the following command:

```
dig @rs.internic.net . ns > named.ca
```

The next section describes the sitename.com zone:

```
zone  "sitename.com" {
        type master;
        file  "sitename.zone";
};
```

The zone type, master, means that your DNS server will be the main one, with the rest only verifying and caching DNS information. The information about this zone will be stored in the sitename.zone file in the work directory, which is /var/named in this case.

The next section describes reverse lookup of the 190.12.10.* IP addresses into host names:

```
zone   "10.12.190.in-addr.arpa" {
       type master;
       file  "10.12.190.in-addr.arpa.zone";
};
```

The zone type is master again.

11.5. Zone-Description Files

According to the /etc/named.conf configurations file, there should be three files in the /var/named directory. These are the following:

❒ named.ca — Links to the root servers are stored in this file. This file is downloaded from the **intenic.net** server; therefore, it should not be edited, and I will not be considering it.

❒ sitename.zone — This file is responsible for resolving the **sitename.com** name to its IP address.

❒ 10.12.190.in-addr.arpa.zone — This file is responsible for resolving the 190.12.10.* network addresses to their corresponding host names.
The sitename.zone file contents may look like the following:

```
@      IN      SOA     ns.sitename.com  root.sitename.com (
                       1 ; serial
                       28800 ; refresh
                       7200 ; retry
                       604800 ; expire
                       86400 ; ttl
                       )
       IN      NS      ns.sitename.com.
       IN      MX      10 mail.sitename.com.
       ns      A       190.12.10.1
       mail    A       190.12.10.2
```

The functions of the main directives used to configure DNS records are the following:

❒ *Start of authority* (SOA) — Specifies the main information, including the administrator's email address and such information as the frequency, with which records are updated, the TTL of cached records, and so on.

❒ *Address* (A) — Indicates the computer name and IP address.

❒ *Canonical name* (CNAME) — Specifies a synonym for the real domain name in the type A record.

❒ *Pointer* (PTR) — Shows a domain name by its IP address.

☐ *Text* (TXT) — Denotes freestyle descriptive information.

☐ *Responsible person* (RP) — Specifies the email address of the person responsible for the operation of the service.

☐ *Host information* (HINFO) — Designates information about the computer, such as the operating system type and equipment installed.

For security reasons, the HINFO and TXT records are not used; therefore, they will not reveal any information to hackers. Hackers should not be given any information about the computer, however innocent it may seem, and information about the computer's operating system and equipment is far from innocent. The HINFO and TXT records are purely informational and do not contain any data affecting the server's operation.

Now, return to the sitename.zone file and consider its contents. In the first records (of the IN SOA type), the zone is described. First, the name of the DNS server (ns.sitename.com) and the person responsible for the record (root@sitename.com) are given. The parameters in the parentheses are each specified on a separate line for convenience. The first parameter is the serial number. Increment this parameter by 1 after each modification or replace it with the date the record was last modified. By this value, other servers will find out whether the record was modified.

The refresh parameter sets the frequency, with which other servers must update their information. In case of an error, the server has to try again after the period specified in the retry parameter.

The expire parameter specifies when cached-zone information will no longer be valid. The ttl parameter defines the entry's minimum TTL on caching servers.

These parameters inform the rest of the DNS how to refresh the information about the zone controlled by your DNS server.

The next record is of the NS type; there can be several such records. In this case, NS stands for name server. This record describes the DNS servers responsible for this zone. All other DNS participants will use these servers to resolve the **sitename.com** symbolic name to its IP address.

Next, mail exchange (MX) records can follow. DNS servers use these records to determine where to send mail that comes to the **sitename.com** domain. In this example, this is the **mail.sitename.com** server. The number in front of the server name specifies the MX entry's priority. If there are multiple MX records, they will be used in the order of their priorities.

NOTE

The NS and MX entries must terminate in a period.

The last records are used for the reverse lookup. They are of the following format:

```
name   A       address
```

There are two such records in the example:

```
ns     A      190.12.10.1
mail   A      190.12.10.2
```

This means that the **ns.servername.com** and **mail.servername.com** symbolic names resolve to the 190.12.10.1 and 190.12.10.2 IP addresses, respectively.

11.6. Reverse Zone

The format of the reverse lookup file (used to resolve an IP address to its corresponding host name) is similar to the following:

```
@       IN     SOA    ns.sitename.com  root.sitename.com (
                      1 ; serial
                      28800 ; refresh
                      7200 ; retry
                      604800 ; expire
                      86400 ; ttl
                      )

        IN     NS     localhost.

1       PTR    servername.com.
2       PTR    mail.servername.com.
```

You already know the purpose of the larger part of the file and only need to consider the last two records. These map IP addresses to their corresponding host names. Don't forget that the file is responsible for the 190.12.10.* network. The asterisk is replaced with the number from the first field, and the name corresponding to this IP address is given in the last field. The file defines the following mappings:

190.12.10.1 = **servername.com.**

190.12.10.2 = **mail.servername.com.**

It is mandatory that symbolic names end with a period.

You can find additional information concerning DNS in the RFC1035, RFC1712, and RFC1706 documents.

11.7. DNS Security

Glancing at the DNS mission, it may seem that it cannot be compromised by hackers. This is a misperception. There have been cases of DNS servers being taken out of commission. This made it impossible to use symbolic host names, and network programs could no longer function. Users are not used to using IP addresses, so DNS becoming unavailable is a kiss of death for their Internet activities.

Other than putting DNS servers out of order, hackers can extract too much information about the network structure. To prevent this, it is desirable to use two DNS servers as follows:

❑ One DNS server is publicly available and contains only the mapping information necessary for remote users to work with shared resources.
❑ Another DNS server is available only to local network users and contains all mapping information the users require for their work.

The firewall on the local DNS server can be configured to recognize local traffic only and ignore access attempts from the Internet. This will make it problematic for hackers not only to obtain information from the DNS database but also to disrupt the operation of this server. In this way, when the firewall is functional, all local users will be protected against disruptions in DNS operations.

You could install a secondary server for each primary server. This will distribute each workload between two servers, reduce the response time, and enhance the system's robustness. Moreover, if one of the servers fails, the other will pick up its workload and keep the DNS service operational.

Pairing up servers allows productivity and security to be enhanced. Linux-based DNS servers are undemanding to the hardware. I have four Red Hat-based DNS servers running in text mode on 400-MHz to 700-MHz Pentium machines. These used to be office computers, but when their capabilities became insufficient to handle office tasks, I turned them into DNS servers. These machines are, and will be for the next several years, more than enough for this task. In this way, old computers can be given a second life, and quite a long one. The important thing is that this solution saves the company money.

But, in addition to offering the described advantages, doubling DNS servers can be dangerous. Hackers can use the `host` utility to obtain the contents of the main server's database in the same way the secondary servers do this to update their databases.

The following is an example of how this can be done:

```
host -l server.com ns1.server.com
```

This will produce all database records about the **server.com** server. To prevent this, the addresses of the secondary servers have to be explicitly specified in the named.conf file. This is done by adding the following entry to its `options {...}` section:

```
allow-transfer {192.168.1.1;}
```

This can also be done in the descriptions of the individual zones, but it is preferable to do this once in the global options. If you do not employ a secondary DNS server, prohibit data from being transferred to the secondary zone by adding the following entry:

```
allow-transfer {none;}
```

DNS servers can be subjected to DDoS attacks. The most notorious DDoS attack on Internet DNS servers was carried out in November 2002. Several root servers were attacked simultaneously. If only one server had been employed to provide DNS services, the Internet would have become inaccessible shortly after the attack started. This did not happen for the following reasons:

☐ Server redundancy, which makes duplicates of the DNS information available
☐ Caching servers
☐ Proxy servers, which also cache DNS records

Other aspects of securing a DNS server are identical to securing any other service and the operating system. As already mentioned, the most secure server is one that performs a narrowly-specified task. There are fewer open ports and fewer running services on such servers, which makes them more difficult to compromise. The only problem with this approach is that numerous servers make the process of updating the operating system more complex. Linux has its fair share of bugs that have to be fixed, and when updates are made available, all servers, including DNS servers, have to be updated.

Chapter 12: System Monitoring

The administrator's initial task is to install the system, properly assign access rights, and configure all necessary services. This done, many administrators believe their duty is fulfilled, and they start chasing monsters in the virtual dungeons of whatever version of Doom they have. If you are among these administrators, sooner or later your system will be hacked and you will face the music for letting this happen.

To reduce the chances of unauthorized outside entry or to secure yourself from nefarious users of your own network, you have to maintain continuous control over your server. The majority of successful break-ins are successful because the administrators do not update some service or do not install patches on time. Hackers often learn about a new vulnerability and start hacking all servers they run across with this vulnerability.

A good administrator can and should learn about vulnerabilities affecting his or her server before hackers do, and take whatever steps are necessary to prevent any potential attack exploiting these vulnerabilities. To this end, administrators should monitor their system and conduct vulnerability checks regularly. After penetrating the system, hackers sometimes do not reveal themselves by any actions for a long time. You should be able to unearth these moles and kick them out of the system before they do any harm.

If you have been hacked, your task is not just to recover gracefully but also to prevent this from happening again. I have seen many administrators who after a break-in simply restore deleted files and continue in the same way, hoping that lightning will not strike in the same place twice. This is mistake, because unlike lightning, a computer hacked into once is much more likely to be hacked into again; the hacker already knows how to enter the system and move around it.

So instead of hoping that the hacker had all the fun he or she wanted and will not return, you should take for granted that the hacker *will* return and have a proper reception party prepared. Find out as much information as possible about the hacker, the ways used to penetrate the system, and how you might block the attack. You also have to peruse the latest Bugtraq lists for information about bugs in your operating system and services installed.

Do no wait until you have a hacker in your system. In this chapter, I will consider measures to enhance system security that you can undertake before and after your system is hacked.

Hackers sometimes leave back doors (e.g., setting the SUID bit of a program that is not supposed to be set), and you should regularly conduct security sweeps of the system as described in the ensuing material. It is especially applicable right after installing and initially configuring the operating system, installing new application software, updating the system software, or experiencing a break-in.

12.1. Automated Security Monitoring

Practically every day, computer security professionals discover vulnerabilities, holes, and gaps you could drive a truck through in various systems. All this information is published in BugTraq reports on various servers. One of the sites where these reports can be found is **www.securityfocus.com**. But besides the new vulnerabilities, there are plenty of old ones that may not have been patched on the server you are dealing with. How can you find out, which vulnerabilities the given server has? Is there a way other than downloading all the exploits and trying them manually? Of course there is. There are a great variety of programs to automatically test a server for vulnerabilities, the most common of these being SATAN, Internet Scanner, NetSonar, and CyberCop Scanner.

I will not recommend any specific program. There is no utility that has a database of all existing vulnerabilities. So download various programs and test the server using them all. This way your chances of discovering paths that could be used for a break-in become much greater. I do recommend that you use software from Internet Security Systems (ISS) (**www.iss.net**), because this company's scanners (Internet Scanner, System Scanner, and Database Scanner) use all three scanning techniques. (I will describe these techniques later.) The ISS personnel work closely with Microsoft and regularly update their vulnerabilities database. Even though a larger part of the company's software products are intended for detecting vulnerabilities in Microsoft software, they also produce security software for other servers.

ISS has developed a suite of utilities named SAFEsuite. The suite contains not only system-security testing utilities but also intrusion-detection utilities and utilities to check the configuration of the main server operating systems.

Security scanners are similar to antivirus programs: They protect only against known threats. Any new vulnerability will not be detected until the program is updated. For this reason, I don't recommend that you rely only on the automatic security scanners; supplement them by manually checking for the latest vulnerabilities described in Bugtraq.

The automatic scanners are good for performing initial scanning for old vulnerabilities. If you are a system administrator and scanning detects vulnerabilities in your system, you should update the software component containing the vulnerability or check one of the security sites (e.g., **www.securityfocus.com**) for ways to neutralize the vulnerabilities discovered. Almost always, the description of the remedy for the vulnerability is given with a description of the vulnerability. The way to neutralize the vulnerability may also be suggested by the scanning program if it has this in its solution database.

Why can't you be certain that the server has no vulnerabilities even after the most exhaustive and thorough scanning comes out negative? In addition to new vulnerabilities, there is the factor of the server's configuration. Each server is configured differently, and under certain conditions a vulnerability that can be easily detected manually may be overlooked by an automatic scanner.

Each scanner employs individual techniques and means, and vulnerabilities missed by one scanner may be detected by another. Computer-security professionals like to use the apartment analogy. Suppose you came to visit a friend, ringed his doorbell, but nobody opened the door. This, however, does not mean that there was no one at home; the owner, for example, may not have heard the doorbell or it may have been out of order. But if you had called him on the phone, he might have heard it and answered. Or it could be the other way around: The friend could miss the phone call but hear the doorbell.

In the same way, one vulnerability-detection technique may produce positive results, and another may show negative ones. To return to the automatic scanners, one scanner is like the phone call and another one is like the doorbell. They both produce results, but with different server configurations one may be better than the other.

There are three methods of automatic vulnerability detection: scanning, probing, and imitating. During scanning, the utility collects information about the server, scans the ports to find out what services are installed, and — based on these scans — produces a report about the potential vulnerabilities. For example, a scanner can check a server and discover that port 21 is used by the FTP service. After the scanner attempts to connect to the port, the server issues an invitation prompt, by which its type can be determined (provided that the prompt has not been modified). The scanner then checks its database for vulnerabilities for the given server version and, if it finds any, produces a corresponding message.

Automatic scanning is far from an exact science and can be fooled easily; moreover, automatic scanning may produce false alarms showing a vulnerability where there is none. Some vulnerabilities can only be detected with certain configurations and will not be noticed with others.

During the probing process, the utility does not scan the server for open ports; it scans its programs for vulnerable code. This process is similar to the way antivirus programs work, which scan all programs for virus code. Here the same thing takes place, only the object of the search is vulnerable code. The method is an effective one, but the same type of error (e.g., a buffer overflow) can be present in programs written in different languages. The scanner will not detect this type of error.

The imitation method involves the utility imitating attacks that it contains in its database. For example, the FTP server may produce the buffer-overflow error when a certain command is executed. The scanner will not try to detect the server's version but will execute the command instead. This will hang the server, but you will know for certain whether the server has this particular vulnerability. This method is the lengthiest but also the most reliable, because if the utility can break some service, then a hacker can also do it.

If you have a new FTP server installed that is unknown to the scanner, it will be tested for errors that other FTP servers have. Different programmers often make the same errors. Simple scanning will not detect these vulnerabilities because they are not listed in the database for the given version of the FTP server.

Always disable the firewall when conducting a system scan. It may block access and the scan may not scan the necessary service. In this case, it will report no vulnerabilities when they may exist. These vulnerabilities are not critical because they are protected by the firewall, but if a hacker finds a loophole through the firewall, they will become critical.

Give the scanner all it needs. For example, some people think that remote scanning, when the scanner imitates an attack over the network, is the most effective. Although this is so, it begets a question: How much time it will take to check the strength of the account passwords? A lot! And such checks as registry and file system scans will become impossible. This is why local scanning may be more productive and reliable.

In remote scanning, the scanner only attempts to enter the network. This type of analysis can be used to evaluate the server's capability to withstand outside attacks. But statistically, most break-ins are inside jobs (carried out by disgruntled employees or simply unscrupulous users) by a perpetrator who already has some access rights but enlarges them and obtains access to off-limit areas. Hackers can also obtain an account with minimal access rights, which they can then raise to take advantage of the vulnerabilities in the access-rights assignment procedures. Consequently, you should apply both remote scanning to detect loopholes that can be used to enter the system and local scanning to detect configuration errors that can be used to expand access privileges.

Automatic scanners scan not only programs for vulnerabilities but also accounts for password strength. A scanner utility contains a database of the most often used account names and passwords and tries to use them to enter the system. If the attempt is successful, the utility informs the administrator that the employed password is too easy. Such passwords must be changed, because hackers can use the same method and learn the account parameters with ease.

Both hackers and administrators can use security analyzers. Hackers use them to detect vulnerabilities they can get hold of to penetrate the system and administrators use them to close such vulnerabilities. If you are an administrator, your task is to find and patch the vulnerabilities before they are found and used by hackers.

Later I will consider manual system-security checking techniques and utilities used for this. Which of the available security techniques and utilities should you use? As I already said, as many of them as possible. You should check your system in as many different ways as possible. Using only one method, you are running a risk of missing a potential vulnerability that hackers will use to break into your system.

12.2. Shutting SUID and SGID Doors

If you are an administrator or a security specialist, you should know your system inside and out. You already know that one of the potential security problems is SUID or SGID bits. You have to clear these bits for all programs that you are not using. But how can you find programs that have these bits set? Use the following command:

```
find / \( -perm -02000 -o -perm -04000 \) -ls
```

This command will find all files that have 02000 or 04000 rights, which corresponds to the SUID or SGID bits set. The following is an example of the command's execution:

```
130337  64 -rwsr-xr-x  1 root root  60104 Jul 29  2002 /bin/mount
130338  32 -rwsr-xr-x  1 root root  30664 Jul 29  2002 /bin/umount
130341  36 -rwsr-xr-x  1 root root  35040 Jul 19  2002 /bin/ping
130365  20 -rwsr-xr-x  1 root root  19072 Jul 10  2002 /bin/su
...
```

The most dangerous thing security-wise in this list is that all of the programs have root permissions and can be executed by a user or a group member. There are programs with SUID and SGID bits set that belong to other users in the system, but most have the root ownership.

If you do not use a program, either delete it or clear the bits. If you think that there are no unnecessary programs in your system, think again. Perhaps, there is something you can do without. For example, if a program is not a must for a server, its SUID bit can be cleared.

If, after the initial paring, there are still many privileged programs left, I recommend clearing the bits for all programs. This will make it impossible for users to mount devices or change their passwords. But do they need these services? If some of them need some of these services, you can always give them these by resetting the SUID bit.

You can also change programs' ownerships to less privileged accounts. Even though this is difficult to implement, because you will have to change quite a few permissions, you will sleep better at night.

Why is it so important to regularly check files for SUID or SGID bits set? Because after penetrating a system, hackers often try to fortify their positions in it to remain invisible yet retain maximum privileges. The easiest way of achieving this is setting the SUID bit on the bash command interpreter. This will result in the interpreter executing any user's commands with the root rights, meaning that the hackers can have guest rights but perform operations requiring root privileges — that is, anything they may feel like.

12.3. Testing the Configuration

I have presented quite a few system configuration rules, and it is difficult if not impossible to remember all of them. System configuration is a complex process, and it is easy to set some wrong settings. But the configuration rules make it possible to automate the testing process.

There are many utilities for automated configuration checking. Some of them are outdated; others are more recent and check a limited number of parameters.

The LSAT Utility

The first automated configuration-checking utility I will consider is the Linux Security Auditing Tool (LSAT). It does not have a long track record, but its capabilities have been expanded by frequent updates and the modular architecture makes extending capabilities an easy and rapid process.

The LSAT program comes as the source code, and can be downloaded from **http://usat.sourceforge.net**. When this book was written, version 0.9.2 of the program was available. Both TGZ and ZIP archives are available. I recommend the former, because the TGZ format is native to Linux and is easier to install.

The program is installed by executing the following sequence of commands:

```
tar xzvf lsat-0.9.2.tgz
./lsat-0.9.2.tgz/configure
./lsat-0.9.2.tgz/make
```

The first command unpacks the archive. Your file name can be different depending on which version of the program you download. The second command starts configuration, and the last one builds one executable file from the source code.

The program is launched by the following command:

```
./lsat-0.9.2.tgz/lsat
```

Now you can brew a pot of coffee and have a few cups of it. The checking process is quite lengthy, especially on older machines. The utility can be run with one of the following options:

- ❑ -o <filename> — Specifies the file, into which to place the report. The default report file is lsat.out.
- ❑ -v — Produce a verbose report.
- ❑ -s — Specifies the silent mode, which is convenient when running the utility with the cron service.
- ❑ -r — Specifies to check RPM integrity. This option is valid for the Red Hat or Mandrake distributions only. The option is used to verify the distribution package validity.

The LSAT utility is optimized for running Red Hat systems because it has a built-in feature for working with a database or RPM packages, which are a distinctive feature of Red Hat Linux and its clones.

When the utility is running, the check it displays messages like the following:

```
Starting LSAT...
Getting system information...
 Running modules...
 Running checkpkgs module...
```

```
   ...
   ...
 Running checkx module...
 Running checkftp module...
Finished.
Check lsat.out for details.
Don't forget to check your umask or file perms
when modifying files on the system.
```

These messages provide no security information and only inform you which modules are being checked. The scanning results are saved to the ./lsat.out file. I ran the utility on my system right after a fresh install and it packed 190 KB of information into this file. That's plenty of information to pore over and get to know your system better.

There are many recommendations in the output file. At the beginning, there are recommendations about which packages should be deleted, as in the following:

```
*****************************************
Please consider removing these packages.
sendmail-8.11.6-15.asp
portmap-4.0-41
bind-utils-9.2.1-1.asp
nfs-utils-0.3.3-5
pidentd-3.0.14-5
sendmail-devel-8.11.6-15.asp
sendmail-cf-8.11.6-15.asp
ypbind-1.10-7
ypbind-1.10-7
```

Indeed, some packages are not reliable. For example, bugs are constantly discovered in the sendmail program; therefore, LSAT suggests removing this program.

There was the following comment in the output file that I especially liked:

```
default init level is not set to 5. Good.
```

The utility's developer reckoned that graphical operation mode is less secure. Indeed, running a graphics shell means running additional programs, and you already know that any additional program is an extra chance for something to go wrong. The text mode uses less memory, requires fewer resources, and runs fewer programs, which means that it is a faster and more secure.

Further down the output file listing, there is a list of all SUID and SGID files in the system.

Still further, there is a list of files accessible to everyone:

```
*****************************************
This is a list of world writable files
/var/lib/texmf/ls-R
/var/www/html/cache/archive/index.html
```

```
/var/www/html/cache/categories/category.cgi
/var/www/html/cache/categories/index.html
/var/www/html/cache/download/download-2-1.cgi
/var/www/html/cache/download/download-3-1.cgi
/var/www/html/cache/download/download-4-1.cgi
```

Any user, even the one with the humblest access rights, can modify these files. Right below this list, there is a list of files, to which users of any groups can write. Check whether all of these files should be available for writing to all users. Ideally, there should be no such files. Any file should be accessible for writing for its owner only, or for a user of the owner group at the worst, but in no case should they be writeable for everyone.

The output file is in a convenient and easy-to-read format; at the end, however, there is a fly in the ointment. Perhaps, it's more of a mosquito than a fly: The report section on the modifications in the file system detected since the previous check is difficult to understand. All changes are heaped into one pile without differentiating, which are serious and which are unimportant. For example, deleting or adding files to the /tmp directory is not that important from the security standpoint, because this is done constantly in this directory. Changes in the /etc directory are much more important to security and ought to have been set off.

The Bastille Utility

The Bastille project (**http://bastille-linux.sourceforge.net**) was created by Linux security specialists and has been around for a long time. The developers also intended to write a more secure version of the operating system, but it seems like they overestimated their capabilities for this task. It's a pity, because the Bastille utility is an excellent security product.

The program checks the system for potential vulnerabilities and creates a report of what it finds. The utility can also automatically fix the discovered vulnerabilities.

The program is so intuitive and easy to use that I will not even consider this aspect. Unlike similar programs, Bastille can work in both the text and the graphical modes. The program can be either installed from an RPM archive or compiled from the source code.

12.4. Detecting Attacks

A good administrator must do everything to nip in the bud any attack attempts on his or her system. What is the first thing hackers do to break in to a system? They collect information about the system, as was discussed at the beginning of this book. Hackers try to learn as much as possible about the system they want to break in to, and administrators must do everything to give as little information as possible about their system or, even better, throw hackers off the track with some false information.

The simplest and initial information-gathering technique is port scanning. To determine who tried to scan ports on your machine, when, and from where, you have to detect any nonstandard port events. Doing this manually is difficult, and a good specialized program is called for.

Automated port-scanning detection programs are a rather good attack-detection tool but, unfortunately, not in all cases. For example, popular servers are scanned often. I believe that such servers as **www.yahoo.com** or **www.microsoft.com** are scanned thousands if not millions of times a day. It is useless to pay attention to each of these countless scans. The most important thing is that automatic attack detection consumes computing resources, and sometimes a quite substantial amount. If every scanning attempt is logged, hackers can devise attack-imitating packets. Then all the server will do is handling these supposed attacks. The effect will be a classical DoS attack, because the server will no longer process client requests.

However, detecting scanning attempts on a company or home network server is a certain way to prevent a break-in.

Another shortcoming of automated scanning detection is that you will not be able to use your own security-scanning utilities, because their activity will be interpreted as an attack by the scanning-detection utilities. Consequently, when you perform scanning yourself, you have to disable the scanning-detection utilities for your scanning to work.

The Klaxon Utility

One of the simplest and most effective scanning-detection utilities is Klaxon (**www.eng.auburn.edu/users/doug/second.html**). The utility monitors ports unused by the system, and when it detects attempts to access them it gathers as much information as possible about the IP address, from which the scanning is conducted, and saves it in a log file.

The program is simple to install. After installing the program to the /etc/local/klaxon directory, add the following lines to the /etc/inetd.conf file:

```
#
# Local testing counterintelligence
#
rexec    stream  tcp  nowait  root    /etc/local/klaxon klaxon rexec
link     stream  tcp  nowait  root    /etc/local/klaxon klaxon link
supdup   stream  tcp  nowait  root    /etc/local/klaxon klaxon supdup
tftp     dgram   udp  wait    root    /etc/local/klaxon klaxon tftp
```

The preceding directives redirect services to the Klaxon utility and you can log who and when attempts to access these services.

This is useful because the remote command execution (REXEC) service is not needed for regular users and is mostly sought by hackers to penetrate the system. If an attempt, even an unsuccessful one, to access the REXEC service was made from some address, you should make a note that someone from this IP address is casing your server for vulnerabilities, and keep your eyes open for it.

I recommend installing Klaxon on no more than three services, because too many ports may cause the hackers to become suspicious. Moreover, with Klaxon installed on more than five ports, repeated scanning can divert system resources to Klaxon, resulting in a successful DoS attack.

The PortSentry Utility

This program comes in source codes and has to be extracted from the archive at sourceforge.net/projects/sentrytools and compiled. This should present you with no difficulties.

Extract the program by executing the following command:

```
tar xzvf portsentry-1.2.tar.gz
```

In my case, the program was extracted into the portsenty_beta directory. The directory name may be different on your machine because the program version may have changed by the time this book is published. The extraction directory and the file being extracted are displayed during the extraction process in the `directory_name/file_name` format.

Open the newly-created directory with the source codes and execute the following command in it:

```
cd portsentry_beta
```

The PortSentry program works under all UNIX-like system, such as Solaris, FreeBSD, OpenBSD, and, of course, Linux. When compiling the program, you have to explicitly specify the operating system installed:

```
make linux
```

By default, the program is installed into the /usr/local/psionic directory; the install directory, however, can be changed by specifying the necessary directory as the value for the `INSTALLDIR` parameter in the Makefile file. The executable file is built by the following command:

```
make install
```

To view the logs created by the utility, you also have to install the Logcheck program. It is available from the same site as the PortSentry program. It is installed in the same way as the PortSentry utility using the following commands:

```
tar xzvf logcheck-1.1.1.tar.gz
cd logcheck-1.1.1
make linux
make install
```

By default, the Logcheck program installs into the /usr/local/etc directory. The directory can be changed by editing the `INSTALLDIR` parameter in the Makefile file.

The program's configuration settings are located in the /usr/local/psionic/portsentry/portsentry.conf file. By default, all settings are commented out and you have to remove the comments from the necessary settings.

For example, for monitoring ports the configuration file contains three port-monitoring options. To enable monitoring of the selected ports, remove the pound sign (#) from the corresponding entry. For example, the uncommented third port-monitoring option looks like the following:

```
TCP_PORTS="1,11,15,79,111,119,143,540,635,1080,1524,2000,5742,6667"
UDP_PORTS="1,7,9,69,161,162,513,635,640,641,700,32770,32771,32772"
```

In addition to the monitoring capabilities, the program has an excellent security feature: When it detects an attack attempt, the utility can configure the firewall to prohibit any traffic from the address, from which the attack was attempted. By default, this feature is also disabled and is enabled by removing the comments (the pound sign) from the corresponding directives.

The firewall most often used in Linux is `ipchains`. It is configured by the following directive:

```
KILL_ROUTE="/sbin/ipchains -I input -s $TARGET$ -j DENY -l"
```

Before doing this, make sure that the firewall is installed at the specified directory (/sbin/ipchains). This can be done by executing the following command:

```
which ipchains
```

If you are using the `iptables` firewall instead of `ipchains`, it is configured by the following directive:

```
KILL_ROUTE="/usr/local/bin/iptables -I INPUT -s $TARGET$ -j DROP"
```

I consider the capability for an automatic firewall configuration in response to attack detection powerful indeed. On the other hand, any program can make a mistake and disallow access to someone that should not be blocked. Hackers can imitate an attack as coming from another user's address — your boss's, for example. PortSentry cannot tell who is hiding behind any address and will cut your boss off from the Internet. This will not be a welcome development.

I conducted an experiment in my test system and tried to throw packets requesting connection to various ports at the server with the source IP address set to different addresses. This rendered the server inaccessible from those IP addresses. You, however, should control how the monitoring program configures the firewall; otherwise, hackers can flood your server with requests and deny other computers access to it.

The monitoring program is launched by the following commands:

```
/usr/local/psionic/portsentry/portsentry -atcp
/usr/local/psionic/portsentry/portsentry -audp
```

The first command launches monitoring of the TCP ports, and the second one starts monitoring of the UDP ports. All activities of the program are saved in a log file, which can be viewed using the Logcheck program. I recommend that this program to be scheduled execute regularly (no less frequently than every 15 minutes) and inform the administrator about system happenings.

Start by configuring the Logcheck program. Open the /usr/local/etc/logcheck.sh file and add the following entry to it (if it is not already in there):

```
"mailto:SYSADMIN=admin@server.com"
```

Replace `admin@server.com` with the email address, to which you want notification messages about log entries created by PortSentry to be sent. To run the /user/local/etc/logcheck.sh script every specified period, use the `crontab` service.

To test the program, I configured it as described previously and started the CyD NET Utils (**www.cydsoft.com**) port scanning utility. It showed only the first two ports as opened. Even though more than one port had been open, the rest of them were closed for the port-scanner program. On the Linux server, I executed the `cat /etc/hosts.deny` command to view the /etc/hosts.deny file, which stores the IP addresses of all computers prohibited to connect to the server.

The last entry in the displayed file contents was the IP address of the computer, from which I conducted the port scanning:

```
ALL:    192.168.77.10
```

The PortSentry program reacted rapidly and efficiently, adding to the /etc/hosts.deny file a prohibition for using any service from the 192.168.77.10 address. This prohibition can only be removed by deleting the corresponding directive in the /etc/hosts.deny file.

It must be said that some ports can be used intensively enough in the process of normal operations for the program to interpret this as a break-in attempt. Such are the ident (113) and NetBIOS (139) ports. It is best if these ports are not included in the list of ports to monitor. Find the `ADVANCED_EXCLUDE_TCP` and `ADVANCED_EXCLUDE_UDP` entries in the /usr/local/psionic/portsentry/portsentry.conf file and add the necessary ports to the lists. By default, the following ports are excluded from monitoring:

```
ADVANCED_EXCLUDE_TCP="113,139"
ADVANCED_EXCLUDE_UDP="520,138,137,67"
```

As you can see, ports 113 and 139 are already excluded from being monitored.

The LIDS Utility

Even though I do not like to patch the kernel, I consider the Linux intrusion detection/defense system (LIDS) packet worthy of consideration because it offers comprehensive capabilities and makes it possible to enhance system security significantly.

The configuration files are encrypted, which makes modifying them difficult. It is not that easy to shut down the utility, because it requires knowing the system administrator's password.

Detection of port scanning attempts is a small fraction of what this utility packet can do. One of the handy LIDS features is being able to limit file access not on the user level but on the program level. This expands the rights-assignment capabilities and enhances the overall security. For example, the `ls` and `cat` programs and text editors can be disallowed to work with the /etc directory. This will make it difficult for hackers to view the /etc/passwd file.

Installing LIDS is not an easy task because it requires patching the kernel source code, compiling the patched codes, and installing the kernel. Here is where some problems may be encountered, because there is no guarantee that the patched kernel will work as intended. The source codes may become corrupted and not compile. When a new kernel version is introduced, it should be tested on a test machine before installing it on the production system. There still is a chance that the new kernel will not work properly on the production machine even after it has been checked on a test machine. But not updating the kernel is not an option, because failure to do this may result in faulty operation in the future.

You can obtain detailed information on LIDS at the utility's official site (**www.lids.org**).

12.5. Logging

Linux activities are recorded into several logs, and the information logged can reveal many interesting things. For example, you can use the log information to discover hackers, when they entered your system, where they came from, what they did in the system, when they left, and other important things. Because logs are one of the security tools, I will consider them in more detail. This information will allow you to exercise tighter control over your domain.

12.5.1. Main Commands

Information about current system users is stored in the /var/run/utmp file. However, trying to view this file — using, for example, the cat command — will not produce any legible results. Data in the file are stored not in the text but in the binary format and can be viewed only with the help of special commands (programs). Some of these commands are given here.

The who Command

The who command shows who is currently logged into the system and how long they have been logged in. The information is extracted from the /var/run/utmp file. It is displayed in the following format:

```
robert tty1  Dec 8 10:15
root   tty2  Dec 8 11:07
```

The first entry tells you that user robert is using terminal one (tty1) and entered the system on December 8 at 10:15.

Most hackers execute this command when entering a system to see whether the administrator is logged in. If they see that the root user is in the system, beginning hackers hightail it because they are afraid their knowledge is not sufficient to remain in the system undetected.

This is yet another reason you should not log into the system as root. You are better off logging in as a regular user; you can always switch to a privileged user when you need more rights. For a privileged user in my system, I created a user account named something other than root and set its UID to zero. Using this account, I have complete access to the system yet do not advertise being there. This way I can lay in wait for unsuspecting hackers and observe their actions to learn how they obtained access to my system.

The users Command

The users command displays user names of all users currently logged into the system.

This information is also stored in the /var/run/utmp file, but only while the user is logged in; it is deleted when the user logs out. The permanent history of logins is stored in the /var/log/wtmp file. This is a binary file, and its contents can only be viewed using special programs.

The last Command

The `last` command shows when a certain user logged into (and logged out of) the system. The command takes a user name as the parameter. For example, the following command shows the login history for user robert:

```
last robert
```

The command's execution produces results looking like the following:

```
robert tty1  Thu Dec 2 12:17 - 12:50 (00:33)
```

From this entry, you can tell that the user took the tty1 terminal, logged into the system on December 2, and remained logged for 33 minutes, from 12:17 to 12:50. If a user logged into the system over the network, information about the host, from which the login was made, will also be shown.

Executing this command for regular user, such as yourself, will produce quite a lengthy list, containing records of all logins for the specific user since the /var/log/wtmp file was created. The number of displayed entries can be limited by specifying it with the -n key. For example, the following command displays information about the last five logins for user robert:

```
last -n 5 robert
```

The lastlog Command

The `lastlog` command displays all users and their last login times. An example of the listing produced is shown in Listing 12.1.

Listing 12.1. Listing produced by the lastlog command

```
Username         Port      From             Latest
root             ftpd2022  192.168.77.10    Mon Feb 21 12:05:06 +0300 2005
bin                                         **Never logged in**
daemon                                      **Never logged in**
adm                                         **Never logged in**
lp                                          **Never logged in**
sync                                        **Never logged in**
shutdown                                    **Never logged in**
halt                                        **Never logged in**
mail                                        **Never logged in**
news                                        **Never logged in**
uucp                                        **Never logged in**
```

```
operator                                       **Never logged in**
games                                          **Never logged in**
gopher                                         **Never logged in**
ftp                                            **Never logged in**
nobody                                         **Never logged in**
vcsa                                           **Never logged in**
mailnull                                       **Never logged in**
rpm                                            **Never logged in**
xfs                                            **Never logged in**
apache                                         **Never logged in**
ntp                                            **Never logged in**
rpc                                            **Never logged in**
gdm                                            **Never logged in**
rpcuser                                        **Never logged in**
nscd                                           **Never logged in**
ident                                          **Never logged in**
radvd                                          **Never logged in**
squid                                          **Never logged in**
mysql                                          **Never logged in**
flenov        ftpd2022 192.168.77.10   Mon Feb 21 12:05:06 +0300 2005
named                                          **Never logged in**
robert        tty1                     Mon Feb 21 12:10:47 +0300 2005
```

The list is divided into the following four columns:

❐ User name taken from the /etc/passwd file
❐ The port or terminal, to which the connection was made
❐ The computer's IP address for network logins
❐ The login time

This command can be used to control system accounts. Their latest login time is shown as **Never logged in**, because these accounts cannot be used to log into the system (they have dummy command-interpreter shells such as /bin/false, /dev/null, and /sbin/nologin). If you notice that one of these accounts was used to log into the system, this means that hackers changed the account's configuration settings and are using it to work in the system.

Simply changing the command shell for the /etc/passwd file will create a back door unseen by the administrator. But executing the lastlog command will bring these machinations with the system accounts to light.

Pay attention to the connection type and address. If something is suspicious, this may be an attack at the inception stage.

The lsof Command

The lsof command can be used to determine, which files and by which users are currently open. The result of its execution looks similar to the following:

```
COMMAND PID  USER   FD   TYPE  DEVICE   SIZE     NODE NAME
init      1  root   cwd  DIR    3,2     4096       2 /
init      1  root   rtd  DIR    3,2     4096       2 /

init      1  root   txt  REG    3,2    26920   635256 /sbin/init
init      1  root   mem  REG    3,2    89547   553856 /lib/ld-2.2.5.so
init      1  root   10u  FIFO   3,2             195499 /dev/initctl
keventd   2  root   cwd  DIR    3,2     4096       2 /
keventd   2  root   rtd  DIR    3,2     4096       2 /
kapmd     3  root   10u  FIFO   3,2             195499 /dev/initctl
```

But this list is far from being complete. Even if there is only one user currently logged into the system, there can be a couple of dozen files open. But if there are several users logged in, the number of open files increases, because the same file can be opened more than once by different users. These are mostly system configuration files.

12.5.2. System Text Logs

The next logs considered are text format files. They can be viewed using the cat command or any text editor.

The /var/log/messages file contains the main information about user logins, failed authorizations, launches and shutdown of services, and so on. Information about all of these events cannot fit into one file and is split into several messages.X files, where X is the file number.

This is the most important log for any administrator. If hackers try to pick the password to some account, you will be able to notice this because the file will grow rapidly and contain numerous failed authorization entries. Fig. 12.1 shows an example of the contents of this file.

Another text log is stored in the /var/log/secure file. This is the most important file and you should check it as often as possible, paying close attention to each entry. This file contains information about remote logins to the system: who, when, and from what IP address. For example, you may discover an entry of the chief accountant connecting to the FTP server but from an address that does not belong to him. This is enough to sound the alarm.

The same file contains information about changes to the user and group lists. Hackers seldom use the root account for their dirty deeds, creating an inconspicuously-named but zero UID account. If such an account was created not manually, by editing the corresponding files, but with the help of Linux commands, this activity will be logged in the /var/log/secure file.

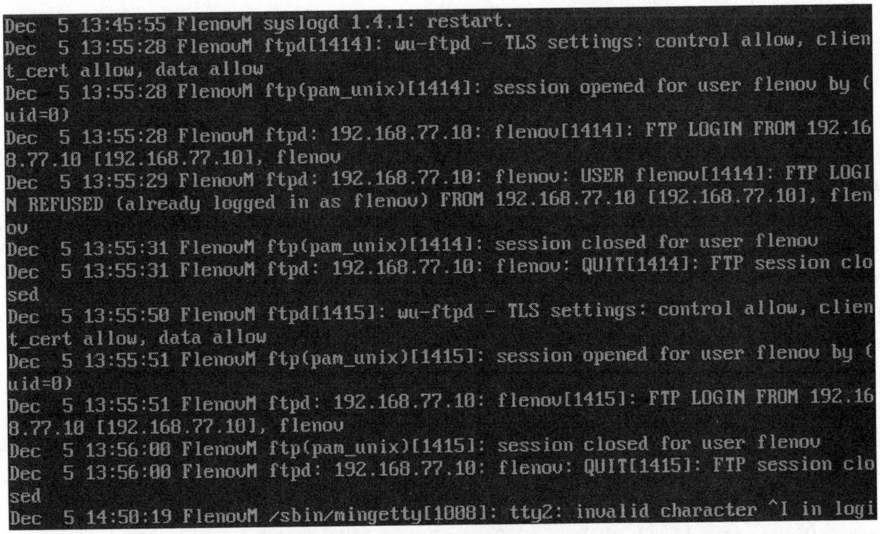

```
Dec  5 13:45:55 FlenovM syslogd 1.4.1: restart.
Dec  5 13:55:28 FlenovM ftpd[1414]: wu-ftpd - TLS settings: control allow, clien
t_cert allow, data allow
Dec  5 13:55:28 FlenovM ftp(pam_unix)[1414]: session opened for user flenov by (
uid=0)
Dec  5 13:55:28 FlenovM ftpd: 192.168.77.10: flenov[1414]: FTP LOGIN FROM 192.16
8.77.10 [192.168.77.10], flenov
Dec  5 13:55:29 FlenovM ftpd: 192.168.77.10: flenov: USER flenov[1414]: FTP LOGI
N REFUSED (already logged in as flenov) FROM 192.168.77.10 [192.168.77.10], flen
ov
Dec  5 13:55:31 FlenovM ftp(pam_unix)[1414]: session closed for user flenov
Dec  5 13:55:31 FlenovM ftpd: 192.168.77.10: flenov: QUIT[1414]: FTP session clo
sed
Dec  5 13:55:50 FlenovM ftpd[1415]: wu-ftpd - TLS settings: control allow, clien
t_cert allow, data allow
Dec  5 13:55:51 FlenovM ftp(pam_unix)[1415]: session opened for user flenov by (
uid=0)
Dec  5 13:55:51 FlenovM ftpd: 192.168.77.10: flenov[1415]: FTP LOGIN FROM 192.16
8.77.10 [192.168.77.10], flenov
Dec  5 13:56:00 FlenovM ftp(pam_unix)[1415]: session closed for user flenov
Dec  5 13:56:00 FlenovM ftpd: 192.168.77.10: flenov: QUIT[1415]: FTP session clo
sed
Dec  5 14:50:19 FlenovM /sbin/mingetty[1008]: tty2: invalid character ^I in logi
```

Fig. 12.1. A screenshot of the /var/log/messages file contents

Hackers know about this and, therefore, add users manually. After all, this is not that difficult: All it takes is to add a single entry to the /etc/passwd and /etc/shadow files. But even then, spotting a user logging in that you did not create, you can suspect something goes wrong.

Yet to spot suspicious entries, you have to be vigilant. The most experienced and, therefore, the most dangerous hackers have some ingenious tricks up their sleeves. For example, a hacker can see that there is a regular user named robert on your system and create a user account named rodert. The difference may seem obvious, but with scores of user accounts to keep track of, you have to pay too close attention to notice it.

The log of the sendmail mail server is stored in the /var/log/maillog file. The information in the file is stored in the following format:

```
Jan 16 13:01:01 FlenovM sendmail[1571]: j0GA11S01571: from=root,
size=151, class=0, nrcpts=1,
msgid=<200501161001.j0GA11S01571@flenovm.ru>, relay=root@localhost
```

The file contains information about by who, when, and to whom messages were sent.

I remember an administrator of a server hacked who manually inspected directories for foreign files. In my opinion, it would have been much easier to examine log records for this. If the hackers did not clean up the logs before leaving the system, you can gather lots of information from them.

But although logs can be informative, they cannot be relied on. Smart hackers always clear away their tracks and delete incriminating records from the logs; thus, inspecting directories manually may be useful, but check the log first.

12.5.3. The FTP Server Log

After breaking in to a system, hackers often upload their own programs on the server to raise their privileges or create back doors. They can use FTP for this purpose. Information about connections to the FTP server can be obtained from the /var/log/secure file, and the uploaded files are recorded in the /var/log/xferlog file.

Information is stored in the FTP server log in the text format, the same as in the mail server log. From my experience, the FTP server is the most frequent source of security-related problems. The server program is quite good, but hackers most often try to take over a user account that has FTP capabilities to be able to upload their hacking tools on the server. Examining the FTP log file, you can expeditiously determine what was uploaded to your server and by whom.

The following is an example of the contents of the log file:

```
Sun Jan 16 13:21:28 2005 1 192.168.77.10 46668 /home/flenov/
sendmail.cf b _ o r flenov ftp 0 * c
```

The preceding entry tells you that a user from address 192.168.7.10 downloaded the /home/flenov/sendmail.cf file at 13:21 on January 16, 2005.

FTP is the most dangerous protocol because it can be used to download confidential data (for example, password files), or upload a hacker's data to the server (for example, a rootkit or a Trojan horse). You should learn to understand each record in the log to know what happens to files in the system. The function of each parameter in the log is as follows:

❑ A full date showing the day of week, month, date, time, and year.
❑ The session duration or time taken to download or upload the file.
❑ The name and IP address of the remote host.
❑ The file size in bytes.
❑ The full path of the uploaded or downloaded file.
❑ The transmission type — a for ASCII or b for binary.
❑ File manipulations — c means the file was compressed, U means the file was uncompressed, T means the file was process with the tar program, and _ means no file processing took place.
❑ The transfer direction — o for download or i for upload.
❑ The user type — a for anonymous, g for guest, or r for real.
❑ The local user name. For anonymous users, this will be the ID string.
❑ The service name, usually ftp.
❑ The authentication method — 0 for no authentication or 1 for RFC931 authentication.
❑ The user identifier. If the user is not determined, the ID is an asterisk.
❑ The transfer outcome — c for successful or i for interrupted.

If you have never worked with the FTP log before, I recommend that you do this now and study carefully the example entry and entries from your own FTP log. You always have to approach a problem already prepared and not study it after it arises; otherwise, you are doomed to lose.

12.5.4. The Squid Proxy Server Log

The main log of the squid proxy server is stored in the /var/log/squid/access.log file. This is a text file, in which each entry consists of the following fields:

- The starting time of the connection or event.
- The session's duration.
- The client's IP address.
- The results of the request processing. It can be one of the following:
  - TCP_HIT — The necessary copy was found in the cache.
  - TCP_NEGATIVE_HIT — The object was cached negatively; the object request returned an error.
  - TCP_MISS — The object was not found in the cache.
  - TCP_DENIED — The service request was denied.
  - TCP_EXPIRED — The object was found but is outdated.
  - TCP_CLIENT_REFRESH — A forced refresh is requested.
  - TCP_REFRESH_HIT — During the refresh attempt, the server indicated that the object had not changed.
  - TCP_REFRESH_MISS — After the refresh attempt, the server returned a new version of the object.
  - TCP_REF_FAIL_HIT — The object in the cache is outdated, but the attempt to obtain a fresh copy failed.
  - TCP_SWAPFAIL — The object should be in the cache but is not there.
- The number of bytes received by the client.
- The request method — GET, POST, HEAD, or ICP_QUERY.
- The URL of the requested object.
- The ident field (- if not available).
- The result of the request to the other caches — PARENT_HIT (object found), PARENT_UDP_HIT_OBJECT (object found and returned in a UDP request), or DIRECT (object requested from the original server).
- The type of the MIME contents.
  There are two other proxy server logs. These are the following:
- cache.log — This log stores information about the cache, saved and deleted object, and the like. I have never experienced a need to consult this log.
- useragent.log — This log stores records of the User Agent field from request headers. This information can be faked easily, and I have already shown that this file can be easily changed for squid requests.

12.5.5. The Web Server Log

Apache server logs are stored in the access.log and error.log files located in the /var/log/httpd directory. These logs contain information about user accesses and activities.

Logs are in the text format and can be viewed by anyone, including hackers. Because logs contain user passwords, they constitute a security danger.

It is impossible to dispense with keeping the logs, because they are necessary. But you should do everything possible to make them inaccessible to unauthorized people. At the least, I always change the logs' default directory. From my experience, hackers seldom examine the httpd.conf file but look for the logs in their default directories. If the logs are not there, hackers think that they are disabled.

In the /var/log/httpd directory, create the following empty files: access_log, access_log.1, access_log.2, access_log.3, access_log.4, error_log, error_log.1, error_log.2, error_log.3, and error_log.4. To add a touch of authenticity to the files, slap copies of some actual data into them, only make sure that they don't contain anything important. Any hacker worth being called a hacker will easily see that the data are old by the file change date and the dates inside the file but will be unlikely to suspect something fishy about this. The important thing is for the file change date to be the same as the dates in the file's entries.

To simplify creating such files, you can temporarily enable the logs in the default directory to have them collect some information and disable them afterwards.

Then modify the ErrorLog and CustomLog directives in the httpd.conf configuration file to point to another directory to store these logs. In this simple way, you'll have most hackers scratching their heads trying to figure out the story with the log files.

12.5.6. The Log Keepers

Logs in the /var/log directories are kept by the syslogd and klogd daemons. Only the former is on the list of automatically started services in the setup program, with its start-up parameters also determining the start-up parameters of the klogd daemon. If yours is a standalone system or you simply do not require system events logging, you can disable these services to save processor resources. For a server system, however, I do not recommend disabling these services. If you do not see the necessity for using logs now, when you run into the first problem or break-in, you will see all the advantages they offer.

The syslogd program logs systems messages. The klogd program is used to log kernel messages. The log settings are stored in the /etc/syslog.conf file. Listing 12.2 shows an example of this file's contents.

Listing 12.2. The contents of the syslog.conf file

```
# Log all kernel messages to the console.
# Logging much else clutters up the screen.
#kern.*                                        /dev/console
```

```
# Log anything (except mail) of level info or higher.
# Don't log private authentication messages!
*.info;mail.none;authpriv.none;cron.none        /var/log/messages


# The authpriv file has restricted access.
authpriv.*                                       /var/log/secure


# Log all the mail messages in one place.
mail.*                                           /var/log/maillog


# Log cron stuff.
cron.*                                           /var/log/cron


# Everybody gets emergency messages.
*.emerg                                                *


# Save news errors of level crit and higher in a special file.
uucp,news.crit                                   /var/log/spooler


# Save boot messages also to boot.log.
local7.*                                         /var/log/boot.log
```

The directives' functions can easily be deduced from the corresponding comments. All directives have the following format:

```
name.level
```

The `name` part is the name of the parameter to be logged. These are the following:

- `kern` — Kernel messages
- `auth` — Security and authorization-violation messages
- `authprith` — Privileged-access use messages
- `mail` — Mail programs messages
- `cron` — Messages from the `cron` and `at` task schedulers
- `daemon` — Service-generated messages
- `user` — Messages from user programs
- `uucp` — UNIX-to-UNIX copy (UUCP) messages, which are rarely used today
- `news` — News messages
- `lpr` — Print messages

The level can be one of the following (lowest to highest level):

- `*` — Logging all system messages
- `debug` — Debugging information
- `info` — Informational messages

- ❏ `notice` — Notices
- ❏ `warn` — Warnings
- ❏ `err` — Errors
- ❏ `crit` — Critical messages
- ❏ `alert` — Requiring immediate operator intervention
- ❏ `emerg` — Emergency, so further operation is not possible

Messages of the specified level and higher are logged. For example, specifying the `err` level means that messages of the `err`, `crit`, and `emerg` levels will be logged.

The more errors logged, the greater the hard disk workload and the more resources used. To enhance the system's productivity, it is advisable to place the /var partition, in which the logs are stored, on a separate hard drive. In this way, system events can be logged in parallel with the system's operation. Make sure, however, that the /var partition is large enough to hold all logs.

Moreover, in my systems, I move logs from their default location to make it more difficult for hackers to find them and delete the information about their activities in the system. But this is not enough. An experienced hacker will examine the /etc/syslog.conf file and discover the new location of logs.

But you can pull a better one on hackers with only standard Linux means. In my system, I have a task scheduled in the `cron` service that every hour makes a backup copy of the /var directory. In this way, even if the hackers clean up the log I can always find out about them from the backup log copies.

It is even better if you can have another Linux server installed in the network. Then you will be able to send all log messages to this server, which will make it even more difficult for hackers to reach them. In this case, hackers will have to break in to another server to be able to clean up the logs. If the server where the logs are stored is dedicated to this mission only and there are no unnecessary ports open, breaking in to it may turn out to be too difficult.

To send the log over the network, the /etc/services file has to contain the following entry:

```
syslog 514/udp
```

Moreover, the following entry has to be added to the /etc/syslog.conf file:

```
messages        @address
```

The `messages` parameter specifies, which messages are to be sent to the server. Specifying it as `*.*` will send all messages. To send only critical messages, this parameter has to be set to `*.crit`.

The `@address` parameter is the address of the server, to which the messages are to be sent. For example, the following entry sends all messages to the **log.myserver.com** server:

```
*.*     @log.myserver.com
```

But there is one problem here: To determine the IP address, DNS is necessary. However, when the system is booted, the `syslog` service starts before DNS, making determining the IP address impossible. This problem is solved by entering the server's name and its corresponding IP address in the /etc/hosts file.

Finally, the syslog service has to be started with the -r option, which allows the server to receive messages from the network and record them in its logs. For this, the script for launching the service has to be changed on the server. As you should remember, all scripts are stored in the /etc/rc.d/init.d directory; the script for the syslogd service is stored in the syslog file. Listing 12.3 shows the main contents of this file.

Listing 12.3. The contents of the /etc/rc.d/init.d/syslog file

```
#!/bin/bash

. /etc/init.d/functions

[ -f /sbin/syslogd ] || exit 0
[ -f /sbin/klogd ] || exit 0

# Source config
# Loading the configuration file
if [ -f /etc/sysconfig/syslog ] ; then
        . /etc/sysconfig/syslog
else
        SYSLOGD_OPTIONS = "-m 0"
        KLOGD_OPTIONS = "-2"
fi

RETVAL=0

umask 077

start() {
        echo -n $"Starting system logger: "
        daemon syslogd $SYSLOGD_OPTIONS
        RETVAL = $?
        echo
        echo -n $"Starting kernel logger: "
        daemon klogd $KLOGD_OPTIONS
        echo
        [ $RETVAL -eq 0 ] && touch /var/lock/subsys/syslog
        return $RETVAL
}
stop() {
# Commands to stop the service
```

```
}
rhstatus() {
# Commands to output the status
}
restart() {
        stop
        start
}
...
...
```

The most interesting information is in the following lines:

```
if [ -f /etc/sysconfig/syslog ] ; then
        . /etc/sysconfig/syslog
else
        SYSLOGD_OPTIONS = "-m 0"
        KLOGD_OPTIONS = "-2"
fi
```

Here, in the `if` block, a check is performed on whether the /etc/sysconfig/syslog file exists. If so, the loading parameters are taken from this file; otherwise, they are specified explicitly in the `else` block:

```
SYSLOGD_OPTIONS = "-m 0"
```

The parameters are specified within the quotation marks. The `-r` option is added, modifying the directive as follows:

```
SYSLOGD_OPTIONS = "-m 0 -r"
```

If the /etc/sysconfig/syslog file exists, it will contain the `SYSLOGD_OPTIONS="-m 0"` entry and you will only have to modify this entry, without having to tamper with the /etc/rc.d/init.d/syslog launch script.

Using a dedicated server is a two-edged sword: Although it enhances system security by providing backup copies of logs, it endangers the same security by exposing the logs to the public. The problem is that log messages are sent over the network in plaintext. This presents no problem if your network is protected from the Internet with a firewall and hackers cannot penetrate it. But if hackers manage to compromise at least one computer in the network, they can install a sniffing program and intercept all log messages.

This problem is easily solved by encrypting the message traffic, sending it through an SSL tunnel. The simplest way of doing this is as follows:

1. In the configuration file of the server sending log messages, specify the local computer as the one, to which all messages should be sent as follows:

    ```
    *.*     @localhost
    ```

2. This will result in all messages being sent to the local computer to UDP port 514. The server must not be operating in the message receiving mode; that is, the -r option must not be specified in the launch script. Otherwise, port 514 will be busy, which is not what you need.

3. Start the `stunnel` client on port 514 of the local computer as follows:

```
stunnel -c -d 127.0.0.1: 514 -r logserver:1050
```

All messages received at this port will be encrypted and sent to port 1050 of the `logserver` computer, where `logserver` is the address of your log message receiving server.

4. On the `logserver` server, create an `stunnel` service as follows:

```
stunnel -d 1050 -r 127.0.0.1:514
```

This will result in the `stunnel` service on the `logserver` server receiving encrypted data on port 1050 and redirecting them in plaintext to port 514. The `syslogd` service on the `logserver` server must be started with the -r option to receive log messages at port 514.

Now, all log messages will be sent over the network encrypted.

12.5.7. The Logrotate Utility

To keep log files from bloating, Linux uses the Logrotate utility. I will demonstrate its operation using the /var/log/messages log as an example.

1. When the size of the /var/log/messages file exceeds the maximum size, or when a certain period lapses, the contents of the current log are transferred to the /var/log/messages.1 file, and the /var/log/messages file is cleaned and reused to log messages.

2. The next time one of the threshold values is reached, the contents of the /var/log/messages.1 file are transferred to the /var/log/messages.2 file and the contents of the /var/log/messages file are transferred to the /var/log/messages.1 file. The process is repeated every time one of the critical values is reached.

In this way, log messages are stored in separate files, each of which does not exceed a certain size, making logs convenient to view.

The configuration file of the Logrotate utility (/etc/logrotate.conf) is shown in Listing 12.4.

Listing 12.4. The configuration file of the Logrotate utility (/etc/logrotate.conf)

```
# See "man logrotate" for details.

# Rotate log files weekly.
weekly
```

```
# Keep 4 weeks worth of backlogs.
rotate 4

# Create new (empty) log files after rotating old ones.
create

# Uncomment this if you want your log files compressed.
#compress

# RPM packages drop log rotation information into this directory.
include /etc/logrotate.d

# No packages own wtmp -- we'll rotate them here
/var/log/wtmp {
    monthly
    create 0664 root utmp
    rotate 1
}


# System-specific logs may be also be configured here.
```

The following parameters can be specified in this file:

- ❑   weekly — Specifies that log files are to be rotated weekly. If the server's workload is light, this value can be changed to monthly.
- ❑   rotate — Indicates the number of files for storing the logs. In this case it is four, meaning that there will be four numbered log files — /etc/log/name.1 through /etc/log/name.4 — in addition to /etc/log/name.
- ❑   create — Notes that a new log file is to be created immediately after the rotation.
- ❑   compress — Specifies to compress the old versions of the log files. This option is useful for servers with heavy request workloads, generating bulky logs. Because logs contain text information, compressing them reduces their size by 70% and more.

The default values are described at the beginning of the file. Afterwards, necessary values for particular logs are specified. In this configuration file, specific parameters are set for the /var/log/wtmp log file:

```
/var/log/wtmp {
    monthly
    create 0664 root utmp
    rotate 1
}
```

Here, the maximum log file size is not specified; this, however, can be done using the `size` parameter. For instance, in the following example the maximum size of the log file is set to 100 KB:

```
/var/log/wtmp {
    monthly
    size = 100k
    create 0664 root utmp
    rotate 1
}
```

Now the log file will be rotated whenever one of the following two events occurs:

- ❑ Monthly
- ❑ When the file size reaches 100 KB

The file-rotation capability presents both conveniences and shortcomings. For example, the hackers can wipe out their tracks after the attack even if they have no direct access to the log files. All they have to do is to flood the log with trash messages, causing it to exceed the maximum size and be deleted by the system.

Attempting to protect the log file by increasing its size is useless, because hackers will not generate messages manually but can use a simple Perl program or even a script containing shell commands. The latter program is really simple. All it has to do is loop through the `logger` command (which logs messages), as follows:

```
logger -p kern.alert "Message_text"
```

Running this command in an endless loop will make the system to destroy the log file.

To prevent log data from being destroyed, you can specify a script to send the log to the administrator's email address as follows:

```
/var/log/wtmp {
    monthly
    size = 100k
    create 0664 root utmp
    postrotate
      The script command for mailing the name.1 journal
    endscript
    rotate 1
}
```

In this case, after the log file is rotated and the main log file is renamed to name.1, the script is executed to send the latter file to the administrator's email address.

When emailing log files, make sure that your mailbox is large enough. For example, if the maximum size of the log file is 10 MB but your mailbox can only take 5 MB of messages, you will never receive this file because it will be deleted by the system.

12.5.8. User Logs

All commands executed by users are logged in the .bash_history file (when the /bin/bash command interpreter is used), which is located in the user's home directory. If you know which user account hackers used to break in to the system, you can trace all their actions with the help of this log.

You will be able to tell what commands or programs were run, and this information may be helpful in determining how the hackers penetrated the system and what they may have changed in it. If the hackers added a user or modified some important system file, you will be able to see this, return everything back to normal, and close the holes in the system used by the hackers to get in.

Professional hackers who earn their living breaking in to computer systems know this and do everything possible to hide their tracks and regularly clean up this file. Extraneous changes in the .bash_history file may serve as an indication that this account was used by the hackers to break in to the system.

You should also regularly check and clean user logs yourself. Users, including yourself, may make a mistake when issuing a command and include your password with it. Hackers can discover this password when analyzing the .bash_history file and use it for nefarious purposes.

If you specified the root password when entering a command, take your time to delete the corresponding entry from the user log. Leaving it there may cost you dearly.

Administrator passwords can also be entered in the command line when working with MySQL. For example, if you executed the /usr/bin/mysql -uroot -ppassword command, it will be recorded in the log. If hackers obtain access to the bash command log, they will have an opportunity to discover the password entered with the command. If they do learn this password, they will be able to use the MySQL database with root rights. This will be the best case scenario. The worst case will be if you use the same root password for MySQL as for the system: This will give the bad guys complete control over your server.

NOTE

Never enter a password as a parameter when executing commands from the command line. If for some reason you do this, then delete the corresponding entry from the bash log. With MySQL, only the /usr/bin/mysql -uroot command should be entered. The server will reply, requesting the password. Entering the password will not record it in the log; only the /usr/bin/mysql -uroot command will be recorded.

If you work with a MySQL server, there will be the .mysql_history file in addition to the .bash_history file in your home directory. This file stores all commands executed in the MySQL configuration program. If any passwords were entered during the MySQL configuration process, their corresponding records must also be cleaned from the mysql log file. Even though a database is not the system, it can serve as a beachhead for breaking in to the system; moreover, databases can contain confidential data, such as passwords to restricted sections of Web sites.

12.5.9. Things To Heed

In this section, I want to consider what things must be paid attention to in security logs. These are not only the entries recording unauthorized system access. When you see that there was unauthorized access to restricted information, the break-in has already taken place. The idea is to use the information in the logs to detect attacks in the inception stage, and to prevent them.

If logs started suddenly growing in size, it means that there is some irregular activity going on. Perhaps a DoS attack is being perpetrated. You should immediately react to and investigate the causes of this increased activity without waiting for the situation to develop to the point where the server will be overwhelmed and cease servicing visitors. Moreover, if logs fill the disk, the system may crash, so make sure you have enough disk space for logs.

The computer should not reboot on its own. If this happens, check the logs to find out why and when it rebooted. You can use the uptime command to find out how long the system has been running.

Keep an eye on repeating entries, especially on those related to authorization. Too many failed authorization entries are an indication of a possible password-picking attempt.

If you notice some of the suspicious activities just listed, you should establish where the potential threat comes from, namely, the IP address and the location of the attacker's network. To prevent further actions by the hackers, you can change the firewall policy by adding a rule prohibiting any connections from the attacking host address.

When analyzing logs, pay attention to every little thing. For example, to pick a password, hackers can use different camouflaging tricks, such as making false log entries.

If hackers try to pick a password using the enumeration method, there will be many unsuccessful entry attempts by a certain user in the log. An unsuccessful system login attempt generates the following entry in the /var/log/messages log:

```
Feb 12 17:31:37 FlenovM login(pam_unix)[1238]: authentication failure;
logname=LOGIN uid=0 euid=0 tty=tty1 ruser= rhost= user=root
```

The login (pam_unix) parameter indicates that the hacker was only trying to login. If the hacker was already in the system but used the su command unsuccessfully, the logname field will contain the user name, under which the hacker entered the system, and the login (pam_unix) string will be replaced with su (pam_unix).

By this entry, you can easily determine that it was generated by hackers, and easily locate them. But hackers can also easily insert fake entries in the log pointing to another user, making it difficult to pinpoint the real ones. For example, executing the following command, hackers can add an entry to the log identical to an authentication failure entry:

```
logger -p kern.alert -t 'su(pam_unix)' "authentication failure ;
logname=robert uid=0 euid=0 tty=tty1 ruser= rhost= user=root"
```

The preceding command will create an entry similar to the following in the log:

```
Feb 12 17:31:37 FlenovM login(pam_unix)[1238]: authentication failure;
logname=robert uid=0 euid=0 tty=tty1 ruser= rhost= user=root
```

Now imagine that hackers executed many such commands but with a different `logname` field in each. It will be practically impossible to determine, which log entries are real and which are fakes.

A less experienced hacker may mess up and not use the `-t` option when using the `logger` program, instead entering the command as follows:

```
logger -p kern.alert "authentication failure ;
logname=robert uid=0 euid=0 tty=tty1 ruser= rhost= user=root"
```

This will generate the following entry in the log:

```
Feb 12 17:31:37 FlenovM logger: authentication failure;
logname=robert uid=0 euid=0 tty=tty1 ruser= rhost= user=root
```

The keyword `logger` before the error message tells you that the entry was generated by the `logger` program and is, most likely, a fake.

But even if the hackers have no access to the `logger` program, they can use a program of their own to place fake entries into the log. To prevent this, only the root administrator should have write rights for the log files.

12.6. Handling Logs

By now, you know what system logs there are, where they are stored, and the nature and format of their contents. All this information is useful, but analyzing several megabytes of text is inconvenient and difficult.

In a system processing numerous requests, logs grow rapidly. For example, the daily log on my Web server can exceed 4 MB. This is a lot of text information, in which finding a specific entry within short time is practically impossible.

This is why programmers and administrators have written and continue writing log-analyzing software. Logs should be analyzed every day or, preferably, every hour. To maintain a secure system, you cannot afford to miss any important messages.

The most effective log-analyzing programs are those that analyze log entries as they are recorded in the log. This is relatively simple to implement, especially on a remote computer that receives log entries from the server over the network. As entries come in, they are analyzed and recorded in the log files for storage and more detailed future analyzes. It is usually difficult to detect an attack by one system message, and sometimes a dynamic picture is necessary. For example, one failed authorization attempt does not mean anything, while ten or more attempts look quite suspicious.

Unfortunately, all known log-analyzing software cannot do effective dynamic analysis. Most of this software only create rules, according to which certain entries are considered either suspicious or not. Therefore, all failed system login entries are considered suspicious and are subsequently analyzed manually. Every day, at least one user hits the wrong key when entering the password, especially if it is a complex one. It would make no sense to react to all such messages.

There is another shortcoming to analyzing logs line by line. Suppose that the log-analyzing utility issued a message informing of an attempt to access a restricted disk area.

Such log entries for most services will contain only information about the attempt, not information about the user account used.

For example, a log entry recording unauthorized access to the ftp directory will contain the IP address of the client but not the user account. To find out, which user produced this failed login attempt, you have to open the log and look over the connection history from this IP manually. This problem can be avoided by dynamic log analysis.

The Tail Utility

When I am working directly at the server, I launch the following command in a new terminal window:

```
tail -f /var/log/messages
```

This command displays updates to the log file in real time; that is, whenever a new entry is added to the log, the utility displays it.

This is convenient if only a few entries are recorded into the log. In this way, you can work in one terminal and periodically switch to the other to check the new log messages. But if there are too many system messages (e.g., many users are working with the server), checking all new entries becomes impossible. In this case, you need a special utility to filter the messages and display only those deemed suspicious.

The Swatch Utility

This is a powerful Perl log message-analyzing utility. This is a rather simple language and many administrators know it, so you can easily modify the program and add new functions. The program can be downloaded from the site **http://sourceforge.net/project/swatch**.

The program can analyze log entries on the schedule (if the program is scheduled in the cron task manager) or immediately upon their being entered into the log.

The installation process is different because Swatch is a Perl program. This is done by executing the following sequence of commands:

```
tar xzvf swatch-3.1.tgz
cd swatch-3.1
perl Makefile.PL
make test
make install
make realclean
```

That the program is written in Perl is also its shortcoming. I had already mentioned that any software that can be used by hackers to enter the system should not be installed on the server unless necessary. The Perl interpreter is necessary for a Web server using scripts written in this language. In other cases, I recommend against installing a Perl interpreter because hackers often use this language for writing their own rootkits.

The Logsurfer Utility

This is one of the few programs that can examine logs dynamically. The program can be downloaded from **sourceforge.net/projects/logsurfer**. As was said, most log-analyzing programs do this line by line, which is ineffective because lots of trash is produced.

The powerful features of the program make it more difficult to configure. This is a shortcoming, because configuration errors may result in an important event going undetected.

The Logcheck/LogSentry Utility

This is the easiest program to use. It was developed by the programmers who developed the PortSentry utility considered earlier. LogSentry uses various templates to filter out the suspicious log messages.

The program is user-friendly, but I am concerned about its future. It looks like there will be no more updates, and sooner or later the current features will not be enough and a substitution will be necessary.

But I have high hopes for the prospects of the program. Its operation was considered in *Section 12.4*, when considering the operation of the PortSentry program.

12.7. Log Security

I want to conclude the system-message logging topic with a section about their security. Even though the original purpose of logs was to monitor the system and detect attacks, they can also be used to break in to the system.

Consider a classical break-in example using logs. As you know, when a failed authorization attempt is logged, the password, albeit an incorrect one, is not saved, so as not to give hackers a starting point in figuring it out. But suppose that the user accidentally enters the password instead of the login. This happens often, especially in the mornings, and especially on Monday mornings. Logins, unlike passwords, are recorded in log messages; thus, the password will become available to hackers who obtain access to the message log file.

Therefore, it is important to make logs inaccessible to unauthorized people. Check the access permissions of the log files by executing the following command:

```
ls -al /var/log
```

The results produced by the command look similar to the following:

```
drwxr-xr-x    9 root     root         4096 Jan 12 13:18 .
drwxr-xr-x   21 root     root         4096 Jan 24 23:00 ..
drwx------    2 root     root         4096 Jan 12 11:14 bclsecurity
-rw-r-----    1 root     root        83307 Jan 12 13:18 boot.log
-rw-r-----    1 root     root        89697 Jan  6 09:01 boot.log.1
-rw-r-----    1 root     root        48922 Jan 30 11:45 boot.log.2
-rw-r-----    1 root     root        64540 Jan 23 19:55 boot.log.3
```

```
-rw-r-----   1 root     root       36769 Jan 16 12:36 boot.log.4
-rw-r-----   1 root     root        8453 Jan 12 13:18 cron
-rw-r-----   1 root     root        8507 Jan  6 09:06 cron.1
-rw-r-----   1 root     root        7189 Jan 30 11:50 cron.2
-rw-r-----   1 root     root        6935 Jan 23 20:01 cron.3
-rw-r-----   1 root     root        4176 Jan 16 12:41 cron.4
...
...
```

The owner of all files should be root. Also, make sure that only the administrator has full access rights, with the rest of the users unable to work with the files.

By default, the read rights for most files belong to the owners and the members of the owner group. The logs most often belong to the root group. If in your system only the administrator belongs to this group, you have no cause for alarm. But if this group comprises several users, which I am against, a special group with minimal rights has to be created and all logs must be switched to this group.

The following sequence of commands creates a new group, named logsgroup, and changes the group membership of all log files to this group:

```
groupadd logsgroup
cd /var/log
chgrp -R logsgroup .
```

Only the administrator should have the read and write rights to the files in the /var/log directory. The group users should only have the read rights, with the others having no rights. To set these permissions to all log files, execute the following sequence of commands:

```
cd /var/log
find . -type f | xargs chmod 640
```

The first line consists of two commands. The first command — find . -type f — searches the current directory for all f-type objects, that is, for all files. The second command — xargs chmod 640 — changes the access permissions of all objects found by the first command to 640. These permissions can even be lowered to 600 to give the read and write rights to the administrator only.

Moreover, no user should have read rights to the /var/log/ directory, so as to prevent unauthorized deletion of the log files. If hackers cannot modify log records, they may settle for the second best: deleting the logs themselves. True, deleted logs are a strong indication that someone unauthorized visited your system. But it's a small consolation, because without the log information you will not be able to learn how the break-in was perpetrated and find the culprit.

Remember, if hackers can read the logs, they can use the information recorded in them accidentally to raise their rights in the system. If hackers can modify the logs, they can cover their tracks by deleting all entries pertaining to their activities.

But it is not enough to provide maximum protection. The essence of logging is that the operating system only adds new entries to the log files; it neither deletes the files nor modifies the entries already logged in them. Thus, log files can be further protected from being deleted or modified with the help of file attributes. File attributes in the Ext2 and Ext3 files systems can be expanded with the help of the `chattr` command. One such expanded attribute is that the file can be only added to. It is set by executing the `chattr` command with the +a option. For example, the following command sets this attribute to the /var/log/boot.log file:

```
chattr +a /var/log/boot.log
```

Now, trying to delete or modify the file will be unsuccessful. The only shortcoming of this attribute is that you will not be able to clean the file. Log files have a tendency to grow constantly and rather rapidly, but usually it is not necessary to save a record of events that took place a month or even a year ago. To clean up, remove the add-only attribute as follows:

```
chattr -a /var/log/boot.log
```

Just don't forget to set it again after you are done.

In addition to protecting logs, programs used for analyzing them have to be protected. After all, what's the use of protecting log files from reading if they can be viewed using these programs? Log-analyzing programs are protected from unauthorized users by making sure that their SUID and SGID bits are not set.

12.8. Network Security

Making your server secure is a complex task requiring you to control the operation of the entire network. The least you have to do is monitor all communication channels to know, which of them are being used.

The easiest way of doing this is to use the `nmap` utility. It allows the `ping` command to be executed for the entire network, thus revealing, which servers and computers are currently accessible. If some computer has not responded, you have to investigate the causes of this. Perhaps, this is only because of a power loss or unscheduled reboot. But it may also be caused by a successful DoS attack, and you should be the first one to know about this.

The `nmap` utility is extremely handy for a one-time check but inconvenient for constant monitoring. I prefer using the CyD NET Utils (**www.cydsoft.com**) utility for this purpose. The utility, however, has a serious shortcoming: It only works under Windows.

Unfortunately, despite my extensive search on the Internet, I have not been able to find any comparable Linux program and I assume there is none. Thus, until one is developed, the `nmap` utility remains your only choice for network monitoring under Linux. Despite its inconvenience, it is better than nothing.

Chapter 13: Backing up and Restoring Data

If you work in the information technology field, you must have run into data loss problems more than once. But this problem is usually given rather superficial attention.

Many administrators are just too lazy and place their trust into equipment instead of backing up their data. No argument: Modern equipment is more reliable than that of just a few years ago. However, in the last couple of years, I witnessed several hard drives dying, five computers stolen from the office, and even one server rack burned up — along with the room it was housed in. And who among the occupants of the great New York towers could have imagined that terrorists would decide to vent their anger on their offices? Of course, the loss of information doesn't come anywhere close to comparing with the loss of human lives. I am just using this case to call your attention to how data loss can result from unanticipated causes. You should take every precaution to preserve it regardless of the situation.

Data backup copying, or simply backing up, involves making a temporary copy of digital information for recovery purposes. Backing up data regularly allows you to restore lost data from the backup copy and continue working with negligible losses.

13.1. Backup Fundamentals

To minimize material losses that can stem from losing data, you should know what may cause data loss. In addition, you should analyze the data being backed up to establish how often to back them up and what methods to use for this.

How quickly you recover your system's operability after a data loss depends on how prepared you are for such a development. Using a test system, you have to rehearse all possible situations and work out a recovery process in advance. This will save you the headache of having to learn how to do this when disaster strikes.

To gain a clear understanding of why backup is necessary, consider the following situations that it can alleviate:

❑ *Accidentally modifying or deleting files* — When an inexperienced computer user is connected to a server, his or her often-clumsy actions may result in data loss. With a proper security policy in place, only this particular user's files are lost, but even they can be of value to the company.

❑ *Equipment failure* — When I was just cutting my teeth in the computer field, 5-inch diskettes and hard drives of no more than 20 MB were used to store information. Although hard drives were sufficiently reliable, diskettes were constantly failing. Switching to 3.5-inch diskettes did not change the situation much, but the reliability of hard drives continued to improve. When the capacity of hard drives started measuring in gigabytes, the bad block problem arose. At one time, I had to change three hard drives, from 10 GB to 20 GB, from different manufacturers. This was like a data-destroying locust incursion. After a certain period of hard drive failures, their reliability began improving. It cannot, however, be called ideal, and there is always a chance of a hard-drive failure.

❑ *Natural disasters and equipment loss* — Many destructive events can cause equipment loss. If you look at the period from the end of 2004 to beginning of 2005, you will notice that natural disasters — floods, tornados, earthquakes, hurricanes, tsunamis — have been hitting our planet at an increased rate and with a greater intensity. Natural disasters can destroy houses, buildings, and even entire cities, as was the case with New Orleans. You may say that against the background of life and property loss inflicted by such disasters, data loss is insignificant and irrelevant. I disagree, because every little thing salvaged is of help. And if the data lost were accumulated over years, their loss is quite significant.

❑ *Hacker and virus attacks* — These are facts of the information technology field that cannot be ignored and have to be protected against. But no matter what is done to fight viruses, they always have the upper hand. Why is this so? Because the most common defense against viruses is to examine suspicious software for code characteristic to known viruses. The keyword here is *known*. But hackers constantly keep developing new viruses and ways to get around antivirus software. And it is new viruses that inflict the most damage, because for a certain period after they appear there is no defense against them. Losses inflicted by computer viruses are becoming greater each year. They can, however, be minimized with the help of data backup.

This list can have many items added to it, but I hope I have been able to convince you of the necessity to have a backup copy of all of your important data. I consider important the following types of data:

❑ *System configuration files* — At first, it may seem that these files are not important because they contain no confidential company information. But without such a backup, it will take you a long time to restore your computer or server from scratch. This means losses caused by service unavailability, which for some companies can amount to tens of thousands of dollars for every hour of downtime.

❑ *User documents* — User directories often contain documents of certain value. These are such documents as financial reports or data and specialized user programs.

❑ *Databases* — Corporations keep their data in databases that make the information convenient to work with; should these data be lost, the corporation would suffer greatly.

❑ *Web sites* — Any dynamically developing Web site, from personal to corporate, contains files and scripts, the loss of which can be felt financially.

Database backup depends on the backup tools provided by a particular database. This subject is broad and will not be considered in this book. But most of the theory considered in this chapter can be applied equally well to files and to databases.

13.2. Constant Availability

The most probable causes of data loss are hacker attacks or equipment failures. In the first case, data can be restored by simply replacing the destroyed files with the backup copies; in the latter case, the equipment may have to be replaced and the system may need to be installed from the ground up. So that the restoration process will not take too much time, it is best to have a spare set of parts most likely to fail: hard drive, memory, motherboard, and processor.

If it is unacceptable for your network to allow even a minute of a server downtime, you can either build a cluster of servers or maintain backup servers.

Building a server cluster may be a more reliable choice. In this case, if one of the cluster servers fails, its workload is picked up by another server in the cluster. This allows almost 100% failproof system operation to be achieved. But building server clusters is a rather complex and expensive task; therefore, companies try other, less expensive ways to make their data secure.

Most industrial software already offers cluster operation tools, which are easy and inexpensive to use. One of the network servers is assigned the role of master, with one or more other servers being slaves. The master server regularly sends information to the network about its operability status; it also sends information about database changes to the slave servers so that all servers have an identical copy of the database. If the master server fails, the slave servers take over the operation.

In addition to enhanced reliability, clusters may enhance productivity if all servers work in parallel and the slave servers handle part of the workload. This makes for more efficient equipment and network bandwidth use.

A less expensive way is to use reserve servers equipped with a Redundant Array of Independent Disks (RAID). In this case, the hard drives of a server are organized into mirroring RAID, that is, RAID 1 or RAID 1+0. Here, data are protected by the RAID system, which saves data to two hard drives in parallel. If one of these drives fails, the second hard drive is placed into operation.

But what if the motherboard or processor fails? Replacing these takes time, which in this scenario was declared unacceptable. To minimize the downtime in such a situation, a backup server of the same hardware configuration as the main one is maintained. When some hardware of the main server fails, simply connect RAID to the backup server and switch the network cable to continue operating. Because the hardware of the reserve server is the same as that of the main server, RAID will work on the backup server without forcing the administrator to edit the configuration files.

If there are several identically-configured servers in your network, one backup server can be used for any of them. Assuring data safety in this way is much less expensive than building a server cluster.

I saw an interesting solution in this respect at one company. All client computers were equipped with a small hard drive holding only the operating system and the necessary utilities and application software. In addition, each of these computers was equipped with a large hard drive installed in a mobile rack, allowing the drive to be easily replaced. Every evening, the administrator removed the large hard drives and backed them up at his computer. In case of a hardware or software failure, the large hard drive would be connected to another computer prepared especially for this purpose.

13.3. Saving Backup Copies

Even if a server is equipped with RAID 1 or operates in a server cluster, its data still have to be regularly backed up. But where is the backup copy to be saved? Once I was called to restore data from a failed hard drive. The hard drive was beyond restoration, so I asked for the backup copy. The answer was as simple as the computer owner's mind: The backup copy was stored on the same physical hard drive but on another partition. Some people just don't get it that no matter how many logical drives a physical drive may be divided into, if the physical drive fails, all of the logical ones do, too.

The saddest part of the story is that the drive had been failing for some time. The system was issuing access errors when backups were performed, but these were simply ignored. The hard drive started failing with the partition used for storing the backup copies, and with time all of the blocks went bad.

The moral of this story is that you should always store the backup copy on a separate medium. This can be a separate hard drive, especially because their prices are constantly dropping, or any removable media of a sufficiently large capacity.

Storing backup copies on separate media protects against equipment failures, but the media themselves have to be protected. I am always amazed by administrators who store useless pieces of paper in a safe while the backup media are stored in a desk drawer. I would like to ask them, "What is the sense in protecting the server by all available means if the backup copy can be easily stolen?"

Don't be one of these administrators; always store your backup copy in a secure place. The best place is a fireproof safe, which will protect your data even against most natural disasters — in addition to those authored by man.

Another way is to take advantage of one of the Internet services offering online storage, which lately have been picking up again. Having placed your backup copy on such a drive, you can be sure that it is safe. The owners of these services use RAID technology on their servers, which gives a high degree of protection to the data stored on them.

I am convinced that this type of service will continue to grow. One of the reasons for this is the iDisk technology from Apple, which offers easy-to-use Internet disks to MAC OS and Microsoft Windows systems users. Other similar systems are being developed and should be available soon. More information about the iDisk technology can be found on Apple's site at **www.mac.com/1/iTour/tour_idisk.html** (see Fig. 13.1).

Fig. 13.1. The iDisk site

If you cannot afford to use online storage, you will have to provide media for storing your backup copies yourself.

You have a large choice of media for this purpose, including removable hard drives, magnetic tape, CD-R/RW, DVD-R/RW, and Jaz and ZIP disks. Which of these you choose depends on the amount of data you must back up and the speed, at which you must do this.

Currently, portable, large-capacity external USB and FireWire hard drives are available. I use one of such drives at home, dumping data from my notebook to it.

13.4. Backup Policy

The backup speed and the extent, to which the data will be restored, depend on how you perform the backup. If your data take hundreds of gigabytes of disk space, it will take a long time to back them all up; moreover, this will put a great workload on the server. If backup copying is carried out over the networks, it will also load the network's bandwidth, reducing the server's availability for other clients.

Your task is to organize the most effective backup procedure, one that takes the minimum amount of time and preserves all necessary data.

When planning the backup process, you should keep in mind that in case of a hard drive failure, all changes made since the last backup will be lost. This means that especially important data should be backed up as often as possible, but remembering that this process is burdensome for the server.

The answers to the questions of how many media you will need for backup purposes, how often, and how to use them depends on many factors, including the following:

- ❐ The amount of information to be backed up
- ❐ How often this information is modified
- ❐ Whether it is possible to restore large amounts of the lost data manually
- ❐ How long the server can be down
- ❐ Which data are modified most often

This list can be continued, but the items given here will suffice. I'll consider them starting with the last one. You should have a clear idea of which data in the system are modified and how often. Group these data into three categories: rarely modified, frequently modified, and those modified at certain time intervals.

The following are the main directories that should be backed up:

- ❐ /etc — Contains configuration files
- ❐ /home — Contains user files
- ❐ Directories containing Web files

Other directories are seldom used to store documents or files. It makes no sense to back up programs from the /bin and /usr directories, because they can be easily installed anew, especially if the configuration has been saved.

13.4.1. Rarely Modified Data

Configurations files (those stored in the /etc directory) can be placed into the rarely-modified data category. They are rarely modified because in most servers the main and the most extensive configuration changes take place at the server installation stage. Afterwards, the server can work for years with the configuration changing only when the software is updated or corrections to the configuration are made.

To back up the configuration files, a slow, small rewritable medium will suffice. I use ZIP or Jaz disks to back up the configuration files, which takes only one diskette.

Because the configuration does not change often, modified files can be saved right away. Only the modified files have to be saved to the disk.

The restoration process should start with restoring the configuration files, with the /etc/passwd and /etc/shadow files being the first on the list. If these files are not restored before the other files, without the necessary users, programs will not be able to set the proper access rights.

This will lead to the rights being restored incorrectly, especially if you are using third-party right-assignment utilities. Before making the restored system available for use, you should ascertain that all files are in the same state they were in before the failure; this especially concerns their permissions.

13.4.2. Frequently Modified Data

Into the frequently modified data category can be placed databases and the main user files and documents (those in the /home directory). Most of these are modified every day. This data can and should be backed up every day. If the backup process takes too long, it should be performed after work hours or during lunch break, when the load on the server is reduced. The backup can be performed using scripts executed as scheduled tasks. Perform backup twice a day (once at lunch time and once after work) so that in case of a disk failure only half a day's worth of data will be lost.

To back up this type of data, I use seven rewritable media, one for each day of the week. Every Monday, data from all of the media is saved to a read-only media, such as a CD-R or DVD-R, and the media is reused for the daily backup.

13.4.3. Periodically Modified Selected Data

Far from all files in the /home directory are changed every day. Most of them may not be changed for years. So as not to waste your time saving these data, you can perform backup using commands that allow only the changed data to be backed up. The simplest way of doing this is to select for backup only those files modified within a certain period.

When this policy is employed, the backup procedure is as follows:

❐   At the end of week, the entire /home directory is backed up.
❐   Only files that have been modified are included in the daily backups.

In this case, restoring should be carried out in the same order as the backup: First, the weekly backup files are restored, and then each of the daily backups, starting with the oldest. Not following the order carries a risk of rewriting a file with its older version.

Performing backup by the file modification date is convenient but not always possible. Most backup utilities only update an existing copy, replacing the old version of the file with the new one. In this case, first all files are backed up and then the update is specified with a special key. Only files that have been modified are updated in the complete backup in this way.

This is a handy method, but it replaces all old files. This makes it impossible to roll back to the contents before the last backup. To allow rollback, every day the complete backup is updated, it is saved to a separate medium. In this way, the main backup copy reflects the state of updates up to the current date, and its daily copies allow rollback to a specific date.

Because only changed files are backed up every day and few files are modified every day, backup can be performed sufficiently rapidly and even during the regular server operation. But in the latter case, you are running a danger of corrupting files. Suppose that there are two hard-linked files, information in which has to be linked. For example, data written to one file also have to be entered into the other file. If when one file is being backed up another file is changed, the backup of the first file will not reflect the changes. This will cause serious problems after the restoration, because the integrity of the files is disrupted.

13.4.4. Other Periodically Modified Data

Data that are modified periodically have to be backed up depending on the frequency of the modifications. For example, some files can be used when monthly reports are prepared. As a rule, such files are quite large and it makes no sense to back them up regularly. It is more effective to back them up when the report-preparing activity is over and to not waste resources on backing up data that do not change.

13.4.5. Image Backup

The most reliable way to back up is to create an image of the entire hard drive. In this case, the information is saved irrespective of the disk's file system, because the file system is bypassed and the tracks are copied directly. Restoring from an image guarantees that all access rights will be restored properly and the system is ready to use right away.

This method, however, has quite a few shortcomings, such as the following:

- ❐ It takes lots of time to create a disk image, especially of large drives.
- ❐ It puts a great workload on the server.
- ❐ It cannot be implemented in Linux, because most distributions do not offer the necessary tools.
- ❐ All files, even those that are not necessary, are backed up, such as files from the /tmp directory.

Disk imaging is convenient to use for moving data to another computer or to replicate the configuration on other computers. For example, you have to set up several client computers with the same configuration. Configure one computer, create an image of its hard drive, and then replicate the image on the hard drives of the other computers. This is more reliable than simply copying files from one computer to another.

13.4.6. Backup Media

Now consider how many media you will need to store all of your backup copies. Each type of data considered previously requires its own media, because they are backed up at different frequencies. These are the following:

- ❑ *Configuration files* — As already mentioned, ZIP or Jaz disks can be used for backing up these data. It is a good idea to make two copies, because all diskettes are easily damaged and fail more often than hard drives.
- ❑ *Periodically modified data* — These backups are stored for a year or longer. I use CD-Rs to back up this type of data. CD-Rs are large enough for my data and cannot be erased accidentally or maliciously. I back up all periodically-changed data every month and keep the medium for a year. In this way, during the year I always have a backup copy of data for any reporting period.
- ❑ *Frequently modified data* — In this case, the decisive factor in choosing the medium is the backup speed, because most often these data are bulky. The backup should take as little time as possible, so as not to put a prolonged extra workload on the server.

As you can see, a backup policy depends on many factors. I have tried to demonstrate the main principles, on which you should base your particular backup policy. These principles may not be equally suitable for all systems, but they can be used as the foundation for a specific backup policy.

13.5. Backup Capabilities in Linux

I will consider only those backup capabilities available in standard Linux distributions. These are simple copying and archiving commands that can be automated by scheduling them for execution in the task scheduler. If several commands are required for a particular backup task, these commands can be recorded into a script file, which then can be run as a scheduled task.

13.5.1. Copying Files

The simplest way to make a backup copy is to use the cp command, which is used to copy files. However, file permissions must be preserved in the process. The following command saves the /home directory to the /mnt/bkupdisk device used especially for backup purposes:

```
cp -a /home /mnt/bkupdisk
```

In this case, the -a option is used, which is equivalent to specifying options -dpR. The functions of these options are as follows:

- ❑   -d — Never follow symbolic links. The directory is copied as is.
- ❑   -p — Preserve the specified attributes (mode, ownership, and time stamps).
- ❑   -R — Copy directories recursively to back up all subdirectories.

Thus, the previous command is identical to the following command:

```
cp -dpR /home /mnt/bkupdisk
```

This command backs up all files and subdirectories in the /home directory to the /mnt/bkupdisk device. Files from this directory that were modified after the backup was performed can be copied with the help of the same command, but specifying the -u option, as follows:

```
cp -au /home /mnt/bkupdisk
```

13.5.2. The tar Utility

Backing up one file at a time is inconvenient. It is much better to back up the entire directory as one file. Linux has a utility, called tar, which allows several files to be gathered into one. This process is called archiving; but you should not confuse this with compressing, which tar does not do. If several files totaling 2 MB are archived, the size of the resulting file will be slightly larger than 2 MB (the sum of all files plus the tar header).

The sense of collecting several files into one is that a single file is easier than several small files to control and compress using specialized programs.

Archiving file using the tar utility is performed by executing the following command:

```
tar cf archive.tar directory
```

The functions of the command's two parameters are the following:

- ❑   c — Specifies that an archive is to be created.
- ❑   f — Specifies the archive file and the device; by default, /dev/rmt0 is used.

Thus, the /home directory can be archived by executing the following command:

```
tar cf backup.tar /home
```

When the cf options are used at archiving, the paths of the archived files are preserved. Extracting the archived /home directory reconstructs the /home directory hierarchy in the current directory. For example, if extraction is performed into the /home directory, the path to the extracted /home directory will be /home/home. And if extraction is performed into the /etc directory, the path to the extracted /home directory will be /etc/home.

Thus, to restore files properly, extraction should be performed into the root directory. This is done by executing the following two commands:

```
cd /
tar xf /home/backup.tar
```

Here, the first command changes the current directory to the root directory, and the second command extracts the archived backup files from the /home/backup.tar file.

The `tar` utility also uses the following options:

- ❑ v — Lists verbosely files being processed.
- ❑ z — Detects and properly processes `gzip` archives during extraction.
- ❑ p — Specifies to extract all protection information.
- ❑ d — Specifies to find differences between the archive and the file system.
- ❑ t — Lists the contents of the archive.
- ❑ u — Specifies to append only files newer than the archive copies.
- ❑ N date — Specifies to archive only files newer than the specified date.
- ❑ P — Specifies not to strip the leading / character from file names. In this case, regardless of the directory, from which the extraction command is executed, the files will be extracted into their initial directories.

The `tar` utility can be used to archive more than one directory at once. The following command archives the /home and /etc directories into one file:

```
tar cf backup.tar /home /etc
```

The contents of the archive can be viewed by executing the following command:

```
tar tvf backup.tar
```

This will list all directories and files contained in the archive, along with their ownership and permissions. An example of such a list is shown in Listing 13.1.

Listing 13.1. An example of listing archive contents

```
drwx------ 504/504    0 2004-11-27 20:24:05 home/adr/
drwxr-xr-x 504/504    0 2004-11-27 20:24:05 home/adr/.kde/
drwxr-xr-x 504/504    0 2004-11-27 20:24:05 home/adr/.kde/share/
-rw-r--r-- 504/504    118 2004-11-27 20:24:05 home/adr/.gtkrc
-rw-r--r-- 504/504    24 2004-11-27 20:24:05 home/adr/.bash_logout
-rw-r--r-- 504/504    191 2004-11-27 20:24:05 home/adr/.bash_profile
-rw-r--r-- 504/504    124 2004-11-27 20:24:05 home/adr/.bashrc
-rw-r--r-- 504/504    5 2004-11-27 20:24:05 home/adr/text
-rw-r--r-- 504/504    2247 2004-11-27 20:24:05 home/adr/.emacs
```

Note that there is no leading / character in the paths of the archive files in the last column. To properly restore files from this archive, the command to extract it has to be executed from the root directory; otherwise, the files will be extracted into the current directory.

13.5.3. The gzip Utility

Unlike the `tar` utility, the `gzip` utility compresses archived files. The resulting archives are of a much smaller size than the sum of the uncompressed files, meaning that they can be stored on a smaller medium.

Most often, data that have to be backed up are documents, whose size can be reduced by 90% by compressing them. Unlike programs, text files yield to compression extremely well.

Compressing, however, places a great workload on the processor, and it may take a long time to fully back up a large directory.

Because the size of a compressed archive is much smaller than that of a noncompressed archive, it takes less time to copy the archive over the network or to write it to removable media.

Before compressing files, you should place them into a `tar` archive. Then compress the obtained `tar` file as follows:

```
gzip -degree file.tar
```

The `degree` parameter specifies the degree, to which the file is to be compressed. The maximum compression degree is 9. The `file.tar` parameter specifies the `tar` archive file to be compressed. For practice, compress the `tar` archive of the /home directory, applying the maximum degree of compression. Execute the following command:

```
gzip -9 backup.tar
```

Now list the contents of the directory (using the `ls` command). Note that there is no more backup.tar file. It was replaced by the backup.tar.gz file, which is much smaller.

A compressed file is decompressed using the same `tar` command, but with the `xfz` option specified:

```
cd /
tar xfz /home/backup.tar.gz
```

The first command changes the current directory to root. The second command first decompresses the `gzip` file and then extracts files from the `tar` archive. To simply decompress a `gzip` file without extracting files from the `tar` archive, execute the following command:

```
gzip -d /home/backup.tar.gz
```

This will replace the backup.tar.gz compressed gzip file with the backup.tar tar archive file.

Now you are ready to write a script to archive directories to be backed up in a tar archive and then compress this file into a gzip file. You can redirect the results of the tar command into the gzip command as follows:

```
tar cvf - /home | gzip -9c > backup.tar.gz
```

Here, the command part before the | character creates a tar archive of the /home directory. The | character pipes the results to the second command part, which then compresses the tar file and stores it as a gzip file.

Another Linux compressing utility is compress. It, however, does not compress as well as gzip; moreover, it has been a subject of scandals and litigations concerning the license. Most administrators have switched to gzip, and I recommend that you start using this utility from the get-go.

13.5.4. The dump Utility

The utilities considered so far in this chapter are not specialized backup utilities. Their main function is to simply copy, archive, and compress files. The initial purpose of the dump utility was to back up the Ext2 file system.

To create a backup copy, at least the following parameters have to be specified:

❒ -n — This parameter takes values from 0 to 9 and specifies the backup level. The value of 0 means that a full backup is to be performed. Levels higher than 0 specify that only files newer than the last backup of a lower level are to be backed up.

❒ -u — This option specifies that the /etc/dumpdates file, which records backup dates, is to be updated after a successful backup.

❒ -f file — This option specifies the file or device, to which the backup is to be stored.

The simplest command to perform a full backup looks like the following:

```
dump -0u -f /home/backup.bak
```

To back up only files newer than the full backup, a level greater than 0 is specified, for example, as follows:

```
dump -1u -f /home/backup.bak
```

Files are restored by executing the restore command. Before executing it, however, make sure that you execute it from the directory that has to be restored.

The only required parameter for the restore command is -f file, which specifies the file to be restored. The -i option runs the command in the interactive mode, in which you can also specify the files to restore. The interactive mode is similar to the command line, in which you can browse the archive and execute the following commands:

❒ help — Displays brief help options for the available commands.

❒ ls — Displays the contents of the current directory.

- ❑ pwd — Displays the name of the current directory.
- ❑ add directory — Adds the directory specified in the directory parameter to the list of files to be extracted.
- ❑ cd directory — Changes the current directory to the one specified in the directory argument.
- ❑ delete directory — Deletes the directory specified in the directory argument from the list of files to be extracted.
- ❑ extract — Extracts all files on the extraction list.
- ❑ quit — Quits restore.

13.6. Securing Backup Media

It makes no sense to secure the system if you leave the backup media unsecured. The backup media store all of the main data from your computer, and if they fall into wrong hands there will be no need to break into the computer.

In one company I witnessed the procedure, by which confidential data from a secure server were copied hourly to a simple user computer configured to the default settings that could be compromised within 5 minutes.

You should approach the business of securing backup media with all due responsibility. The simplest way to secure the media is to store them in a safe. But a better way is to encrypt the backup archive before copying it to a medium. You can use the OpenSSH package for this by executing the following command:

```
/usr/bin/openssl des -in /home/backup.tar.gz -out /home/backup.sec
```

This will create the backup.sec file, which should be the one to write to a medium. Afterwards, don't forget to delete backup.tar.gz and backup.sec from the computer.

When restoring the backup archive, it first has to be decrypted as follows:

```
/usr/bin/openssl des -d -in /home/backup.sec \
-out /home/backup.tar.gz
```

After the archive has been decrypted, the files can be restored as usual.

Chapter 14: Advice from a Hacker

In this chapter, I consider various attack and break-in techniques. To protect your system, you should know how it can be broken into, just as to break into a system you should know how it is protected. These rules apply not only to the computer world but to other areas of life as well. How can you protect against burglars if you don't know how they are most likely to sneak into you house, apartment, or office? If you fortify the most likely entries, the potential burglars may just leave your place alone and move on, looking for an easier prey. Even should they take your defenses as a challenge to their professional skills, your defenses will slow them sufficiently for the police to arrive.

In this chapter, I will present techniques used by computer criminals so that you can develop antidotes against these methods for your defense arsenal.

Some of the questions are considered in a general sense, because it is not always possible to describe precisely a method that has many variations. Take, for example, virus attacks. At first, everything seems simple: Viruses are malicious software that must be sought out and destroyed. But there are different types of viruses requiring individual approaches to neutralizing them. Some general rules can be formulated that can be applied to detecting and neutralizing viruses. Even though these rules may not produce 100% satisfactory results, they will, at least, give you some leverage in your fight.

Experienced users and administrators may consider some of the recommendations offered here outdated. They are mistaken in this respect, because nothing is outdated and everything new is just something old that has been forgotten. There are many Johnny-come-lately users and administrators on the Internet who know modern technologies and events but do not know much from the Internet's recent history. I have noticed that hackers recently started successfully using methods from 10 and even 20 years ago.

Why are old hacking techniques successful? Experienced administrators simply forget about them, and rookies don't know them yet.

With the huge number of users and servers in the today's Internet, there are bound to be at least 1,000 computers whose users will be taken by the simplest break-in techniques. This has to do with the low education level of the average Internet user. By education, I don't mean formal school education but rather computer security savvy. Nobody teaches security to regular users, and most administrators are either too lazy or just don't want to spend money for training to raise their security-level skills.

14.1. Security Fundamentals

Before continuing further study of Linux, you should learn some general security principles. Some aspects that will be considered are only applicable to Linux, and others can be applied to any operating system and computer or server.

There are certain rules applicable to whatever operating system or service/daemon is being protected. These rules are considered in this chapter and are referenced in other chapters.

In this chapter, I intend to destroy some of the myths concerning security and will supply numerous examples from my personal experience as a network administrator.

Why is it necessary for you to take additional steps for protecting your system? Aren't operating systems and server software supposed to be inherently protected? Unfortunately, they are not; on the contrary, they are more vulnerable than secure. Again, God helps those who help themselves.

What is a vulnerability as related to computers? A vulnerability is an error (a.k.a. a bug) in a program that can be used to obtain unauthorized access to the system's files or capabilities.

All software has bugs because it is written by people and people have a propensity to making mistakes. Even the most protected software will have bugs; it's only a matter of time before they are found. Ask any hacker about which Linux kernel is the most secure, and you will be told that the latest kernel version is excellence itself without any bugs. Ask the same question a month later and you will find out that the kernel praised a month ago is buggy and it is recommended that you patch it before continuing working with it.

With every new Windows version, the Microsoft people tell us how reliable and secure it is, but a month later the same people tell us what a great service pack they've created for us to patch the holes and get rid of the bugs in this so-called secure and reliable operating system. Throw Internet Explorer and Microsoft Office applications into the mix and you get a good idea of the extent of the problem. Software bugs are as inevitable as death and taxes, and you have to accept this. Accepting does not mean resigning, so be ready to update regularly and religiously.

Most vulnerabilities cannot be called errors, because they have no negative effects on the program's operation; it's just that, to achieve their own goals, hackers use certain pieces of code in ways the developers never intended them to be used. To envision how every twisted mind may decide to use a program is more difficult than to ensure that it works as intended; the only thing developers can do is circumscribe the program's capabilities to the minimum necessary to perform its main function so as to minimize the number of unintended uses it can be put to.

14.1.1. Responsibility

The first step in securing the system is establishing who is to be responsible for system security. In most organizations, this task is entrusted to the system administrator, which is a mistake. The administrator who configures the system may not have the necessary security training and simply will not see his or her mistakes in this respect.

Administrators often fall victim to classical optical illusions. I have written quite a few books and constantly run into the classical problem of any author: When you read your own text, you tend to see it the way it is supposed to be and not the way it actually is. To give a simplest example, you can write "their" instead of "they're" because it sounds the same. Even though you know that it's wrong, you simply overlooked the spelling going by the vocalization only.

A spelling mistake of even one letter in a configuration file may have grievous consequences. Going through voluminous configuration files, you may fail to see it because to speed up the check you tuned your perception more to the sounds of words and not to their spelling. Besides, when checking their own work most people, no matter what they may think consciously, subconsciously think that they did everything right and do only a perfunctory check. It takes a special training to view one's own work as someone else's. But someone who sees the text for the first time and not in its primary context will notice the error right away. It is preferable that this someone be a security specialist.

The administrator should configure and service the system from the performance standpoint, and the security specialist should check the configuration from the security standpoint and test it for vulnerabilities. These two specialists have to interact and cooperate with each other, because a perfectly secure system may not necessarily be one that can deliver any meaningful performance, and vice versa. They can even substitute for each other when necessary, but no single person should be responsible for both areas, especially in large companies, meaning large networks.

Highly skilled security professionals demand a high price for their services, but you should not scrimp on security. It is better to spend a few extra dollars for a security specialist's salary than a few thousand dollars to recover from a hacker attack.

14.1.2. One Man's Trash Is Another Man's Treasure

Many security specialists recommend protecting only active work areas. Indeed, you may think: What's the use of protecting the wastebasket if the information in it was discarded as unnecessary? The first thing that comes to mind in this respect is the movie *Hackers*, whose characters did quite a bit of dumpster diving. What were they looking for in there?

For various bits and pieces of papers their owners thought were no longer valuable and discarded into trash cans without a second thought about what will happen to them. Quite often, users write passwords on pieces of paper or are given access information written on paper slips. After they write the information onto more permanent information storage media, such as notepads or notebooks, the bits of paper, and the information they contain, usually go into the trash can.

The same principle applies to the file system. A directory containing seemingly trashy information may turn out to be a mother lode of information for hackers. Once I conducted a security check of a system that had only one directory open, which contained only text files with song lyrics of group Dune. Seemingly an innocent thing, because what can be done using text files with this type of information?

I started a password-cracking program to pick the root password by the dictionary method and specified these text files as the dictionary to use. Imagine my surprise when within seconds the program informed me that the root password was the name of the group — Dune!

Administrators often keep information related to their personal interests in open folders. If they also create their passwords based on their interests, this information may greatly facilitate picking of the password.

Once hackers obtain any sort of access to the system, they can raise their privileges. This can be done using various exploits, which can be found on the Internet in droves. Every day, new ones are created. If hackers have no access to the system, it will be much more difficult for them to break into it.

Currently, there aren't that many ways to break into a computer remotely, but with local access hackers' chances of raising their access privileges increase manyfold. It is easier to protect against break-ins perpetrated over the network; the main defense method here is using a firewall. But if hackers obtain some sort of access, what they can do depends only on the access-rights allocation policy. If it is not well thought out, hackers can even obtain administrator privileges.

The main targets attacked by hackers after accessing a system are the following:

❑ *Vulnerable operating system utilities.* If you look at security reports, you will see that vulnerabilities in various utilities crop up almost weekly and programmers and administrators have a hard time keeping up with patches.

❑ *Third-party software.* The developers of distributions go to great lengths to test all application-software packages included with their distribution. But third-party developers usually test their software only with their own distribution; thus, there is no guarantee that such a program will work reliably and securely under all Linux versions. Moreover, the professionalism of some third-party software developers — and, thus, the quality of their software — leaves a lot to be desired, as was explained in *Section 1.3*.

❑ *Scripts and programs written by the system administrator or company programmers.* To expand the functionality of the operating system, administrators often write their own scripts (mostly using the Perl interpreter), and quite frequently hackers break into the system through holes in such scripts. Only a professional programmer possessing a good knowledge of security principles and secure coding techniques can create a secure script or program. Beginning programmers and regular administrators do not give proper attention to checking arguments and parameters, which results in low-quality code.

To summarize, there should be "important" and "unimportant" areas where security is concerned. Although more important data should be allowed better protection, up to being encrypted, the whole system should be protected as well.

You can fortify the server containing restricted information and open another one for public use. In this case, however, there should be no trust relationship between these two servers, and user names and passwords must be different. But humans, being such a lazy bunch, typically make the root passwords for all servers the same or, if they differ, make them similar enough that they will be easy to remember. If you can discipline yourself to follow all pertinent security rules, assigning different physical servers for different tasks is a correct approach to securing your network.

You can start by strictly following the rule that the root user password should be different for each server.

14.1.3. All Users Are Created Equal

Being a network administrator in a large company with many departments is the most difficult chore psychologically.

Most administrators direct their security measures toward protecting the network from outside attacks. But statistically, most and the worst break-ins are perpetrated from inside by company workers, their friends and acquaintances, and the like. It is much easier to perpetrate an internal break-in, because administrators often cannot resist pressure from friends and coworkers to give them some password or access to a certain resource. You should not yield to any entreaties or demands of this type. A friend given expanded privileges may repay the kindness in the form of a break-in. It may be purely accidental or intended as an innocent prank, but cleaning up the consequences may be as difficult as after a real break-in.

Security means not only hardening your system against break-ins but also making it impervious to improper user actions. The simplest example is what I call the boss effect. Many administrators consider that their direct boss or the company director should have the right to view any information in the system. There may be a legitimate need for this, but once a boss is given rights to view information, he or she usually starts demanding the write rights also. This is much more likely to create problems, especially if the boss is a klutz with computers. And it is usually bosses of this type who ask for the maximum rights. If you yield to someone pulling rank, there is a good chance that their use of these rights will result in serious data loss. Guess who will be left holding the bag?

Another problem stemming from giving extra privileges to friends and bosses is that it is impossible to protect their passwords. If there is only one maximum-privileges user in the system, the root, it is relatively easy to protect his or her password. But keeping track of the passwords of ten high-privileged users is a more difficult task. Any of these users can select an easy password or simply write a strong password on paper. In either case, the password will become vulnerable with the corresponding consequences stemming from it being compromised.

14.1.4. Protecting Workstations

Protecting workstations is no less important than protecting the operating system and its services. When I worked as a programmer for a major company, I was responsible for developing industrial equipment data-collection software, configuring workstations, installing workstations with the software into the shops, and doing operational maintenance. For each computer I devised an individual strong password.

Seemingly, I took good care to make the workstations secure, but when one day I came to one of the shops to service one of the computers I saw the password written with a permanent marker on the monitor case. So, all my efforts at creating strong passwords were nullified by one lazy computer operator, who made the password available for any company worker or even a stranger to see.

Beginning computer users do not like to remember strong passwords, so they write them on the monitor, the keyboard, or Post-It notes, which are then stuck on the same monitor or keyboard. It is unnecessary to say what this turns the administrator's best efforts to secure the system into.

Thus, you should pay the same attention to securing workstations as to securing the network. Based on my experience, I can say that most break-ins have their roots in the lackadaisical attitude of users.

You can protect workstations by following these recommendations:

- ❑ Never write down passwords on paper and, even more so, never leave these near monitors or keyboards. Take a little time to memorize the main passwords.
- ❑ Leaving the computer, block the keyboard (e.g., using the `vlock` or `xlock` utility) or log out of the system, so that no one can use the computer while you are away.
- ❑ Changing the password takes just a few seconds, so never rely on a screensaver because someone can take advantage of your momentary absence and change the password. Thus, you can lose control over your account. I disable the screensaver on my computers so as not to be tempted to rely on it; instead, I have developed a habit of always blocking the keyboard when leaving the computer even for a short time.
- ❑ If you work in the graphical mode, never place any shortcuts other than the default ones on the desktop. For example, a shortcut to another computer provides a wealth of information for hackers.
- ❑ Put a password on BIOS. If hackers obtain physical access to the computer, they will be able to reboot it in the single-user mode and proceed to break the root password.
- ❑ Use a boot loader password to protect against unauthorized booting (see *Section 3.2*).
- ❑ Disable the <Ctrl>+<Alt>+<Del> key combination by deleting the corresponding entry in the /etc/inittab file to prevent accidental or unauthorized boots.

14.1.5. Security Documentation

Many administrators consider documentation the domain of bureaucrats, and categorically refuse to issue any documented instructions. There was time when I was like that myself and preferred to keep everything in my head and issue only oral instructions. This continued until the system grew too large and complex to be managed this way and was eventually hacked.

Consider a simple example of using documentation to make your system more secure. Suppose hackers broke into your system and obtained root privileges. You close the hole and change the root password, but the hackers return in almost no time. How could they manage this? It is possible that the hackers stole the password file and decrypted the passwords in it. To prevent this type of situation, all user passwords should be changed after a break-in. This can be done in one of the following two ways:

❑ Generate new passwords yourself and distribute them to the users. This approach is convenient for a large network to ensure that all passwords are changed. However, there could be problems distributing passwords.

❑ Prepare a security memo instructing all users to change their passwords when instructed by the administrator. All users should be familiarized with this memo.

In practice, however, it would be preferable to use a combination of these two methods. That is, users are instructed to change their passwords themselves, but if they don't do this within a certain period (for example, 3 hours) after having been instructed to, you change the passwords. This solves the distribution problem: The users will come to you to discover their new password.

The security memo should also instruct users to create strong passwords of a certain minimal length. Most importantly, you should ensure that users use strong passwords.

Documentation can also be used to make various department heads help you maintain system security. For example, network administrators usually don't know when a worker's employment is terminated. A former employee can give his or her login information to another person, who may not even be a company employee and who then can use this information for an illegitimate purpose.

Also, a fired worker may decide to get even with the administration for the firing and use his or her login parameters to do some unscheduled creative maintenance on the system. There are numerous examples of this happening. I witnessed one such case when the network administrator was fired but the new administrator did not change the passwords. Two days later he wished that he had not had so much faith in human decency: The server's hard disk was wiped clean. At the time I worked as a programmer at that company and had my share of overtime restoring the destroyed data.

14.1.6. Passwords

All passwords must be periodically changed. I change passwords monthly for my Web site; the same goes for the servers, with the important ones having their passwords changed weekly.

Even though this adds certain inconveniences when remember the new passwords, the security this provides is worth it.

The only password I don't change is the Windows password on my notebook, because I am the only one who uses it.

Once they obtain access to the system, many hackers do not engage into any malevolent activities. They simply explore the system to figure out its organizations and ways for staying undetected. Only those hackers intent on destroying data will move fast, because they don't intend to hang around long. Fortunately, there aren't that many break-ins of this type.

So it is possible for you not to notice a hacker lurking in your system. But if you change passwords every month, after a regular password change the trespasser will lose his or her rights and will have to break the password again.

Changing passwords regularly makes cracking them more difficult. Here is how. Many automated security systems can easily detect an attempt at password cracking by several unsuccessful authorization attempts in a row, usually three. To circumvent such protection, hackers insert some delay before trying the next password. This makes the break-in process longer, but unless the password is difficult and changed periodically, the attack will ultimately succeed. If the password is periodically changed, the possibility to pick it before the next change becomes very low.

For example, suppose that the password contains only digits. Further, suppose that the password is 7000000. By a brute-force search, the hacker tried combinations from 0 to 6000000, at which point the password was changed to 5000000. Further combination picking can go on indefinitely without any results, because the range, in which the new password is located, has already been passed.

Another advantage offered by regular password changes is that it may take the hacker so long to pick a strong password that by the time he or she succeeds the password will be changed, throwing the hacker back to stage one.

How can you make users change passwords periodically? You can make use of the `chage` utility, executing it as follows:

```
chage parameter user
```

The `parameter` value can be one of the following:

- ☐ `-m N` — Sets N as the minimum number of days between password changes. Setting this value to a few days smaller than the maximum value, you can protect against unauthorized password changes, meaning that if hackers take over an account, they will not be able to change its password. They can get around this by executing the `chage` command themselves, but they will need root privileges for this. A difference of 3 to 4 days between the maximum and the minimum number of days before a password change should give the user enough time to change the old password. The difference ought not to be less than 3 days to account for weekends. The default value is –1, meaning the user can change the password any time before it expires.

- ☐ `-M N` — Sets N as the maximum number of days, during which the password remains valid. The default value of N is 99999, meaning that the password never becomes invalid.

- ❐ -d N — Sets the date the password was last changed. The N parameter is the number of days from January 1, 1970. The date can also be expressed in the YYYY-MM-DD format.
- ❐ -E date — Sets the date, on which the user's account will no longer be accessible.
- ❐ -I N — Blocks the account if it has not been used for N days. I recommend setting the N value to no fewer than 3 days but no more than 4 days to block the account while the owner is on vacation or sick leave.
- ❐ -W N — Displays a warning that the password is about to expire, starting N days before the password expiration date. This should be set to no less than 3 days for the user to be able to change the password if the expiration falls on weekend.
- ❐ -l user — With this parameter, the command can be executed by any user but only to find out when his or her password expires. For example, executing chage -l root displays the expiration date of the root password and other pertinent information. The execution results look similar to the following:

```
Minimum:      -1
Maximum:      99999
Warning:      -1
Inactive:     -1
Last Change:          Feb 04, 2004
Password Expires:     Never
Password Inactive:    Never
Account Expires:      Never
```

The meanings of the entries in the preceding listing are as follows:

- ❐ Minimum — The minimum number of days between password changes
- ❐ Maximum — The maximum number of days before the password change
- ❐ Warning — The number of days before the password expiration that a warning message starts to be issued
- ❐ Inactive — The number of days the account remains inactive before it is blocked
- ❐ Last Change — The date the password was last changed
- ❐ Password Expires — The password expiration date
- ❐ Password Inactive — The date the password became inactive
- ❐ Account Expires — The account expiration date

Changing a password too often results in users simply not being able to remember or get used to them. Consequently, they start writing strong passwords down or simply change the new passwords to the old. To prevent this development, users should not be made to change passwords too often. A period of 60 to 90 days between password changes is considered acceptable.

But how can you make sure that users select strong passwords or that they do not simply reuse the old passwords? This can be achieved with the help of the pam_cracklib.so module. This module performs basic password checking for stronger passwords. For example, the module will not allow the user to specify the old password or a password containing too many characters from the old password.

The `pam_cracklib.so` module is enabled by adding the following entry to the /etc/pam.d/passwd file:

```
password  required  pam_cracklib.so retry=5 minlength=8
```

The first part tells the system to use the pam_cracklib.so library. The `retry` parameter sets the number of attempts to enter the new password to five. The `minlength` parameter sets the minimum password length.

14.1.7. BugTraq

To tell the truth, there aren't that many real hackers in the world. Most break-ins are perpetrated by teenagers who have nothing better to do and who want to try their skills somewhere. This sort of hackers is not too strong on the theory of programming and mainly uses ready-made techniques designed and perfected by real hackers. This means that you should keep track of new break-in techniques and newly-discovered vulnerabilities. I use the **www.securityfocus.com** or **www.cert.org** sites for this purpose. They regularly publish information about new security holes, how to use them, and how to protect against their use.

The discussions concerning the need for sites like **www.securityfocus.com** have been carried on for a long time. On one hand, they allow administrators to protect their systems by learning about new vulnerabilities, but on the other the hackers can use this information for diametrically opposite purposes. I don't see any problems with such sites and, what is even more, believe they are a good idea. The problem is that most administrators simply do not visit these sites and they learn about the weak spots only when their site, network, or server has been broken into. Even if you consider a security hole discovered in 1990s, computers and servers can still be found on the Internet that have this hole unpatched. If I had my way, I would sack such administrators without thinking twice.

If you think that regularly updating your system can make it impervious to break-ins, you are sadly mistaken. A considerable length of time may pass from the time a new security hole is discovered until an update with a patch for it comes out, during which your computer can be compromised. Any hacker who has learned about the new hole can successfully attack your computer. To keep this from happening, you must learn about the new vulnerability before hackers do and undertake your own security measures to keep your computer secure until the official patch comes out.

Not only services but also the kernel can contain bugs. Bugs in application software can be fixed by installing a fresh version. Fixing kernel bugs is somewhat more complicated. Updating it involves recompiling the kernel source code, which is a rather intricate procedure. But updating using RPM is no more difficult than installing any other program.

14.1.8. Patching the Kernel

In addition to the official kernel updates, there are many patches written by third-party developers (e.g., SELinux, lcap, and LIDS). All of them are intended for securing the system on the kernel level. For example, the kernel can prohibit executing code from the stack, which will make many stack-overflow attacks impossible. There are kernel patches to prohibit viewing files in the /proc directory, monitor system processes, protect against port scanning, and so on.

You may ask why examples of third-party kernel patches weren't considered earlier in the book. The reason is that most of such patches require you to recompile the kernel, do not work with all Linux kernel versions, and require serious effort to install. Although kernel patches enhance system security, they may make the system less stable because they are produced by third-party developers and Red Hat Linux may simply not support all of their requirements.

This is why this subject is not included in the book. However, you should know that such patches exist; you may decide that the security features offered by a certain patch are just what your system needs, and install it. But you should realize that you will be doing this at your own risk. You should also be aware that updating the kernel to a new version may cause problems. Moreover, as with all new software, new kernel versions have bugs that will have to be patched.

14.1.9. Raising the Professional Skill Level

One of the most important components of effective administration is constant improving your professional skill level.

Many computer specialists do not have special education and are self-taught. I have rather extensive experience dealing with administrators and can tell from the contents of administrator's computer the professionalism level of its owner. In a nutshell, if there are games on the administrator's computer, there is a 90% chance that the administrator spends too much time fighting monsters. If the computer has no games and only administrating software, the administrator is a good one or on the way to becoming such.

The computer field is in the state of constant development, and if you spend more time running through dark hallways and machine-gunning monsters, your computer skills will become obsolete faster than rapidly. You have to be constantly raising the level of your professional skill and learning something new every day.

Special education is a good thing, but it only gives the base that you can learn from professional literature in a month or so. Specific knowledge becomes obsolete way before you graduate from college, and unless you constantly refresh your body of knowledge, you stand good chances of becoming a simple advanced user.

All work and no play makes Johnny a dull boy, so shooting a monster now and then is no sin. But you should remember that computer-security specialist responsibilities include not only taking care of present tasks but also raising your qualification level.

The preceding was just a general outline of security concepts. Other sections of the book consider the operating system and its various services from the security standpoint in more detail. But the general rules always apply regardless of the operating system and hardware.

14.2. Buffer Overflow

Buffer overflow is one of the most popular and widespread yet one of the most difficult-to-use vulnerabilities. First, consider why programmers commit errors that make buffer overflow possible.

Programming languages like C++ allocate a memory buffer of a certain size for working with the data supplied by the user. User data are placed into the buffer by simply copying them to it. Most programmers calculate the maximum size of data that can be passed by a user to the program and allocate this much memory, perhaps with a little to spare, for the buffer. Most of them do not check for the exact size of the data entered by the user.

This makes it possible to pass the program too much information, which will simply not fit into the memory allocated to hold it and cause a program crash.

How can too much passed information crash a program? I will not burden you with programming and machine code intricacies, but simply consider a simplest buffer overflow example. A program can be thought of as occupying a single continuous memory block as follows:

```
Code
Code
A 50-byte data buffer
Code
Code
```

As you can see, the programmer allocated 50 bytes for the buffer to store user data, and placed this buffer in the middle of the code. But what will happen if the user passes, for example, 70 bytes to the program instead of 50 bytes? In this case, the extra data will overwrite the program code following the buffer. When the time comes to execute the code following the buffer, there will be no code to execute and the program will crash.

In older Windows versions, some buffer overflow bugs could crash the operating system itself. Windows 2000, XP, and Linux are hardened against buffer overflow errors and are more difficult to crash. But programs still crash.

The program crashing itself is only half the trouble. The other half is that experienced hackers can pass such data to the program, in which the first part, corresponding to the buffer size, is trash while the part following it is executable code written by the hacker to perform certain operations. This will make the program code look as follows:

```
Code
Code
A 50-byte data buffer
Hacker's code
Hacker's code
```

In this case, the buffer overflow will cause much greater damage than a simple program crash. If the program executes with root privileges, the hacker's code can perform any operations that require root privileges.

Buffer overflow bugs are becoming less common because of automatic code-checking utilities, but many of them are still around. There aren't that many good hackers able to use the buffer-overflow bug to insert their own code into a program. But programs exploiting the buffer-overflow bug written by such hackers can be used by anyone, which presents a major danger.

In addition to crashing the stack by exploiting the buffer-overflow bug, program code can be corrupted by improper formatting. Some functions may present a security threat if used in a certain way. Hackers may pass to them such information that when processed by the program will change the program's code. The principles of preventing the adverse effects of these errors are the same as those for preventing buffer-overflow effects, so I will not go into much detail on this aspect; moreover, users and administrators don't usually deal with machine codes.

What you should know is that when you find out that one of the services is vulnerable to a buffer-overflow attack and you can temporarily do without it, you should disable the service. If the service is not a necessary one, you can simply delete it.

If you need the service, the first thing you should do is visit the developer's site. Follow any recommendations on how to fix the error that you may find there. Sometimes, all you have to do is modify some configuration files, but sometimes a new version of the program has to be installed.

In 90% of cases, buffer overflow errors are fixed by updating the program. This is because such errors stem from incorrect code logic that can only be fixed by correcting the source code and recompiling the program.

If the developer offers no solution to fix the problem, limit the program's rights as much as possible. If a program belongs to root and its SUID or SGID bit is set (that is, the program executes with the root privileges even if run by a guest user), this bit must be cleared.

As universal protection against buffer overflow bugs, I can recommend the `libsafe` utility (available from **www.research.avayalabs.com/project/libsafe**). This is a library that creates a buffer layer between the application software and the operating system. When system functions that may cause buffer overflow are called, the library substitutes these functions with its own versions. These are functional analogues of the system functions but are protected against buffer overflow.

The library has one shortcoming: It causes a slight productivity drop. But the library's advantages overweigh this shortcoming in many ways. The library does not protect against a certain program or a certain error, but against most potential problems. As you already know, it is impossible to protect against everything, because hackers constantly come up with new tricks, so the library does not provide 100% protection against buffer overflow errors. But the protection it does provide will allow your system to work uninterruptedly for a much longer period than it would otherwise.

14.3. Rootkits

Having obtained access to the system, hackers strive to fortify their positions and to obtain maximum privileges. Once in the system, a hacker will never be satisfied with regular user privileges and will seek the capability to execute commands with the root privileges.

The hacker can go about obtaining this capability by obtaining file-loading capabilities and then uploading and installing a special program for raising privileges to root, called a *rootkit*. After this, any command issued by the hacker is executed as follows:

❐   The command has regular user permissions and is sent to the rootkit program.
❐   The rootkit program has root permissions and executes the hacker's program as the root.

But how does the rootkit program obtain root permissions? With the help of the same notorious SUID or SGID bit.

Moreover, the ownership of the rootkit program must belong to the root user. There are two ways of changing a program's ownership to root and setting its SUID or SGID bit. These are the following:

❐   Use the chown and chmod commands (if such an opportunity exists).
❐   Substitute the rootkit program for an existing program with root permissions and the SUID or SGID bit set.

This is why SUID and SGID programs should be tightly controlled. Each such program is a hole in system security, but unfortunately sometimes these programs are necessary. You should closely monitor such programs and immediately delete any new ones that are not installed by yourself. You should also monitor changes to the legitimate SUID and SGID programs. A size change of an SUID or SGID program is a cause to sound the alarm, because this may be an indication of the legitimate program having been substituted with a hacker version.

Pay close attention when checking SUID and SGID programs. Hackers know that administrators monitor such programs, and they resort to various tricks to prevent their infiltrated or subverted SUID and SGID programs from being detected. For example, you may see nothing alarming in that the /mnt/mount program has the SUID set because the mount program does require this. However, the legitimate mount program is located in the /bin directory, and the one in the /mnt directory is without a doubt a cuckoo egg. If you are going over the list of the SUID and SGID files in a hurry, you may not notice the directory difference or may not even be looking at the directories in the first place.

Moreover, hackers can substitute letters in the names of legitimate programs with letters similar in appearance. For example, they can add the /bin/1ogon program masquerading as the /bin/logon. The difference is that the letter "l" in the legitimate version is substituted with the digit "1" in the counterfeit one. You likely will not notice the difference, because the legitimate version does not have the SUID and SGID bit set and only the fake one will show in the SUID and SGID list. And even though the login program should not have this bit set, you, most likely, will not suspect this program is anything malicious.

In addition to making it possible to execute commands with root permissions, rootkit packages provide other functionality. These can be utilities such as network sniffers, log file manipulators for cleaning up hacker's tracks in the system, and other hacker tools.

Once hackers have a rootkit package installed in the system, they can always come back even if you find and patch the hole used to enter originally. Thus, you should be able to locate and neutralize rootkit packages.

You can use the chkrootkit program for this purpose (available from **www.chkrootkit.org**). Currently, it can detect more than 50 different popular rootkit packages.

But, as usual, the protection from an automated tool is limited and a sweep by chkrootkit will not guarantee your system a clean bill of health. The problem is that only beginning hackers use readymade rootkit packages. Professional hackers are good programmers and create their own tools. It is not that difficult; they only have to know some programming and the way Linux operates. Therefore, you should be able to detect and neutralize rootkit packages manually yourself.

One of the ways of detecting rootkit packages manually is to scan the ports, because to open a back door to the system a rootkit opens a port, which it monitors for the hacker to connect.

One of the best Linux scanning tools with extensive functionality is the already-mentioned nmap utility. To scan all 65,535 ports, the program is launched as follows:

```
nmap -p 1-65535 localhost
```

The -p parameter sets the port range to be scanned. In this case, the entire range of existing ports from 1 to 65,535 is specified.

The following parameters can also be used:

❐ -sT — Standard TCP connect scan. This is the slowest scanning, opening a connection to every port on the scanned machine. Any antiscanning utility will detect this scan (see *Section 12.4*). This is the default scanning mode if the program is run with the regular user permissions.

❐ -sS — TCP synchronization (SYN) scanning. This is the default scanning mode for root users. It is faster than the sT mode and is detected by fewer antiscanning utilities.

❐ -sF — TCP finish (FIN) scanning. Pursuant to RFC 793 specifications, closed ports must reply to a FIN packet (sent by a client to the server to initiate connection termination) with an reset (RST) packet. Consequently, receiving no RST packet in response to a FIN packet indicates that the given port is open. This, however, applies to Linux systems only. Windows creators, as usual, decided to ignore the standard and do it their own way, so the scan will not work against these systems.

❐ -sX — TCP Xmas tree scanning. This scan is similar to the TCP scan, only the URG and PUSH flags are set in addition to the FIN flag.

❐ -sN — TCP null scanning. This scan is similar to the previous two scans, only no flags are set.

❐ -I — Ident scanning.

❐ -sU — UDP scanning. UDP ports are different from TCP ports and must be scanned separately.

The idea of scanning consists of obtaining some sort of reply from the server. Depending on the scanning method employed, a positive or negative reply indicates that the given port is closed or open.

A faster way to determine open ports is to use the `lsof -i` or `netstat` command; however, these can only be executed on the machine whose ports are being scanned.

In addition to checking the system for rootkit packages, you should check for the presence of extraneous loadable kernel modules. You can use the `chkproc` utility for this purpose, which is included in the `chkrootkit` package. The packet also includes the `ifpromisk` utility, which is used to detect network sniffers.

Finally, check for the presence of extraneous processes by executing the `ps -aux` command to list all currently running processes. Pay close attention when inspecting the process list. Remember the trick of swapping the digit "1" for letter "l," which is probably the most widely-used trick. Giving just a cursory once-over, you may not notice the difference.

Combined use of all of these utilities will allow you to detect rootkits that `chkrootkit` misses.

After you identify the files belonging to the rootkit program, you have to stop their operation and delete them from the system. This will suffice unless the rootkit has modified some system files. If, however, it has, you will have to determine, which programs have been modified, and reinstall them. In Red Hat distributions, which support RPM packets, this can be done by simply executing the following command:

```
rpm -U -force packet_name.rpm
```

Here, `packet_name.rpm` is the name of the program to reinstall.

14.4. Back Doors

After penetrating a system, quite often hackers install in it a back-door program for logging into the system that bypasses the regular login procedure. The general operating principle of such programs is the following:

❑   The back-door program opens a port and listens on it for a connection.
❑   When the hacker connects to this port, the program opens a command shell on the port, thus giving the hacker the ability to execute commands.

The back-door operation is similar to the way Trojan programs work; however, Trojans have to be launched by the user to be installed, and back doors are uploaded to the target computer and installed by the hackers.

There is also a similarity with the way rootkit programs work. There is no clear-cut distinction among different hacker tools, with one program having the functionality of what used to be separate utilities. Rootkit and back-door utilities have been combined in a single package for a long time, although separate utilities can still be found.

Hacker utilities are not the type of software you can purchase at a store where regular software is sold. Hackers write these programs for their own use; nevertheless, they can be downloaded from some private sites.

Hackers do not like to make their utilities public, because in that case the loopholes they use to penetrate systems will be closed.

Because the main goal of this book is to teach you how to create a secure system, I will not consider creating and installing back-door software. What I will consider is how to detect and neutralize it.

The simplest and quickest way to find a program that does not belong is to check the current processes and open ports. As already stated, a back-door utility waits for the hacker to connect to the computer it is installed on, meaning that there has to be a process for this program. The current processes can be viewed by executing the ps command. Open ports are checked using a port-scanning utility or the netstat program.

When using the ps utility to check the current processes, make sure that it has not been modified by hackers. Because Linux source codes are open, hackers can modify the ps utility in such a way that it will not display the process of the back-door program. Thus, they can slip the doctored version into your system.

The source codes being open means that any other program can be modified to perform other functions in addition to the legitimate ones. For example, the telnetd utility can be modified in such a way that it can be used to enter the system without having to go through the regular login procedure. Thus, make sure that the executable files for all running processes have not been modified.

Moreover, some daemons can support loadable modules. Thus, hackers can write and load their own module instead of or in addition to the standard modules of a service. Detecting this module will be more difficult, because the main process file is not changed.

Modifying program source codes is a rather difficult task, and you have to possess good programming knowledge; consequently, even though this method is among the most dangerous ones, it is not that widespread. Still, it should not be dismissed, because even though there are few high-class hackers, they do exist.

Pay close attention when inspecting the process list. There may be two utilities with the same name in your system, for example, telnetd. One of these will be the genuine utility, and the other will be a back door planted by hackers.

If you server is never turned off, hackers can simply start their back door program and leave the system knowing that they can come back any time they wish. But if the server is periodically turned off or rebooted, they will have to make arrangements for the back door to start upon reboot to keep it functioning.

Consequently, you should check all boot scripts for changes. This may prove to be a complex task, because there are quite a few such scripts in Linux and hackers can modify any of them. Scripts for loading services are located in the /etc/rc.d/init.d directory.

Even if you do not find any extraneous processes or any modified service or program file, there still may be a back door in your system. Processes can be hidden from viewing by kernel modules.

Of late, the Linux kernel has become truly modular. This is convenient because while earlier the kernel had to be recompiled to add a new functionality, now this can be done by simply executing a few commands to load the necessary module.

So how can the kernel be used to hide a process? The ps program, and others like it, uses the kernel to determine, which processes are running. The kernel has all information about what is being currently executed. Hackers have written various modules that prevent the kernel from disclosing information about certain processes, thus keeping those processes hidden from the administrator's eyes. This is why you should not stop after inspecting processes and executable files even if you don't find anything suspicious.

In addition to starting a process, a back-door program has to open a port, on which to wait for the hacker to connect. Your task is to find this port.

The quickest method of determining that a service is waiting for connection is to use the netstat command. But because this command is a part of a standard Linux distribution, its source code can be tampered with. The most reliable way to search for extra open ports is to use a port scanner, even though this takes longer.

The best way to hide a back-door from network analyzers is to program it using raw sockets, the way sniffers are programmed. The installed back-door program monitors all traffic going through the server and, if it sees specially-marked packets, executes the instructions specified in them. The hacker can then send broadcast packets marked this way and the back door will filter them out and execute the instructions in them.

The netstat utility and port-scanner utilities cannot detect sniffer programs. However, to monitor traffic, a network card has to operate in a special mode, called promiscuous, which can be easily detected by checking the state of the network interface with the help of the ifconfig command. When in the promiscuous mode, the network card passes on to the operating system packets addressed to any machine in the network.

The only sign of there being a sniffer in the system is the increased workload on the server because of all the packets that pass the network card passed on to the operating system for processing.

But even then back-door programs can be detected. In this case, you follow the "like cures like" principle. To be more specific, start a sniffer of your own and check what is passing through you network card. Packets sending confidential information, such as passwords, are a sure indication of a back-door program doing its filthy job. But if the back door encrypts the information it sends, you will not be able to detect this with a sniffer program.

The best protection against a back door is a properly-configured firewall. If your default policy is to prohibit everything, allowing access to public resources only, even if a malware program opens some port it will be impossible to connect to it without changing the firewall filters. Keep an eye on firewall filter files to make sure that they are not modified, and all of a hacker's efforts will be in vain.

14.5. Monitoring Traffic

As already mentioned, the most popular tools used for local network break-in are sniffer programs, that is, traffic monitoring. Even though using these programs on the Internet is a more difficult task, it is not impossible. In this chapter, I consider the theory of implementing attacks using sniffers and explain how to detect traffic-intercepting sniffers in a network.

As you know, sniffers intercept packets addressed to other computers. Because most protocols are created at the dawn of the Internet and transmit data in plaintext, confidential information (passwords, credit card numbers, etc.) can easily be gathered from transmitted packets.

The initial purpose of sniffer programs was to be an administrative tool. But hackers found other applications for it, turning it from a simple network traffic analyzer into a powerful hacker weapon.

Sniffers can work in active and passive modes, both of which are considered in this chapter. However, to have a better understanding of the subject, you will have to learn the basic concepts of the Open Systems Interconnection (OSI) model.

14.5.1. The OSI Model

When data are sent over a network, they are directed from one computer to another. But how exactly is it done? You may guess that a special network protocol is used, and you would be right. But there are many protocol varieties. When is each of them used? How do they work? These and other questions I will try to answer in this section.

Before getting down to the protocols, you have to learn about the OSI model, developed by the International Standard Organization (ISO) to describe how information moves from one computer through a network medium to another computer. According to this model, all network interaction is broken down into the following seven layers (Fig. 14.1):

1. The *physical* layer is responsible for transmitting data over physical network media (e.g., coaxial, twisted pair, and fiber-optic cables). It defines physical environment characteristics and electrical signal parameters.
2. The *data link* layer provides transit of data between any nodes in typical topology networks or between adjacent nodes in random topology networks. Addressing employs MAC addresses.
3. The *network* layer defines the network address, which differs from the MAC address. The layer provides unreliable communication, meaning the delivery of packets is not guaranteed.
4. The *transport* layer is responsible for delivering data across the network with the specified delivery-reliability level. The layer provides for establishing a connection and buffering, numbering, and sequencing packets.
5. The *session* layer establishes, manages, and terminates communication sessions. The layer sets the currently-active communications party.
6. The *presentation* layer provides data coding and conversion functions.
7. The *application* layer provides a set of network services (FTP, email, etc.) for users and applications.

If you paid attention when reading the descriptions of the OSI layers, you probably noticed that the first three levels are implemented in hardware, such as network cards, routers, hubs, and bridges. The last three layers are implemented by the operating system or applications. The fourth layer is implemented in both hardware and software.

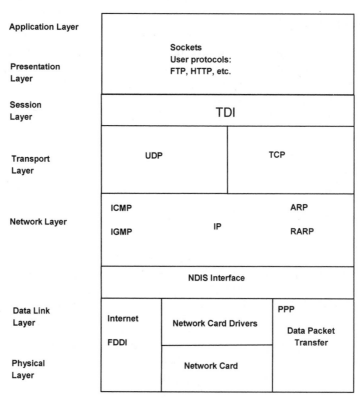

Fig. 14.1. The OSI model

How are data transmitted according to this model? The process starts with the application layer, where packets are added a header. The application layer then transfers the resulting packet to the presentation layer. The application layer communicates any necessary control information required by the application layer of the destination machine by prefixing a header of its own to the packet. The process is repeated for each successive layer up to the physical layer, which places the packet on the network media.

The process is reversed on the destination machine, with each layer stripping the header added by the corresponding layer on the source machine and passing the resulting data unit to the next layer until only pure information, without any service data, is handed to the application layer.

Data transmission does not necessarily start from the physical layer. If the protocol used works on the transport layer, the packet's downward travel starts at this layer. The number of layers used by a protocol defines its needs and data-transfer capabilities.

The higher a protocol (the closer to the application layer), the more capabilities it has and the more overhead involved in data transmission (more headers, which are also more complex).

14.5.2. Passive Sniffing

Passive sniffing involves monitoring packets that pass directly through your network card. This method can only be used on the common-bus and star-topology networks. (Network topologies are described in *Section 5.2.*)

Passive sniffing is the easiest to implement. All network packets that pass through a network card are checked for being addressed to that card. The network card compares the destination address in the packet header with its own MAC address and, if they match, passes the packet to the operating system for further processing. Packets whose address does not match are rejected. The operating system uses the header information to determine the port, to which the packet is directed, and the program that opened the port and must process the packet.

Processing to filter out packets addressed to a particular computer is carried out on the network card level. But a network card can be placed into a special mode, called promiscuous, in which all packets are passed to the operating system and can be processed using specialized programs. It should be noted that not all network cards can be switched into the promiscuous mode, but at least all modern cards can.

This trick, however, cannot be pulled on the Internet and networks using routers, because only packets addressed to a particular network card reach that card. All other packets are filtered out by switches or the provider's routers. In this case, active sniffing is resorted to.

At first, it may seem that administrators cannot detect sniffing, making engaging in this activity safe for hackers. Acting on this belief, some beginning hackers launch their sniffing programs and keep them running all day long, waiting for secret passwords to start coming their way. But administrators can and should detect sniffing activity in their networks, even passive sniffing, and discover and punish the perpetrator.

Passive sniffing is detected by sending ping requests to all network computers, in which the correct IP address but an incorrect MAC address is specified. In the regular mode, the network card checks each packet's MAC address and rejects those packets that are not addressed to it. But if the network card is switched into the promiscuous mode, it will pass any packet it receives to the operating system, which will check the packet's IP address. Because the packet's IP address is correct, the operating system will respond to it with an echo reply. This explicitly indicates that the given computer's network card is switched into the promiscuous mode.

But hackers are not that stupid and operate from behind firewalls. All the hacker has to do is prohibit outgoing ICMP traffic, and his or her computer will not reply to the administrator's ping requests.

An indication of a sniffer in a system can be increased average processor workload. This is caused by the network card passing all network traffic to the operating system.

To find out whether your network card is operating in the promiscuous mode, execute the following command:

```
ifconfig -a
```

If the PROMISC mode is set, your card can monitor all network traffic.

14.5.3. Active Sniffing

Active sniffers redirect other computers' traffic to themselves. This is done by modifying routing tables and fooling network equipment, which is more difficult to implement.

To understand how active sniffing works, you have to understand how packets are transmitted at the low layers. To transfer packets on the Internet, network devices use IP addresses. If the destination IP address is within the current network, the packet is delivered using the MAC address; otherwise, it is sent to the default gateway, which is either a router or a computer forwarding packets to the router. The router uses the packet's IP address to determine the necessary destination network. When such a network is found, the packet is passed to this network, where it is delivered to the destination by its MAC address.

Spoofing the MAC Address

Thus, inside networks, packets are addressed using only the MAC address. This is because network cards, hubs, and most switches work only with MAC addresses.

Here is where the OSI model comes into the play. Network cards, hubs, and most switches operate on the level of the data link layer. Receiving a packet, they check its data link header, operating only with MAC addresses. These devices can neither see nor understand other layer headers. Routers and more advanced (third-layer) switches disassemble packets to the network layer, where IP addresses are used.

Thus, within a network that has no third-layer switches, packets can only be addressed using MAC addresses. But how is it done exactly? Users never specify the MAC address, and you cannot simply place a packet on the network addressed using the IP address.

How, then, does the source computer find out the MAC address of the destination computer? It first sends a broadcast request to all computers in the network, asking something like this: Whose IP address is *XXX.XXX.XXX.XXX*? The request is sent using ARP. Also, packets are addressed using a special broadcast address as the destination MAC address, and all network cards must accept such packets and pass them for processing to the operating system. The operating system examines the packet on the network-layer level, where ARP is employed. If the IP address being inquired about belongs to the particular computer, the operating system replies to the requester informing it about its MAC address. Now the source computer has the IP address mapped to the MAC address.

But what is to prevent your computer to answer ARP requests directed to another computer and pass itself off as that computer? Nothing. ARP does not have any authentication mechanism. It blindly accepts any replies to any ARP requests without further questions.

But this is not the worst thing. The source operating system caches responses to its ARP requests, and the next time it has a message to a resolved IP address, it does not send a broadcast ARP request but uses the cached MAC-mapping information. And here is the worst thing. Some operating systems (I will not name names) cache not only replies to its own ARP requests but also replies to ARP requests issued by any other host. Thus, a hacker's computer can send ARP replies mapping its MAC address to another computer's IP address to all network's computers, and they will cache this fake MAC-to-IP mapping information.

You can view the current ARP cache by executing the `arp` command. The results of its execution look similar to the following:

```
Address         HWtype  HWaddress          Flags   Mask    Iface
192.168.77.10   ether   00:03:0D:06:A4:6C  C               eth0
```

The most interesting columns are the following:

- `Address` — The computer's IP address
- `HWtype` — The remote device type
- `HWaddress` — The MAC address of the remote device
- `Iface` — The network interface

Thus, if a host has to address a computer with the IP address 192.168.77.10, it uses its ARP table to determine that the computer with this address can be found at the `eth0` network interface and that its hardware (network card's) address is 00:03:0D:06:A4:6C.

If you discover fake IP-to-MAC mapping information in the ARP table, you should delete it; afterwards, you can use the MAC address to find the miscreant.

You can delete entries from the ARP table by executing the `arp` command with the `-d` option and specifying the necessary IP address. For example, the ARP entry in the preceding example can be deleted as follows:

```
arp -d 192.168.77.10
```

This will result in the MAC address being replaced with (`incomplete`):

```
Address         HWtype  HWaddress          Flags   Mask    Iface
192.168.77.10           (incomplete)                       eth0
```

ARP table entries added to the cache by ARP are dynamic, meaning they are periodically deleted. Hackers know this and may periodically mail fake ARP replies. So simply deleting fake entries from the ARP table will not be effective. You have to find and go after the miscreant.

You can use Reverse ARP (RARP) for this. This protocol requests the IP address from a known MAC address. You should receive replies from all IP addresses, for which there are entries in your ARP table. Keep in mind that more than one IP address can be mapped to one MAC address. For example, the network card on my computer has two IP addresses mapped to its MAC address to work in two logical networks concurrently. So this is a normal situation. But if a certain IP address does not answer, you should delete the corresponding entry in the ARP table.

For working with ARP tables in Windows, I recommend using the CyD NET Utils utility (**www.cydsoft.com**).

Keep it in mind, however, that it is difficult to spoof ARP mapping in Windows. Broadcasting fake ARP replies mapping IP address 192.168.77.1 to your MAC address will result in the computer with this IP address issuing an error message that this address is already used by another network device and disconnecting from the network. This can be avoided by sending fake ARP replies to only one computer instead of broadcasting them.

Sending fake ARP replies is a rather involved task. It is much easier to simply change the network card's MAC address if its driver supports this operation. This can be done using the already familiar `ifconfig` utility with the `wh` option followed by the hardware class and the new MAC address.

If switches can be easily fooled by using fake ARP entries, this is not the case with routers. Routing devices operate on the network layer level, that is, on the IP address level. To fool routers, faking MAC addresses will not do; it takes faking IP addresses. For this purpose, hackers break into routers and reprogram them to serve their needs.

The only way to resist fake ARP information is by employing programmable switches to organize the network. These switches can permanently assign a certain MAC address to each of its ports. But this is only a partial solution to the fake ARP reply problem.

The complete solution is to use static ARP table entries, that is, to manually fill out the ARP table on each client computer. But this is not that convenient to put into practice, because ARP tables on all computers will have to be edited when there is any network equipment change on a single computer. It's alright if you have, say, five or even ten computers in the network, but what if there are dozens or even hundreds of them? Every time you add or replace a network card, you will have to update the ARP tables on all of the network's computers.

To facilitate the task of manually updating ARP tables, you can create a script. The script is located on the server, and each client should run it at booting.

Flooding Switches

Hubs are devices that replicate all traffic that arrives to the incoming port to all outgoing ports. Switches are intelligent devices that route incoming packets to their corresponding MAC addresses. This means that a switch will send an incoming packet only to the port, to which the packet's recipient is connected, not to the rest of its ports.

Thus, sniffing is impossible on a network built using switches. But switches have one peculiar feature: When a switch cannot analyze all packets it receives, it switches to operating as a simple concentrator, replicating all incoming packets to all computers connected to it.

So you have to flood the switch with so much traffic that it switches into the broadcasting mode. The best way of doing this is by throwing a bunch of packets with wrong MAC addresses at the switch. It takes too much of the switch's resources to analyze such packets, and it cannot handle the workload.

The only way to defend against switch flooding is by using more powerful equipment. At present, switches from 3Com and Cisco are sufficiently powerful to handle even the maximum load of fake packets. I haven't had an opportunity to test equipment from other manufacturers.

Fooling Routers

Routers can also be fooled; to be more exact, computers acting as routers can be fooled. Suppose that your network consists of several subnetworks connected using routers. Fig. 14.2 shows an example of such a network.

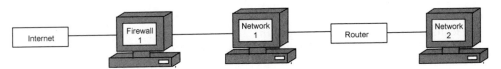

Fig. 14.2. A network with two routers

If a computer from Network 1 sends a packet to another computer in the same network, this packet, as you know, is forwarded using the MAC address without resorting to the routers. If a packet is addressed to another network, it is sent to the default gateway. Suppose that such a default gateway is the firewall computer. In this case, if the packet is addressed to the Internet, the firewall computer forwards it there without much ado. But if the packet is addressed to a computer in Network 2, the firewall computer will not necessarily forward it to the router. The firewall, acting as the default router, may send an ICMP message to the source computer, suggesting that it negotiate directly with the router connecting Network 1 to Network 2.

Because ICMP does not employ any authentication or encryption mechanisms, hackers can send such a message to any computer, asking it to use their computer instead of the legitimate router. This will give them the opportunity to view all traffic.

I recommend disabling the routing redirection feature by means of writing 1 to the /proc/sys/net/ipv4/conf/all/accept_redirects file. This is done by executing the following command:

```
echo 1 > /proc/sys/net/ipv4/conf/all/accept_redirects
```

This parameter can also be changed by adding the following line to the /etc/sysctl.conf file:

```
nt.ipv4.conf.all.accept_redirection=0
```

If there is only one router in your network, disabling routing redirection will only enhance the system's security. But even if there are more routers in the network, the network operation will not be affected much. At the worst, traffic will have to go through two routers instead of taking the direct route.

Because ICMP is necessary for carrying out the routing redirection attack, this protocol can be prohibited by configuring the firewall accordingly. This will make it impossible for hackers to send messages to redirect routing.

14.5.4. Hijacking the Connection

The first computer attack using connection hijack was carried out several decades ago. But even now, the only effective method to oppose this attack is to encode packets. At the initial stage of establishing a TCP connection between computers, two counters are created that are incremented with each sent packet. These counters can be intercepted with the help of network sniffers, and at a certain moment hackers can hijack the connection, becoming its owner and replacing the legitimate client in communications with the server. The legitimate client loses the connection.

In this way, hackers circumvent all authorization mechanisms. The legal client is initially authorized at the server, but then its connection is hijacked by hackers, who use it for their own purposes.

The reason for the connection vulnerability lies in the TCP/IP suite being obsolete. Its creators did not anticipate that someone may eavesdrop on network traffic or try to take over the connection. The problem is expected to be solved with the introduction of IPv6.

14.5.5. Protecting against Eavesdropping

Even though it is possible to detect that you are being eavesdropped on, sometimes this knowledge may come too late. While you are discovering the hackers, they may intercept packets with passwords and break into the system. If sniffing is being conducted by a program installed on a zombie computer, you will be able to find out only this computer and its owner but not the hacker who installed the sniffer program.

Consequently, detecting sniffing and going after the perpetrator is not effective against sniffing. You should make sniffing unproductive for hackers so that they would not even think about resorting to it. The way to achieve this is to encrypt all traffic.

You cannot trust the network and send your data in plaintext over it. The times when networks were used only by professionals and only as intended are long gone. Nowadays, you can meet all kinds of people on the Internet, from children to retirees, from school students to scientists. What is more pertinent, there are not only good guys out there but also those bent on mischief.

In *Section 5.2*, techniques to encrypt any service communications were considered. Thus, you can encrypt any connection — and must do this if confidential information is being transmitted.

But before you start encrypting channels on your own, look around for an existing solution. For example, there already exists an HTTP version that supports encryption: HTTPS. You can use HTTP for transmitting public data, such as Web pages, and use HTTPS for transmitting confidential data, such as credit card numbers.

Even if hackers intercept a packet with encrypted data, they will not be able to decrypt it right away unless they have the private key, which is extremely unlikely. They can attempt to break the key, but this process will take too much time; by the time the packet is decrypted, if it is decrypted, its data will be of no value. Moreover, the data may be of no interest to the hackers to start with, but to find this out they will have to spend time decrypting it.

14.5.6. Sniffing Tools

Reading this chapter, you may get the impression that sniffing is inherently harmless and is exclusively a tool of hackers. It may even seem that hardware manufacturers ought to make their equipment sniffing-proof on the hardware level.

This is not quite the case. Sniffer software was initially developed as a programmer and administrator tool, and it is a handy means for debugging various protocols.

I will not consider all sniffer programs, because there are many of them and each has its own advantages and disadvantages. But I can recommend taking a look at my favorite and one of the most powerful of such programs: hunt. It can be used to monitor traffic, replace ARP records, and even intercept connections.

Another popular and in some cases more convenient is the dsniff utility package. This package comprises more than ten utilities and can be used to solve any task, both by administrators and hackers. A more detailed description of the package is given in *Appendix 2.*

14.6. DoS and DDoS Attacks

One of the most destructive attacks is the DoS attack. In my opinion, this is the stupidest thing that hackers could come up with. When they cannot break into a server, they try to put it out of commission by various methods, including flooding its communication links with trash messages.

As you should remember, the idea of a DoS attack is to make the server unavailable to legitimate clients. There are various ways of achieving this, and the main ones will be considered in this section. The DDoS attack is a variation of the DoS attack that uses multiple computers to carry it out.

The worst thing about these attacks is that sometimes it is impossible to protect against them, especially against the DDoS variety. If the number of requests received by a server exceeds the number it can handle, it will no longer be able to handle other requests and even crash. Imagine if all computers on the planet simultaneously addressed the most powerful server (a server cluster). There is simply no communications channel with the bandwidth capable to let through so many connections, so even such powerful servers as **www.yahoo.com** and **www.google.com** will not be able to handle this flood of requests, or, rather, their data links won't be. In this way, users attempting to hit the site will not be able to do so.

The following are short descriptions of the main DoS and DDoS attacks and ways of protecting against them.

14.6.1. Ping of Death

You already know that the ping utility is used for checking connections with remote systems using ICMP. When the server being tested receives an ICMP echo request message, it has to respond with an ICMP echo response message.

Some operating systems could not handle certain types of ping packets. The reason is that developers of ICMP never anticipated that it might be used in ways other than intended and did not take any steps to protect against such uses. In particular, the protocol expected users to send packets only of a certain size. The reliance on users' conscientiousness turned out to be misplaced and resulted in the Ping of Death attack. For this attack, packets are formed that do not follow the protocol specifications. Servers cannot process such packets and hang. The most notorious attack was the one implemented by sending a packet more than 64 KB in size. If only 64 KB are reserved to receive data, this is not sufficient to receive oversized packets and the server hangs. Thus, this is essentially a variety of the buffer overflow attack.

The only defense against such attacks is to use a firewall configured to prohibit receiving ICMP echo request packets. All new operating systems and appropriately patched older ones are not susceptible to this attack.

14.6.2. ICMP Flood

Another variety of the DoS attack is ICMP flood, in which, as the name suggests, the server is simply flooding the target with ICMP packets. The perpetrator only needs a channel half the bandwidth of the channel of the attacked system.

Thus, to fully load a 64-Kb/sec bandwidth channel, hackers only need a 32-Kb/sec bandwidth channel. The attack is carried out by simply sending an uninterrupted stream of ping packets to the server. (If hackers want to remain anonymous, they'll have to take care that their real IP address is not shown in the packets.) If hackers load 32 Kb of the server channel's bandwidth with ping messages, the other half will be loaded with the server's replies to these messages, effectively taking the service out of commission and making it unavailable to service legitimate requests.

The defense against this attack is the same as against the Ping of Death attack, namely, prohibiting ICMP traffic. This will not result in much inconvenience, because this protocol is not really necessary, especially for incoming Internet traffic.

14.6.3. TCP SYN

The number of connections that most servers can open is limited. In some cases, this has to do with the limitations of the technology used, but these can also be software limitations imposed by the configuration settings of a particular server.

The attack's essence consists of sending numerous TCP packets with the SYN flag set to the server. Packets of this type are used to establish server connections. Once the limit on the number of in-progress open connections is reached, the server stops responding to requests for new connections.

This sort of attack is practically impossible to defend against by your own means. You can configure the firewall to prohibit SYN packets, but this will be of little use.

As a temporary solution, the size of the in-progress connection queue can be increased by modifying the configuration file accordingly. This will not increase the server workload, because connections are only initialized and do not load the server with any requests or traffic. But the number of in-progress connections is not always controlled by a configuration file and may be hard-set by the software's technology.

Another way to fight off this attack is to decrease the timeout length for partially-open connections. Some programs allow the timeout length of a partially-open connection to be changed by modifying the corresponding parameter in the configuration file. Decreasing the timeout length to 10 seconds will make it impossible to flood the server with SYN packets, because although new connection requests are placed into the in-progress connection queue, old ones in the queue will time out and be removed from the queue. This may create problems with establishing connections for legitimate users, who may have to try to establish a connection with the server several times, but at least the server will not be paralyzed and will remain mostly functional.

The best defense can only be implemented programmatically. At the least, the program should offer an option to change the size of the in-progress connection queue and the timeout for partially-open connections. It should also give an option for prohibiting establishing several connections from the same IP address.

14.6.4. TCP Flood

This attack is similar to the ICMP flood attack. If a hacker is not smart enough to find a vulnerability in the system, he or she may decide to flood the server with trash TCP packets. The efficiency of TCP packets is sometimes lower than that of ICMP packets. While with ping echo requests the server pinged is required to answer with echo response messages, with TCP the response messages are not always required. Consequently, the hacker's channel must be of the same bandwidth or even wider than that of the system being attacked.

Using HTTP attackers can overload a server even if their own communications link is narrower than that of the target. This is achieved by sending the server requests that require the server to dedicate numerous resources to processing them. For example, a server can be overloaded by loading its search system with a large number of requests to search for especially popular words. If the server's search scripts are not programmed efficiently, processing these requests will take long enough to make the server unavailable to service other requests.

HTTP can be used to flood a server with requests to download a large file. Combined with ineffective caching, this can make the server unavailable to servicing legitimate requests.

But TCP has an advantage. In most networks, outside ICMP traffic is blocked by firewalls, but TCP traffic to public resources cannot be blocked if such resources are to remain available to the public.

It is impossible to pull off a successful attack on a powerful server from a single computer, but it is quite possible to carry out any sort of attack using a large number of computers.

14.6.5. UDP

Bugs in UDP programs are especially dangerous, because this protocol does not establish a virtual connection. This protocol simply sends packets into the network and has no data authenticity-verification mechanisms. While it is difficult to fake IP address in TCP communications, doing this with UDP communications is too easy.

Fortunately, UDP is seldom used on public servers and it can be prohibited by appropriate firewall settings. If the protocol is necessary, protection can only be implemented programmatically by creating some sort of UDP-based authenticity check of received packets.

14.6.7. DDoS Attack

It can be said that DoS attacks with a future are the DDoS attacks. Bugs in programs that made it possible to disable a server with a few packets are getting fewer every day, because programmers are devoting more attention to security aspects when writing network programs. But DDoS attacks do not rely that much on bugs, and there is no really effective and universal defense against this type of attack.

However, it is difficult to implement a really massive DDoS attack, and large companies even used to think that such attacks were practically impossible. Even the largest hacker group with the widest bandwidth channels cannot approach the computational resources of such servers as **www.yahoo.com** or **www.microsoft.com**. But where is a will, there is a way, and hackers keep on coming up with new tricks.

An excellent example of a successful DDoS attack is the one perpetrated using the MyDoom worm. Starting on August 22, 2003, for 3 days this worm was attacking the site of the SCO software company from numerous infected Internet computers. Some time later, a similar attack on the Microsoft site was attempted using the MyDoom.B virus. The second attack was less effective; I say this because there were fewer computers infected with this worm on the Internet, and the worm's code was far from the ideal.

DDoS attacks often are carried out using powerful zombied machines with wide bandwidth channels. This gives hackers all they need for successful DDoS resources.

We can expect new, more effective, and original DDoS attacks in the future. Administrators are powerless to prevent such attacks, and here law-enforcement agencies should step in.

14.6.8. Effective DoS Attack

If you consult Bugtraq frequently, you should notice that bugs that can be used to carry out DoS attacks crop up regularly in network programs. These bugs are often of the buffer-overflow type that can be used to disable a server.

The buffer-overflow issue was covered in *Section 14.2*, and you already know that these errors can be dealt with without even waiting for the software bugs to be fixed. All that has to be done is to patch the kernel prohibiting code from the stack to be executed.

A strange thing is that the number of bugs does not decrease with time. Identical errors can be found in different programs — sometimes committed by the same programmers. Buffer-overflow problems are well described in voluminous literature, yet programmers continue to make the same old mistakes. This is telling about the low quality of programmer education.

I believe that the low quality of software is due to outsourcing programming, especially from underdeveloped countries. The general education level in many of these countries is low, and many workers are ready to work for low wages. Software-developing companies are attracted by the low-wage factor but overlook the poor-education one. As a result, administrators constantly have to deal with the same problems in different software.

The problem can be solved if software-developing companies start to use higher-quality human resources.

Linux is an open-source operating system, and any homegrown programmer can make changes to it. Back when Linux was being developed by many different Linux enthusiasts, it contained many bugs because of the lack of systemized quality control.

Currently, few distributions are created by hodgepodge efforts. All programmers who wanted to produce quality software have organized companies and instituted strict quality control. Now changes proposed by a lone programmer will make it into an official distribution only if the distribution's developer decides that the code is safe and useful. This contributes to the overall reliability of Linux; however, this reliability does not extend to its individual components.

14.6.9. DoS and DDoS Defense

As usual, the most effective defense against DoS attacks based on software bugs is updating software regularly. But attacks directed at overloading server resources are difficult to defend against. Still, you can make it more difficult for the hacker.

First, the server's weakest point has to be determined. This is done by making the server work at the maximum workload. This can be achieved by recruiting lots of users to access the server as frequently as possible, or by running a special program emulating this process.

When the computer is working at the maximum workload, check which resources are in short supply. Take note of the following aspects:

- ❏ The network's bandwidth
- ❏ The bandwidths of the network equipment
- ❏ The processor workload
- ❏ The hard-drive workload
- ❏ The operating memory workload

Determine the spots in your system that can become bottlenecks, and take steps to fortify them. It would make no sense to build up your external communication channels to 100-Mb/sec bandwidth if you local network works only at 10 Mb/sec. Hitting the server with 10 Mb/sec of traffic will consume all your local network resources no matter how wide your outside channel is. This is why it is so important to determine the potential bottlenecks in your system.

Configure your network interfaces and the operating system for the maximum productivity (see *Section 14.11*). This means that there should be no resource waste, especially of the network resources. The expenditures for processing network traffic and the traffic itself can be reduced by completely prohibiting ICMP traffic.

14.7. Penetration through Trusted Systems

When hackers cannot penetrate a system via its server, most often they resort to looking for weak spots in trusted computers in the network. Not all computers in a network can be protected equally well, and hackers will attempt to find one that will yield to their probes.

When looking for vulnerable spots in a system, you have to establish IP addresses of all computers in the network. This can be done using the classical `ping` utility, manually pinging each IP address of the target network. A better way, however, is to use the `nmap` utility, which can scan a specified IP address range automatically.

A range of IP addresses can be scanned by issuing the following command:

```
nmap -sP 192.168.1.0/24
```

The IP address is followed by the net mask specifying how many of the address bits define the network ID. In this case, all computers in the network are specified. This will make the program send a ping request to all IP addresses in the network and will show, which of them are used by computers.

Using the ping packets is a handy and quick way to scan a network, but it can produce incorrect results if the target network is protected by a firewall configured to prohibit ping packets.

Thus, if you are an administrator and have no special need for using ping packets, you should configure your firewall to filter them out. But a firewall can only protect the network from outside scanning. To protect against scanning originating within the network, each of the network's computers has to be equipped with a properly-configured firewall. You could disable the service that responds to ping requests, but there is nothing that can be done about port scanning.

After the IP addresses of all computers in the network have been determined, each of these computers is scanned for vulnerable services. It is much easier to break into a network than into a single computer, because at least one of the network's computers will yield to a determined assault.

After breaking into one of the network's computers, the network can be scanned for computers again, this time from the compromised machine. This scanning may produce more precise results because it is not hindered by the firewall.

Having obtained control over one of the network's computers, further taking over the network becomes easier because of the following factors:

❑   The computer broken into may have trusted relations with the server. In Linux, computers can be specified that can be trusted; that is, they can connect to the server without undergoing the authentication procedure. Never use trusted relations, because this is a huge blow to security. This is why the subject of using trusted relations is not considered in this book.

❑   The login password for the compromised computer may be the same as that for the main server. Also, the /etc/passwd file often contains information for users that work with the server. Users normally don't like remembering the password for each server or computer and use the same parameters for connecting to any computer in the network.

There is no guarantee that information will contain the login information for the main server administrator. But quite often all you need is to get your foot in a cracked door to take over the whole system.

Regular users are not the only ones using the same password for accessing different servers; administrators also are guilty of this practice. For example, an administrator may change the user name for a different server but use the same password. Hackers collect all passwords they come across and then use them to crack the root password.

To tell the truth, I am guilty of using the same password for different services. I, however, use a different login password for each system. I only use the same password when using harmless services, for example, when registering on forums or on sites collecting some statistics.

You should protect each computer equally well and use different passwords for users who have root privileges.

14.8. Dangerous Network File System

The Network File System (NFS) was developed by Sun Microsystems in 1989. The idea behind it was great. Any user can mount a server's directories in his or her file system and use them as if they were located on the user's machine. This is a handy feature for networks. User catalogs can be located on the server and can be connected to the client machine as required. In this way, all files are stored in one central location but can be used as if they were located on a local machine.

But, as I have already said, convenience and security are two incompatible things, and NFS is just too convenient. NFS includes the showmount utility to show, which directories are mounted by which users. This is important information for administrators. Executing the showmount -a localhost command produces information similar to the following:

```
All mount points on localhost:
robert:/home/robert
econom:/home/john
buh:/home/andrew
roberet:/usr/local/etc
econom:/usr/games
```

The entries consist of two fields separated by a colon. The first field contains the name of the computer, on which the partition is mounted; the second field shows the path to the mounted resource on the server.

Although it is handy to have an option for displaying such detailed information, it is also dangerous because the command can be executed remotely. Thus, any hacker can execute it and obtain the following information:

❑ In the preceding example, various directories from the /home partition are mounted. Most often, directory names coincide with user names. This makes it easy to determine the actual user names on a given system without consulting the /etc/passwd file. Knowing user names makes it much easier to pick passwords for them.

❑ The list shows the names of the network's computers. If you have gone to great lengths to secure your DNS server, you nullify all of your efforts by running NFS on one of the servers. One command will show the names of the network's computers. Even though not all computers will be shown, but only those working with NFS, this information may be enough for the hacker. This makes probing the network with ping requests unnecessary, because the computers in the network are already shown.

❑ In Linux, program directories can be named as the program name and its version, for example ./jail 1.0. If any of such directories is mounted, the hacker can find out what programs users work with and, most important, the program versions.

Depending on which directories are mounted, much more information can be gathered. Thus, NFS utilities disclose too much information, which should not be allowed.

If you decide to use NFS, take care that it is not available from the Internet. For this, you will have to configure the firewall to prohibit outside connections to the UDP and TCP port 2049. But the firewall will only protect the system from outside connections. If hackers have already broken into one of the network's computers and can execute commands within the network, the firewall will be of little use.

The /etc/exports file contains a list of directories that may be shared with NFS clients, the clients that can share these directories, and the clients' access rights. Never allow complete access to the entire system. For this, make sure that the file does not contain the following entry:

```
/        rw
```

The paths to the directories allowed to be mounted by a user should be explicitly specified. If users are allowed to mount home directories, the /home rw permission is dangerous and should not be used.

Why is it dangerous? Not all user home directories should be allowed to be mounted remotely. For example, if you are an administrator but work under a user account, there may be a program used to administer the system in your user home directory. This directory should not be accessible to unauthorized people, even for viewing. Allow only specific users that actually mount their file systems remotely to connect, as in the following example:

```
/home/Robert       rw
/home/FlenovM      rw
/home/Aubrey       rw
```

Most security specialists share the opinion that NFS should not be used. If you decided to use it only because software on the workstations was centrally installed, you should overcome your laziness and install software on each computer individually.

If the documentation has to be publicly available so that users could share one directory, you can consider using the Samba network service. This service is not as talkative and may offer a solution to your needs to share server directories.

14.9. Detecting Break-ins

Timely break-in detection is important for organizing effective server defense. The earlier you find out that your system has been penetrated, the earlier you will be able react and avert negative consequences of the break-in. Remember that any system can be, and likely has been, broken into, but you should be able to detect these break-ins.

How can you go about this? There are many methods. I will consider the most interesting and effective of them.

4.9.1. Aware Means Protected

I often use an effective but difficult-to-implement method, which consists of informing the administrator when potentially dangerous programs are launched. The difficulty of the method is that you have to know how to program in Linux in at least one language. The preferable language is C, but Perl will also do. As a last resort, being able to write scripts (batch files) will suffice.

So, what does this method consist of? After entering the system, the hacker always starts looking around and trying to find a way to fortify his or her positions to remain in the system as long as possible and unnoticeable to the administrator. To this end, the hacker most often uses the who, su, cat, and similar commands. Your task is to place traps on these commands. For example, the code of the su program can be changed so that a message is mailed to the administrator every time it is invoked.

A message that a high-risk command has been executed by a user other than the administrator is a good cause to check the system for the presence of an intruder in it.

If you cannot program, you can manage only with the operating system means. Suppose that you want to be informed every time the who command is executed. Hackers often execute this command upon entering the system to find out whether the administrator is currently logged in. The directory, in which the command is located, can be found by executing the following command:

```
which who
```

The displayed path will usually be /usr/bin/who.
Next, find out the file permissions by executing the following command:

```
ls -al /usr/bin/who
```

The permissions for the who command file should be -rwxr-xr-x, or 755 in the numerical notation.

Rename the /usr/bit/who file as /usr/bin/system_who. This is done by executing the following commands:

```
mv /usr/bin/who /usr/bin/system_who
chmod 755 /usr/bin/system_who
```

Now, to execute the who command, it has to be invoked as system_who. The new file may become unexecutable, so the second command restores its file permissions.

Now create a dummy for the who file. This will be a file named who in the /usr/bin directory that will be executed when the who command is called. This is created by first executing the following command:

```
cat /usr/bin/who
```

Now, everything entered from the console will be recorded into the /usr/bin/who file. Enter the following two lines:

```
/usr/bin/system_who
id | mail -n -s attack root@FlenovM
```

Exit the entry mode and save the file by pressing the <Ctrl>+<D> key combination. Change the file permissions of the just-created who file to -rwxr-xr-x, or 755 in the numerical notation.

Execute the who command. This will produce the expected results but also will send a letter to the administrator's mailbox. The letter will contain all parameters about the user who invoked the command as returned by the id command (Fig. 14.3).

The mechanism that produces this result functions as follows: When the who command is invoked, the custom who file is executed. This file contains two commands.

The first command — /usr/bin/system_who — executes the real system file who renamed as system_who.

The second command — id | mail -n -s attack root@FlenovM — executes the id command and redirects its results to the mail program mail, which in turn sends them to the **root@FlenovM** mailbox. The -s option specifies the subject of the letter. The -n option inhibits reading of the /etc/mail.rc file upon the mail program start-up. I recommend specifying only these two options so that nothing would be displayed to alert the hacker that something is not right when the modified who command is executed.

In this way, all high-risk programs that should not be available to regular users can be modified.

Hackers most often do not check the utilities they launch, even though the telltale information can be readily discovered by executing the regular cat command:

```
cat /usr/bin/who
```

This is where the shortcoming of using scripts becomes apparent: They can be viewed as regular text files. Programs written in C and then compiled into an executable file can show only the queer garbage when viewed in a text editor or other text viewers.

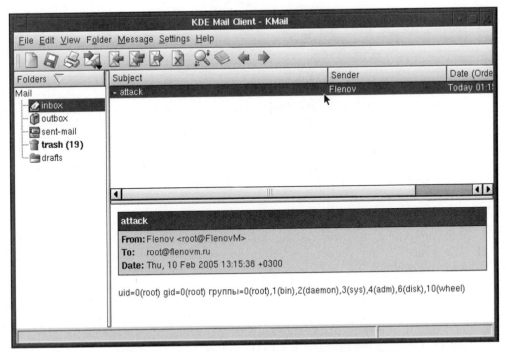

Fig. 14.3. An example of an attack notification email

4.9.2. Honey Pot

In *Section 4.11.7*, I considered the subject of organizing a network, in which the public resources are hosted on separate servers and are protected separately from the main network. I also touched upon the subject of creating sham servers to throw hackers off track. In this chapter, I will consider the subject of sham servers and networks, known as "honey pot" technology in the parlance, in more detail.

Its essence is as follows: A computer, or even a subnet of computers, is set up in a network that is filled with information to attract hackers' attention but that is useless. The computer, or the network, is made relatively easy to crack. The main function of such a computer or network is to track outside access and to register any break-ins.

Fig. 14.4 shows how a classical honey-pot network is organized. This network is protected from the Internet by a firewall. Behind the firewall are public resources and sham servers and workstations. This sham network is separated from the actual private network by another firewall.

When a hacker swallows the bait and starts rummaging in the honey-pot network, administrators can investigate where he or she came from without running the risk of destroying important data.

Fig. 14.4. Honey-pot network construction

To prevent your trap from snatching everyone who touches, as well as from generating false alarms, its protections should be hard enough not to be circumvented by hackers using exploit programs. Otherwise, there will be hundreds, if not more, hackers caught in it every day, because a popular resource is scanned countless times daily.

I configure my honey-pot servers for maximum security but let the firewall protecting them (Firewall 1 in Fig. 14.4) pass practically all traffic into the public network. This kills several birds with one stone:

- ☐ Hacker's suspicions are not aroused. A professional will immediately become suspicious if the protection is too weak and will not touch such a network with a ten-foot pole.
- ☐ The system is not triggered by every beginning hacker who is using commonly-available exploits.
- ☐ If the honey-pot system, which is protected as well as the real system, has been broken into, this means that the private network is also vulnerable. I can learn about this vulnerability by examining the techniques used by the hacker to penetrate the honey-pot network. In this way, attacks unknown to the security community until now can be detected and defense methods against such attacks can be devised.

As soon as I notice that the honey-pot server has been compromised, I undertake the following steps:

- ☐ Analyze the vulnerability used by the hacker to obtain access. Having found the weak spot, I look for a patch and install it on the computers in the private network, to prevent the hacker from using this vulnerability to break into the sensitive area.
- ☐ Determine the source of the break-in, such as the IP address or street address, and pass all this information on to law-enforcement agencies.

Because honey-pot systems do not process actual user requests, they do not require powerful hardware. Obsolete hardware that no longer can be used for modern applications will suffice. Any administrator always has old junk piled up in the office and used for spare parts.

If you don't have any old computers, you can use public servers for the honey-pot network. In essence, public servers are already supposed to maintain powerful monitoring and logging systems, differing from honey-pot servers only in that they should not have known vulnerabilities and easy passwords.

To prevent hackers from suspecting trickery and make them interested in the honey-pot systems, equipping such a system with strong defense is not enough. The computers have to do something and process some traffic. This can be achieved with the help of specially-developed utilities that imitate network operation on the honey-pot system. A computer that is just sitting there doing nothing sticks out like a sore thumb, and only a dummy will try to break into it.

14.10. Cracking Passwords

There are two methods of picking passwords: by using a dictionary and by trying all possible combinations. In addition, passwords can be cracked remotely or locally.

14.10.1. The Dictionary Method

First, a file with words most commonly used for passwords is prepared. Next, a password-picking program tries each of the words in the file against the login password.

The advantage of this method is that if the password is in the dictionary, it can be found quite quickly. If the password is a simple word that can be found in any English dictionary, the number of possible passwords will not exceed 20,000, the approximate number of the most often used words in the English language.

The hacker's task is to prepare the dictionary using the most effective potential passwords. First, all possible information about the administrator is collected: his or her name; the names of his or her spouse, friend, relatives, and pets; hobbies; favorite music and movies; and so on. Passwords built based on this information are placed in the beginning of the dictionary. Practice shows that most people use passwords of this type, and most often those related to their hobbies.

But the chance that a strong password, which is made up of digits and symbols in addition to letter and uses both uppercase and lowercase characters, will be included in the dictionary approaches zero; consequently, the time spent picking the password using a dictionary will be wasted. In this case, the enumeration, or brute-force, method is resorted to.

14.10.2. The Brute-Force Method

The program goes through all possible combinations of letters, digits, and symbols in both uppercase and lowercase. There are billions of possible combinations, the exact number depending on the password length. The longer the password, the more possible combinations there are and the more time needed to pick it.

The method is 100% successful. But this method is time-consuming; it can take weeks to months, if not years, to crack a really strong password. Moreover, if passwords are changed monthly, when a hacker cracks a password, it may no longer be valid.

14.10.3. Cracking Remote Passwords

A hacker tries to crack the password when logging into a system remotely. This is the most dangerous method for the hacker, because each unsuccessful attempt is recorded in a security log. If the administrator at least occasionally inspects the log, the break-in attempt will be discovered in the early stages and nipped in the bud by prohibiting connections from the hacker's IP address.

Another problem with remote password cracking is that the password discovered will be to a certain service only and there is no guarantee that another service will use the same password. To make password cracking more difficult, most services are configured to limit the number of password entry attempts, for example, to three. If no correct password is supplied within three attempts, the connection is broken off and has to be established again. Establishing a connection takes extra time, which also increases the time necessary to crack the password using the dictionary method.

To make password cracking a lengthy process, some services insert a delay after an incorrectly-entered password before allowing another login attempt. A good example of this is the operating system. When an incorrect login or password is supplied when logging into the system, the verification process takes longer than when the correct parameters are provided. The delay may seem insignificant when you simply mistype a parameter once, but it adds up when you are going through thousands of variations.

The delay is easy to bypass by launching several threads of a password-cracking program, which will connect to the server and try to crack the password in parallel.

The most effective method to prevent multithread cracking is to configure the firewall to prohibit connections to the server from this IP address.

14.10.4. Cracking Local Passwords

Because it is so difficult to crack passwords remotely, hackers strive to obtain a copy of the /etc/shadow file so that they can work on breaking the passwords it contains on their own machines. In this case, the process is much faster for the following reasons:

- ❐   The real names of the users registered on the server are known.
- ❐   The server-protection mechanisms against password cracking are no longer effective.
- ❐   Because passwords in the file are encrypted, each possible password also has to be encrypted before it is compared with the password stored in the file. The encryption process adds to the overall time necessary to crack a password; however, its negative effects depend on the number of passwords in the file. Instead of trying all possible password combinations against one encrypted password, each combination is first tried against all entries in the password file. The greater the number of password entries in the file, the higher the chances that the combination will fit one of them.
- ❐   Also, the larger the password file is, the greater the chances are that at least one of the users chose the account name for the password.

Local password cracking is much faster and safer for the hacker than the remote method. But it has its own problem, which is obtaining the /etc/shadow file. The only user that has the read and write rights to this file is the administrator, with the rest of the users having no rights to it.

14.10.5. Protecting against Password Cracking

In principle, there is not, and can't be, 100% protection against password cracking. If a hacker obtains access to the /etc/shadow file, you can take it for granted that at least one password will be broken. But you can make password cracking more difficult or prevent its negative effects by following these rules:

☐ Change passwords monthly. If hackers are cracking passwords remotely, this can make hitting the right combination impossible. If hackers are cracking passwords locally, by the time they pick a password it may already have been changed.

☐ Check your passwords for resistance against the dictionary method. Make users change passwords vulnerable to picking.

☐ Use strong passwords to make password picking by the dictionary method impossible.

☐ Protect the /etc/shadow file by all possible means. Although all users have to have read access rights to the /etc/passwd file to be able to use numerous utilities, they have no need for the /etc/shadow file.

☐ Regularly examine the security log for an abnormal number of failed system logins.

Following these rules, you will lower the chances of your system being broken into by the brute-force method of password cracking.

In *Section 2.6*, I mentioned the importance of choosing strong passwords and offered some recommendations on how to create them. Now I want to offer another interesting method using encryption. It works as follows:

☐ Create a file named, for example, pass.txt, and enter into it the text to be used as the password. For example: `echo "password" >> pass.txt`.

☐ Encrypt the file by executing the following command: `openssl des -in pass.txt -out pass.txt.s`. The key to be used for encrypting does not matter; you can enter any word.

☐ The text saved in the pass.txt file will be encrypted and saved in the pass.txt.s file. Open this file, choose readable characters, and build a password from them. This password cannot be cracked using the dictionary method; the brute-force method has to be used.

An excellent method for protecting against remote password breaking can be using PAMs, considered in *Section 3.3*. One such module is /lib/security/pam_tally.so. It blocks access after a certain number of unsuccessful login attempts. Consider using the module on an example of Linux login authorization. The login configuration settings are stored in the /etc/pam.d/login file. To limit the number of attempts on entering the password to five, add the following entry to the file:

```
account required /lib/security/pam_tally.so deny=5 no_magic_root
```

Five is the optimal number. Giving users fewer chances may cause problems for especially forgetful users. But unless a user suffers from amnesia, if the correct password is not entered after five tries, there is a good chance that password breaking is taking place.

14.10.6. John the Ripper

Now it's time to consider some practical password-cracking techniques. This is necessary to understand how passwords are cracked and to be able to do this yourself to test the passwords of your users for meeting the strong-password criteria.

John the Ripper is the most popular password-cracking program among most hackers and administrators. The program supports the main encryption algorithms: MD5, DES, and Blowfish.

The password-cracking process is started by executing the following commands:

```
unshadow /etc/passwd /etc/shadow > pass.txt
john -incremental pass.txt
```

The first command matches user names with their corresponding passwords and stores the pairs in the pass.txt file. You could do this manually, but for a large number of users this task is better left to the program, unless you have masochistic tendencies.

The second command starts John the Ripper. If you want to use your own dictionary file, specify it using the following command:

```
john -wordfile:filename pass.txt
```

Here, filename is the name of the dictionary file. Linux has a built-in dictionary, stored in the /usr/share/dict/words file. At the dawn of the Internet, the famous Morris worm broke into the largest, at the time, number of computers using only the UNIX dictionary (there was no Linux yet). The Linux built-in dictionary is specified by executing the following command:

```
john -wordfile: /usr/share/dict/words pass.txt
```

A large collection of dictionaries that you can use to test your password for meeting the security criteria can be found on the **www.packetstormsecurity.org** site. If you can crack any of your passwords using one of these dictionaries, hackers can also do this.

While John the Ripper is hard at work, pressing any key will display information about the status of the process. To interrupt the program, press the <Ctrl>+<C> key combination. To resume work, execute the following command:

```
john -restore
```

The file with the cracked passwords can be viewed by executing the following command:

```
john -show pass.txt
```

14.11. Tuning Linux

In this section, I will sum up all previous sections concerning configuring Linux and its services for secure and efficient operation. I will also consider several other, more sophisticated techniques for making your system more secure and productive.

I already stated that the best way to enhance security and efficiency is to load only the most necessary programs and services. The more services loaded, the more memory and processor resources consumed.

After you have decided on the services to use and cut their number to the minimum, you have to configure each of these services for maximum productivity. The minimization principle applies here. For example, the Apache service loads lots of modules that most sites do not need. Each unnecessary module is a blow to security and efficiency.

Minimizing the number of modules for each service allows the greatest performance to be achieved. This said, consider how you can fine-tune your system.

14.11.1. Kernel Parameters

Start by opening the /etc/sysctl.conf file, which stores the kernel parameters. Listing 14.1 shows an example of the file's contents.

Listing 14.1. The contents of the /etc/sysctl.conf configuration file

```
# Kernel sysctl configuration file for Red Hat Linux.

# For binary values, 0 is disabled, 1 is enabled. See sysctl(8) for
# more details.

# Controls IP packet forwarding.
net.ipv4.ip_forward = 0

# Controls source route verification.
net.ipv4.conf.default.rp_filter = 1

kernel.sysrq = 1

kernel.core_uses_pid = 1

#net.ipv4.tcp_ecn = 0

kernel.grsecurity.fifo_restrictions = 1
kernel.grsecurity.linking_restrictions = 1

# Audit some operations.
kernel.grsecurity.audit_mount=1
kernel.grsecurity.signal_logging=1
#kernel.grsecurity.suid_logging=1
kernel.grsecurity.timechange_logging=1
kernel.grsecurity.forkfail_logging=1
kernel.grsecurity.coredump = 1

# Lock all security options.
#kernel.grsecurity.grsec_lock = 1
```

I'll consider the function of the parameters saved in the file, using as an example the `net.ipv4.tcp_ecn` parameter. This is a path, relative to the /proc/sys directory, to the tcp_ecn file, namely: /proc/sys/net/ipv4/tcp_ecn. Execute the following command to view the contents of the file:

```
cat /proc/sys/net/ipv4/tcp_ecn
```

The system will display 0 or 1, which is the value of this parameter.

You can change the value manually, but it's more convenient to do this by executing the following command:

```
sysctl -w paramater_name = new_value
```

The same command can be used to view the value of the kernel parameter:

```
sysctl parameter_name
```

For example, the value of the `net.ipv4.tcp_ecn` parameter, which is stored in the /proc/sys/net/ipv4/tcp_ecn file, is displayed as follows:

```
sysctl net.ipv4.tcp_ecn
```

The values of most parameters are Boolean, meaning they can be either 0 (disabled) or 1 (enabled).

The following are the parameters that should be changed. If they are not in the sysctl.conf file, they should be added to it.

- ❑ `net.ipv4.icmp_echo_ignore_broadcasts` — When this parameter is enabled, the system ignores broadcast ICMP echo packets.
- ❑ `net.ipv4.icmp_echo_ignore_all` — When this parameter is enabled, all ICMP echo packets are ignored. You can use this parameter if you don't want to fool around with the firewall. Prohibiting echo-request packets reduces the traffic, albeit not by much, and makes ineffective any attacks based on using ping packets.
- ❑ `net.ipv4.conf.*.accept_redirects` — This parameter controls accepting router-redirection messages. (I covered this subject in *Section 14.5.3*, saying that enabling router redirections is dangerous because this gives hackers a chance to fool the router and monitor the target machine's traffic.)

The asterisk character is a wild card and stands for any directory name. There can be several subdirectories in the net/ipv4/conf directory, one for each network interface. There should be at least four such subdirectories in your system:

- ❑ all — Contains configuration files for all interfaces
- ❑ default — Holds the default values
- ❑ eth0 — Holds configuration files for the first network card
- ❑ lo — Holds configuration files for the loopback interface

The asterisk indicates that the parameter must be set for all interfaces whose parameter files are stored in the subdirectories of the net/ipv4/conf directory. In most cases, the all directory can be substituted for the asterisk, but sometimes all existing subdirectories have to be specified.

- ❑   `net.ipv4.conf.*.secure_redirects` — When set, this enables ICMP redirect messages to be accepted only for gateways listed in the default gateway list. It is advisable to enable this parameter only if there is more than one router in your network; otherwise, it should be disabled.

- ❑   `net.ipv4.conf.*.send_redirects` — This parameter allows a computer acting as a router to send ICMP redirect messages to other hosts. If there is more than one router in the network, it is advisable to enable this parameter, so that you can distribute the workload among the routers and not try to route all traffic through the main gateway.

- ❑   `net.ipv4.conf.*.accept_source_route` — This parameter controls whether source-routed packages should be accepted or declined. I already mentioned that such packets can be used to bypass your firewall; thus, you should disable this parameter.

- ❑   `net.ip_always_defrag` — When set, all incoming packets are defragmented. I already explained how the firewall can be bypassed using fragmented packets. It just happens that the firewall checks only the first fragment of the packet and considers the rest of the fragments allowed if the first one passes the check. When this parameter is set, all incoming packets are defragmented, thus making bypassing the firewall using this method impossible.

- ❑   `net.ipv4.ipfrag_low_thresh` — This specifies the minimum amount of memory allocated to reassemble fragmented packets. The higher this value, the fewer memory-allocation manipulations necessary. The default value is 196608. Setting this parameter too high will cause extra memory to be allocated and may result in the server running out of resources for processing data. It is advisable to leave the default value.

- ❑   `net.ipv4.ipfrag_high_thresh` — This specifies the maximum amount of memory allocated to reassemble fragmented IP packets. The default value is 262144. If this value is exceeded, the operating system starts tossing out incoming fragmented packets. In this way, a server can be flooded with trashy fragmented messages causing it to no longer react to fragmented packets.

- ❑   `net.ipv4.ipfrag_time` — This indicates the time in seconds to keep an IP packet fragment in memory. The default value is 30 seconds. This is too much, because during this time hackers can flood the entire cache. In case of an attack on the system, the value should be lowered to 20 or even 10 seconds.

- ❑   `net.ipv4.tcp_syncookies` — This controls whether to send out SYN cookies when the SYN queue of a socket overflows. It is advisable to enable this parameter to ward off SYN flood attacks.

These are some of the main kernel parameters. There are too many of them for each to be considered in this book. I advise you to consult the pertinent documentation for information on parameters not included in the preceding overview.

14.11.2. Tuning the Hard Disk Drive

For a long time, Direct Memory Access (DMA) support for hard-drive access was disabled in Linux, although almost all motherboards have had this support since the first Pentium processors. The operating system had DMA disabled by default to be compatible with older computers, so this feature had to be enabled manually.

In modern distributions, DMA support is enabled by default, but it is still possible to optimize the hard drive for more efficient operation. The hdparm utility is used for testing and configuring hard drive in Linux. The hard drive speed can be tested by executing the command with the -t option:

```
hdparm -t /dev/hda
```

The program will display a message of the following type:

```
Timing buffered disk reads: 64 MB in 3.02 seconds = 21.19 MB/sec
```

To display the parameters of the hard drive, the partition is specified as the parameter:

```
hdparm /dev/hda2
```

The results produced look similar to the following:

```
/dev/hda2:
 multcount    = 128 (on)
 IO_support   =   0 (default 16-bit)
 unmaskirq    =   0 (off)
 using_dma    =   1 (on)
 keepsettings =   0 (off)
 readonly     =   0 (off)
 readahead    =   8 (on)
 geometry     = 2088/255/63, sectors = 32515560, start = 1028160
```

The most interesting parameters are the following:

❑ multcount — The number of words read in one cycle. This parameter must be enabled, and it advisable to set its value to 128. Doing this can raise the efficiency 30% to 50%. The value is changed using the mX option, where X is the new value.

❑ using_dma — DMA use. The DMA mode is enabled by using the d1 option.

❑ IO_support — The drive access mode. The default can be the 16-bit mode, but currently the 32-bit mode can be used. This mode can be enabled by the c3 option.

The preceding three parameters can really enhance hard drive efficiency. To set them to the recommended values, execute the following command:

```
hdparm -m128d1c3/dev/hda
```

As you can see, I simply listed all necessary keys and specified the disk, to which they apply. Note that there are no digits, for example, hda1, in the disk name. Digits used with a disk name specify a disk partition, but access can only be changed for the whole disk and not its individual partitions.

The modified parameters have to be saved as follows:

```
hdparm -k1 /dev/hda
```

Now, execute the disk read speed-testing command: `dhparm -t /dev/hda`.

In addition to the parameters displayed by the `hdparm /dev/hda2` command, there is also the access mode parameter. Currently, three Advanced Technology Attachment (ATA) modes are supported: 33, 66, and 100. Consult your hard drive manual for information about which access mode it supports.

The access mode is changed using the X option as follows:

- ❒ X34 — Corresponds to ATA33
- ❒ X68 — Corresponds to ATA66
- ❒ X69 — Corresponds to ATA100

For example, ATA66 is enabled by the following command:

```
hdparm -X68/dev/hda
```

As strange as it may sound, the parameters you set are lost on reboot. To make them permanent, the commands setting them should be saved in the /etc/rc.d/rc.local file. Add the following commands at the end of the file:

```
hdparm -m128d1c3/dev/hda
hdparm -X68/dev/hda
hdparm -k1 /dev/hda
```

14.11.3. Automount

If your exposure to the world of computers started with Windows, you may find having to mount file systems and especially CD-ROMs manually absurd. Although this can be lived with on servers, because discs are seldom used there, on workstations this becomes a real pain in the neck, because CD-ROMs and diskettes are used quite extensively on them. I sometimes have to change up to 20 different discs a day, and I quickly tire of having to mount and unmount them.

Because Linux is striving to move in to the home computer area, its latest distributions include the default automatic mounting option. This is done with the help of the autofs service. Check that this service runs on start-up; if it does, you can start configuring it.

The service's main configuration file is /etc/auto.master. The following are its contents:

```
# $Id: auto.master,v 1.2 1997/10/06 21:52:03 hpa Exp $
# Sample auto.master file
# Format of this file:
# mountpoint map options
# For details of the format, look at autofs(8).
/misc   /etc/auto.misc      --timeout=60
```

Only the last entry in the file is supposed to do something, the rest are only explanatory comments. This entry may be commented out in your system; uncomment it to use the automatic mounting feature.

The configuration entry has the following format:

```
mountpoint  map      options
```

In this case, `mountpoint` is the /misc directory. This circumstance is somewhat of a problem, because the /mnt directory is the default directory for mounting devices manually. The second parameter specifies the mount map. In this case, it is the /etc/auto.misc file. The file's format and function are similar to those of the /etc/fstab file used for the mount command. Listing 14.2 shows the contents of the /etc/auto.misc file.

The last parameter, `--timeout=60`, is the idleness period. If during this period there is no activity in the directory, into which the device is mounted, the device is unmounted. The default timeout value is 60 seconds. In most cases, this is an acceptable value.

Listing 14.2. The contents of the /etc/auto.misc file

```
# $Id: auto.misc,v 1.2 1997/10/06 21:52:04 hpa Exp $
# This is an automounter map, and it has the following format:
# key [ -mount-options-separated-by-comma ] location
# Details may be found in the autofs(5) manpage.


cd            -fstype=iso9660,ro,nosuid,nodev      :/dev/cdrom


# The following entries are samples to pique your imagination.
#linux        -ro,soft,intr        ftp.example.org:/pub/linux
#boot         -fstype=ext2                          :/dev/hda1
#floppy       -fstype=auto                          :/dev/fd0
#floppy       -fstype=ext2                          :/dev/fd0
#e2floppy     -fstype=ext2                          :/dev/fd0
#jaz          -fstype=ext2                          :/dev/sdc1
#removable    -fstype=ext2                          :/dev/hdd
```

There is only one entry not commented out in the /etc/auto.misc file. This entry mounts the CD-ROM:

```
cd      -fstype=iso9660,ro,nosuid,nodev    :/dev/cdrom
```

The first parameter in the command specifies the subdirectory in the /misc directory, into which the device will be mounted. The second parameter specifies the parameters of file system of the device to be mounted and the options to be used for mounting. For a CD-ROM, the `iso9660` file system is used; the file system is mounted for read only, and SUID and DEV are prohibited. The last parameter specifies the device to be mounted.

As you can see, everything is simple. If an attempt is made to access the /misc/cd directory and there is a disc in the CD-ROM at the moment, it will be automatically mounted. There is one idiosyncrasy when working with file systems mounted automatically: Linux command line commands should be used. For example, to view the directory, execute the `ls /misc/cd` command. If you try to view the /misc/cd directory using Midnight Commander, the program will not see the automounted disc.

14.12. Miscellaneous Recommendations

In the course of the book, I have considered numerous aspects of the task of creating a secure system; however, some of the recommendations I would like to offer could not be placed into any of the topics considered. Therefore, I decided to place all of them at the end of the book.

14.12.1. Packet Defragmentation

Packet fragmentation is often used to carry out attacks on servers. Linux can be configured to defragment incoming packets. If your kernel is monolithic (i.e., lacks module support), this can be achieved by writing 1 to the /proc/sys/net/ipv4/ip_always_defrag file. This can be done by executing the following command:

```
echo 1 > /proc/sys/net/ipv4/ip_always_defrag
```

For newer kernel modules, which support modules, the `ip_conntrack` module has to be loaded using the following command:

```
modprobe ip_conntrack
```

14.12.2. Source Routing

As you should remember from *Section 14.5.3*, inside a network packets are moved using MAC addresses, and between networks they are moved using IP addresses. In the latter case, a router is necessary to move packets to the proper address. Routers determine the route for sending packets from the source to the destination. However, these devices are programmable, and there are several methods of sending packets over specific routes. One of these methods is source routing.

Source routing involves specifying the route, over which a packet is moved from the source to the destination. Sometimes, this is a handy option, but, as you already know, what is convenient usually is not secure. The source-routing feature is better disabled, and it would be the best if it had never been invented.

So how does source routing affect security? Suppose that you detected an attack attempt from address 192.168.1.1 and took countermeasures by configuring the firewall to prohibit connections from this address. Because routers send all packets from the hackers through this address, the hackers can no longer connect to your system. But they can use the source-routing feature to specify the route, by which their packets are to be moved to your system and to exclude the router, or a server playing the role of a router, with the disallowed address from this route.

Unfortunately, you cannot disable the source-routing feature on a hacker's computer; but you should disable it on your own computer, and even more so on the computer used as the Internet gateway (the proxy server or firewall). This can be done by writing 1 to the /proc/sys/net/ipv4/conf/all/accept_source_route file as follows:

```
echo 0 > /proc/sys/net/ipv4/conf/all/accept_source_route
```

14.12.3. SNMP

The Simple Network Management Protocol (SNMP) is used to control network devices, such as routers, programmable switches, and even home appliances connected to a network.

There are three versions of this protocol. The first version was developed a long time ago and does not employ encryption. The encryption option was added to SNMP in the second version. Therefore, you are recommended not to use the first version of the protocol; in the best case, it should be disabled altogether.

Another drawback of SNMP is that it uses UDP as the transport. This means that SNMP packets are transmitted as payload inside of UDP packets. Because UDP does not support virtual connection and just send packets without any authorization, any fields of its packets can be faked.

I recommend not using SNMP, because most tasks do not require it. The encryption feature added in the second version has raised the protocol's security significantly, and it can be used for especially important tasks. You have to make sure, however, that the second or a higher version of the protocol is on hand before using it for tasks requiring data protection.

14.12.4. Absolute Path

When running some utility, most users and even administrators simply enter the command's name, which may lead to a break-in. Thus, you should specify the complete path when launching any program.

The following is an example of how using short names can be used to compromise the system:

1. A file with the same name as the target program, let it be ls, is created in a public directory, for example, /tmp.

2. A script to carry out specific actions is saved in this file. For example, the following:

```
#!/bin/sh
# Changing access rights to the /etc/passwd and /etc/shadow files
chmod 777 /etc/passwd > /dev/null
chmod 777 /etc/shadow > /dev/null
# Executing the ls program
exec /bin/ls "$@"
```

The script contains only three commands — or, rather, only two because the first two commands are the same, just applied to different files. These first two chmod commands change access rights to the /etc/passwd and /etc/shadow files. Moreover, any system messages that may be produced when these commands are executed are redirected to the /dev/null device and are not displayed on the screen. The second command in the script file executes the legitimate ls system command from the /bin directory.

Now, set the file's execute permission so that it can be executed by any user:

```
chmod 777 /tmp/ls
```

The fake ls file is ready. But now it has to be made to execute instead of the system's legitimate ls file. This is an easy enough task: Simply add the /tmp directory at the beginning of the PATH system environment variable. Now, if the ls command is executed without its full path specified, executed instead of it will be the script file, which will try to change access rights to the password files. If the user who executes the command has enough privileges for this, the attempt will be successful and you can consider the system as good as cracked.

The conclusion that should be drawn from this example is that you should regularly check the contents of the PATH environment variable for potential modifications. If you find that the variable has been changed, you can consider your system compromised and should initiate the post-break-in procedure.

14.12.5. Trusted Hosts

The .rhosts file contains names of trusted hosts. Users of these computers can connect to your computer remotely using such programs as Telnet or FTP without having to go through the authentication process.

The security aspects of remote connections are described numerous times throughout this book, so by now you should easily see that the source address can be easily faked. Once this is done, your computer becomes a public thoroughfare.

14.12.6. Password Protection

The main thing for protecting a Linux password is to safeguard the /etc/shadow file. In addition, you should also make sure that users have strong passwords. To this end, you should regularly run password-cracking programs using popular dictionaries that can be found on the Internet, which are what hackers usually exercise. If the passwords are strong, then even if hackers manage to get their hands on the /etc/shadow file, it will take them too long to decrypt the passwords in it for the passwords to be of any use, that is, if they can decrypt them at all.

But not everything is as easy as it seems to be. Where system login passwords are protected by the operating system and have mandatory encryption, passwords used in other programs may not be afforded this protection. For example, user programs to access certain services, such as FTP or POP3, may not use encryption. In this case, their passwords may be stored in a configuration file in plaintext.

Before installing any program, determine where it stores its passwords and whether they are encrypted and how. Set such file permissions that only the specific user and the administrator can have access to them. It is desirable that groups are assigned zero rights, especially if there is more than one user in a group.

If a separate group is created for each user, the group may be given some rights. Nevertheless, I would recommend against this, because you never know what may become of a group in the future. A hacker may add himself or herself to a group, or you may join several users into one group.

I recommend to all my users not to save passwords in programs. This means, for example, that the password has to be supplied every time a user checks his or her mail. This is inconvenient, especially if you have more than one mailbox, which nowadays is a norm. But even with only one mailbox, users are difficult to convince to memorize passwords and not save them in the system.

But passwords have to be entered directly into the program; ideally, they should not be displayed on the screen. This means that passwords should not be specified in the command line, which displays all data entered into it.

There are many methods to oversee a password being entered, for example, the ps utility. A good example of a proper way to enter a password is the login utility. When you are logging into Linux, the password entered is not displayed on the screen.

Passwords may be stored in plaintext in databases, which is where the most important data of any company are stored. Databases are a separate subject that requires a book in itself and is beyond the scope of this book. Databases, however, always should be kept in mind.

14.12.7. Redirecting Services

Services used by a limited number of users should work on nonstandard ports. This will protect the system from many potential problems.

One of the most common security threats presented by using standard ports is that they can be scanned. For example, a hacker discovers that there is a bug in a particular database. Suppose that this database uses port 1457. All the hacker needs to do to find vulnerable databases is to scan the network for computers with port 1457 open. Having detected such machines, the hacker can write a program that exploits the vulnerability on all of these machines.

The problem is easily solved by reconfiguring the service to use another port and removing any banners that may be displayed when a connection to this port is being established. This will prevent the hacker from learning what port the program uses and how to work with it.

If services are used by a limited number of people, the ports of the most vulnerable services (e.g., those that allow users to upload files to or execute commands on the server) can have their places switched. For example, make the FTP service work on port 80 and the Web service on port 21. Unfortunately, public services cannot be made to work on different ports. For example, making a Web server work on port 81 instead of the standard port 80 would require that every potential user of this service be informed of this change. This defeats the purpose of port switching, because a hacker is also a potential user.

14.13. You've Been Hacked

If you discover that there is stranger in your network while the server stores information that may be disastrous to lose, I recommend disconnecting the server from the network at once and analyzing the system logs. It is better to make the server services unavailable for a couple of hours than to lose control over it altogether.

Start log analyzes by checking the system's configuration as explained in *Section 12.3.* The reports of the log-analyzing programs before and after the break-in should be compared. This will help you determine what the hacker has done in the system. Remove any rootkits you discover.

As the next step, verify the checksums of all main files, especially of the configuration files from the /etc directory and of the executable files from the /bin directory. These files can be changed by hackers to plant a back door to the system and to remain in it unnoticed. Having found all changes, try to restore the affected files to their initial state.

Next, check the integrity of the installed modules. For this, execute the following command:

```
rpm -qa | grep kernel
```

Now, check all installed application packages. Restore any changed application packages to their initial state.

Next, check the integrity of updates for Linux and all services. Most break-ins are made possible because of outdated software. Update all software. Web scripts used by the Web server also have to be updated, because they also are common sources of break-ins.

If your server provides Web server services, I would not put the server back online until all of the Web scripts have been checked. Only then can you put the server back online and start close monitoring of the system.

Here is where you start analyzing logs to determine how exactly the hacker performed the break-in, simultaneously monitoring the running system. If the hacker tries to surreptitiously enter the system again, you should be able to detect this and stop this attempt before it's carried out so that you would not have to analyze and clean the system again.

While you are analyzing the logs, all users have to change their server login passwords and their passwords to all services.

You should determine the following from the log analyzes:

☐   The services used by the hacker and in which logs the hacker's activity in the server is recorded

☐   The parameters of the accounts the hacker was able to discover and use

☐   The commands the hacker has executed

You should learn as much as possible to determine whether you have taken all steps necessary to prevent a subsequent break-in. Some administrators simply restore the server operation and some time later suffer the consequences by having to restore it again.

It is desirable to obtain as much information as possible about the hacker and to turn this information over to law-enforcement agencies. Don't try to always fight hackers on your own, because you cannot always win. Feeling invulnerable, hackers will continue breaking in, and with each break-in the chances increase that they will get what they are after. Ask the law enforcement agencies that have the appropriate jurisdiction and facilities to find and stop the hacker.

Conclusion

I hope that this book has helped you to learn more about security in general and about Linux security in particular. In it, I described at length various computer attack methods and defenses from those attacks. This may make you form an impression that all every administrator is doing is fighting off bad guys trying to break into his or her system. My opinion is that there are no hackers and crackers. This is a scary tale invented to frighten administrators.

In any field of activity, there are strong and weak players. Most hackers are young people who simply happen to know more than others and can use their knowledge. For some reason, the information technologies field is considered a domain of gurus possessing almost supernatural knowledge. Perhaps, there was some truth to this conception at the dawn of the computer era, but it ceased to be this way a long, long time ago. Computers have become an inseparable part of our lives, as commonplace as telephones and television sets. Thus, they should be treated accordingly.

When you soup up your car, you may not be breaking any laws. The manufacturer certainly cannot prohibit you from doing this. The warranty, of course, will be voided, and there is no guarantee that the modifications will not kill the car way before its time. But you likely will not be persecuted for being an auto hacker.

All this means is that the main weapon for fighting hackers should be knowledge. If your system has been compromised, it does not necessarily mean that you should devote your outmost efforts to sending to prison the person who did this. You simply should give more attention to your server's security. If the overall level of knowledge and expertise and, correspondingly, the level of Internet services can be increased, there will be far fewer break-ins.

Constantly enhance your knowledge base, raise the level of your expertise, and expand your information store. Don't just rely on ready solutions to protect your system. Leaving your system full of holes is the same as leaving the canary cage's door open in a room with a hungry cat. Don't rely on the law to protect your system: The most law-enforcement agencies can do is catch the villain who stole your confidential information or destroyed it. But other than giving you some moral satisfaction, this will hardly be of any help. So you should be the one to protect your system. Remember, God helps those who help themselves.

APPENDIXES

Appendix 1: FTP Commands

The following commands are necessary when connecting to an FTP server with a command line client:

- ☐ `cd path` — Change the current directory to the specified one. The `cd ..` command takes you one level up; the `cd directory` command takes you to the specified directory on the next level down.
- ☐ `exit` — Terminate the connection and exit the system.
- ☐ `chmod permissions file_name` — Change file permissions. For example, to set permissions for the passwd file in the current directory to 770, execute the `chmod 770 passwd` command.
- ☐ `get -P remote_file local_file` — Download a file. The `-P` switch is optional and is used to preserve the file permissions on the local system, making them the same as on the server. This switch does not function if a file is transferred among different operating systems, because Windows uses a different file-permission mechanism. The `local_file` parameter specifies the absolute path, to which the file will be downloaded.
- ☐ `put -P local_file remote_file` — Upload a file to the server.
- ☐ `help` — Display the list of the available command.
- ☐ `pwd` — Show the current directory on the remote machine.
- ☐ `delete file_name` — Delete a file on the remote machine.
- ☐ `rmdir directory_name` — Remove a directory on the remote machine.
- ☐ `mkdir directory_name` — Create the specified directory.

Keep it in mind that different FTP servers and clients may process commands in different ways.

Appendix 2: Useful Programs

- ❏ hunt (**lin.fsid.cvut.cz/~kra/index.html**) — This is one of the popular sniffer programs. It also has built-in functions to send fake ARP packets to fake MAC addresses and to intercept connections.
- ❏ dsniff (**monkey.org/~dugsong/dsniff/**) — This is a utility package for traffic monitoring and related tasks. It comprises the following utilities:
  - dsniff — Intercepts passwords (the main utility). The utility monitors the network for authorization packets. When it detects such a packet, the utility extracts and displays the password. Authorization packets for all of the main protocols — Telnet, FTP, POP, etc. — are supported.
  - arpspoof — Sends ARP reply packets to fake IP addresses.
  - dnsspoof — Sends fake DNS packets. If the target machine requests that a host name be resolved to its IP address, you can switch the reply from the DNS server to make the target connect to your computer instead of the requested host.
  - filesnaf — Monitors traffic, waiting for NFS file transfers.
  - mailsnaf — Monitors traffic, waiting for POP and SMTP mail messages.
  - msgsnaf — Monitors Internet pager and chat messages, such as ICQ and IRC.
  - macof — Floods a switch with packets with generated MAC addresses. If the switch fails to handle the route-resolution workload, it starts functioning as a simple hub, replicating the incoming traffic to all outgoing ports.

- tcpkill — Terminates a third-party connection by sending an RST packet.
- webspy — Monitors Web connections and creates a list of sites visited by a specific user.
- webmint — Emulates a Web server to carry out a man-in-the-middle attack (see *Section 7.9*).

□ ettercap (**ettercap.sourceforge.net**) — In my opinion, this is the most convenient traffic-monitoring program. Its main function is to look for passwords in packets of all popular protocols. Administrators will also appreciate the function to detect other sniffing programs.

□ LSAT (**usat.sourceforge.net/**) — This utility is used to check the system configuration (considered in *Section 12.3*). It analyzes the server's configuration, displaying potential faults, and in some cases can give recommendations on how to fix them.

□ Bastille (**bastille-linux.sourceforge.net/**) — This utility detects potential server-configuration errors. It can automatically correct configuration errors and faults.

□ Klaxon (**www.eng.auburn.edu/users/doug/second.html**) — This is an attack-detection utility (see *Section 12.4*).

□ PortSentry (**sourceforge.net/projects/sentrytools**) — This utility monitors ports for port-scanning activities (see *Section 12.4*). It can automatically configure the firewall to prohibit connections with the computer, from which port scanning was detected.

□ Swatch (**sourceforge.net/projects/swatch**) — This is a handy program for analyzing system logs on a schedule (see *Section 12.6*).

□ Logsurfer (**sourceforge.net/projects/logsurfer**) — This is one of the few utilities that can analyze security logs dynamically (see *Section 12.6*).

□ John the Ripper (**www.openwall.com/john/**) — This is the most famous password-cracking program.

□ POP-before-SMTP (**popbsmtp.sourceforge.net/**) — This service allows email to be sent only if the user first checks the POP3 mailbox.

□ nmap (**www.insecure.org/nmap/**) — This is a port scanner with numerous features.

Appendix 3: Internet Resources

- ❐ **www.redhat.com** — The official Red Hat company site. The latest versions of the kernel, application software, and patches are available for downloading from here. It also provides information about the history and future prospects of this operating system.
- ❐ **www.kernel.org** — A site is devoted to Linux kernels. The latest versions of the kernel can be downloaded from here.
- ❐ **www.securityfocus.com** — A security site. It offers descriptions of numerous vulnerabilities and how to fix them.
- ❐ **www.cert.org** — Another IT security site.
- ❐ **www.insecure.org** — A site offering voluminous security information, articles, and software.
- ❐ **www.novell.com/de-de/linux/suse/** — The site of SUSE Linux, one of the most user-friendly Linux distributions.
- ❐ **www.linspire.com/** — The developers at Linspire are working on creating a Linux-kernel operating system to run Windows programs.
- ❐ **www.debian.org** — The official site of the Debian Linux distribution.
- ❐ **www.slackware.com** — The official site of the Slackware Linux distribution.

Index

Visit us on the Internet at: http://www.alistpublishing.com

Hacker Debugging Uncovered

by Kris Kaspersky (ISBN 1-931769-40-0, $44.95, 624 pp, June, 2005)

*How To Analyze Programs
and Minimize Errors Using a Debugger*

This book concentrates on debugging concepts, disclosing secrets that will aid practical use of debuggers (such as NuMega SoftIce, Microsoft Visual Studio Debugger, and Microsoft Kernel Debugger) with minimum binding to a specific environment. What are the advantages of using debuggers? From an economic perspective, they prevent unexpected losses. Conversely, without debuggers, no company would be able to profit from software product sales. Society will be unable to do without debuggers for at least the next two decades. This book shows how the debugger operates, what is under its hood, and how to overcome obstacles and repair the debugger in the process. The main topic covered in this book is the use of debugging applications and drivers under the operating systems of the Windows and Unix families on Intel Pentium/DEC Alpha-based processors. This book not only extends the opportunities for job hunters and improves skill level; it also stimulates thoughts of abandoning these traditional concerns and favoring personal satisfaction and enjoyment. Simply speaking, the surrounding world contains so many wonderful and interesting things that the petty problems of the workaday routine regress to the background. The everyday needs of hackers become insignificant. The purpose of this book is to make readers love their jobs and find pleasure in debugging. The companion CD for this book contains the source code of all listings provided in the book, high-quality color illustrations, and useful utilities. This book covers all aspects of debugging, including the sources of bugs and errors and methods of minimizing their numbers. Various debugging techniques (from the origin of debugging to the present) and hardware and software tools that support debugging technologies by the processor and operating systems are explained. The book covers techniques for efficient debugging strategies, secrets of investigating programs distributed without source code, and much more.

Brief Table of Contents: Introduction; Part 1. Goals and Tasks of Debugging; Part 2. Practical Debugging; Part 3. No Source Code, or Face-to-Face with Alien Code; Part 4. How To Make Your Programs More Reliable; Part 5. How the Debugger Works.

A-LIST Publishing
295 East Swedesford Rd, PMB #285, Wayne, PA 19087
e-mail: mail@alistpublishing.com
www.alistpublishing.com
Fax: 702-977-5377